THE LATE SHIFT

LETTERMAN, LENO, AND THE NETWORK BATTLE FOR THE NIGHT

BY

BILL CARTER

HYPERION
NEW YORK

ISBN 0-7868-8907-1

Original book design by Joel Avirom

FIRST MASS MARKET EDITION

10 9 8 7 6 5 4 3 2 1

To Beth, with love always

ACKNOWLEDGMENTS

The primary source material for this book is my own firsthand reporting. I conducted several hundred interviews with more than one hundred people connected with the business and the programming of late-night television. Every important figure in the story spoke with me at least once; most agreed to be interviewed several times. The level of cooperation I received was truly extraordinary.

I supplemented my reporting with information from various newspaper and magazine articles. Most helpful were articles from the *New York Times,* the *Los Angeles Times,* the *Boston Globe,* and the *St. Louis Post-Dispatch.* Among the many magazine articles I consulted the most useful came from *Time, Newsweek, Esquire, Rolling Stone, GQ, People, Success, M,* and *Buzz.* I was also aided by the reporting of the ABC News program, "20/20." Two pieces from *The New Yorker* magazine, one on Helen Kushnick by Peter Boyer and one on the courting of David Letterman by Ken Auletta, were also very helpful.

Helpful books included *King of the Night* by Laurence Leamer, *The World of Jay Leno* by Bill Adler and Bruce Cassiday, and *Arsenio: Prince of the Night* by Aileen Joyce.

I wish to thank first and foremost my agent Kathy Robbins for her faith in me and for her hard work and support in making the book happen. I am also grateful to her colleague Elizabeth Mackey for all her efforts, especially for her boundless encouragement. I also wish to thank my editor Brian DeFiore for his enthusiasm in pursuing this project.

Two other editors made crucial contributions to this effort: Martin Arnold, the Media Editor of the *New York Times* and Peter Kaufman, the Deputy Media Editor of the *New York Times*. They are much more friends than bosses.

Many individuals provided significant help in assembling the information for this book. Some who have asked not to be included by name have my profound thanks.

The long list of people I would like to thank by name for their important contributions includes: Alan Baker, Cindy Berger, Phil Beuth, Susan Binford, Curt Block, Teri Garr, Michael Gartner, Jules Green, Brad Grey, Arsenio Hall, Peggy Hubble, Mark Kern, Dan Klores, Ken Kragen, Lucy Kraus, Merrill Markoe, Conan O'Brien, Steve Rivers, Bud Rukeyser, Lucie Salhany, Garry Shandling, Stu Smiley, Jeff Sotzing, Hayley Sumner, and, for his always unique insight into how the television game is played, Brandon Tartikoff.

I had essential assistance from numerous individuals at both of the networks involved in this story. From CBS I am most deeply indebted to Howard Stringer, who was generous with time, thoughts, recollections, and emotions. I would also like to give special thanks to Ann Morfogen, Susan Tick, Tom Goodman, Gail Plautz, Michael Silver, and the rest of network's public relations staff, as well as Ed Grebow, Tony Malara, Rod

Perth, David Poltrack, and George Schweitzer. And certainly not least, this book could not have been completed without the voluminous and extremely gracious contributions of Rosemary Keenan, first of NBC, then of CBS, but always of the Letterman show. She has my heartfelt thanks.

From NBC I am grateful for the considerate assistance of the network's public relations professionals, including Beth Comstock, Ed Markey, Mary Neagoy, Rosemary O'Brien, and especially Pat Schultz and Judy Smith. Numerous NBC executives provided invaluable help. I would like to thank Sissy Biggers, Dick Ebersol, Betty Hudson, Pier Mapes, Robert Niles, Don Ohlmeyer, and Jeff Zucker. And from the General Electric Company, I would like to thank chairman Jack Welch for his generous comments.

Three NBC executives made indispensable contributions for which I am enormously grateful. John Agoglia was graciously open and helpful. Warren Littlefield was candid, colorful in his accounts of events, and exceptionally generous in every way. And Bob Wright very kindly made his network and himself accessible to me.

From the Creative Artists Agency, I wish to thank Anna Perez for her warm, facilitating help, and Lee Gabler and Michael Ovitz for their thoughtful assessments and candor.

From "Saturday Night Live," executive producer Lorne Michaels was an important, and always cordial, resource.

From the "Tonight Show Starring Johnny Carson," I am greatly indebted to Johnny Carson for contributing his time and insights. His lawyer, Ed Hookstratten, made special efforts on my behalf and I thank him enormously as well.

From the "Tonight Show with Jay Leno," I would like to thank Jay's writing partner and my old college friend, Jimmy Brogan, and Jay's cheerful and accommodating assistant, Helga Pollock.

I also wish to express my deep appreciation and thanks to Helen Kushnick, who gave freely of her time, her analysis of the business, and her opinions on late-night television.

From "Late Show with David Letterman," I was lucky enough to receive the most gracious and helpful support of Julie Bean and Susan Shreyar, the assistants to the executive producers, and Laurie Diamond, David Letterman's executive assistant. I owe great appreciation to Ken Lerer for his extremely valuable help and ideas. I would also like to thank Jim Jackoway for his significant contributions. To Peter Lassally and Robert Morton, I owe my deepest thanks for their welcoming openness, their abiding thoughtfulness, and their endless generosities.

This book could not have been written without the willing participation of Jay Leno and David Letterman. Both stars shared their thoughts and opinions freely and with spectacular grace and generosity. I am profoundly in their debt for their professionalism and their kindness, and for all the fun they have provided me—on and off the air—in the past year.

In the course of pulling this project together, many friends, relatives, and colleagues have played vital roles. I wish to thank two of my journalist comrades, Marc Gunther, my former co-author, and especially Eric

Mink, who was invaluable in sharing ideas, information, and overall strategy. And for special help with getting me where I had to be, thanks to Diane Guercio.

My fondest thanks also to Denise and Phil Andrews, Deirdre Carmody, Rich and Nikki Carter, Richard and Teresa Carter, Kathy and Tony Garrett, Frank Guercio, James Houston, Catharine and Thomas Keating, Nancy Keating, Patrick and Julie Keating, Aine and Paul McCambridge, Diego and Mary Lou Merida, Frank Murphy, Catherine and Dan O'Neill, Lori and Thom Peters, Jeanne Shatter, and Gerard and Jan Uehlinger.

Certainly the most important contribution to my work was made by the members of my family, who sustained this intensely consuming effort with unending supplies of patience, support and love. And so I thank most of all my children, Caela and Daniel Carter, whose laughter and love surpass all other forms of inspiration, and my wife, Beth Keating Carter, whose extraordinary skills at editing, encouraging, life and family managing, and loving without limit are reflected in every word on these pages.

CONTENTS

NO MORE
TO COME

Tucked behind a podium on the far left of the deep, elegant stage of Carnegie Hall, Warren Littlefield was finishing up his debut as maestro of NBC's entertainment programming. It was May 23, 1991, a sparkling spring afternoon in Manhattan. In front of a full-house audience of advertising agency executives and station managers from NBC's affiliated stations, Littlefield was bringing onto the stage the full roster of NBC stars—Ted Danson, Jane Pauley, Bill Cosby—trying to complete with a flourish his first presentation of the upcoming fall television schedule.

NBC's ratings fortunes had, in the previous television season, started a steep plunge after six years of dominating prime time. (Or, as Preston Beckman, an NBC research executive, described it: "Our ratings took a bungee jump off the Empire State Building.") Now NBC's executives had assembled their most important constituencies in the grandeur of Carnegie Hall and, in an effort to impress, they were reaching for rabbits from every conceivable form of headwear.

More than two hours earlier, the session had started

with a rambling satellite interview between NBC anchorman Tom Brokaw and President George Bush, who, a year prior to the start of a new presidential election season, was pressing a little flesh electronically with the managers of local television stations. This group was one of growing importance to politicians seeking access to local newscasts. Littlefield, at that point pacing offstage, found the interview interminable and unfathomable. He relished the chance to introduce the next act: Jay Leno, permanent guest host of the "Tonight" show, who in the last several years had polished his reputation as the best backup to Johnny Carson NBC had ever had on its "Tonight" show depth chart. Leno came out and did ten minutes of crackerjack stand-up.

Danson did a warmly received walk-on, minus his hairpiece, which few in the crowd seemed to notice. And Cosby, NBC's leading man since the mid-eighties, turned up to voice his appreciation for all the support his "Cosby Show" had received, helping make him a millionaire another couple of hundred times over.

Littlefield had the stage to himself as he introduced these stars and others from the new shows he had picked for NBC's fall schedule, shows like "Eerie, Indiana," "Pacific Station," and "Man of the People," all of which were being celebrated as the new wave from the House of Hits.

As the long ceremony wound down toward its close, it was a moment of some triumph for the thirty-nine-year-old Littlefield, one he had been aiming for all his professional life; not because he had ever longed to walk out into the spotlight at Carnegie Hall, but because he had waited a decade to walk out from under the tall shadow of Brandon Tartikoff. Tartikoff, who had been named chairman of Paramount Pictures a month earlier, had led NBC's charge from doormat to king of the prime-time hill in the mid-eighties, piling up annual profits of up to $500 million for the network. Along the way Tartikoff had charmed the powers of Hollywood—and even more importantly the press—to carve for himself a legend as the premier showman of the living-room box.

Littlefield, shorter, redder-faced, with a neatly trimmed, carrot-colored beard and a taste for conspicuously colorful ties, had been Tartikoff's principal lieutenant, standing like the dutiful little brother at Tartikoff's side at previous fall season presentations. What had once been a close relationship had grown fractious toward the end, with the two men often disagreeing on program and casting choices. At one Hollywood party, Tartikoff was overheard calling Littlefield and another NBC programming executive, Perry Simon, the "Milli Vanilli of programming," after the singing duo who were exposed for lip-synching songs sung by other people. Littlefield, who had always had a vulnerability and sweetness about him, tried to shrug the insult off, saying, "Brothers fight, and brothers at times want to inflict a punch that hurts."

Fearing his big show had drifted on too long and that he might soon lose a large part of his audience to long-delayed trips to the restroom, Littlefield urged a final round of applause for the whole "NBC family of stars" he had introduced that afternoon. He promised a "final special visitor from the West" as the last celebrity member of the NBC prime-time family exited the stage.

"I've waited my whole life for this," Littlefield said, revving up his thin, somewhat high-pitched voice: "Ladies and gentlemen, the king of late-night television, soon to begin his thirtieth season on NBC . . . here's Johnny!" The theme song, "Da-Dat-Dat-DA-DA," as familiar to anyone who owned a television set as the National Anthem was to anyone who'd gone to a ballgame, rose to match the applause. Johnny Carson strode in his elegant, stiff-legged style to center stage. The audience kept up the applause, rolling it toward the stage in waves, as though trying to embrace him in warmth and enthusiasm. They were genuinely surprised; Carson's appearance had been totally unbilled and effectively kept from the press by the few NBC executives who'd planned it.

As much as American television audiences had come to love Carson, the managers of NBC's television stations had several million stronger reasons for their ardor. Almost thirty years into his nightly role as the nation's chief cultural color commentator, Carson was the single biggest money generator in television history. He was also the greatest individual star the medium had ever created.

Carson smiled broadly as he drank in the applause, touched by its evident sincerity. "Thank you very much," he said. "That's very nice of you and I'm very grateful." And then after a perfectly timed pause: "Gee, what a fast-paced afternoon!" As the huge laugh was just dying down, Carson stretched it: "You folks must be just short of a coma."

And he was off and running, tossing off quick-hit jokes about Ivana Trump, the cheapness of NBC's corporate parent General Electric, even the afternoon's host: "You get a little awestruck being on this stage, to think of all the great men who have graced this stage at Carnegie Hall: Jascha Heifetz, Vladimir Horowitz, Isaac Stern, and today (pause) Warren Littlefield." He tacked on a rebound laugh with: "Kind of knocks hell out of Darwin's theory, doesn't it?"

Then he shifted to Jay Leno, the latest in a seemingly unending line of presumed successors. "Jay Leno kept driving me nuts backstage, coming up every few minutes: 'How you feeling? Feel okay? How's your thyroid? Your thyroid okay?' I like Jay Leno, and as a matter of fact, he *is* very concerned about my health. In fact, he insisted that I jog through Central Park about midnight tonight."

Leno didn't hear the cracks. He was long gone, having bolted the theater immediately after his own stand-up spot to grab a limo to the airport. There, a private plane commissioned by NBC would take him back to Lake Tahoe and the gig at the hotel he had interrupted to open the NBC festivities. As Johnny was speaking, Jay was already somewhere over Pennsylvania, working, as always, on more jokes.

Carson's next target was also absent: Brandon Tartikoff, the NBC entertainment executive Carson had come to like best and respect most. "I love Brandon Tartikoff," Carson said. "He talked me into staying and then he jumped ship."

For some who knew Carson well, the last statement didn't sound entirely like a joke. They believed that Carson felt somewhat abandoned when Tartikoff decided to leave NBC for Paramount, though Johnny himself never said that was the case. But with Tartikoff gone, Carson was sharing his Burbank headquarters with a group of executives that he was not nearly as close to.

Carson did have some reason to be disenchanted with NBC: The network had seen fit, for the first time in his run as sovereign of late night, to challenge his hard-earned prerogatives. The previous February, during the Persian Gulf war, NBC had responded to its stations' requests for more local news time by pushing the starting time for the "Tonight" show back five minutes, to 11:35 P.M. in the East. It was a convenient excuse for the stations to start squeezing more commercials into their newscasts.

NBC could have fought the stations to hold the line at 11:30, but the network didn't want to take the risk. NBC's executives believed the move to 11:35 was necessary to maintain the loyalty of the stations to the "Tonight" show. With syndicated shows like "Entertainment Tonight" and reruns of "Cheers" churning out big profits for non-NBC stations in the late-night time period, it was becoming increasingly difficult for NBC to hold together the lineup of stations that provided full national clearance for the show. That 100 percent clearance rate was the backbone of the "Tonight" show's dominance of late night.

NBC had been under pressure for some time from stations that wanted to delay the start of "Tonight" until midnight so they could plug in one of those syndicated shows. The syndicated programs were enticing for a couple of reasons: The stations got to sell all the time in those shows, while NBC gave them only half the commercial minutes in the "Tonight" show; and the stations had noticed that the audience for Carson was starting to gray along with the star.

That was a potentially fatal trend. The television business had become so youth-oriented that viewers over the age of fifty were all but worthless. Advertisers bought commercial time almost exclusively on the basis of the demographic makeup of the audience. A show needed good young "demos" to make big profits because advertisers had concluded that only young customers were likely to switch brands. Carson still had the biggest audience in late night, but the game had changed: The point was no longer to have a big audience, but to have the *right* audience.

NBC's entertainment executives had been nervously eyeing Johnny's demos for several years. The Gulf war provided a somewhat graceful way to take a little piece out of Johnny to placate the station managers, who were starting to wonder what sort of young female demos they could get with "Love Connection" at 11:30.

As Carson saw it, the stations were simply eating up the first five minutes of his access to the public, and he didn't like it. It was certainly a slap in the face to Carson, who had always resisted every network effort to tamper with his show. If it had happened earlier in his career, Carson would have threatened to quit and stopped this encroachment dead in its tracks. He understood the television business as well as any executive who had ever worked in it. He knew you could never permit the stations to start nibbling at your show, because the next year they might decide they'd like to nibble you back to an 11:45 start. And after that it would be an easy jump to dropping in a rerun of a sitcom at 11:30, pushing the "Tonight" show back to midnight. Carson would never have allowed himself to be nibbled to death that way if he hadn't concluded his time on the show was growing short anyway. That made the threat to quit a bit pointless. So Johnny decided not to bother; though he let NBC know it surely didn't make him happy.

But Carson had not come to New York to win back his five minutes; he was there to deliver a special monologue, and a special message. And he had more jokes to attend to before he got down to business.

He took a few shots at Paramount, then more at GE for not having a clue about the entertainment business. He noted all the pregnancies at the "Today" show and suggested that even Willard Scott had morning sick-\ ness.

Then, without breaking his comic rhythm, he shifted gears. "We've been doing this show many, many years. I've had a few problems. I've never talked about them on the air, but since this is my last year, I might let you in on a few things that have happened."

He had dropped the line in so smoothly, so seamlessly, that it stirred not even a ripple of reaction in the big audience—except down in the front row, where the NBC executives sat. There quizzical looks fogged over a few of the faces. To Betty Hudson, the head of corporate public relations, it was like a faint buzzing in the ear that you couldn't quite identify.

Johnny was onto stories about advertisers he'd offended over the years: the Sara Lee bakery, with his suggestion on the air one night that Sara was actually a "little hooker from Cleveland who made those cookies on the side." Later he learned from the president of the company that Sara Lee had been named after the man's daughter.

Carson was most amused by the reaction of Forest Lawn, the famed Hollywood final resting place, to his comment about their $39.95 funeral: "They take you out, stand you on tippy toes, and drive you into the ground with a croquet mallet. You don't even get a headstone. They just leave your hand up, holding your Diners Club card." The call the next day from the director of Forest Lawn was delivered in an especially otherworldly voice. "Mr. Carson: We shall have the last laugh."

That drew Johnny's biggest laugh of the day. He might have stopped there and saved the row of NBC executives from further squirming, but the responsive crowd and the setting and the emotion of the moment seemed to be making him nostalgic. So Carson rolled amiably on, reminiscing about the seven presidential administrations he'd made fun of, reserving some special thanks that Dan Quayle had come along to provide so much monologue material. Then he recalled a recent bit he'd done on the show about "least-uttered expressions in the English langauge," including: "That's the banjo player's Porsche," and "Oh, you're a Jehovah's Witness. Come on in!"

The audience was totally his now. Every line went off like a fireworks shell. Finally he came around to his point:

"I know you've had a long afternoon, and I would

like to say for one thing here, as you well know, this is the last year that I am doing the 'Tonight' show, and it's been a long, marvelous run."

Now the rumble rolled through the audience, not a single member of which knew that this was supposed to be Johnny Carson's last year on the air. Heads began to turn, one to the other, in the row of NBC executives. Just offstage, Warren Littlefield could suddenly feel his shirt sticking to his back.

Backstage, Dick Ebersol, the president of NBC Sports and a longtime friend of Carson's, heard the words and remembered that Johnny, sitting around a table with Ebersol, Danson, and Cosby a while earlier, had said something about going out and telling them all he was leaving soon. Ebersol had no idea he'd meant *that* soon.

John Agoglia, the executive vice president of NBC and the man who conducted every major talent negotiation for the network, sat up and leaned forward in his chair.

Carson went on: "Brandon came to me as he has for the last ten years, and we had our annual talk."

The murmur in the audience started to spread.

"He wanted me to go into the thirtieth year, and I said I would be delighted. I said, 'Can we make it a year from now?'—meaning this month of May."

Carson had quietly been leaning toward his thirty-year anniversary in October 1992 as a logical endpoint. But he knew that NBC would be preempting the show for its late-night coverage of the Barcelona Olympics for two weeks in July 1992 anyway. Viewing levels were always down in summer as well, and it was always hardest to book guests in the summer months. He always considered June, July, and August the show's dog days. So he simply looked backward on the calendar and realized May was the next closest "sweep" month, a special ratings period of most importance to the local stations—and thus to the networks as well. And if he stepped down in May, he could relax the rest of the summer and take his wife Alex to the French Open and Wimbledon.

The full meaning of what was happening was sinking into the intently listening NBC executives: The king was about to abdicate.

"And so we're going to go into next May," Carson said, "and my last show is going to be May 22, 1992."

Agoglia's face went totally white. He saw the head of Bob Wright, his boss, the president of NBC, jerk around to look at him. Wright had become a good friend of Carson's; they'd scheduled a dinner together that night. Yet Carson had said nothing before about this. All Agoglia could do was shake his head at Wright and look as surprised as everyone else.

This wasn't in the script. Agoglia had been at that same luncheon meeting with Tartikoff, Carson, and Carson's agent, Ed Hookstratten. As always it had been at the Grill restaurant in Beverly Hills. For some time Carson had been working year to year, making his own call every time about whether he wanted to go on with the show. NBC actually sold the show to advertisers on a two-year basis, so Carson was technically signed for two years. But that was just a paper clause. He had an option every year if he wanted to get out.

What Agoglia had heard at the lunch didn't sound to him as if Johnny was definitely setting the date for his finale. It sounded more like another "maybe next year should be the last year, maybe we should call it quits at that" from Carson, lines that Agoglia had heard several times before, always leading to another year on the show. Nor had Tartikoff said anything different to Wright in the months since the lunch. If he and Carson had really agreed on May, Tartikoff hadn't let his boss in on the secret.

Though some NBC executives had been anticipating for some time that Carson would soon make the call to step down, he had not revealed to anybody at NBC his intentions to use the Carnegie Hall appearance to break the biggest television news in years. Nor had he told any of his "Tonight" show staff. Only Alex Carson knew what Johnny was going to do before he left Los Angeles the night before. The guest of honor had decided to stage his own farewell surprise party—and had pulled it off with his customary effortless mastery.

Now Johnny wrapped up his comments, with a strong endorsement of the continuation of the "Tonight" show, because young performers needed a place to make their mark on the nation. Then he thanked the advertisers and station managers for their support through the years.

The row of NBC executives was now completely agitated. They had no press release to hand out; they had no official comment ready; they had no prepared words of praise for their outgoing star. And they knew this story was going to explode across the country.

Warren Littlefield was suddenly struck by the fact that he had just heard one of the biggest announcements in the history of broadcasting. He thought: "And it happened on my stage, at my party." But there was no one close to him in the wings to talk to about it.

On stage, Johnny had come to the end: "So I just wanted to thank you, and I am very grateful and I bid you good-bye. Thank you."

After just a few seconds acknowledging the applause, Carson walked briskly past Littlefield, who returned to his podium for a single, desperately anticlimactic remark: "That's our show. Down the hall and to the right, you'll find the bathrooms . . ."

Agoglia was the first one out of his seat. He went vaulting up the steps to the stage, determined to catch Carson. Johnny knew he had touched off a media frenzy, but he had another appointment, so he wasn't about to stick around explaining himself. Backstage, Carson took just a moment to confirm the news for any doubters in the NBC hierarchy. "This is real, this is real," he said. "I just said it; the world just heard me. It's real." And then he headed for the exit.

Agoglia headed for the nearest phone. The other NBC executives were moving, too. Littlefield and Perry Simon had cars waiting to take them to the airport. They would be making the same presentation to advertisers in Chicago the next day, and the show in New York had run late. At that moment, getting to Chicago to sell "Pacific Station," "Man of the People," and the rest of the fall season shows seemed much more important than dealing with the implications of Johnny Carson's announcement.

Susan Binford, NBC's PR vice president for the West Coast, was quickly conferring with her boss, Betty Hudson. Even if their executives were heading out to the airport, they knew what would come next for them: The press reaction would be a roaring fire, besieging offices on each coast for information. "My office phones are going to light up like a Christmas tree," Binford told Hudson.

But neither of them had anything they could tell the press. Before they could even move out of the hall, the two women were surrounded by the suddenly energized reporters who had sat numbly through the long event. All the reporters were yelling the same question: "Who's getting Johnny's job?"

Neither Binford nor Hudson had the answer to that question at hand; and the guys who were in charge of that decision—Littlefield and Agoglia—had already disappeared from the scene.

Agoglia was on the phone to Ed Hookstratten. "Did you know about this, Ed?" he asked the agent. Agoglia was steaming. He asked Hookstratten why he hadn't called to tell him so the network could have been prepared. "We all have egg on our faces here, Ed," he said. Hookstratten told him that Johnny had kept the decision to himself.

The announcement had put Agoglia in a spot he had not planned to be in—and hated being in. It was not that he was about to mourn the passing of Johnny Carson from the late-night scene. It was the messy surprise he objected to. Agoglia was a man who prided himself on going about his business mechanically, making sure each part of a deal was in working order before it left his hands. This announcement would surely force to the front the question of succession; Agoglia knew all it meant was going with the still secret plan that was already in place. But he was irked because some complications remained unresolved.

The main complication, he knew, was going to be David Letterman.

Letterman was NBC's other late-night star. His 12:30 show, "Late Night," had been on for a decade, turning into a critical triumph and a financial bonanza for NBC, extending the network's dominance of the late-night landscape. Letterman had once been the only logical choice to succeed Carson. But that was before Jay Leno replaced Joan Rivers as the show's permanent guest host.

Agoglia hadn't faced the Letterman issue head-on yet—and he wasn't about to at this moment either, because he simply felt he didn't have to. He hadn't thought an announcement by Carson was imminent, and besides, he had Letterman locked into a contract for another two years.

As for Bob Wright, the only information he'd ever got on David Letterman was that he had never really pushed to be considered for the "Tonight" show job. So Wright simply didn't think of calling Letterman to discuss the news of Carson's announcement with him.

No matter how much press this story was going to generate, the entire executive hierarchy of the NBC entertainment division felt it had better things to do at that moment than worry about the ruffled feathers of some late-night star.

Ten blocks away, in studio 6A of the GE Building, David Letterman was in the middle of taping his "Late Night" show, talking to his lead guest, actress Susan

Sarandon. When the show opened ten minutes earlier, Carson had been finishing up his remarks at Carnegie Hall and Letterman didn't know what Johnny had said.

But during the next commercial, Letterman got word from the control room of the developments at Carnegie Hall. He didn't have time at that moment for the full impact to sink in. As he came out of the break, he began to speak again, pretending to introduce his next scheduled guest. He had been aware since the day before that a special walk-on was scheduled for immediately after this break. Letterman knew who it was, too, and now he had an extra reason to be excited.

As Letterman addressed the audience, he looked to his right, and out from the blue exit doors next to his desk walked Johnny Carson, holding an enormous piece of cardboard. Letterman feigned surprise at the walk-on, but his delight was genuine: Carson meant more to him than any other figure in show business.

Carson's prop was a big check, the kind his bumptious sidekick, Ed McMahon, gave out in his Publishers Clearing House commercials.

"Ed couldn't be here, so he asked me to deliver this," Johnny said to a wide-eyed Dave. "Oddly enough, it seems you are the million-dollar winner."

It was the first time Johnny Carson had walked into the studio since he last broadcast the "Tonight" show from New York in 1973—and he had just announced his retirement date from the "Tonight" show. But Letterman didn't dwell on the nostalgia of the moment. He took his lead from Carson, who he thought looked haggard. If Johnny wanted to address the retirement issue, he would. So the two men chatted amiably.

After a few jokes, Carson said he'd come to New York "to do some business with the affiliates." Then he again dropped in the news almost casually, saying, "It's all coming to an end next year. I've always wanted to be a shepherd."

After the show, Letterman sat in his office ready to review the show with his producer and friend, Robert Morton. He told Morton how amazing he thought Carson was, how Carson had just announced that he'd be retiring after thirty years, and even after doing something that emotional, he was able to come over, do his guest spot, get laughs, and be so at ease. When they replayed the tape of the show and got to the moment where Carson said he was in town to do some business for the affiliates, Letterman couldn't contain his amazement. "You quit!" he shouted at the screen. "That was the business you came into town for: You quit!" Letterman marveled at Carson, but then he had always marveled at Carson, the man whose career had inspired him—and whose job he had always dreamed of getting.

That evening, David Letterman had no calls from the management of NBC.

Halfway to Nevada, Jay Leno's plane dropped down on a runway at a refueling depot near Kansas City.

In Los Angeles, Helen Kushnick, Jay Leno's manager for seventeen years, had already received a call at her office from a contact who attended the affiliate meeting in New York. She now knew what Carson had said, and what it meant. Kushnick first tried to see if Leno was reachable in flight, and was told the private plane was scheduled to make a refueling stop in Kansas City.

While Kushnick waited for Leno to land, she was more apprehensive than excited. The phrase she'd heard so often from her mother kept running through her head: "Be careful of what you wish for; you might get it." Still, she was not wasting a second in trying to reach Jay with the news.

As he got out of the plane to stretch his legs, Leno was told he had a call in the depot office. When he picked up the phone, he expected to hear Helen's voice.

"Johnny announced he was quitting today," she told Leno the second he was on the line.

"What? What do you mean?" he said. "Today, at the NBC thing in New York? What did he say?"

"He said he's doing one more year and that he's quitting next May."

They didn't have to fill in any blanks. Both of them knew what Carson's decision meant for them: They would begin work on the "Tonight" show the following May, on the Monday after Carson's exit.

Leno's emotions, as usual, were muted. "It is official?" he asked.

"No, NBC hasn't made it official."

"So we still have to keep it quiet," he said.

Leno had only told the news to his wife, Mavis. Helen had told nobody. Only they and the very top NBC executives knew what had happened just seven days earlier in the NBC corporate offices in Burbank: Jay Leno had signed a contract, worth more than $6 million a year, with the NBC television network that guaranteed him the job as host of the "Tonight" show as soon as Johnny Carson stepped down.

It was the biggest job in television, on the longest-running show in television. As of this day, Jay Leno had it; and Helen Kushnick had gotten it for him.

NBC eventually got around to authorizing an official statement a day later. Summoning up the collective eloquence of the company, the statement said: "Obviously the 'Tonight' show will continue. For now we're delighted that our association with the king of late-night television will continue for another year. We will spend the immediate future reflecting on the statement Johnny made yesterday. No immediate announcement is planned!"

2

THE EMPIRE OF THE NIGHT

T he producer of an upcoming late-night talk show ran into Johnny Carson, then late in his career, at a network party. The producer would never presume to solicit advice, but Carson knew and respected the producer, and he asked him how the planning for the new show was going.

Carson listened politely for some time to the mostly general ideas the producer tossed back at him—some suggestions about comedy sketches, how the music would be integrated, what kinds of guests they would try to book. When the producer was finished, Carson paused, cocked an eyebrow, and offered one sentence: "These shows are about the guy behind the desk."

For almost forty years, millions of Americans had stayed up later than they intended watching a guy behind a desk tell jokes, comment on the news, and schmooze and banter with celebrities. The creation was an undeniable American original: the late-night talk show.

And it was the exclusive property of one network, NBC. The "Tonight" show began in 1954 when Sylvester (Pat) Weaver, the president of NBC, decided to expand the network's programming past the 11 P.M. local news. Weaver wanted his nighttime entry to be something along the lines of "Today": some news and light features with interviews. At that time a comic-musician named Steve Allen was doing a much-talked-about ninety-minute show on WNBC, the network's flagship station in New York. After settling some disagreements about the format, NBC offered the "Tonight" job to Allen. The show went on the air September 27, 1954.

Pat Weaver had put it on the NBC network, but Steve Allen defined the "Tonight" show: It was a nightly mix of comedy, music, and show business chatter. Allen's "Tonight" show had many conventional elements—the familiar celebrity faces, familiar singers singing standard songs. But what started keeping people awake past midnight was the star's high-energy wit and his appreciation for how the emerging medium could lend itself to spontaneous, original humor. Allen put cameras on the street and tried to find unscripted comedy in random interviews with passersby. He was a comedy adventurer, jumping into vats of funny stuff like Jell-O, or dressing up in a suit of tea bags and lowering himself into a giant cup of hot water.

Success came fast, and once the show's producer, Jules Green, successfully made a deal that paid all guests, no matter how big, the union scale (then $265.50 per appearance), the show quickly established the highly efficient economics of late-night talk. The star could command a massive salary—Allen got up to about $3,500 a week during his tenure—but the other costs were modest and mostly fixed. The total original budget was $11,000 a week. With the amount of commercial time in a ninety-minute, five-night-a-week show so abundant, "Tonight" instantly set itself up as the champion cash cow in the network pasture.

Live every night, the "Tonight" show was the freshest entertainment on television. It proved to be so fresh and entertaining, in fact, that NBC decided to try Allen in the bigger arena of prime time. Just a little over two years into his "Tonight" run, Allen picked up the show and moved it more or less whole to Sunday night at eight, where he did battle with some success against "The Ed Sullivan Show" on CBS.

After a quick, embarrassing flop with a new show called "America After Dark," NBC decided to revive the "Tonight" format with a different host. Several were considered, but the network quickly settled on an offbeat monologuist and frequent game show guest named Jack Paar.

Like Allen, Paar, who took over the show in July, 1957, tooled the "Tonight" show to the specifications of his own talents. For Paar that meant stirring public opinion like an overheated cauldron. He took on causes, like Castro's Cuba; took on censors; even fought his battles with his enemies right on the air. Paar's show was constantly embroiled in controversy or silliness; he cried, he quit, he fired people. Paar's show mesmerized the country; it was the first "water cooler" show, the first television program whose impact could be measured by the amount of talk it generated around the nation's offices the next morning.

Paar made the "Tonight" show a phenomenon. After him, NBC would never again consider any other form of programming in late night. But Paar's fragile emotions and the intensity of his nightly performances consumed the star long before the nation was tired of watching him. Paar announced he was quitting in 1962.

Possible successors had been rumored before, because Paar was so often close to quitting. Johnny Carson's name would always come up because he had so smoothly filled in during occasional assignments as guest host. After a short winnowing process that included a tryout performance in which Carson's stand-up act electrified an audience of advertising executives at the Greenbrier resort in Virginia, NBC had a clear choice.

Carson had already turned down the job once. He had earlier expressed doubts about comedians appearing too frequently, how that could wear out the public's interest in them. He had also heard advice that following a figure of national fascination like Paar amounted to professional suicide. Carson had a good thing going. He was the host of "Who Do You Trust?," a hot ABC game show, which had become a comedy show thanks to Carson's rapid-fire byplay with his often absurd guests.

But NBC came back a second time: Carson was the "type" they were looking for: He was lightning fast with ad-libs (even though many of his game-show quips were scripted), he was boyishly good-looking, and he was clearly a Waspy midwesterner. No one ever articulated why that mattered. But much of television comedy was still the province of ethnic comics, and this was a national show being sent into homes where a sizable portion of the audience was either already in bed or heading that way. The intimacy that implied seemed to underscore the need to find a star who was comfortable to the mass of viewers—and their mass prejudices.

Carson's contract with ABC committed him to the game show for twenty-six more weeks. NBC was willing to wait; the network was sure it had the right man.

Carson stepped onto the stage as the host of the "Tonight" show on October 1, 1962.

Johnny Carson conquered America from bases on either side of the country, but his roots were deep in the middle. Born in Corning, Iowa, in 1926, Carson grew up in Nebraska in a solidly middle-class family.

When he was twelve, Carson sent away for a mail-order magic kit—and he never had to think again about what he wanted to do with his life. Soon he was "The Great Carsoni," performing for bridge clubs and church socials.

After the Navy in World War II and the Univerity of Nebraska on the GI bill, Carson began his career on radio in Omaha. He paid his dues as a television broadcaster beginning in Omaha, and eventually moved to Los Angeles. After a series of failed attempts to break into network television, Carson finally found the right vehicle, "Who Do You Trust?"

Carson had a hit; he was in the right place, New York, at precisely the right time, when the television business was exploding. When Paar went on vacation, Carson got a shot behind the "Tonight" desk. No one ever glided more smoothly into his element.

From his first night on the air as the new permanent

host Carson was a smash. His ratings quickly eclipsed Paar's. Of course, Carson wasn't doing Jack Paar's show; he was doing Johnny Carson's show, taking bits and pieces of his earlier TV work and fleshing them out with his growing talent for stand-up comedy. Like Allen and Paar before him, Carson put his own imprint on the show. In a short time, nobody talked about the "Tonight" show in terms of either of the old stars anymore. Johnny Carson *was* the "Tonight" show.

The nightly Carson monologue quickly became the most consistent five to seven minutes of entertainment on television. As Carson grew into the show, his comedy grew as well; he started dropping his early reliance on slightly risqué material for more substantial comedic commentary on the news of the day. Johnny's monologue became the country's most acutely observed political barometer. Johnny made fun of them all: anyone in politics or show business or public life. But the ones he made *fools* of were truly in trouble.

What stood out most clearly was Carson's ability to communicate with his audience. He gave them exactly what they wanted in the minutes before they ended their day: good laughs, big stars, a little music, sometimes a kind of naughty pleasure. His strengths were his ear for language, his timing, and his uncanny sense of how far he could take the show and when he needed to pull back. He had such extraordinary skill at presiding over this odd form of entertainment that he made it look effortless. This was his ultimate magic trick.

On the air, Carson projected complete authority. Paar may have been called the "king of late-night television," but Carson turned the show into an empire, the most powerful seat in all of show business. Guests paid homage. Nobody crossed Johnny; careers could be at stake. More than anyone, comics came to see Carson's show as their main chance. To kill on the "Tonight" show was to be launched toward stardom. The "Tonight" show became the one altar at which everyone in show business worshiped.

Carson accomplished all this despite being often racked with self-doubt. The most confident, smoothest man on television, the idol of millions of young men— especially those who thought they too could make people laugh—would sometimes, among his closest associates, blurt out how terrified he was that it might all disappear at any moment.

For NBC, Carson was the key to the mint. The show poured out cash, many years grossing more than $100 million and providing as much as 15 to 20 percent of the profits recorded by the entire network. Carson's own income quickly set the standard for television performers, reaching $1 million a year before he had finished a decade on the air. As his hold on the country's bedtime habits grew, so did his hold on the NBC treasury. All the leverage in future contract negotiations lay with Johnny. In the mid-seventies he passed $3 million a year. But he never stopped validating his worth. The other networks noticed the profit machine NBC had built in the midnight hour, and sought to build their own prototypes. They tried, with Joey Bishop, Merv Griffin, Dick Cavett. Later, syndicators tried with Merv again, and also with David Brenner and Alan Thicke.

Carson swept them all away with the same apparent nonchalance he displayed in the middle of a monologue. He was a late-night gunfighter with a perfect record. The only time a network established any kind of success against him was when it deliberately moved away from challenging him at his own game. ABC found an audience for news viewers starting in 1979 with "Nightline," a nightly news and discussion program. Ted Koppel's matchless interviewing skills helped ABC grab a piece of late night, but mostly that piece came with new viewers. Johnny held his own.

In 1980, in a showdown with NBC president Fred Silverman, Johnny used his ultimate power: He threatened to quit the show. That was all he needed to wring an unprecedented deal out of NBC. In addition to more than $5 million a year in salary, Carson got series commitments from the network for his production company, and most important, he gained ownership over the "Tonight" show. From then on, everything Carson did on the "Tonight" show belonged not to NBC, but to him. In total, the deal was estimated at more than $50 million. No one in television had ever received anything close to that amount. And at the same time, Carson got something else he wanted: The show was cut down from ninety minutes to one hour.

By that time, NBC had started to build from the lush vine of the "Tonight" show the most fruitful garden in television. With its base in the unassailable Carson, NBC turned late night into an expanding industry. In 1973 the network added an eccentric interview show at 12:30 A.M. called "Tomorrow." And in 1976 it created another landmark comedy show, "Saturday Night Live," spreading NBC's late-night dominance to the weekend.

With a hit six nights of the week, NBC decided that

Johnny's decision to cut out the last thirty minutes of the "Tonight" show created another opportunity: a new comedy/talk show to follow Carson. Silverman first had the idea to fill the slot with a name from the past: Steve Allen. But Carson was not enthusiastic about that idea. He didn't see any reason to allow a show likely to be much like his own to come on the air right after he said good night.

But NBC didn't abandon the idea. Its programmers, led in 1981 by Brandon Tartikoff, saw how effectively "Saturday Night Live" had proved the value of building on strength. Increasingly there was money to be made in the fringe periods of the television day, especially if a show could appeal to young viewers the way "Saturday Night Live" did.

And so it made sound financial sense for NBC to beat the other networks to the punch at 12:30, just as it had at 11:30.

But there was another reason for NBC to push for expansion in late night. This time period had become the clear cultural hallmark of the network. Just as CBS News once stood for tradition and greatness at that network, and ABC made its early name with innovative sports coverage, late night was the signature programming of NBC. From Allen to Paar to Carson and "Saturday Night Live," late night was cutting-edge television—and only NBC had it.

For thirty years NBC had been unerring in choosing its late-night stars. In 1982 NBC found the next link in the late-night chain. His name was David Letterman.

When David Letterman was a boy growing up in Indianapolis, he grasped an essential truth about himself:

He was funny. "I always knew I was a first-class wiseass," Letterman said.

He later figured out the genealogy: His maternal grandfather, once a miner and later a farmer, always came across slyly funny, pretending to be mean, growling at the kids; only later did Dave grasp that it was "always done with a sense of irony." There was also Letterman's father, Joe, an Indianapolis florist. "He was goofy-funny," as Dave described him. "Told a lot of corny jokes, did a lot of silly things, mostly calculated to keep the house in an uproar. I really only noticed after he died that my mother is the least demonstrative person on the planet."

The Letterman house could have been captured in any Wonder Bread commercial from the 1950s: mid-American, middle-class, honest, shop-owning, white-bread-eating folks. Dave was born on April 12, 1947, the middle child between two sisters. When he was not yet ten, Letterman got a Tinker Toys set as a gift; the first thing he built was a microphone, just like the ones he saw Arthur Godfrey and Garry Moore use on television. When he watched Johnny Carson on "Who Do You Trust?" and later Steve Allen on his post-"Tonight" syndicated comedy show, the young Dave came to envision himself someday being a similar kind of wise guy on television.

At Broad Ripple High School in Indianapolis, in the midst of getting mediocre grades and goofing around, Letterman enrolled in speech class. "It was the only thing other than girls that got my attention." Letterman had found a major for college and a direction to pursue for life: broadcasting. "I knew from the time I was a sophomore in high school what I wanted to do."

He was single-minded and extremely disciplined in his approach toward building a career. That trait would never leave him.

At Ball State University in Muncie, Indiana, Letterman practiced his craft at the campus radio station and landed a real job even before graduating. WLWI-TV, channel 13, the ABC affiliate in Indianapolis, hired him as a booth announcer for the summer. He was twenty years old and he was already a broadcaster. The experience was invaluable. Letterman read some news ("I knew that was all wrong for me") and hosted a kids' show and the late-night bad-movie program. He soon became the weekend weather anchor, always taking every opportunity to squeeze in a joke.

Letterman was in his hometown, married at twenty-one to his college sweetheart, Michelle Cook, and he was getting some recognition for working at a big-time television station. He was even making some decent money—about $17,000 a year, enough to buy himself a sweet, red 1972 Olds Cutlass, complete with black vinyl top and sports wheels ($4,300 new), and a 1973 red, half-ton Chevy pickup ($2,700 at a fleet sale). But none of that was satisfying; Letterman wanted more.

At night, at home with Michelle, Dave would sit at a typewriter and pound out scripts for "The Mary Tyler Moore Show" and "The Bob Newhart Show." He didn't have a clue what he was doing; the scripts were long enough for a full-length movie. But he had to do it. What he didn't tell anyone, not even Michelle, was that in writing sitcoms he was still submerging his real desire: to perform, to stand up in front of an audience and be funny, to be on television. "My family didn't understand because I never explained it to them. I was too embarrassed to admit to myself that this is what I wanted to do."

For a year Letterman tried talk radio, an excruciating experience at a minuscule, 5,000-watt, daytime-only station. Through an ad in a Hollywood trade paper, he got the name of a Hollywood agent who actually responded to his letter and promised to represent him if he ever came to L.A. Letterman had already decided he had to go there, had to try. Michelle supported the plan and helped convince him he could do it. She arranged to quit her job on precisely the day he said they'd be leaving, only to have her husband get cold feet and stay at the radio station for another three months.

On Memorial Day weekend, 1975, Dave and Michelle Letterman closed up their Indianapolis lives, packed up the Cutlass and the truck, and pointed them west. They drove tandem though the plains and desert, with Letterman staring at the alien landscape, his stomach refusing to unknot, wondering what the hell he'd done.

The Tuesday after they arrived, Letterman turned up at the agent's office, only to learn he wouldn't be much help; the agency had shut down its business as of that morning.

After a couple of nights at the Safari Motor Inn on Vineland Avenue, Dave and Michelle settled into a semidetached house in a Hispanic section of town. Their landlady, Gladys, was riddled with arthritis and needed frequent trips to the hospital for care. Dave had to lift her into his truck because her knees were locked. "I had time to do this because I wasn't doing anything else, and I thought, all right, at least I'm being decent to this woman."

Michelle quickly got a good job as an assistant buyer for the May Company. That took care of keeping them alive, and allowed Letterman to chase his muddled muse. The second Monday after he arrived in Los Angeles, he showed up at the Comedy Store on Sunset Boulevard. It was amateur night. He took the flimsy material he had prepared, stared into the blinding beam of the spotlight, and stepped forward onto the stage.

Within seconds he felt a surge of exhilaration like nothing he'd ever before experienced. All that terror—the decision to quit his job, to drive across the country—hadn't been for nothing. Letterman thought: "At least you put the gun to your head and you didn't flinch."

With a boyish face that seemed to convey an impish temperament (dozens of writers would later compare him to Huckleberry Finn), Letterman was tall, skinny, young, long-haired, red-bearded, and extremely raw. But he clearly had something. Mitzi Shore, the club owner, told him, "Ah, you should come back next week." Letterman, convinced he'd bombed, held on to the words as he went out into the night, looked out across the lights of L.A. spread out below Sunset Boulevard, and thought: "How did I get to this bizarre place?"

Jay Leno saw him at the club soon after; he knew a new voice had arrived. "A lot of times on amateur night, guys constantly do things like 'What if Bob Dylan was a tree,'" Leno said. "But all of a sudden this new guy from the Midwest gets up and he has this really clever, hip material. He knocked everybody out."

Leno was then already a prince among the stand-up frogs. The others saw him as a polished, powerful stage presence, honed from years of working comedy clubs in Boston and New York. He was younger than many of the new comics at the Comedy Store, including Letterman, but he seemed to be so far ahead of them, they'd never catch up. They stood in awe of Leno.

Letterman was so impressed by Leno's ability as a stand-up that he told himself he ought to go back to Indianapolis, "because he was doing it the way I wanted to, and I thought I'd probably never do it as well."

But Letterman learned by watching Leno. "Jay filled in a huge blank for me. What I learned from Jay was you can do almost anything if you have a consistent attitude." He also took note of how Leno connected himself to the audience. "I get it: We're all Jay's hip friends," Letterman said.

And so he started absorbing Leno's attitude and moves. The act improved quickly. Letterman's material was always strong—smart and sharp and verbally creative. The geek from Broad Ripple High in the Speedway City, the speech major from Ball State in Muncie, started sounding like the smartest guy in the room.

But the more deeply he immersed himself in Hollywood, the more Letterman found himself cringing. Even in his fringe association with show business, Letterman was growing repulsed by the sleaziness of it, the phoniness and the shameless self-aggrandizement. He resisted hiring an agent or manager, and when he did, the manager he picked, Helen Gorman (later Kushnick) had a volatile temperament that Letterman could not long abide. Helen had seen Dave performing in the clubs at the same time she'd seen her other big client, Jay Leno. She thought Dave was clever, good-looking (he'd dropped the beard), and had a lot of promise. But after only about a year working together, Dave's business relationship with Helen ended.

Even without managers, his career accelerated. The other comedy clubs wanted him. Talk of television had started. Then he picked up management he could live with: Jack Rollins, a classy New York manager of acts like Woody Allen and Billy Crystal, took him on. Rollins told Letterman exactly what he wanted to hear: His future was in television.

All was going well—except the marriage. Michelle Letterman never stopped supporting her husband in his climb. She had been the only believer at one time. But Letterman, in his words, "behaved badly." He started performing at a Comedy Store in Pacific Beach. Out late every night, Dave loved the camaraderie with the other comics as well as the attention he was getting from some of the customers. Eighteen-year-old college girls from San Diego filled the place. Letterman, married at twenty-one and still mostly a naive Hoosier, succumbed to the abundant temptations. He drank, he caroused, while his wife waited at home. "It was embarrassing and superficial," he said. Letterman, the man who despised shallow show business posturing, had been seduced by his first taste of public popularity. As the good life with the beach girls beckoned, Letterman decided he wanted out of his marriage, a decision that had a devastating effect on his wife. She had given up her life in Indiana to allow him to pursue his dream of making strangers laugh.

"I ruined the marriage," Letterman said. "For what I put her though, I felt like I should burn in hell for the rest of my life." The guilt lingered long after the marriage ended. Much later he learned that she was happily remarried, and he hoped that might help "flush the horrible memory for her." His conclusion: "It was just me being a dork: Hey, young girls! It took a long time for me to reconcile the guilt."

Still, the breakup had one creative side effect for Letterman: Merrill Markoe entered his life.

Markoe had been teaching art at Southern Cal when she decided to try comedy writing. She tried television writing, but found it alienating to see her work fed through the sausage-making process that produced television comedy. Looking for her own voice, Markoe tried stand-up at the Comedy Store, where she quickly noticed this tall guy from Indiana. Dave was the second-best guy at the club, Markoe concluded. Like everyone else, Merrill thought Jay was the best. "He had the attitude, the cleanest attitude," she said. "Jay started all that ironic stuff that you then started to see everywhere."

It certainly turned up in David Letterman's act, some of it written by Merrill Markoe. After they started to go out, she began giving him some of her jokes. That was the beginning of a collaboration that would produce ground-breaking television, a ten-year personal relationship, and, in the end, a lot of unhappiness for Merrill Markoe.

Dave didn't open himself to many people. But Merrill was quickly a special person to him. "We were on one of our first dates," Letterman said. "I was drunk, of course, and I told her. She was the only person I ever told." And so Merrill Markoe got to hear David Letterman's dream. Step one: get to the "Tonight" show, do a killer spot, and then sit next to Johnny Carson, who was his idol. Step two: succeed Carson as the host himself some day.

"All the time I knew him," Markoe said, "Dave dreamed of going on the 'Tonight' show, and of being the host." Letterman resisted doing the "Tonight" show until he was convinced he was totally ready. He'd seen other guys go on once with their best four or five minutes, do well and then be asked back, only to bomb because they only had 4 or 5 good minutes. Letterman wanted to have at least a half hour of A-quality material before he took the biggest step of his life. In November 1978, he was ready.

The nerves Letterman felt that night would have reduced him to a puddle of perspiration if he had not perfected his routine to the point where he could have performed it in a coma. "I knew I had that one cold. Unless there was an earthquake or a power outage or an assassination, I knew I had that one slick. I did it and it worked beyond my wildest dreams, and I sat down and Johnny Carson is sitting right there, and you're just talking and talking and praying to God that it's over soon, and you're looking around and you're seeing stuff that you've seen on TV for years. And you can't let yourself think for a second or, you know, your head would explode. So you're talking and talking and just praying, Oh please go to a commercial, please go to a goddamn commercial! And the next thing you know you're out of there and it's just, Holy Christ, I was on the 'Tonight' show!"

Letterman's spot struck everyone who saw it the same way: A new star had just emerged. "When he walked through the curtain on the 'Tonight' show for the first time, I got chills," said Tom Dreesen, one of Letterman's closest comic friends. "I knew he had found his home. He did the strongest first shot I'd ever seen."

Letterman's life changed instantly. "I was in a different dimension. It's like West Point graduation and your hat's in the air. All those years hanging around the Comedy Store and driving around in your truck and heating up burritos at the 7-Eleven, and drinking warm quarts of beer. All of a sudden it's changed. You're on the 'Tonight' show. It was like a miracle. It turned me upside down. I go to the Comedy Store now and I was an important guy because I had been on the 'Tonight' show. I was one of the chosen few."

Letterman made just two more "Tonight" appearances—and then was asked to guest host. It was the all-time record for fastest trip to Johnny Carson's chair.

Fred Silverman, about to be honored at a B'nai B'rith dinner in early 1980, needed to provide some entertainment from his NBC stable of stars. Naturally he asked Carson first, but that was a futile gesture. He inquired about Bill Cosby and some others, but no one was available. Silverman was in a characteristic black rage when one of his PR executives, Alan Baker, mentioned that he had just seen David Letterman at a club and he had been very funny.

"He damn well better be funny," Silverman told Baker.

The night of the event, Baker held his breath when Letterman was introduced as the evening's entertainment. Two minutes into Letterman's performance, Baker let out a gasp of relief. Laughter cascaded through the banquet hall. Afterward, Silverman happily accepted congratulations all around the room for the superior entertainment. As he left that night he said to Baker, "We've got to get this kid a show."

Silverman soon decided what it was to be. He wanted Letterman to start a daytime talk/service show with a regular "family" of performers, ninety minutes live every morning at ten from New York. Arthur Godfrey's name was mentioned as what to shoot for.

Dave and Merrill didn't care what Fred Silverman wanted; they had their own vision of what their show would be: funny, inventive, groundbreaking. Everything daytime television had never been. Merrill, the head writer, was forced, thanks to a last-minute resignation, to take over as producer, a job she had never done in her life. Nobody on the show knew how to find cue cards to write on, so they used enormous pieces of cardboard. They stumbled onto the air in June 1980.

The show only righted itself after a new producer, Barry Sand, brought in to impose some order, suggested they dump everything else and concentrate on Letterman. And the new director, Hal Gurnee, who had once worked with Parr, brought a sense of inventive style to the show's look. Markoe, freed up to write for a cast of one, created strong point-of-view pieces that she and Letterman liked: Dave out in New York at some bizarre shop, Dave observing Valentine's Day in the cafeteria. One day they even set the show on fire—

by mistake. Letterman thought they would all get kicked out of show business for that one.

They didn't—but they certainly weren't setting the business on fire. The ratings never even built up a pulse. After a few weeks a few viewers noticed that Letterman was starting to hit his stride. But the situation was already hopeless. Stations started dropping him in favor of syndicated game shows. Letterman got on the phone and begged station managers to give the teetering show a chance. Nothing he did mattered. The show was canceled, and given four weeks' notice.

If Letterman had taken time to think about it, he would have been devastated. Instead he was devastated later. He still had a show to do, and once out from under the burden of NBC's expectations, the show really cut loose. Dave took the show live to the home of a family in Cresco, Iowa. He roamed the halls of NBC looking for wilder stories, finding them in unlikely subjects like the grotesque food available in the sixth-floor vending machines. He flew in a farmer from Missouri named Floyd Stiles and gave him a gooey, show business–style tribute.

Merrill came up with one idea because she and Dave loved their dog Bob so much. Merrill thought she could make a segment out of the stupid things people do with their pets. She called it Stupid Pet Tricks.

"The David Letterman Show" lasted nineteen weeks on the air. Letters poured into NBC condemning the cancellation. College kids hitched across the country with petitions to save him. A group of housewives from Long Island tried to block traffic in Manhattan in protest. The show won two Emmy Awards.

None of it made any difference, not even to soften

the blow for Letterman. For the first time in his career, something had gone totally wrong. He had failed, and it only confirmed his deepest doubts about himself. Letterman didn't think in terms of a show being over; he thought his career was over.

Within weeks Westinghouse Broadcasting was talking about an offer for a syndicated show. NBC acted swiftly, signing Letterman to a holding contract—he was paid to do nothing. Letterman, still shell-shocked from the cancellation and needing to prove he was still worth something, told one reporter it was a million-dollar deal. It was, in one respect. NBC agreed to pay Letterman that much as a penalty if it didn't come up with a new show for him before the contract ended. In reality he made several hundred thousand dollars, still not bad for doing nothing.

Not that it salved the wound. Letterman knew of other contracts signed in order to keep talent off the market, and the talent sometimes never resurfaced. Letterman went back to California, where he and Markoe shared a Malibu beach house, and stewed. He worked the clubs, and subbed for Carson some more.

The NBC holding deal had one other side effect: It helped fuel speculation that Letterman might be in line to succeed Carson. There was always speculation about the "Tonight" chair; it went with the royal metaphor: If somebody is king and rules late-night television, then it must follow that somebody else is next in line. Of course, the others presumed to be in the line with Letterman at the time included such names as Richard Dawson and Burt Reynolds.

But Carson himself seemed to be sending signals about what he thought of Letterman. Unlike previous heirs apparent, whom Carson tended to freeze out, Letterman seemed to have ingratiated himself to Carson. And Carson even dropped his name on the show. In his monologue on April 8, 1981, Carson said recent developments in Washington had him wondering: "If I quit, what would the line of succession be? Would it be Letterman, Bush, Haig, or would it be Letterman, Bush, Tip O'Neill, and then Haig?"

A few months later, on a night when the monologue was falling flat, Carson said, "Why don't I just go on home and we can bring Letterman in right now?"

The buzz about the line of succession was Letterman's first opportunity to reveal his feelings about someday getting Johnny Carson's job. He shrank from the prospect, either dismissing the speculation as nonsense or even occasionally declaring he really had no interest at all.

Partly this was simple respect: Letterman idolized Carson and found the idea of looking as if he was pushing him out of the "Tonight" show completely repugnant. But the other part was strategy; nobody had ever got far openly coveting Johnny's job. "I knew there was no future in making an enemy of Johnny Carson," Letterman said.

NBC had that million-dollar penalty payment forcing the issue of finding a show for Letterman. The network program executives didn't have to think too hard about a program that would suit Letterman's talents. The idea of extending the late-night comedy franchise another hour had not gone away. And the show Letterman wound up doing in the morning had struck everyone who saw it as a misplaced late-night talk show.

NBC made the link between the shows closer by giving Carson Productions a weekly fee to cover the cost of making sure the shows didn't duplicate each other in guest bookings. The weekly fee of $5,000 paid the cost of hiring an executive from Carson Productions, David Tebet, a former NBC talent manager who was close to Carson. Tebet served as the liaison between the two shows.

Still, a few other issues had to be resolved. In the months before Letterman took his new show to late night, he had a meeting with Tebet, who spelled out the late-night rules: First, no monologue. Second, the band could have no more than four members. Third, the bandleader, or whoever was going to qualify as Letterman's Ed McMahon, could not sit down at the panel with the host.

With those stipulations, the new show would have Johnny's blessing.

Merrill Markoe couldn't have cared less. She wanted the show to be as different from "Tonight" as possible anyway. They'd call what Dave did in the show's first minutes "opening remarks." A four-man rock band was far more to their own taste than Doc Severinsen's big-band sound. And Paul Shaffer, the new bandleader, would stay in the band area and banter with Dave from there.

The rest would be a show grounded in the same comic sensibility that Dave and Merrill brought to the daytime show, only with a bit more organization to it. Much of the staff carried over from the morning show.

It was as though they'd had a nineteen-week out-of-town tryout for the real run in New York. And now they were ready.

No one would have confused the show that went on the air at 12:30 A.M. on February 1, 1982, with the "Tonight" show. It was fresher, livelier, more inventive—younger. It was also ragged and a bit unkempt. Letterman didn't step into late-night stardom whole. Even with the morning show and all his "Tonight" experience—by then he had guest hosted twenty-nine times—hosting the new show generated much more anxiety. Letterman looked a bit spooked as he walked onto the stage at NBC's studio 6A for the first time. Bill Murray filled most of the hour ranting around the stage doing calisthenics while singing "Physical" in his bad lounge-singer voice.

But "Late Night" had time, plenty of time, to find its own voice. At that hour there was no serious competition, other than a good night's sleep. The network's ratings expectations were extremely modest. And Letterman's act, with its post-sixties ironic sensibility, was pitched to the right audience: the college crowd. As Dave put it: "Our audience doesn't have to get up at eight in the morning."

Murray, who had made his name on "Saturday Night Live," fit into a category of young comics that "Tonight" simply didn't book. Letterman would become the place to see such talent: Richard Lewis, Michael Keaton, Sandra Bernhard, Jeff Altman.

And the whole show was infused with attitude, Dave's attitude; wry, cynical, goofy, smart-ass Dave. "Dave was saying, 'We're not part of the entertainment world,' " said one of his managers, Stu Smiley. " 'We're part of you. We're part of the viewer.' "

Dave, thinking like a broadcaster first and a comic second, found ways to use the fact that they were on television to invent comedy: He took the camera on a behind-the-scenes tour of the studio on the very first night. Two months later he introduced elevator races in the RCA Building. Later that year they held a real bar mitzvah on the show.

One night they did a show in which Dave and his guests had their voices overdubbed by British actors. Another night they decided to strap a camera to a monkey's back and have him roller-skate throughout the studio (the monkey also bit Sandra Bernhard). On the 360-degree-rotation show, the picture of Dave on the screen rotated 90 degrees during each segment—halfway through, Dave and guest Peter Ustinov were exactly upside-down.

They never set out deliberately to parody the conventional talk show; they only tried to be different. But the result was something like the reverse image of a talk show (and yes, they did a reverse-image show, too).

Dave paid homage to Steve Allen in a series of stunts modeled after Allen's jumps into tubs of Jell-O. In the most memorable one, Letterman wore a Velcro suit and stuck himself to a wall. In another he wore a suit covered in Alka-Seltzer tablets and jumped into a 1,000-gallon tank of water. In a suit of tortilla chips, he jumped in a tank of yogurt dip. He even tried a suit of Rice Krispies in a tub of milk so he could snap, crackle, and pop.

Each stunt was followed by a slow-motion replay.

Letterman was playing the medium like a newly discovered instrument. Other stunts were just goofy, juvenile ideas made hilarious by Letterman's pervasive anarchic attitude. He dropped watermelons off the roof; he squashed gooey things in a hydraulic press; he crunched a Smurf doll under a steamroller; he smashed the Energizer bunny to smithereens with a baseball bat. The show held dog races in the sixth-floor halls.

Letterman also displayed his growing verbal virtuosity by calling people on the phone and wringing comedy out of them, or sending remote cameras to places like photo stores and restaurants and starting conversations that somehow presented the mundane as hilarious. Letterman's writers soon discovered that they didn't always have to write material; they could just come up with a goofy premise, drop Letterman in the middle of it, watch him fix his brain on it, and turn it into laughs.

They started calling what they were doing "found humor"; it wasn't scripted, it was just Dave finding something funny in whatever situation they placed him in.

Merrill also found strange places for Dave to go for pretaped pieces; stores that only sold lampshades, or only sold lightbulbs. He went to a store that called itself the Mattress King and asked if there was a mattress queen. ("Yes, and several mattress princes.") He visited a dry cleaner with a fashionable address and asked how certain celebrities liked their dry cleaning.

In one memorable remote piece, Dave got a letter from a young female viewer who criticized his running shoes. He and a crew went to her house on Long Island.

When he didn't find her at home, he got out the lawn mower and cut her lawn. When her brother showed up, they all visited the sister's room and Dave went through her closet. A burly, slovenly crew member sat on her frilly bed. Then Letterman went to Sears, where the woman worked. He talked a customer into taking over the young woman's spot at the jewelry counter while he took her to the shoe department so she could pick out new running shoes for him.

Perhaps the most famous remote piece took place just after the General Electric Company bought NBC in 1986. Letterman and crew went to GE's headquarters looking to drop off a welcoming basket of fruit. Rebuffed by guards outside, Letterman took advantage of a moment of confusion to get himself in the building, went up to the board of director's floor, and then encountered a truly nasty security chief, who refused the basket and snatched his hand away when Letterman offered to shake hands—a moment that forever became known as the "GE handshake."

These pieces created a new late-night form: journalistic humor. They were helped enormously by Letterman's skill as an editor; he found just the right cuts in the pieces to give each one pace and punch. As Letterman described it, "We want viewers at home to look at each other and say: 'What the hell was that?' We want to pierce that flat TV screen."

The program's initial weakness was its last remaining link to the talk-show convention: interviews. Letterman struggled with them early on; with some guests he seemed not to care, and with others he seemed to try much too hard. The interviews improved when the show's comedy vision carried over. Guests were preinterviewed and told that all that was expected of them was to have a funny story or two to tell.

In the search for laughs, Letterman often struck some viewers—and interview subjects—as mean-spirited. Cher called him an asshole on the air. He sent Jane Seymour packing, in tears. He went into full interview meltdown with Shirley MacLaine, who refused to do a preinterview, came spoiling for a fight, and got one. She said Cher had been right; he said sayonara forever.

"Late Night" started building its own repertory company of guests; they weren't the traditional Hollywood stars, but sports figures and news anchors, offbeat comics and sometimes obscure actors. Television names were much more likely to appear than movie names. "Late Night" wasn't about plugging the latest movie; it was about comedy and, mostly, it was about David Letterman.

Thanks to the reliable laughs he generated, as well as the spontaneity of his interaction with Dave, one comic became the signature "Late Night" guest: Jay Leno. They had been linked from their earliest days together in the comedy clubs. Now they helped each other establish reputations as the two funniest guys with attitudes on television. Jay appeared almost forty times on "Late Night," and the staff almost always felt these shows were the funniest of the season.

Praise arrived before ratings. Letterman was first called refreshing, and later brilliant. "Late Night" was labeled the show of the eighties. Emmy Awards rolled in. Dollars followed. Letterman's audience grew modestly, but steadily, up toward 4 million viewers a night.

And these were highly prized viewers: mostly young, mostly male, mostly people who were not being reached by many other television shows and certainly not in so dense a concentration.

NBC had built the ideal franchise: two hit shows back to back, while no one else in television had even one entertainment show working in late night.

When Letterman first came to late night, NBC gave advertisers a deal that made them buy some commercials for his show if they wanted to buy into the "Tonight" show. That's how they protected the new entry.

By the mid-1980s the positions had reversed. Many advertisers, especially for products like beer and running shoes, now wanted to buy into Letterman first. NBC began packaging the two shows to help "Tonight." Advertisers could get a better deal if they bought some "Tonight" commercials in addition to the ones they wanted to buy in "Late Night." By 1985 Letterman, starting at an hour formerly occupied by test patterns, had accomplished something truly remarkable: He was selling out every commercial in the program. Suddenly NBC's $50 million-plus take in late night had become about a $70 million take.

The timing of the show's growth coincided with an explosion in sales for videocassette recorders. The A. C. Nielsen Company always reported that "Late Night with David Letterman" was among the most taped programs on television.

Jack Rollins, Letterman's manager, noticed all the stories. He went to Letterman and asked if the star wanted to renegotiate his contract, which was then paying him about $1 million a year. But Letterman, who still despised anything that smacked of show business sleaze or double-dealing, declined, saying: "I signed the contract. I'll live up to it."

The heat generated by the show only intensified the presumption that Letterman was at most one more contract away from the big chair in late night. On "Late Night" it was taken for granted. "We were the farm team, ready to be called up," one staff member said.

By 1986 Johnny was undergoing one of his periodic reinvigorations. The inspiration: Joan Rivers. Rivers had negotiated a deal with the new Fox network for her own late-night show. In so doing she had committed the ultimate affront to the man who had given her the opportunity to shine on television: She didn't tell Johnny beforehand. She simply made the three-year deal, which she said was worth $15 million.

Carson cut her off like a traitorous child. In a demonstration of just how powerful Carson still was, Rivers found herself one step removed from leper status in Hollywood. Guests had to risk the wrath of the "Tonight" show to go on with Joan. She did herself no favors by trying to turn into a hipster, booking rock-and-roll acts half her age and singing "The Bitch Is Back" with Elton John. The show was doomed and disappeared in six months.

Johnny Carson had prevailed again. The competition was humbled again. But the rationale for Fox's assault remained. Carson's show, to many observers both outside and inside NBC, was getting stodgy and out-of-date. Johnny himself still seemed strong, especially in his monologues, which were as sharp and contemporary as anything on television. But the guest list took on a rigid, old show-business cast. Some of Johnny's own staff members wondered why he didn't book new young actors like Kevin Costner.

One headliner comic told his friends: "When you go on that show, you can smell the polyester."

"I blame Brandon a little bit," one longtime producer of television comedy shows said of the NBC entertainment boss, Brandon Tartikoff. "He could have provoked Johnny, 'cause I think Carson is a real competitor. Brandon could have said, 'I need you and you're not going anywhere, and spruce up that fucking show. Get back into it.' Instead it was always, 'Whatever you want, whenever you want to leave, let us know.'"

The quick demise of Joan Rivers may have renewed the network's confidence that Carson was impregnable. But with the show's drift toward older audiences apparent to everyone in the business, it only encouraged the plotting of new challenges to NBC's late-night fortress.

In 1988 a CBS late-night executive named Michael Brockman believed he'd hit on the most promising Carson challenger in years. With a smash hit in syndication, "Wheel of Fortune," and lots of experience as a funny weather guy in Los Angeles, Pat Sajak struck Brockman as CBS's first hope in a generation to get something started in late night.

The CBS strategy was simple and straightforward: Get Sajak on the air, let him settle in comfortably somewhere just behind Carson in the ratings, and then let him grow until the moment Carson finally retired.

Then CBS would have the incumbent show in place, ready to take command of late night.

Some doubters inside CBS questioned the choice. Rod Perth, who was the manager of the CBS-owned station in Chicago, stood up at a closed-door session during a CBS affiliates meeting and asked, in a loud voice: "Why Pat Sajak?"

To Perth, Sajak was the host of a syndicated show watched primarily by ladies with blue hair who lived in trailer parks and went to bed early. Brockman suggested Perth check the ratings for "Wheel of Fortune." Perth's protests didn't sway anybody. Pat Sajak had a late-night show on CBS, beginning in January 1989.

Sajak would present no threat at all to Johnny Carson, especially with those younger viewers that Carson apparently was losing. But Sajak didn't jump into Carson's talk-show ring by himself. At the same time, a syndicated group of stations agreed to begin running another entry, a Paramount Television production hosted by a young black comic from Cleveland named Arsenio Hall.

The changes in late-night television were only beginning.

3

THE CAMPAIGN

Rod Perth felt slightly ridiculous riding the Triumph Bonneville motorcyle across Sunset Boulevard in a suit and tie—and no helmet. But CBS's late-night situation had gotten desperate—and it called for desperate measures.

Perth had sounded like the smart guy at the CBS affiliate meeting the year before, predicting how bad Pat Sajak would be as a late-night talk show host. Now, as the new head of CBS's late-night programming, he was fighting a losing battle to keep "The Pat Sajak Show" show breathing. He was trying to stem a tidal wave of station defections away from Sajak to Paramount's new talk show, starring Arsenio Hall. Having helped stir up that wave, Perth felt a special twinge of irony.

When he first complained about Sajak, Perth had been the general manager of WBBM, the station CBS owned in Chicago. As soon as Sajak's ratings started their inexorable nosedive, Lucie Salhany, the head of Paramount Television, had called Perth in Chicago, telling him he had twenty-four hours to buy into the suddenly scalding-hot "Arsenio Hall Show." WBBM had strong ties to Paramount, and Salhany was respecting those ties by giving Perth first crack at Arsenio Hall in the Chicago market. Perth had jumped at the chance, putting Arsenio on the air immediately after Sajak.

Having a station that CBS owned snap up Hall only gave the restless CBS affiliates more reason to sign on for Arsenio themselves. But most of them used Hall to *replace* Sajak. By December 1989, more than fifty CBS stations had made the switch, dooming Sajak even as they coronated Arsenio as the first truly viable challenger to Carson and the "Tonight" show.

Several months later, the top CBS management had complicated Perth's life by promoting him to an executive job at the network. CBS wanted Perth to ride to the rescue and assume responsibility for the fiasco that the network's late-night schedule had become.

When he arrived in L.A. that August, Perth's first mission, whether he chose to accept it or not, was to try to fix and save Sajak. Perth quickly discovered he was not going to get much help from the star. Sajak seemed unaccountably laid-back to Perth. Before he'd agreed to take the job, Sajak had made just one, very L.A. demand: He had to have a billboard of his face on Sunset Boulevard.

CBS got most of its stations to agree to carry Sajak, promoted the show brilliantly, and sent the host off to a roaring start with a 6.2 rating, a full point higher than Carson's. That didn't even hold up for a week. Sajak was soon sinking through the 3 rating level. It got so bad that the show was having trouble getting audiences to come to the studio for the tapings. Yet Sajak didn't change his demeanor—or his show—at all. Perth came to regard him as one of the least ambitious people in show business, observing that Sajak would come in at noon, tape his show from 5:30 to 6:30 and be out the door by 6:45. The show was collapsing around him. With stations leaving every week, the distribution system was canceling him even before the network did. And yet Sajak remained unruffled.

Perth, on the other hand, faced an abyss: the end to any prospect of CBS ever launching a successful late-night show again. If "Arsenio" ate up all the CBS stations, Paramount would have a network show in late night and CBS wouldn't.

What Perth desperately needed was a name, a talk-show name that would keep the rest of the CBS stations from joining the growing "Arsenio" juggernaut. Working with the kind of financial carte blanche that comes only with true desperation, Perth began drawing up a list of possible hosts, stars who could compete against Johnny Carson and Arsenio Hall in a talk format. But he quickly realized this was the shortest list in Hollywood. There was only one name on it: Jay Leno.

Perth had heard that Leno, then finishing up his fourth year as the permanent guest host of the "Tonight" show, was still working on year-to-year deals with NBC, which paid him only about $1 million a year. He believed NBC was taking advantage of Leno's loyalty, or at least he thought he might be able to sell it that way.

So he called Leno's manager, Helen Kushnick. They had dinner, a sort of feeling-out meeting, where Perth began to broach the idea of Jay jumping to CBS. He didn't let it rest there, however. Perth knew of Jay's passion for restoring and riding antique motorcycles, and in a sweet coincidence, that happened to be Perth's hobby as well. He got to know Jay a little from meeting him on Sunday afternoon rides to the Rock Store, an old gas station turned diner that had become the L.A. gathering place for motorcycle enthusiasts. Perth began to tell Jay about his restored Triumph Bonneville, a bike he knew Jay didn't yet own in his thirty-plus collection. Leno was impressed—and eager to get a look at this treasure. "You gotta bring it over to my house someday," he told Perth.

Perth left out one detail. He didn't actually own such an item; he just knew one existed, in a little motorcycle shop called Adam Ant's in North Hollywood.

The next move for Perth was to meet with Jeff Sagansky, the president of CBS's entertainment division. Perth had kept Sagansky informed of his ongoing gentle wooing of Leno and Kushnick. The problem, both men knew, was that hints of general interest by CBS might be enough for Kushnick to wring a better deal out of NBC. "I think we have to impress Jay somehow that we're absolutely serious," Perth told Sagansky.

"OK, what do you have in mind?" Sagansky said.

"I want to go out to the shop in North Hollywood, buy him the Triumph, and ride it over to his house and give it to him," Perth said. Sagansky liked the idea immediately, but asked what this little overture was going to cost CBS. Perth told him the price: $6,000. Sagansky had the check cut that day.

Perth went straight to the shop, bought the bike, and drove it away. He stored it at a friend's house in Hancock Park while he went on his next errand—to a trophy shop. The gift needed one more touch. Perth had the shop make a brass plaque, just big enough to be attached discreetly to the oil tank on the side of the motorcycle. The last thing Perth wanted, however, was this little shop owner to know CBS was out buying motorcyles for Jay Leno. CBS's public posture was still 100 percent behind Pat Sajak. If *Daily Variety* or the *Hollywood Reporter* got a tip that CBS was giving gifts to Leno, that charade would be over—and so might the dance with him and Kushnick.

So Perth ordered that the message read: "To J.L.—Crank it on up and ride over to CBS . . . forever. Rod Perth and Jeff Sagansky." The next morning he called Leno and told him his Triumph had just been shipped in from his old house in Chicago. Jay's enthusiasm was dependable. He asked to see it right away.

So off Perth rode, in his CBS corporate suit and tie, across Sunset to Leno's large but tasteful Tudor home on the outskirts of Beverly Hills. When he got to the gates, Leno pushed a button to let him in. And Perth got his first look at Leno's downhill brick driveway that led to his enormous, double-stacked, twelve-car garage. It contained just a small assortment of Leno's automotive treasures: a 1955 Packard, a 1967 Lamborghini Miura, and a 1915 Hispano-Suiza.

Jay walked out of the garage in his coveralls, oohing and aahing every step of the way toward the Triumph. The motorcycle wasn't nearly as pristine as most of those already in his collection, but he walked around the machine with a lustful gleam in his eye, offering a few words of advice about what else Perth might want to do—like replace the speedometer, for instance, because it was all wrong for this model.

Finally Leno's eye caught the plaque near the oil tank. He got down on one knee, read the words, and looked up at Perth. "What's this?" the puzzled Leno said.

"It's a gesture from us, Jay," Perth said. "We just want you to know we're dead serious."

Leno's face reddened slightly. He was clearly fumbling for words. "Gee, I can't believe you did this. I don't know what to say."

Perth didn't push at all, knowing Leno wasn't the one he had to negotiate with anyway. CBS's point had been made. Instead, Perth talked with Leno about the machine for awhile, and about his cars, and then got Leno to drive him to work in Leno's replica Cobra, which overheated on the way.

Within a few weeks, after the first of the year, Perth scheduled a lunch with Helen Kushnick. He was bringing some friends. Perth picked a small Italian restaurant called Ronda, around the corner from CBS's headquarters in Television City, because it was not frequented by Hollywood insiders. He knew a lunch that included Helen Kushnick, Jeff Sagansky, and Howard Stringer, the president of CBS, would be noticed—and no one would have to wonder what they were there to talk about.

When the CBS executives walked in, they discovered what seemed like half the television industry sitting around at the tables that afternoon. They tried to find an inconspicuous spot. When Kushnick arrived and saw Stringer, she knew that he hadn't flown in from New York for more small talk about Leno. This was a serious negotiation. And the CBS guys had a serious piece of paper for Kushnick to read.

The offer CBS framed made Kushnick blanch. It was a three-year deal for Jay, at about $6 million a year. He would start in late night on CBS in September of 1990. "Holy shit," she said. "You guys are serious." Then she pushed the offer sheet back at them. "Take it," she said. "I don't want a copy of this." The CBS executives assumed that, if asked, she wanted to be able to say she had no offer from CBS in hand. But everyone at the table knew Kushnick had absorbed every important detail on the paper.

Over the next few months, Perth discreetly checked in with Kushnick, and even more discreetly, with Jay. He respected the close relationship between them and he wanted to be extra careful not to insult Kushnick. When he called her, Helen would say she was dying to move Jay to CBS, that she was tired of waiting for the NBC executives to pull the chair out from under Johnny Carson. She said the same things to Howard Stringer during a couple of meals she shared with him and his wife, Jennifer. Stringer got the feeling that Kushnick was more interested in CBS than Leno was. Perth had the same impression: No matter what Kushnick was saying, Leno was not being won over, not with Carson's crown still looming within his grasp.

What CBS was offering was a late-night job right away, for great money. But the chair being offered had been tattered by Pat Sajak's woeful performance. The network had no history worth remembering in late night. As the days went on, with no positive response from Leno, Perth realized the only thing he might have accomplished with his energetic wooing was to hand

Jay Leno another loud toy to tinker with; and to hand Helen Kushnick the crowbar she needed to pry Johnny Carson out of the most powerful seat in television.

In private, Helen Kushnick often slammed the NBC executives, saying they didn't know a thing about the television business. But that sweeping denunciation didn't include Brandon Tartikoff. Kushnick respected Tartikoff, and he had been friendly and fair with her. So naturally, once she had the firm offer from CBS in hand, she let Tartikoff know that Leno was in play.

Tartikoff, among the most skillful poker players in Hollywood, had managed to keep the "Tonight" show issue from becoming a crisis for most of the decade he ran NBC's entertainment division. Tartikoff knew that the ultimate call on the "Tonight" show would be excruciatingly difficult to make; he knew how volatile the mix was, with three big stars—Carson, Letterman, and Leno—all involved. Tartikoff was also close to all three men. The one top NBC executive with a real gift for talent relations, Tartikoff had insight into each man, and he didn't see an easy solution in any direction. He couldn't hand the "Tonight" show to Leno while Carson still occupied it; but if he didn't, he might lose Leno to CBS. And whenever the show did change hands, Letterman would have to be factored into any resolution. Tartikoff wasn't certain Letterman would jump at the chance to do the "Tonight" show; but he believed the job had to at least be offered to Letterman or the star would quit.

As a hedge against such an uncertain future, Tartikoff had made deals with other comedians he saw as possible future late-night players. He signed Dennis Miller, then doing the "News Update" segments of "Saturday Night Live," to a deal with the network worth about a half-million dollars. And he decided to indulge another comic with a commitment for a sitcom pilot, just to get him under contract to NBC. Tartikoff figured him much more for a late-night star; he didn't have high hopes then for the sitcom project being pitched by Jerry Seinfeld, called simply "Seinfeld."

But those were moves for the long term. The immediate, urgent issue Tartikoff had to deal with was the implication of what he was hearing from Kushnick: Here was Howard Stringer luring Leno with money and motorcycles. If Leno was at CBS instead of Sajak, would Carson still sail blithely along? And when Carson decided to quit, how would a Leno vs. Letterman late-night battle play out?

Tartikoff talked it through with Kushnick. He knew Leno's obvious preference: hang in at NBC and stay in line to succeed Carson. That was the card Tartikoff had to play. But he had to be careful. He knew that Kushnick was a potential loose cannon; she had to be finessed in this situation. One too many promises would probably mean reading the news in the next edition of the *National Enquirer*.

Tartikoff knew John Agoglia already had a deal with Leno that had a penalty payment in place if Johnny were to leave and the show went to somebody besides Jay. Now, a new deal was made for Leno. More money from NBC, more commitment to his future. It amounted to a chunk of financial security for Leno, and that figured to be enough to hold him. The rest of Tartikoff's assignment involved the careful stroking of Kushnick.

He asked her—in a way calculated to get her to agree—if she really wanted him to force Carson out in September 1990. That would deny Carson his 30th year on the show, Tartikoff pointed out. Kushnick backed off, saying, of course, that made no sense. She settled for the deal Tartikoff had brought her.

It wasn't quite what she and Jay wanted—the "Tonight" show right away—and it was not close financially to the deal CBS had offered. But Helen had some consolation anyway—or so she concluded from Tartikoff's skillfully vague stroking. She believed the leverage of the CBS deal had won her the next best thing to the job itself: a verbal commitment from Brandon Tartikoff that Jay Leno had the "Tonight" show as soon as Johnny Carson went away.

Leno had never had any inclination to accept the offer from CBS. He didn't want to go against Carson, nor did he want to go against Letterman. He feared it would look bad: the onetime guest host, the former favorite guest, now biting the hands that once fed him straight lines. He would be cast as the ingrate, the upstart. Leno was terribly uncomfortable with those images. They didn't square with the carefully assembled persona of the all-around good guy, straight shooter, and network team player. Joan Rivers's experience had made an impression on him, too: Crossing Johnny and taking him on head-to-head on was the shortest route to the exit from show business.

And if Helen was right, this offer from NBC would just move them closer to the big prize anyway. Verbal commitment or not, Jay wasn't convinced yet that the job would inevitably be his. But having maneuvered his way into position to be a change of heart away from the best job in television, Leno, always proud of the patience he had shown in developing his career, had every reason to be willing to wait a little longer. Besides, Helen had a plan.

Helen told Jay that all this endless speculation about who was going to replace Johnny Carson missed the point. "No comic is going to replace Carson," she told him. "The affiliates are going to replace Carson." As Kushnick saw it, the NBC station lineup, unified at 11:30 for close to forty years, had the true power over the "Tonight" show chair. And she believed she had the guy who could make the affiliates his strongest constituency. Jay was already the ultimate comedy road warrior. He had performed up to 300 nights a year in clubs and arenas and colleges all over the country. Even after he became the permanent guest host of the "Tonight" show in 1987, Leno continued to work the road in almost all of his free time.

Wherever he went, Helen had him check in with the nearest NBC affiliate, talk to the general manager, and see if he could do a promotion for the local news—or anything else the station might need a celebrity for. At the same time, she had Jay do interviews with the local papers, partly just to get his name out everywhere, partly to hone his skills with publicity and press. And anytime NBC needed something, talent for an event, a performer for a special, a presentation for stations or advertisers, Helen nodded and Jay came running. It was a carefully organized campaign to convince the network, and especially the people who ran the stations that made up the network, that Leno was Mr. Reliable.

The role was not a challenge for Jay Leno; he'd been playing it all his life.

If Leno's ability to work the network and the affiliates made him look like a traveling-comedy salesman, he came by the resemblance honestly. At one point in his life Jay thought he would be a funny insurance salesman, because that's how his Dad, Angelo, supported the Leno family in Andover, Massachusetts.

It was a small family; Jay's only sibling, his brother Patrick, was ten years older, but they had large, somewhat conflicting extensions to the immediate family. The Italian relatives on Angelo's side were typically boisterous, fun and food-loving, while the Scottish relatives on Jay's mother's side believed in restraint in all things. The mix came out about equal in Jay, a big funny guy who kept his emotions under rigidly tight control.

Jay's mother, an immigrant from Scotland at age ten, was forty-one when James Douglas Muir Leno was born on April 28, 1950, in New Rochelle, New York. The family moved to Andover in 1959, soon enough for Jamie, as he was called throughout his youth, to acquire a solid, working-class New England accent.

Early on, Jay admired his father's storytelling ability, often displayed at company conventions where Angelo was usually called on to introduce the vice president. The idea of being able to stand up in front of people and tell funny stories had a powerful appeal to young Jay, though he then could only foresee it translating into being another funny insurance salesman. Jay knew comedians existed, but they had jobs in show business, which in his neighborhood was looked upon as something undertaken by different life forms. "I had this friend up the street and his mom said to me, 'You know, you can't be a comedian because they've got a union and you can only do it if your father's in the union.' I thought you had to be like Milton Berle's son."

But some things are simply foreordained. Jamie Leno had an ear and an awareness for anything funny. Leno struggled in school, only learning later that he was mildly dyslexic. To compensate, he worked on providing schoolmates—and teachers—with laughs. Earl Simon, his teacher in fifth grade, wrote a note on Jay's report card at the end of the year: "If James used the effort toward his studies that he uses to be humorous, he'd be an A student. I hope he never loses his talent to make people chuckle."

Jay was lousy at sports. He had two explanations: He just wasn't interested, and too many sports involved knocking people down. Jay hated to do that. From a very young age, he liked to be liked.

At Emerson College in Boston, Jay picked speech therapy as a major because it called for oral final exams. He simply couldn't bring himself to open the books and read the material, though he retained everything he heard in class. The college had a comedy workshop, which Jay tried to join, only to be rejected—even though he was already making money as a comic. He and a classmate, Gene Braunstein (later to move to Hollywood and produce the sitcom "Who's the Boss?"), formed a comedy team "Gene and Jay, Unique and Original Comedy" and played the Boston coffee-house circuit. After he went solo he began booking himself into any club, bar, joint, or dive that he thought might reasonably be interested in providing entertainment for its customers.

Leno came to specialize in colorful accounts of his early comedy days. The tales included getting lighted cigarettes tossed at him, being protected from hecklers by strippers in a sleazy club, being knocked out cold by another heckler who hit him over the head with a bottle of ketchup, being approached by an agent who wanted to turn him into a combination comedian-wrestler, and playing on the same bill with a performer who called himself the "Personable Yodeling Sensation."

The tales of Leno's wild and woolly early life extended to his determination to work on cars. He needed a regular source of income, so he went to a Rolls-Royce/Mercedes dealership in Boston and asked for a job as a car washer. The owner said no. As Jay related it, he simply turned up for work the next day, put on coveralls, and started washing cars. When the other guys on the job took notice of him, Leno told them he was the new wash guy and they all went on happily for a few days. Finally, the owner noticed him working and asked what he thought he was doing. Jay told him he thought he'd just do a good job for awhile without getting paid, and maybe if the owner liked him he might eventually get hired. Of course, the owner caved in and hired him that day.

The Rolls-Royce job coincided comfortably with his comedy career because Jay got to deliver new cars to customers in the New York area. And he wanted to get to New York as often as he could to appear in the comedy clubs. Leno would drive a car down to Manhattan or Scarsdale or Garden City, pick up a car for the drive back from the Mercedes dealer in Port Elizabeth, New Jersey, and then spend several hours at the Improv waiting for a shot to go on.

His best tale from this experience involved a Rolls he had to deliver to Greenwich, Connecticut. When he got there, the new owner said he was going to pay in full—in cash. The car cost $29,000 in those days, and Jay said he got the whole stash in a brown paper bag. Naturally he went to the Improv. Careful to take the bag of money with him, Leno managed to get on the stage that night and do a killer set. Excited and elated, he took the return car back out of Manhattan, heading home, listening happily to the tape of the performance he'd just completed. He got as far as Greenwich when he remembered something: the cash. Panic-stricken, Leno turned the car around and sped back to the city. He'd been on at about 2:00 A.M., now it was almost four and the club was getting ready to close. Jay burst into the club, looking immediately to the piano where he had left his brown bag. It was still there. "Gee, sorry," Jay said, "I forgot my lunch."

Like many of Leno's early-days recollections, this one was vivid and detailed. But many of his closest colleagues and friends learned that a Leno story was rarely to be taken at face value. They described Leno as a champion embellisher. "Jay's a comic. Storytelling is part of his act," one friend said. "But Jay's so good at it, makes it sound so believable, that sometimes you get to feeling he believes it all himself."

Jimmy Brogan, a comic who met Leno in New York and later became a close friend and writer for him in Los Angeles, became aware of Jay's tendency to put some extra spin on a good story. Brogan once heard Leno telling a reporter about a time when *US* magazine decided to do a story on him. Leno had said: "I called up my dad in Massachusetts and told him that *US* magazine was going to do this story on me and he ought to get a copy so he and my mom could read it. So my dad goes down to the store that sells the magazines, and he asks if they have a copy of U.S. magazine. The guy says, 'You must mean *U.S. News and World Report,*' and he gives my dad a copy. So my dad looks through it and there's no story on me. So he calls back in kind of a huff and he says I don't know what I'm talking about; there's no story about me in this U.S. magazine. So I say, 'No, Dad, it's *US,* like you and me, *US* Magazine.'"

The story didn't have the ring of wild fabrication as Leno told it, but Brogan pointed out that there was just one problem with it: "That happened to *me* and *my* father. That wasn't Jay and his father. So I had to remind Jay to stop telling that story like it happened to him."

For Brogan, who became one of Leno's closest friends in the business, these embellishments amounted to another endearing trait. But another headliner comic was less charitable: "I don't mind Jay and his fabrications as long as he keeps me out of them."

What is certainly true is that Leno began at an early

age to throw every ounce of his interest, energy, and attention into becoming a professional comedian. He worked unstintingly on his act, shaping himself as the always slightly irked observer of the absurdities of American life: airplane food, foreign cars, the phone company. Typical joke: "The Yugo has come out with a very clever antitheft device. They made their name bigger." Jay knew exactly how to hit the last few words really loud, to emphasize the punch line. Leno was also distinctive for the things he didn't do in his act: no drugs, no sex, no vulgarity at all.

Because of his background at the car dealership, Leno was often labeled a comedy mechanic. In truth he was closer to a craftsman. He worked on jokes to find the perfect word, to try to put a sense of meter into each line. "I liked to listen to Bob and Ray on the radio," Leno said. "I would listen to it just for the flow the way other people would listen to a record."

From his earliest days on stage, Leno had a commanding presence. He was tall and broad-shouldered, and he moved somewhat stiffly, like Robo-comic, but he conveyed energy and a consistently aggressive attitude. The robot image was strengthened by his striking jawline, which tended to make his head look slightly oversized. The prominence of his jaw so dominated Leno's looks that it was usually the only thing about his appearance that got remarked upon. In early accounts of his act, he was called "lantern-jawed," "anvil-faced," and even compared to the Frankenstein monster. Those who took the trouble to look past the jaw saw a guy with rather soft features, doughy cheeks, a head of Elvis-like black, wavy hair, and most surprisingly, a pair of arresting aquamarine eyes.

Leno met all the comics on the New York scene in the early 1970s, and most of them regarded him as a comedy savant. He knew how to create a joke, build it, and deliver it better than anyone else.

But most of the comedy business was still in Los Angeles, and in 1974 Leno decided to make his move.

As good as he was on the stage telling jokes, Leno had a hard time putting his career into high gear. An agent at the William Morris agency once told him he just wasn't the kind of guy who could get his name in the papers. A casting director at NBC told him he should dye his hair blond and have his famous jaw rehung surgically because he had a face "that would frighten small children."

Leno tried to turn his early struggles into virtues. When he was rejected, he would just hunker down and work harder, do more gigs, tell more jokes, keep pushing, pushing, pushing. "I watch other people and they like to go on vacations, to go out to dinner, go to athletic events. And I just write jokes. And it's seven days a week and it's fine. It's just that you have to have the stamina to do it. You just do it every day. And I like it."

Leno was aware early that his was not the hyperactive talent of Robin Williams, but the slow, steady, persistent, tortoise-style talent of a guy who would outwork every comic with a flashier act. Leno hadn't been at it long in L.A. before other comics started calling him "the hardest-working comic in show business." That was Jay's identity. It was matched by Mr. Nice Guy. Jay spoke no evil, did no dirt to anybody. He was the choirboy of the comics. He had batches of young comics up to his apartment; they would sit around him on the couch and he would hold court on the craft of comedy, puffing on a pipe. Nobody disliked him, but some thought he laid on the hardworking nice guy bit a little too thick. Mostly, it was hard for anyone to figure Leno out. Everything about him seemed a little more complicated than what he showed on the surface.

Helen Kushnick had seen Leno in the Comedy Store in 1975. She had been managing writers and producers for ICM, then broke away to start her own company. She thought Leno had spunk and spark on stage, and signed him as a client. It was a business relationship that quickly put down deep, entangled roots.

The same year, Carson heard that a hot young comic was in town and came to see Leno at the club. He left unimpressed because Leno's material, while funny, didn't really seem to contain enough true jokes to work in the five-minute stand-up spots on the "Tonight" show. Jay at this point was doing a lot of long-story jokes about his parents, their inabilities to work remote controls and operate the car.

Leno reacted to the Carson rejection with his usual rededication to work: Hit the road, keep building the act. Helen started booking dates for him. When he finally did get an invitation to the "Tonight" show, it was 1977. He had been in L.A. more than three years and he felt as if he were the last comic of his entire generation to get on the show—even though he was only twenty-seven, and he still beat Letterman to the show by more than a year.

Rather than lead to new opportunities, the "Tonight" show experience set Leno back. His first spot, on March 12, 1977, went well; but he had used up most of his best material. When he was invited back a second, third, and fourth time, his material got progressively worse. And on the "Tonight" set, Jay wasn't his cynical self. "As much as I liked Johnny, I was intimidated," he said. "I would call him Mr. Carson—I felt funny calling them Johnny and Ed. So I'd say 'Mr. McMahon.' With Johnny I would feel odd trying to be a smart guy."

Leno's fourth appearance, by this time with a guest host instead of Carson, fell completely flat. It would be his last appearance on the "Tonight" show for eight years.

Helen, who kept trying to book Jay on the show for a time before giving up, didn't believe the offers had stopped coming because of Jay's lackluster performances. She thought the "Tonight" show people were punishing her guy for getting bigger laughs than Carson on one show. But she didn't have much choice. She booked Jay back on the road, in the clubs and the colleges. Confident that his material could work with any kind of audience—and figuring it made sense for him to build his audience into every age group—Kushnick made a deal for Leno to open for Perry Como and Henry Mancini. She never stopped believing in Jay; she still thought he would break through on television. She just had to find the right sledgehammer.

On "Late Night with David Letterman," they were actively looking for guests who weren't getting booked with Johnny Carson. Leno had essentially disappeared from television, except for an occasional spot on Merv Griffin. But Letterman did not forget how much he admired Leno's command as a stand-up. So just two months into his new show on NBC, Letterman brought on his old Comedy Store colleague.

The same night, April 15, 1982, Letterman introduced a new bit called "elevator races." (A woman from Albany, New York, won the "Golden Shaft" award.) Leno came on later and did a killer stand-up, followed by some strong interaction with Letterman at the desk. Leno had no intimidation problems with Letterman; they were contemporaries with similar comedy temperaments.

As good as that was for the show, it was far more important to Jay Leno; he had finally found a way to make an impression on television. Helen Kushnick made a deal that effectively made Jay exclusive on television to the "Late Night" show. Every month to six weeks, she would call the show's producers and say that Jay was ready for another spot. It was the completion of a circle. David Letterman had helped launch his own career by watching Jay Leno work in the clubs. Now Jay Leno was using his guest shots with Letterman to save his career.

Leno's bookings on the road improved; so did his income. He started making more than $5 million a year doing stand-up dates. He had good uses for the money: He bought a new house, and more cars and motorcycles.

The Letterman-Leno act began to generate a lot of good press. Nobody paid closer attention to what he called "buzz" in the media than Brandon Tartikoff. The buzz was valuable to Tartikoff, who never stopped being vigilant about scouting for new late-night talent to protect the NBC signature franchise. Leno was a new name on the late-night horizon. Tartikoff began to include it on the mental list he was assembling, the one he figured he would eventually have to call on whenever it happened that Johnny Carson finally decided to leave the arena.

By 1986, what he had seen of Jay had impressed him enough. Tartikoff contacted Helen Kushnick and made a holding deal for Jay Leno. All the deal did was bind him to NBC. But by that time Joan Rivers was gone and Tartikoff had an idea where Jay Leno might fit in.

In 1987 Tartikoff made a deal for Leno to split the guest-hosting job on the "Tonight" show with Garry Shandling. For Tartikoff it was extra insurance. He knew David Letterman had been auditioning for the "Tonight" job by putting on a great show at 12:30 each night. But even if Carson left and Letterman got the 11:30 job, Tartikoff believed it was smart to keep developing backup talent. After all, somebody would have to go in at 12:30 for Dave.

The two-man backup system only lasted a few months. Shandling, a creatively neurotic stand-up, whom many on the "Tonight" show then preferred to Leno, had started his own comedy series for the Showtime cable network, "It's Garry Shandling's Show," and he was writing and starring in all the episodes. He found the idea of doing both shows at the same time, and dividing up his energy and attention, exhausting and debilitating. So Shandling, with some reluctance, took himself out of the "Tonight" guest-hosting rotation. That left the field free for Leno, who had absolutely no problem giving energy and attention to the "Tonight" show.

The "Tonight" staff found Jay to be a pussycat to

work with. He was friendly, manageable; he worked hard, took suggestions, and almost always brought in a polished monologue that he and couple of writers put together during his week off. Jay would have tried out the material in comedy clubs over the weekend. The only thing that troubled Peter Lassally, the "Tonight" show producer, was that Jay, pleasant as he was, had what he felt was a strange persona. When Lassally would sit in his office talking to Leno, he could see that the comic had trouble expressing his feelings. To Lassally, this necessarily limited Jay as a host because it made his comedy material more mechanical and his interviewing style stilted. Lassally had worked in television a long time—more than twenty years for Carson—and he felt he had developed a true eye for talent—as well as for people. Lassally spent a lot of time with Jay looking for the real person inside to emerge; but he could never find it.

Helen kept her distance from the show; but she advised Jay on all matters. And as Jay's "Tonight" spots improved and he started to get more and more favorable press, she began to turn the heat up on NBC—lightly at first, but full blast was soon to come.

Helen Kushnick had other clients: they included a few television writers, producers, sometimes another comic. But no one who interacted with her missed the compelling force in her life: her mission. She was devoted to Jay Leno. An industry executive who worked closely with Helen said the obsessive commitment was unmistakable. "This was someone who was unbelievably devoted, centered on one thing: Jay Leno. And disciplined enough to say: 'That's it.' That's what she was there for: Jay Leno. That was her life."

Helen knew the goal she wanted for Jay: the "Tonight" show. By 1990, thanks to the CBS offer, she had put him into place at NBC, but that was no reason for her to relax. Johnny Carson still held the power, still blocked the way for her boy. And Helen had too many doubts about the NBC managers to believe nothing could go wrong. Every year that Carson held on was another year something unexpected could happen. The network management could change, the network could be sold. And rumors that GE would dump NBC were all over Hollywood. Besides, Jay turned forty in 1990— not old yet, but certainly the right time in a career to grab the spotlight. Carson had been thirty-six when he took over the "Tonight" show. Letterman was thirty-five when he got "Late Night." As far as Helen was concerned, the time for Jay Leno was now.

Early in 1991, Kushnick still did not have a firm date from NBC for Carson's retirement—and she was getting angry. Almost everything about Carson made her angry, beginning with her conviction that the show had never appreciated her star client. She felt that the Carson people wouldn't let Jay play on their field because he didn't look like he belonged on television. He wasn't blond. He wasn't from the Midwest. So she decided to move the game.

Anger worked for Helen Kushnick. "She's one of those people who are much more comfortable being angry," said one of Helen's close associates. "If you're not angry, you gotta feel comfortable, so let me be angry about something. What she was angry about at that point was: How dare NBC not give this show to Leno? They won't make up their minds. It's getting to be Johnny's thirtieth year. That was the whole big deal with her: how to strategize to get Leno the show—and get Johnny out."

Helen hatched a plan using an industry colleague in New York as her go-between. "She asked me to plant a story somewhere, and I must say I did a great job," this associate said. Indeed, the plan worked beyond their wildest expectations. Helen wanted the story in a New York newspaper; she wanted it to get great play, and to have absolutely no fingerprints—no attribution at all.

The story was to say that top NBC executives wanted Johnny Carson out. His audience was getting too old. Jay Leno was in the wings, attracting much younger audiences when he guest hosted. Therefore, the advertisers liked him more and the affiliates liked him more.

Helen's associate, who was not an NBC executive and had not talked to anyone about this information, called the *New York Post*. The associate asked for a guarantee of front-page play in exchange for exclusivity—and got it. The reporters for the story read the piece back to the source to make sure that absolutely no names were used. Every promise was kept. The *Post* had a complete exclusive, based entirely on information delivered, through an intermediary, by Helen Kushnick.

Helen was on the phone to her accomplice in New York most of the evening. They knew the first edition of the *Post* would be out about 11:00 P.M. Helen called and said, "Look, when you get the story, read it to me and then we'll call Jay. But don't mention to Jay that we had anything to do with this at all, or how it happened."

To the source who so effectively carried out her plan, it was a demonstration of just how far Helen was willing to go to advance Jay's cause. "As devoted as she was to the guy, she wasn't completely honest with Jay," the accomplice said.

In its editions of February 11, 1991, the *Post* story carried the headline: "THERE GOES JOHNNY; NBC Looking to Dump Carson for Jay Leno." It had pictures of the two stars on page three.

They read it over the phone to Leno as planned. Jay sounded a little bewildered. He wondered if this might not mean some problems for him. But typically, he had no strong reaction. He just said okay, and hung up.

The next day NBC was in an uproar. The story hit the network executives like an unexpected brick to the forehead. Nobody knew where it had come from, or who was responsible for it. But that wasn't the issue that had to be addressed. NBC had to first conjure up a statement of support for Johnny Carson.

It was a tortured exercise. On the West Coast, Warren Littlefield and John Agoglia were in charge. (Brandon Tartikoff was incapacitated by a serious automobile accident.) They were upset about the story. But they had a problem drafting a statement of denial the next day. They didn't see an easy way to frame the statement, for the simple reason that the *Post* story had, in its scattershot way, hit on an issue that was being discussed in whispers in some corners of the NBC hierarchy. These voices were raising concerns about what was happening to the "Tonight" show, how much older

Johnny's audience was getting, what significant inroads Arsenio Hall had made. One top NBC executive admitted there was no specific plan in place to force Carson out the door, but there was a general feeling that if it could be worked out smoothly, the time was right for a transition.

So NBC labored over its statement. It couldn't say the network wanted Johnny to stay forever; truly, it didn't. But what could be said short of that so it would sound as if NBC were standing behind the most important star in its history?

The statement that was released made reference to the network's debt to Johnny and how it would always be up to him to decide when he wanted to leave the "Tonight" show. It said nothing about hoping that the king would reign forever. Inside the "Tonight" show, this episode was a dispiriting affront. The staff thought the ugly story in the *Post* had crushed Carson. Most of them were convinced that Helen Kushnick had planted it. But that was secondary to their concern that Carson felt humiliated by it.

Jay, too, heard the rumors that Helen had planted the story. So he asked her directly. Helen told him that "under no circumstances did this come from us." Helen knew there were enough other interests at work in the fight for the "Tonight" show that the finger of blame did not necessarily have to point to her. "It came from the other side," she told Jay. "They're trying to screw you and put you down by leaking the story, and it backfired on them."

Nobody specifically on the other side had to be mentioned. For years Jay had heard Helen rail about the

Carson people and their opposition to Jay. Many times what she said seemed irrational or even hysterical to the mild-mannered Jay, but he never questioned her too strenuously. He was so thoroughly a nonconfrontational personality that he might not have pushed the issue with anybody. And he certainly couldn't with Helen. She ate confrontation for lunch, and besides, he had little reason to question her. Helen's choices had worked quite well for him so far.

But Jay surely recognized that the *Post* story was likely to upset Carson. As usual, he tried to do the right thing, so he called Johnny.

"Listen, Johnny, about that *New York Post* story," Leno said. "I'm sorry it came out. I know you think it came from us, but I don't know where it came from."

"It came from you," Johnny said. His voice was controlled, not hostile. He said it as a given fact.

"No, let me guarantee you," Jay said, earnestly. "I checked with my manager about it and she said under no circumstances did this come from us. I feel terrible about this because I know your people think it came from us."

Johnny didn't prolong the conversation. He just told Jay that in show business you sometimes have to be wary of situations where other people speak for you.

Jay knew he hadn't convinced Johnny that his side wasn't responsible. But he had done what he could. He had tried to be a good guy about it.

For the executives at NBC, the unexpected headline in the *New York Post* was just the first sign that events were moving quickly out of their control.

4

STUPID NETWORK TRICKS

ne morning in December 1990, the producers of the "Maury Povich Show," the latest in a seemingly endless line of daytime talk shows devoted to subjects like "Overweight Women As Sex Objects," took a tour of NBC's studio 6A. The purpose of the tour: to determine if the Povich show would be interested in subletting the space.

When the news of this impending transaction reached the staff of "Late Night with David Letterman," the full-time tenant of studio 6A for more than eight years, questions were asked immediately about exactly what NBC had in mind.

If the deal were made between NBC and Maury, it was patiently explained, stage hands would have to strike the Letterman set after its 5:30-to-6:30 taping each evening and put it back together the next day after Maury and his audience cleared out. That was enough information for Robert Morton, the "Late Night" producer. He pointed out that, among other things, "Late Night" really did use its set some mornings when there were complicated rehearsals to run through. And besides, moving an entire audience through the studio each morning was sure to affect the room temperature. Letterman had made it quite explicit that he wanted his studio air-conditioned down to a frigid 58 degrees to keep the audience awake and alert during his tapings.

In other words, if NBC proceeded with this half-assed plan with Maury Povich, "Late Night with David Letterman" was going to raise another stink.

Relations between Letterman and the management of NBC, never exactly sweet, had soured year by year, especially after the General Electric Company took control of the network in 1986. By the end of 1990, they had turned to acid. Letterman had come to view GE as a forbidding corporate monolith out to penny-pinch his little show into an early demise. On their side, some NBC executives viewed Letterman as whining, querulous, impossible to please, and probably not worth the bother.

The notion that his studio might be invaded by a cheesy talk show seemed to Letterman like the most egregious insult of all, a gratuitous slap in his face by the tightwad GE managers. As Letterman put it, "It was almost this: Dave, when you're done with your ties, would you mind if we take them and rent them out to restaurants where you have to wear a coat and tie? We can make a little money that way."

Warren Littlefield and John Agoglia said the idea of renting out the studio to Maury Povich was a blunder made by an unnamed "low-level executive in New York," a mistake that never actually led to a firm rental offer to Povich. Littlefield said of the incident: "We blew it."

Still, Agoglia believed the Letterman staff reacted

typically, with the "us versus them" peevishness that marked most of the interaction between the show and the network. Once this unnamed NBC executive went through the studio with the Povich people, the situation was instantly out of control, Agoglia said, and for a predictable reason. He believed members of the Letterman staff looked for excuses to "stoke the fire" against NBC. That's how they kept their jobs, instead of simply by doing good work. They maintained their longevity with Letterman, Agoglia said, by "being friends with the guy they worked for and being enemies with everyone he's enemies with." He didn't mention Robert Morton by name, only by unmistakable implication.

Morton, who enjoyed nothing more than a good fight, especially with the network, harassed NBC continually over such things as the nightly promotions for the show. Morton believed that the promos were essential to keep interest up in the show, and he pushed and pushed to get more. Not just for the sake of pushing, but because everything about the show was produced to very exacting standards—standards set by the star himself. "Everything we did was in keeping with David Letterman's overall vision for the show and his desire to make the best show possible," Morton said—a point, he added, that the NBC bosses never grasped. Nothing was too trivial to fight over, because NBC seemed incapable of even minimally stroking its star, the man helping to shove an extra $20 million into their pockets each year. Dave wanted a car phone; Agoglia said no. The bandleader, Paul Shaffer, wanted a new pair of glasses; Agoglia said no.

From the perspective of a network executive, the requests surely seemed preposterously presumptuous. Letterman was making millions and he couldn't afford his own car phone? Shaffer expected a network to pay for his eyewear? But the reflex answer—"no"—was symptomatic of NBC's disdain for the concept of talent relations. Partly it was GE's belt-tightening at work; NBC had once had a full talent relations department charged with remembering birthdays, buying gifts, soothing sensitive egos and anything else that involved the care and feeding of high-priced stars. But that department had been gutted in one of the sweeping workforce reductions undertaken by NBC's efficient, new GE-installed management team.

John Agoglia was a holdover from the pre-GE days, but he was smart and tough, and his hard-nosed negotiating skills were quickly admired by the new regime. Here was a guy who could stand up to the Hollywood cash-suckers, the stars and managers and agents who spun deals and took percentages and wrung out perks from the network as if it were some kind of freestanding beer tap. Agoglia took pride in shutting all that down. Tall, curly-haired, barrel-chested, and with a pencil mustache, Agoglia looked the part of a stylishly dressed California corporate executive in his perfectly tailored suits and crisp white shirts. But his voice had never lost the intonations of his native Brooklyn. The accent gave his words a bluntness that inflated their impact. Agoglia had a hearty Italian laugh, but the voice, the mustache, and a frequently cold, brusque demeanor left an overall impression that this was not a businessman to cross.

Agoglia had worked closely with Tartikoff in a system one producer described as "the accelerator and the brake." Tartikoff (the accelerator) would talk up a show with a producer or star, would be expansive about the project's possibilites, and then turn it over to Agoglia (the brake) to work out a deal. "There might be ten points at issue," the producer said. "And at some point in the negotiation, John would slip point seven into his desk drawer. So if something happened and Brandon decided he wanted out of the deal, John could pull out point seven and say that's the deal breaker. Agoglia's job was to say no."

Especially when NBC was riding high in the mid-1980s, Agoglia knew how and where he could squeeze the dollars in a deal, and he seemed to enjoy it thoroughly. One drama producer, who had once worked for NBC and then saw Agoglia in action on the other side of the table, said, "The thing about John is he's a prick when he doesn't have to be." One comedy producer with years of experience negotiating fine points of contracts and star perks with Agoglia called him "the anti-talent."

Agoglia's power increased after Tartikoff left NBC; he became the head of NBC Productions, NBC's in-house production company. Within the company, suspicion grew that Agoglia had a bigger ambition: to take over the job of head of the entertainment division, which Warren Littlefield had inherited from Tartikoff. But Littlefield himself had functioned for some time as the guy who did the dirty work for Tartikoff, saying "no," saying "not interested," saying "canceled." "With those two guys there, you had two brakes and no accelerator," the producer said. "Neither wanted to give up any power."

But another longtime NBC executive who was regularly involved in the late-night lineup said Agoglia was only part of an overall management style that saw everything as "just business," never considering the implications of any action they were taking. "I always felt it was never being talked out," the NBC executive said. "It sounds so fundamental, but I always felt people weren't getting in a room and saying: 'Well, what if? What if Dave is unhappy about this deal?' "

The Povich question was left hanging because a new issue involving David Letterman came up to occupy the attention of the NBC program department in Burbank. Sunday night had become a sinkhole for NBC programs. The network was pouring out millions in program costs subsidizing chronic failure. So NBC came up with an innovative, and cheap, idea: A show made up of highlights of other NBC shows. They called it "Sunday Best."

Crucial to the concept was including clips of the best moments of popular NBC shows that were not that widely seen, at least by the standards of prime time: the best sketches from "Saturday Night Live," Carson's best monologue jokes, a selection from Letterman's nightly Top Ten list.

On the afternoon of December 11, 1990, NBC initiated a conference call to the Letterman staff in New York. Garth Ancier, a former network executive at NBC and Fox who had been named executive producer of "Sunday Best," was on the line along with several NBC executives. The NBC side tried to explain the concept of the show to Letterman's manager, Jack Rollins, and other members of the Letterman staff in New

York. They emphasized how crucial clips from "Late Night" would be, saying the show would ask Carson to participate, but if he did not agree they would still go on with "Sunday Best." But if Letterman did not share his clips, they said, upping the pressure as much as they could, the new show would probably be dead.

Of course, there was also the little matter of the potential rental of the studio to Maury Povich. Should Dave agree to share his nightly performance with "Sunday Best," it was suggested, the Povich deal just might go away. "This was the relationship we had with the NBC executives," Morton said. "They were trying to bribe us that they wouldn't put Maury Povich in the same studio."

Later that day, pressure came from another quarter. Johnny Carson's people called the Letterman show and strongly suggested they not participate in "Sunday Best." Carson had his own reason for wanting to stick it to NBC at that moment. Just a few weeks earlier, "Saturday Night Live" had done a sketch in which cast member Dana Carvey, known for his devastating impersonations, had starred as "Carsenio," a stinging takeoff in which an aging Carson, struggling to be one part hip Arsenio Hall, looked almost senile and totally out of it. The sketch enraged members of the Carson staff; Carson himself was furious that NBC had allowed Lorne Michaels, the executive producer of "Saturday Night Live," to air the sketch.

Carson's stand helped steel the resolve of the Letterman show. No clips were given to "Sunday Best" by either late-night show, and it died a quick, totally unlamented death. No deal was made for Maury Povich anyway. But the incident gave David Letterman one more reason to make "pinhead GE executives" a running gag and rallying cry.

As tough as Letterman was on his NBC bosses, he made life much worse for one other victim: himself. The cancellation of his short-lived morning show had made Letterman even more vigilant about ensuring that his show was as good as it could possibly be—and that only guaranteed he would be even more searingly self-critical. He sensed failure every day, always because he believed his own performance was so inadequate. Letterman began rejecting more and more material from his writers. Five bits were tossed out for every one he accepted—then the ratio grew. To Merrill Markoe, the head writer, it felt as if she were submitting fifteen bits for each one Dave liked.

The postmortems for each show could be witheringly negative. Letterman wouldn't beat up the staff; he would beat up himself. He was a guy who was hypersensitive to embarrassment in a job where potential embarrassment lurked in every line out of his mouth. On nights when he felt he'd totally screwed up the show and humiliated himself, he would sometimes lock the door to his office as he reviewed the show on tape. The staff would then hear crashing noises coming through the door.

On the set one night, during a commercial break in the middle of a show, the band was playing so loudly that it was impossible for Teri Garr, one of the show's favorite guests, to converse with Dave. When she all but shouted at him: "How are you doing?," Letterman grabbed a pad on his desk and scribbled a note that he passed back to her. The note read: "I *hate* myself." When Garr tried to reassure him that he was, in fact, truly a wonderful guy and talented star, he grabbed the note back, underlined "I *hate* myself" twice, and shoved it back at her.

The best anyone would hear from Dave was: "Well, I guess it stuck to the videotape" or "Nobody got killed today." For Merrill the postmortem would extend to their drive home to New Canaan, Connecticut. Every day, Dave would predict cancellation. The gushing reviews, the awards, none of that sank in for Merrill, because all she knew was that Dave thought they were failing every day.

Before every show, she would feel the terror. Dave would have predicted everything was going to fail, and Merrill would stand in the wings, heart pounding, telling herself not to faint before the first comedy piece started to play. Then the laughs would come washing over Dave on stage and she would feel a slow release from the pressure. The color would start to come back into her face.

She knew that terror, for whatever reason, gave Dave something to work with; but for her it was torture. She felt compelled to find new ideas, breakthrough ideas, because maybe that could keep them on the air, maybe that would please him. All she cared about was pleasing Dave, and maybe squeezing a drop of self-satisfaction out for herself and her writing staff. She didn't want to feel as if their smart, charming star were carrying them along like dead weight.

Eventually the warfare was too intense for Markoe.

Every day she went to Letterman with "what about this?," and it was so often "no, no, no" that she decided for the sake of their personal relationship, she had to pull back, had to let someone else endure some of the rejection. She quit as head writer, staying on as a consultant. She was still feeding Dave ideas, still going a million miles an hour to please him. But it felt wrong. She realized that when you earn a position where you have to grow backward, you're not in a good position. The situation began to feel ludicrous to her.

As much as she tried to make Dave happy, the work thwarted her. Work was everything in their lives. It wasn't that Dave wasn't happy at all, it was just that he had severely narrowed the range of what might make him happy. Most of the staff came to realize: This was a guy happy exactly one hour a day. The hour: from 5:30 to 6:30 on weekday evenings, when he was on stage taping his show.

Dave himself recognized it: "I'm just the happiest, the best I ever feel, from five-thirty to six-thirty."

By the start of 1991, the relationship between Letterman and NBC was chillier than his own studio; soon it would ice over completely. That spring NBC set up yet another deal in search of additional revenue that Letterman saw as coming at his expense.

NBC initially decided to sell off reruns of "Late Night with David Letterman" to the Arts and Entertainment cable channel. As one senior NBC executive saw it, it was an easy way to impress the GE management. "You could generate up to, say, seven million dollars in quick profits and look like a real hero to GE," the executive said. The Letterman reruns were an enormous, unrealized asset. NBC had an ownership position in the A&E channel, so the connections were in place already; the channel's programmers were certainly interested in acquiring such an attractive package. The deal was easy to set up.

It was harder to execute. Letterman had no right of ownership to his old shows, but he was extremely protective of them. He believed overexposure could diminish the value of what he did every night. For that reason he resisted NBC's requests that he do more prime-time specials. But his contract only gave him the right to consult on any NBC decision to sell the reruns of his old shows.

John Agoglia did consult with Jack Rollins and Letterman's Indianapolis lawyer, Ron Ellberger. If they ran it by Letterman, he hadn't grasped the full import of what the deal meant. By the time he did, NBC had an agreement in place with A&E—and David Letterman exploded. "They did it over Dave's objections," the senior NBC executive said. "Dave had consulting rights; that isn't worth anything. Only a right of refusal is worth anything in a deal like that, and Letterman never had it."

Agoglia said he never had a chance to talk the deal through with Letterman himself. "God forbid we had the opportunity to explain why we wanted to do it to Dave; we would never get that. His people signed off on it; they knew the terms and conditions." Indeed, Agoglia said he amended the terms drastically from the original proposal to try to appease Letterman. Instead of a firm four-year deal for a lot more guaranteed money, the deal was scaled back to include options for NBC to cancel after only one year. That greatly reduced the money Agoglia could realize from the deal. Then the Letterman side demanded that they be able to select the shows available to A&E and that they have their own unit to edit the shows, at a cost of $250,000—another frivolous expense as far as Agoglia was concerned. The Letterman people took that reaction as more evidence of how Agoglia just didn't get it. "We saw the show as unique and special, and we devoted our lives to keeping it that way," Robert Morton said. "NBC never appreciated that."

The deal was finally announced on April 25, 1991. Letterman still hated it, still squirmed at the thought that three- and six- and eight-year-old versions of a show he was still uncomfortable doing every night would now be out there for people to see—not to mention the sight of the old versions of himself, sometimes much fatter, sometimes with a lot more hair, always imperfect to his unforgiving eye.

It was then that John Agoglia's picture started turning up on "Late Night" as "GE Employee of the Week." Later Warren Littlefield was similarly honored—and mocked. Even some of Dave's defenders inside NBC believed Letterman was pushing the hostility too far. "The guy is so funny and great and always had the rhetoric, but that was really, really mean," one NBC executive with ties to Letterman said. "That wasn't funny to me. That was offensive. These are behind-the-scenes people. It was sort of unfair for Dave to trot them out like that."

Agoglia and Littlefield were undeniably irked by the

on-air attention. Agoglia felt like a poor slob in the audience who is getting picked on by the insult comic on stage with the microphone. "You're helpless," Agoglia said. "He had this microphone and he felt obligated to take shots at us." As for Littlefield, "Oh, Warren really, really loved it," Agoglia said, rolling his eyes.

Letterman's shots had hit their targets; but the targets also happened to be the men in charge of the decision that would determine the future course of his professional life. And, unlike his competitor on the West Coast, he wasn't exactly courting their votes.

David Letterman never made it easy to get a relationship going—for anybody. As decent and honorable as he was in all his professional and personal dealings, he was not easily approachable, not usually responsive to contact with new people, and the furthest thing from comfortable in social situations. "Everything starts with the fact that he is painfully shy," said a longtime entertainment industry associate whose wife also came to know Letterman well. "That leaves so much room for erroneous analysis of what he's all about, because the first thing, since he's a talent, that he should be judged on is his talent." This associate recalled an incident in which his wife wanted to give a dinner party at their home for their friend Marty Klein, who was then also Letterman's agent. When his wife called and asked, Letterman declined. He said: "You know I never go out. I stay home and I just watch baseball games. I never go out. I never leave my house. I just pick up a pizza. How could you think I would leave my house to go to someone else's house?" For ten years, Letterman's extremely confined social life revolved around his relationship with Merrill Markoe. But after several rocky periods, the romance and professional partnership ended for good in 1987. The aftereffects of what Markoe felt was a very bad breakup lasted for years, at least for her. She could no longer even watch Dave on the show she helped create. For Letterman, who never failed to credit Markoe graciously for the show's crackling originality ("We haven't had a good idea since she left," he once said), the process of living and working with Markoe grew too strained to continue. "She's very disorganized about everything but getting ideas on paper. But the process that leads to that is just like an explosion. In her mind it's quite clear. And it was the beginning of the end of our relationship because I just felt like I was being poked with a sharp stick every day."

Letterman eventually began quietly dating a young woman named Regina Lasko, who had a job in the unit manager's department at NBC. Soon they were living together in Manhattan and Connecticut. After they had been together for several years, he began predicting on numerous occasions that they would soon marry and start a family.

Given his shyness and the limitations of his social skills, it might have been easier for an NBC executive to thread a peacock through the eye of a needle than for anyone to get a relationship going with David Letterman.

"Both parties are to blame," said Peter Lassally, whose relationship with Letterman went much deeper than producer and star. NBC executives would sometimes call to try to stroke Letterman in their clumsy way, but he usually found that intrusive. He resisted compliments from NBC because he believed they were probably insincere. If NBC sent a birthday gift and it was cheap and crummy, he would go on the air and make fun of it, describing how cheap the network was. The next year, if they sent him nothing at all because they wanted to avoid that kind of treatment, Letterman would tell his staff he couldn't believe NBC was snubbing him that way.

Bob Wright, the NBC president, tried several approaches to find the right tone with Letterman. At first he steered clear, thinking that Tartikoff had a special relationship with Dave and that was enough. Once, for Letterman's anniversary, Wright had a cute, playful idea. He got a GE toaster, filled it with flowers, covered the whole thing up, and rolled it in to Letterman's anniversary party. Letterman did get a laugh out of the gift, and as a gag made toast with it on the air for guests for a couple of nights.

But nothing developed from that approach. "I tried, but Dave made it difficult," Wright said. He did not encourage anyone to just drop in and see him. Even Wright had to make an appointment, and frequently when the day came, Letterman would cancel the appointment.

"When you tried with Dave, he made you feel stupid," said one NBC executive. "It was: Leave me alone but love me. You got to the point where you would think: If I go in there to see him, it's going to be so awkward. And so then you don't do it, and you hear Dave wondered where you were."

Some encounters were excruciating or embarrassing.

Sissy Biggers, the NBC entertainment executive assigned to the show, would sometimes have an exchange with Letterman outside his office, and he would cut her off with a remark so sarcastic and rude that it shocked her into total silence. She might try to muster up her best sarcastic bravado to respond in kind, but the remark would be too hurtful to her and she simply walked away. She always quickly forgot what the incident was about and even the remarks Dave made, but she didn't forget that he had made fun of her that way. He once gave Biggers an on-air slam as well, dismissing her as the show's program executive, "if you can call that a program executive."

It did not occur to Letterman that this testy estrangement from his NBC keepers might be sabotaging his own dream of winning the "Tonight" show. His was a different sort of naïveté from Leno's; but it left him no less vulnerable. Letterman still believed that he would earn the job or lose it based totally on how good he was on the air every night.

For many reasons, which boiled down mostly to respect and caution, Letterman always strenuously resisted the heir-to-Johnny talk that started almost as soon as "Late Night" became a hit. In one early magazine interview, he protested way too much: "Hosting the 'Tonight' show was never my desire, dream, or purpose." As late as 1986, Letterman was still dismissing the possibility: "There is no way I'd want to compete with his record."

But by then Letterman was aware of some rumbling behind the scenes: In mid-1986, he got an unexpected call from Dave Tebet, the Carson Productions executive who worked with "Late Night." Tebet said that he and Henry Bushkin, Johnny Carson's extremely powerful attorney, friend, and business partner, wanted to meet with Letterman—by himself, totally confidentially. Letterman had no idea what the meeting could be about, but agreed to show up.

The three men had breakfast at the Dorset Hotel in Manhattan. Letterman was stunned when he heard what they had come to propose: They were offering him the "Tonight" show; they wanted him to take Johnny Carson's job. Bushkin, in his role as head of Carson Productions, said that the company intended to maintain ownership of the "Tonight" show after Johnny stepped down, and now was the time to line up Letterman to slip into Johnny's chair. The details were vague, and to Letterman they sounded deliberately so. He said he was flattered, he listened politely, but his radar was signaling a warning. Neither man told Letterman how or when this ascension would be accomplished, a problem that started sounding even worse when Bushkin advised Letterman that no one at NBC or anywhere else knew of the plan yet—not even Carson.

Letterman, already nervous, now started to feel as if he were getting close to a fire he didn't want to be in the same campground with. Bushkin and Tebet told him that once the plan took effect, Carson might work some vacation weeks or special occasions, but the show would be Letterman's. They asked Letterman not to tell anyone, not even his management. They would get back to him.

The more Letterman thought about it, the more it

sounded like a palace coup. His immediate instinct was to stay out of this, because there was going to be warfare of some sort. He feared Carson would interpret this maneuver as plotting, and he guessed what might happen next: Johnny's best friend Bushkin wouldn't take the fall. Nor would his old crony, Tebet. It would be the punk who got blamed for engineering this.

Letterman broke his promise and called Peter Lassally, Carson's producer, who had booked Letterman on his first "Tonight" show and who had become a close, fatherly friend in the years since. Lassally was shocked by what he heard. He suspected that Bushkin was involved in all sorts of machinations that might or might not have benefited Carson. He thought about telling Johnny, but other attempts to alert the star to questionable activities by Bushkin had been harshly rebuffed. Lassally decided to see what developed and advised Dave to keep Bushkin and Tebet at a distance.

Letterman had a couple of more phone calls from Bushkin and Tebet about the deal; they discussed it with Ron Ellberger, the Indianapolis attorney that Letterman still employed. Tebet blamed the lawyer for muddying up the deal, and eventually said that Carson knew of the plan and had approved of the idea of lining up Letterman for the future.

But Carson had never heard a word about it, and when he did—long after the approach had taken place and Bushkin and Tebet were both long gone—Carson exploded with rage at the thought that this plotting had gone on behind his back. He knew exactly what he would have done if he had learned of it at the time: He would have fired Bushkin and Tebet before another day elapsed. Letterman had guessed right in steering clear of the coup. When he learned that Carson hadn't known what was going on, Letterman was deeply thankful for his cautious instincts.

When the offer from Bushkin melted away, Letterman tried not to give it any second thoughts. Only for the briefest time did he think that he might have walked away from an offer to host the "Tonight" show. The next time, it would not be nearly so easy to take.

Helen Kushnick had no concern about how an offer for the "Tonight" show might arrive. By early 1991, all she cared about was when.

As John Agoglia was battling with Letterman and his representatives over the A&E deal, Helen was pressing for an answer. Kushnick wanted Jay Leno signed once and for all to a contract that guaranteed him the "Tonight" show.

Helen was simply tired of waiting for NBC to put their signatures where their promises were. Agoglia and the others seemed to be stalling. They had countered the CBS offer with real assurances that the show would be theirs, but nothing was on paper yet. Beyond that, Helen wanted some assurances purely of her own. She intended to take over as executive producer of the show, and she wanted to see that on a piece of paper, too.

The same explanation kept coming back from NBC: These things take time; this is simply how long it takes. Meanwhile no one knew, or at least no one was saying, when Johnny Carson was going to quit. But Helen thought that if Johnny were to announce his exit before she got Jay officially signed, NBC could still have found a way to fool around with the deal. In mid-April, she had had enough. She called Agoglia with a simple message: "I want Jay signed."

NBC knew the CBS offer was still viable if Helen wanted to take it. As the months had gone by, the NBC executives had become even more convinced that Jay was now a superstar in late night. Having built him into that, they couldn't let him go across the street to CBS, bringing all those younger viewers with him and leaving them with Johnny's aging audience. The moment for action had arrived.

The lawyers went to work. On May 16, Helen, Jay and their lawyer, Ron Berg, drove to NBC's West Coast headquarters in Burbank. They spent much of the day going in and out of various offices in the legal department of NBC Productions, conferring with lawyers and executives, hammering out the details. In one of her trips to one of the offices, Helen ran into Bob Wright, who said hello in the hall. The process seemed exhaustingly long to those on Helen's side. But finally the papers were in order. Jay Leno signed the deal that formally set up the mechanism to hand him the "Tonight" show upon the departure of Johnny Carson. It was a done deal: Jay Leno would be the successor to Johnny Carson, and Helen Kushnick would be Jay's executive producer. John Agoglia noticed that the mercurial Kushnick was completely focused and composed as she sat there signing the documents. "It was the impossible dream coming true for two people," Agoglia said.

After a brief round of congratulations, Helen said her good-byes and went outside to the parking lot. She had left her gold Mercedes in a "Tonight" show space, and as she walked to it she noticed a piece of paper stuck under the wiper. She opened the note and saw it was from Bob Wright's notepad. "This is a very expensive car," the note read. "Call me. Bob."

Exactly one week later the terms of the contract would be in effect.

Before the deal with Jay Leno was closed, NBC's executives held no discussions about whether David Letterman should still be considered for the "Tonight" show. They all knew that he had a clause in his contract that required NBC to pay a penalty of $1 million if he did not get the job. But like the others, Wright had the impression that "this was more of a negotiating comment offered during times of negotiation, and it wasn't a demand or something he personally aspired to."

For Wright, this seemed to be a wonderful situation for the network: Letterman would stay at 12:30 and NBC would get a new person in the "Tonight" show— the best person to come along, a person with a different sensibility, who would also hold on to the Carson audience. They didn't want to start some approximation of "The Arsenio Hall Show." They weren't looking for some totally hip turnaround from what Johnny had been doing. NBC felt it had established over thirty years an audience that expected certain things, and Jay Leno looked like the perfect successor to that, while David Letterman remained the ideal performer for the 12:30 show. "David was so good convincing us that he was good at twelve-thirty that I don't think a lot of time was spent figuring out how good he would be at eleven-thirty," Wright said.

Warren Littlefield, however, *had* given the choice of Leno versus Letterman at 11:30 a bit of time and thought. Littlefield believed that Leno had an accessibility that the audience embraced, and that even though the 11:30 show was considered a late-night franchise, this audience really was broad-based. When push came to shove for Warren Littlefield, Jay Leno was just more broad-based than David Letterman. Littlefield approved of Leno's work habits, the fact that he was a team player, and what he called his "attitude about what he's willing to do to succeed."

Attitude had come to be a crucial factor in NBC's evaluation of the two stars. For Littlefield, Leno had a club in his bag that Letterman lacked. He defined it as "I'll work all day and night. I'll work around the clock. I'll go to every affiliate that you want me to go to. I'll do anything it takes. I'll work with advertisers. I'll work with our affiliates. I'll work with you guys in the network. I'm not afraid to hear any research data. I'm not afraid to do what it takes."

Jay had done his groundwork exceptionally well. All that campaigning through affiliates and advertisers, every appearance at an NBC event, and everything that Helen had recommended had made an impression. Jay was the go-to guy for NBC.

And then there was Dave—recalcitrant, irritable, uncooperative Dave. That is unquestionably how some executives inside NBC viewed him after his years of "us versus them" comedy. Littlefield was perfectly willing to concede Letterman's brilliance as a comedian, but he was looking for that full bag of clubs. And one club Littlefield thought Letterman did have was hardly a recommendation: the club Dave had used to beat him over the head with on the air, the "nasty Dave" club.

Littlefield thought that Letterman's penchant for what he called "ambushing the guest" would never play with the broad-based audience that came to the set at 11:30. "That sense of nastiness," as Littlefield called it, was only for the college boys who stayed up late and waited for Dave to nail some fool actress, or zing some pinhead from GE, or mock some poor NBC executive as "Employee of the Week." Whether Dave was really nasty to his guests or just funny with them wasn't an issue that Warren Littlefield or John Agoglia had to commission special research to determine; they didn't even have to watch the show to see if it was true. They already knew Dave was nasty, because he'd been plenty nasty to them.

David Letterman always spent the Memorial Day weekend back home in Indianapolis; he had choice seats every year for the 500. But in 1991 he was far from up for the race. A flimsily sourced *New York Post* story had inflicted itself on his life this time. By the time Letterman got to Indianapolis that Saturday, May 25, only two days after Carson's retirement announcement at Carnegie Hall, he had read a *Post* story that declared that Jay Leno already had the "Tonight" show, that it was a done deal, that David Letterman didn't have a chance to get the job. The *Post* didn't even have Helen Kushnick feeding it the news this time. But even if it was nothing but a shot-in-the-dark story, it troubled Letterman. He thought: "Really? Did it happen this quickly?"

He had grudgingly admitted to himself that it was

probably going to happen: Jay was likely to be handed the job without his even getting a chance to speak for it. But Dave didn't believe it was foreordained; he couldn't believe NBC would really have put it in a previously signed contract, which is what it would have taken, he thought, for the deal to be done this quickly.

That Saturday was Warren Littlefield's first day at home with his family in Los Angeles after the long siege of putting the new prime-time schedule together, topped off by advertisers' presentations in New York and Chicago. He had decided to make the announcement about Jay Leno as new host of the "Tonight" show early the following week. Whether from fatigue or just a consistent case of shortsightedness, the idea that he should first break the news to David Letterman simply did not occur to him. The Carson-to-Leno transfer of late-night power seemed like a fait accompli. Littlefield, like so many of the other NBC executives, viewed this as a transition that had already begun months or even years earlier, when Leno started scoring big in his guest-hosting spots.

But a colleague's call that weekend gave Littlefield some pause. The colleague asked point-blank when the announcement of Leno would be made. Littlefield said early in the week. "Have you talked to David Letterman?" the colleague asked. The weary Littlefield said he simply hadn't had time between all the fall season preparations, the travel, then the unexpected announcement by Carson. He said he would call Dave that afternoon.

"This guy has auditioned for this job the past ten years," the colleague said. "He's made like hundreds of millions in profits for the company. Don't you think you should tell him face-to-face?" Littlefield said he'd just got home from the presentations; this was his first chance to be with his family and relax in weeks. It just didn't make sense to fly all the way to New York again to break the news to David Letterman, news Letterman surely expected to hear anyway.

Still, the call got under Littlefield's skin. He was too decent a guy to be able to shrug off concern about Letterman's feelings. But besides his empathy for someone about to be hit with a powerful professional disappointment, Warren had to consider the prospect of Letterman's escalating this event into full-scale, on-air warfare with the company. That loomed as an unpleasant probability. Littlefield made a call to Jack Rollins.

When Rollins reached Letterman in Indianapolis later, he couldn't conceal his glumness. "David, Warren Littlefield wants to see you," Rollins told him. "Are you going to be in California during your vacation?"

"No," Letterman said. "I'm here for the race and then I'm going to the Hamptons for the rest of the week."

"Well, could you go to California?" Rollins asked him.

"I'd really rather not," Letterman said. "What does he want to talk to me about?"

"I think it's about the 'Tonight' show," Rollins said.

"Yeah, what about it?" Letterman said. He knew from the tone of the conversation that Rollins wasn't likely to tell him Warren was about to offer him the job.

"They're going to give it to Jay," Rollins said.

"Are you sure?" Letterman said.

"Well, they didn't say so, but it was made pretty clear to me that that's what this is all about."

The deflated Letterman talked over with Rollins whether he should call Littlefield back. And then the meaning of what was going on swept over him. Here he was on vacation, getting a call and hearing the news he had been dreading for months—the worst possible professional news short of "You're fired." Now they wanted him to interrupt his vacation and fly off to California just so they could dump this on him in person. And Letterman instantly decided: No way am I going to California. If they want to do this to me, they can fly themselves to wherever I am and tell me.

That was the message he gave Rollins to deliver to Warren Littlefield. But it didn't make Letterman feel any better. Because the full realization of what had happened was just starting to sink in. He was not going to get the "Tonight" show. Jay Leno, his contemporary, a comic who had honed his style on Letterman's own show, was going to be the heir to Johnny Carson. David Letterman, forty-four years old, going on ten years on the same show, was going to be . . . what? More of the same? The cult hero to the college crowd? The follow-up act to Jay Leno? It was one thing to be the guy who came on after Johnny Carson, the master, the king; but to follow Jay, whose show was not a generationally different one, that seemed like a prospect with no future at all.

David Letterman started to believe that his time in television was drawing to a close.

Peter Lassally had been Letterman's closest professional mentor since the day he booked Dave as a guest host on the "Tonight" show in 1979. A producer with deep television roots going all the way back to "The Arthur Godfrey Show," which he worked on in the 1950s, Lassally was a man of unusual grace and sensitivity—unusual certainly for the world of show business where those virtues existed almost exclusively in fictional characters. A trim, compact man approaching sixty, with a shock of sandy brown hair that was just beginning to gray, Lassally spoke in sonorous, cultured tones, his words almost always delivered slowly and thoughtfully. Lassally's bearing was so dignified, it didn't seem to fit the world of television comedy; that incongruity was only intensified for most people when they learned that Lassally, born in Hamburg and raised in Holland, had survived a concentration camp as a teenager in World War II. Characteristically, Lassally didn't trade on that personal history in any way. But it certainly helped shape his serene perspective on the foolishness of show business.

Lassally had worked for Johnny Carson for more than twenty years, gaining a reputation as the steadiest hand in the operation. Letterman, who shrank from the fraudulent emotions that saturated most show business relationships and strove to build his career on principles like honesty and integrity, was understandably drawn to a figure of real substance like Lassally. And Lassally saw a performer of real substance in Letterman. He grew fond of sitting back and watching Letterman display the full range of his verbal and comedic gifts. Lassally would beam and unashamedly say, "I'm like a proud father with him."

Lassally's greatest hope was to finish out his own professional career as the executive producer of a "Tonight

Show Starring David Letterman." And as much as he understood Letterman's respect for Carson and the circumspect way Dave approached lining himself up as Johnny's successor, Lassally felt that Letterman waited far too long to drop the necessary hints of how badly he wanted to inherit Carson's chair. Lassally accepted Dave's resistance to having managers and agents surrounding him, chipping off little pieces of his self-respect. But Lassally also knew the show business world well enough to recognize that Dave was leaving himself open to being undone by the very types of people he so disdained: the poseurs and schemers who saw a prize and would do whatever it took to grab it. People, Peter Lassally thought, like Helen Kushnick.

Lassally wanted Letterman to come right out and say he wanted NBC to recognize the great job he had done by giving him Johnny's job when Johnny retired. He wanted Dave to demand it as his right. At first Lassally despaired when Letterman dodged the question in every interview with a remark like "I don't know how anyone could follow Carson." But as the eighties ended he began to see more pieces in the press where Dave would step up to the question and declare that it would mean a lot to him to have a shot at the job. That encouraged Lassally, and he would call Dave and tell him to keep it up. But then Dave and NBC started feuding; he didn't seem quite as hot in the press, and there seemed like a long silence when David Letterman had nothing to say about wanting the "Tonight" show.

Like everyone else, Lassally saw how NBC responded to Jay Leno's performance as guest host for Johnny. Since Lassally himself produced those shows with Jay, he had his own take on Jay's abilities, and he wasn't overly impressed. Jay seemed too much the joke machine and less the completely rounded talent that Carson was, that Letterman was.

At the moment of Dave's deepest despair in Indianapolis, Peter Lassally called. He had seen all the press about the likelihood that Leno would get the "Tonight" show. They talked about the way it seemed to be going. Dave was responding laconically as usual. Finally, Lassally couldn't take it anymore. He blurted out: "Dave, don't you *want* the 'Tonight' show?"

Letterman seemed a bit stunned by Lassally's emotion. But he had the answer Lassally wanted. "Yes, of course I want it," he said.

"Well, what are you going to *do* about it?" Lassally asked. "You can't just want it; you have to *do something* about it."

Letterman seemed at a loss. All he said was that Jack Rollins had mentioned that maybe he should have a dinner with Bob Wright and start a relationship.

The line shocked Lassally. He realized the full consequences of Dave's effort to distance himself from the NBC suits. The "Tonight" show was about to fall into Jay Leno's arms, and David Letterman's side didn't even have a relationship going with the NBC bosses. Lassally knew that Dave had always believed he would get the "Tonight" show for the righteous reason: because he deserved it. But now he had to clue Dave in: It doesn't work that way in show business.

Lassally asked Letterman if he had anything in his contract that guaranteed him a shot at Carson's job. Letterman said no, he only had the $1 million penalty payment.

Lassally knew right away that a million-dollar penalty was meaningless in a deal like this and that Letterman, for all his efforts to keep high-powered show business lawyers away from him, needed one now in the worst way. But at least he had taken the most important step. He had said the words out loud: "I want the 'Tonight' show."

Now it was up to him and Dave to figure out a way, at the twenty-third hour, that they could go out and get it back from Jay Leno.

5

BRIDGES BURNED

A s he talked to Peter Lassally on the phone on the night of June 3, 1991, David Letterman was putting up the usual resistance. There was no time left to play with; the appointment had already been made. Warren Littlefield and John Agoglia were flying in from California and would be in Dave's office the next evening following the taping of "Late Night." And still the idea of needing some sort of slick Hollywood dealmaker representing him in a meeting with the NBC bosses made Letterman's skin crawl. But Lassally kept pressing his points: If you want the "Tonight" show, you have to fight for it. And that means getting yourself someone who'll protect you.

Letterman thought he had steeled himself for months to accept the inevitable. "It's gonna be Leno, it's gonna be Leno, it's gonna be Leno," he had told himself. Yet when he faced the prospect of actually hearing those words spoken officially by NBC executives, Letterman got totally rattled. He had spent his week's vacation in the Hamptons letting the finality of it all sink in, and it hadn't gotten any easier to take.

Now only one night separated him from hearing that

the "Tonight" show was irretrievably gone. Lassally, at home in Los Angeles, called one last time to Connecticut trying to push Letterman into some kind of action. "We have about twelve hours to get you a lawyer," Lassally told him. "Will you accept a show business lawyer? Because I don't want you going into that meeting with your Indianapolis lawyer."

Letterman wasn't sure what good having a show business lawyer would do at this point, but he and Lassally had started talking over a plan. It was a pretty desperate plan, true, but at least it involved taking some form of action instead of passively nodding like a condemned prisoner when the NBC guys said the job had gone to Jay.

They worked out exactly what Dave should say in the meeting and how he should say it. At the least, being a little aggressive might make this encounter a bit more difficult for Littlefield and Agoglia than they were expecting. That finally got Letterman's juices going. He allowed himself to think maybe there was the tiniest chance that he could connect on a Hail Mary pass and pull out the game in the final seconds.

After fighting Lassally to the last possible moment about hiring a new lawyer, Letterman gave in. Taking charge of how he would orchestrate the next day's meeting, Letterman left the lawyer business in Lassally's hands. At 11:00 P.M. West Coast time, Lassally finally reached Jake Bloom, probably the most powerful show business attorney in Hollywood. Lassally knew Bloom's expertise was in movie deals, not television deals, but all he really wanted was a name that might scare Littlefield and Agoglia. "All we want right now is to be able to use your name to the NBC guys," Lassally told Bloom. Bloom agreed verbally to take Letterman on as a client. Everything was in place for the confrontation.

It had not been a great week for Warren Littlefield and John Agoglia, either. They had to deal with non-stop calls harassing them for an answer on when an official announcement would be made about the "To-night" show. Many of these calls were coming from the press, but plenty of them were coming from Helen Kushnick. Helen said that Jay was jumping out of his skin wondering why he hadn't been pronounced the winner yet. The NBC executives weren't sure whether that was really Jay getting antsy or Helen covering her own agitation by referring to Jay, but it didn't really matter. They knew they could hold out on Helen and Jay a little bit longer. They already had their deal; Jay wasn't going anywhere. Littlefield now felt he had to get to Letterman first, before Jay Leno was officially coronated, a point that Helen didn't especially buy: Even if that was Warren's plan, she wanted to know, why not get on a plane, find Dave in the Hamptons, and get the dirty deed done? Littlefield tried to be patient with her, explaining his plan to see Letterman in his office with Agoglia the following Tuesday. But he certainly didn't need the extra aggravation from Helen.

On the plane flying in to New York, he and Agoglia discussed what Letterman might really want. As usual, Agoglia boiled it down to dollars and cents. As he saw it, Letterman might be upset "from a negotiating point of view," which might mean he would hold his breath until his face turned blue, or until he got his price, whichever came first. But then there was the ego aspect,

Agoglia thought, which was a different level of upset and one that wouldn't go away so easily if money were tossed at it. NBC was prepared to take any of several approaches to try to make Letterman happy.

Not that NBC was about to abandon its strategy, which could be reduced to three words: Keep both guys. Agoglia, thinking mechanically, his chosen method, had planned the situation down to its basics. The decision they had made—Jay in for Johnny, Dave staying put at 12:30—was the smart play. Agoglia had a contract, signed by David Letterman, that committed the star to NBC for another two years. So it was guaranteed: pick Leno and get the two guys back-to-back until at least April 1993. As Agoglia saw it: "It was a short-term gain with a long-term problem. And we thought in two years we could solve the problem."

Agoglia did not perceive that settling up with Letterman, even with his fragile emotional state, would prove insurmountable. After all, there had been no pressure on the network from Letterman's representatives all these years, no threats to move to another network, and there were no provisions in Letterman's contract stipulating he get a shot at the "Tonight" show. So how serious could the issue really be? NBC's position had only been enhanced, Agoglia and Littlefield thought, by the newspaper TV columns that had appeared in the week since Carson's announcement. Virtually every television columnist in the country had written pieces saying how the logical choice was Leno.

Littlefield did anticipate a frosty reception in New York from his combative star, but he felt he had come up with some intriguing proposals to run by Letterman.

He didn't foresee the encounter turning into much more than an initially tense meeting that would eventually get around to business and what was best for everybody involved. Warren had been through plenty of those before.

In his office on the fourteenth floor of 30 Rockefeller Plaza, Letterman spent the early part of his day choreographing the meeting. He was joined by his manager, Jack Rollins, who also held the title of executive producer of "Late Night," and his producer and friend, Robert Morton. Letterman assigned each of them a specific seat in the little scene he was creating: Rollins was to sit in a chair on one side of the desk; Letterman would sit in a chair on the other side; and Morton would sit in Letterman's chair behind the desk. Letterman also told them where he would place Littlefield and Agoglia when they arrived—across the room from the desk, on either end of the office's battered couch.

Letterman knew Littlefield reasonably well, because he had had occasion to meet him at NBC functions several times in the past decade. But Agoglia worked for the network in more mysterious ways, negotiating contracts, making business decisions, saying no from afar. Letterman had had no reason to become acquainted personally with Agoglia.

Following that night's taping, the Letterman side gathered in the star's office and waited. After a few minutes, Dave's assistant, Laurie Diamond, buzzed them with the information that Littlefield and Agoglia had arrived. The men all stood as the two NBC executives entered the office. Letterman stepped toward the door to greet them. In his gut he was seething; he thought the two of them looked like such worms. He shook hands with Littlefield first, saying a perfunctory, "Hi, Warren, how are you?" Then, in an exaggeratedly formal way, Letterman turned to Agoglia, reached out his hand and said: "And you are . . . ?"

Agoglia tried to laugh the insult off as he shook hands with Letterman. "Oh, come on Dave, John Agoglia." The other men forced out a small laugh. The tone had been set.

After just a few other strained pleasantries, Letterman steered them all to their assigned seats. Littlefield stepped up the task at hand; he knew it was his responsibility to do most of the talking. So he started off the conversation they were all expecting to hear: The network had analyzed the late-night situation. They knew the day was coming when Johnny would step down. For the last several years they had watched Jay Leno grow into the role as guest host. Obviously NBC had every reason to be proud of what Dave had accomplished on the "Late Night" show. But the choice had to be made. And they all felt Jay had proved he could succeed with the 11:30 audience. And so, Warren said, summing it up in the form of a pronouncement, they had decided to name Jay Leno the new host of the "Tonight" show.

That was Letterman's cue. In a strong but even tone, he started to speak: "Well, I'm sure that Jay will do a great job. But I must tell you," he said, "we've been here for ten years. We're a unit of forty people; we know how to do this show. The next best thing for everyone would have been if we could have done the 'Tonight' show. That's always what we wanted to do; that's what we've had in the back of our minds. This is a real disappointment. But if this is your decision, you can contact my lawyer, Jake Bloom." Then Letterman stood up from his chair, looked directly at Littlefield and Agoglia, and said: "Gentlemen, this is completely unacceptable. I want you to release me from my contract."

The room fell totally silent as Letterman, without a second's hesitation, turned away from them and strode out the door, leaving the two NBC executives staring at his back.

Letterman felt a surge of adrenaline as he disappeared out the door, past Laurie and out into the hall. He felt great, not so much because he believed this grandstand play was going to turn the tide—though that was his wafer-thin hope—but because he had done what he set out to do, and he had done it well: He had been very calm, very articulate, and he thought he had made a meaningful argument. Within minutes, taking refuge in Robert Morton's office down the hall, Letterman was on the phone to Peter Lassally in his "Tonight" show office in Burbank, describing what had happened, what a perfect performance he had given, and how he had stunned them into total silence.

In the twelve years he had known David Letterman, Lassally had never heard the performer prouder of himself.

Inside the room, Morton and Rollins were left to deal with the two wide-eyed NBC executives. They never got to sell any of their new promises to Letterman. "What are we going to do now?" Littlefield asked Morton. "How can we make him happy?

"How can you make him happy?" Morton said. "You heard him. Give him the 'Tonight' show."

"Well, short of that," Littlefield said.

Agoglia jumped in with what had been their intended sales pitch to Letterman: They wanted Dave to know that when Jay took over the "Tonight" show, NBC was going to change the formats of the two shows to create what Agoglia called "a seamless two-hour block." The idea, as Agoglia and Littlefield framed it, would be to emphasize the similarities between the two shows and the two stars, with the nightly promotions always coming on the air in tandem. Sometimes the shows could even have gags that ran over from one show to the next. Over and over, Agoglia and Littlefield pushed the notion of the two-hour seamless comedy block, never realizing that David Letterman's biggest fear was that his show would lose its distinctiveness if it started looking too much like the "Tonight" show. Nor could they have been aware that the biggest fear of Dave's producers was that the lead-in from Jay Leno was inevitably going to be weaker than the lead-in they had had for ten years from Johnny Carson.

The discussion in Letterman's office continued for about forty minutes after Dave's abrupt departure. Then Laurie Diamond buzzed Morton and said he had to take a call at her desk. Morton excused himself and went to the phone. It was Letterman. "All right, wrap it up," Dave said. "That's enough time for those guys." Morton told Dave that Rollins was still inside talking to them. "Well, we need to talk about this ourselves," Letterman said. "Go in there and put an end to the meeting."

Morton figured it wouldn't especially endear him to the NBC executives to walk back in and order an end to the meeting, but that's what his boss wanted; so he did it.

"All right, let's knock this off now," Morton said as he came back into the room. The discussion wasn't really getting anywhere anyway, so the NBC executives didn't protest. They said their good-byes and left, not sure of what the next step was going to be or how they were going to handle Letterman, whose distress about losing the "Tonight" show was far deeper than they had expected. But they were sure of one thing: They had a contract with David Letterman for two more years, they had done nothing to violate any terms of that contract, and no matter how deep his pique, no matter who his lawyer was or what he said, they certainly weren't going to let him out of it.

Within a day, Letterman was full of regret about the meeting. Somebody had tipped the press that he walked out of the meeting in a huff because he didn't get the "Tonight" show. Now the story was "Letterman Goes Ballistic, Threatens to Quit." It became embarrassing, and Dave still abhorred embarrassment. He thought his master plan had backfired, that he had shot himself with his own gun.

And the feeling grew worse. As the days went by, Letterman began to feel overcome with the conviction that he had no future at all in television. He sank into a deep depression. With Jay officially named as Johnny's heir on the "Tonight" show, Dave was left with no viable choices, as he saw it. He could continue at 12:30, but he was forty-four years old, and it was simply logical that the people staying up that late would soon decide they didn't want to see a guy pushing fifty doing a show at that hour. On top of that, Jay was going to be doing a show that Dave expected would be perceived as more similar to "Late Night" than it was to Carson's "Tonight" show. With Carson and "Late Night" it had always seemed like two guys with more differences than similarities; with Jay, that would be reversed.

Letterman asked himself what he could possibly do. It didn't seem as if CBS would be interested in a show, not after their Sajak experience. He couldn't imagine them leaping back into the late-night talk arena again. And he felt that ABC was—and should be—extremely happy with Ted Koppel and "Nightline." That left only syndication, a prospect that gave Letterman true chills. He could envision a sleazy syndication salesman out with a videotape of his wares: "Uhhh, we got Letterman. What the hell ya want? Ya want 'Studs '93?' " Letterman knew he would eat himself alive if he had to sink to that level. His oldest demon, self-doubt, came roaring up inside him again. Suddenly the two years left on his NBC contract started looking like a lifeline.

On their side, all the NBC executives knew was that they had a massively unhappy star. At the same time, they realized they had no one in the network who could easily step in and make it better, because no one had any sort of a close relationship with David Letterman. Even without knowing that Letterman considered him a worm, Littlefield didn't think he was likely to get too far pursuing Dave immediately. So he tried an indirect route. The day after the meeting, he called someone who did have a good relationship with Letterman: Robert Morton.

"I understand he's angry; I understand he's hurt," Littlefield told Morton. He then asked Morton what NBC could do to make Dave enthused about sticking with the 12:30 show. Morton told him one problem was that with Jay as host, the "Tonight" show was going to start doing what "Late Night" did—and was going to book the same guests. Littlefield said that wasn't necessarily so, that Jay had had on guests like C. Everett Koop, the surgeon general, people Dave would never have chosen. Still wondering just what Dave might be up to with this new lawyer, Littlefield said, "If possible, could we get him back in the frame of mind of 'we've got a show to do?' "

To indicate the depth of his concern about Letterman's state of mind, Littlefield told Morton that NBC had given Letterman the news of the selection of Leno even before it had told Johnny Carson. Littlefield suggested that moving the Letterman show to the West Coast would not be a problem, if Dave wanted to do that. Littlefield asked if he and Morton could meet late in the day to talk it out further. But Morton said no; Dave had already told him he didn't want anyone from the show talking to any of the NBC guys. Morton repeated that to Littlefield, and added, "I've worked with him a long time and he always means what he says."

Littlefield pressed on. "Get in the room and talk to him," he told Morton. NBC was still hawking the two-hour seamless block. "This is such a great opportunity. Don't let him blow the opportunity," Littlefield told Morton. The newly combined block would be called

"NBC Latenight," instead of two separate show names, Littlefield said. Morton said he'd do what he could. But that was purely polite business talk: Robert Morton was going to do whatever David Letterman thought was right.

A close friend said Robert Morton could have been a Catskills comic or social director if he hadn't gone into television; there was an unmistakable aura of old-time show business about him. Morton, called Morty so often that he frequently used the nickname himself, displayed the kind of New York style and energy too often reduced to a description like "street-smart." But Morton was a vending machine stacked with smarts; he had stores of savvy and chutzpah, and he loved to play the network political game. Morton was especially smart about television. He started as a page for game shows at the Ed Sullivan Theater in the mid-seventies then got into production with local talk shows in Boston and New York. He was hired as a segment producer for Tom Snyder's "Tomorrow" show in 1978. When Letterman got the morning show in 1980, Morton, who had roomed in college with Stu Smiley, then one of Letterman's managers, had a chance to work on the show. But the woman Morton was dating at the time worked as a segment producer on Letterman's morning show, and he wanted to avoid any potential conflicts. He hooked up with Letterman when the show became "Late Night" in 1982.

Morton sometimes said that Peter Lassally fulfilled the role of Letterman's older brother, while he played younger brother. Certainly Morty supplied a lot of

youthful enthusiasm; he liked to generate fun as well as
have it. In his late thirties, ruddy-faced, with curly black
hair and a stocky build, Morton had every reason to
love his life. He was a prince of the city and attended all
the industry social occasions, invariably with a stunning
female companion. In the summer Morty held court in
the Hamptons, and became a fixture in the social swirl
that centered on players in the media world. On vacations, he often repaired to the villa he leased in Tus-
cany. All of this good life was possible because Morty, a
kid from Long Beach, Long Island, had found his way
onto a hot show with a hot star. He recognized his good
fortune and was grateful and intensely loyal to Letterman. But the notion, held by Agoglia and others inside
NBC, that Morton was little more than Letterman's
lapdog and simply served at his master's whim (one
other NBC executive said Morton filled the role of
"lucky stone or charm" for Letterman) completely
missed the hardworking, professional approach he took
to his job. Morton wasn't the creative genius behind the
show, but he was the guy who got it on and off the air.
He had paid his dues. For years he ran all the production aspects of the show, deciding on bookings, getting
the show taped on time every night from a spot in the
audience just in front of Letterman. Morton was also
the guy who had to face Dave every night in the postmortems, even on those nights when he knew Dave's
mood would be coal black after a lame effort. He did it
because he was well paid to do it, and because it was his
job.

Jack Rollins had the title of executive producer of
"Late Night." His role was mainly to work with Dave;

he didn't involve himself much in the day-to-day mechanics of running the show, though he sat in the control room most nights and frequently met with and counseled Dave. Morty and Jack got along extremely well. Morton waited patiently for his chance to move up, even turning down offers to make the jump to other shows, including "The Pat Sajak Show" and Fox's failed late-night effort that followed Joan Rivers, "The Wilton/North Report." Morton, like many others on the staff, stood in awe of Letterman's comic abilities. He kept the faith.

Morty was also the center of operations for "Late Night." Nobody could get Dave on the phone, so they all called Morty, a guy who never met a conversation he didn't like.

After Letterman's big scene in the meeting with Agoglia and Littlefield, Morton's phone was incessantly busy. The same night the meeting took place, Morty got a call at home from Leno at 1:00 A.M. In the conversation, Leno told him of the deal, set up in April, in which he was to get the "Tonight" show as soon as Johnny chose to leave, and that he had signed a contract with NBC stipulating those terms only one week before Johnny made his announcement. Knowing Jay's inclination toward embellishment, Morton didn't know whether he should believe that story.

At 1:30 the next afternoon, Helen Kushnick called. "From me to you, I'm here and I'm scared to death," she told Morty. Helen then said she had heard the meeting was uncomfortable, but expressed hope that the two shows could coexist without any animosity. She added that she thought the NBC executives were "shit-heads" who would always make the wrong decision. She also revealed to Morty that she would take over the show as executive producer. That, he surely believed.

Several other NBC executives called, including Rick Ludwin, the president of NBC's late-night program-ming. Ludwin said he had recommended they pick Leno but also that NBC take steps to make the news easier for Dave to swallow. Some initiatives should have been put on the table, Ludwin added. Morton thought Ludwin sounded lost and scared.

None of this was changing any of the circumstances, and Morton realized nothing probably could. NBC had made its call; he knew it was a bad call, but as long as the "Tonight" show opportunity had passed, Morton figured it was wise to make the best of it. If the idea of a seamless two-hour block held the prospect of any short-term benefit for his show, he'd be willing to try it. At the least it might get "Late Night" a few more promos.

Helen Kushnick had a year to get ready to run the "To-night" show; she relished every minute of it. She had ideas, of course, most of which involved doing almost everything opposite of the way it had been done under Johnny Carson. She would order a different set, a far different band, and the guests she booked would con-firm just how stodgy a show Carson had been deliver-ing. Initially Kushnick stayed out of the way on those nights Jay was guest hosting during Carson's final year. But gradually she began to exert her influence. No-where was her influence more imposing than with Jay. Helen wanted no one to come to Jay who hadn't spoken to her first. One night, through some mix-up, Leno's aunt was denied permission to get into the audience for the show. The representative of NBC guest relations responsible for the mistake called Jay's aunt and apologized, telling her to come back whenever she was in town. Then, as a courtesy to Jay, the representative knocked on his door, explained what had happened, and apologized for the error. When Helen heard of it she exploded, and told everyone in the department they were never to speak to Jay Leno unless they talked to her first.

Before Jay became the host-designate, Helen steered clear of the bookings, allowing the regular "Tonight" staff to continue to book their own show. But once NBC had named Jay, Helen immediately became more aggressive. She began to make deals with studios and record companies and publicists: In exchange for the biggest names, Helen agreed to put a line of lesser guests on the show. Many on the "Tonight" staff objected to this practice because they had always avoided it. They thought the idea was to make the show entertaining each night, not to feature a big name one night and damage the show another night with a guest who was a virtual unknown. But when they complained to Carson, he told them to back off. "It's their show," he said. "They're in control. Let them book the show the way they want to book it."

Of course, he had also told staff members: "When I go out the door, the product goes with me." To the astonishment of many on the "Tonight" show staff, NBC had never seen fit to consult Carson about the naming of his successor, and he never volunteered an opinion.

But no one close to Johnny had any real doubt about his preference; he never said a bad word about Jay, but they were certain he supported Letterman.

Helen had plenty of business to attend to on the show, but she also had a last deal she needed to make with NBC before Jay began his run. Jay's deal as star was already in place: He was to make a guaranteed $12 million over two years, with some bonus incentives based on ratings performance. And Helen had her own deal to become executive producer. The last point to work out related to the ownership rights to the program. NBC had negotiated ownership of the "Tonight" show away to Carson in his spectacular 1980 contract. Now the network wanted that ownership back, badly. In the years since Carson assumed control of the show, the rest of the television industry had expanded exponentially. Cable systems were already offering fifty channels or more, and the future promised hundreds. All those channels needed programming. Everything on television had become recyclable. So everybody wanted to control the future sales of the reruns.

With Jay as host, NBC would own the show outright again. But with Helen remaining Jay's manager, even as she produced the show, the arrangement became messy. Helen also had a few other clients whose careers might be affected by the "Tonight" show. "There were potential conflicts," Agoglia said. Besides, Helen was making loud noises about selling her management company to somebody else. In a letter to Agoglia, with a copy sent to Jack Welch, the GE chairman, Helen said she had had expressions of interest in her company from Carsey/Werner Productions, the team that had produced two of television's biggest comedy hits, "The Cosby Show" and "Roseanne." If a company like Carsey/Werner got the management rights to Jay, they would then have an interest in how the "Tonight" show was run, who was booked, etc. In the letter, Helen emphasized that she wasn't shopping the management company around, but did point out that she was sure CBS would have bought her out in order to land Jay.

Helen contacted the investment firm of Deloitte, Touche to obtain an estimate of the value of her company. When she got back a figure of just over $7 million, she first took it to Jay to make sure he didn't want to buy her out himself. She told him it was a formality; she was sure he didn't really want the responsibility of running a management company himself. The idea, she told Jay, was to sell the company to NBC to make the network happy that it had a clean deal with Jay. And there was something good in it for each of them as well: Helen would become a rich woman before the show even started; Jay would get his $6 million-plus a year without having to pay any commission at all.

NBC agreed to pay $7 million even for Helen Kushnick's management company. Agoglia labeled it "the price of poker." Even without the formal title, Helen had no intention of relinquishing the role of manager in Jay's career.

The NBC executives did not have any second thoughts about giving Helen Kushnick all this money or all this power, even though her experience in producing television shows was drastically limited. All she had produced up to that point were a couple of specials with Jay. They knew she had a reputation for being volatile, but they had never seen that trait in her negotiations for Jay. In all their dealings with her, she was always totally focused. And what she was asking for wasn't the slightest bit unusual in Hollywood. Managers frequently assumed the title of executive producer on their stars' shows. Letterman himself had made his manager, Jack Rollins, his executive producer. And Garry Shandling, when he did his sitcom, made his manager, Brad Grey, his executive producer.

But beyond that, the NBC executives thought Helen had good, solid, creative ideas about the show. "She had given us notes about how the show would be changed with Jay, and they were very interesting and highly acceptable," Agoglia said. "She also knew everyone in the business, in the music world, and everywhere else. And from an operational point of view, one of the more difficult transitions in network television we thought would be made much easier with her doing it than with a new person coming into Jay's life."

So Helen got her $7 million and NBC regained full ownership of the "Tonight" show. Of course, Helen had designs on that, too. She estimated that with the kind of ratings results she expected Jay to generate, it would take only five years before she and Jay got ownership of the show away from NBC.

As Jay Leno's level of recognition grew, an image started to emerge. He was decent, honest, straightforward, disdainful of pretension, generous to fans, and a friend to almost every comedian in the business. *Time* magazine, in a cover story, called him "the most popular regular guy in America."

But many people close to Jay said the portrait of an uncomplicated, Everyman comic was either superficial or totally inaccurate. "Jay is one of the most complicated human beings I have ever known," a member of the "Tonight" show staff said.

For all his outward warmth with people and his easy approachability, Leno seemed to distance himself emotionally from everyone around him, even close friends. He even disdained the *idea* of having emotions. If people complained about being under stress, Jay said: "What does that mean, stressed? I've never been stressed." When a comic friend, Carol Leifer, was going through a tough period in her life and told Jay she was depressed, she asked Jay what he did when got down. "Down?" Jay asked, as though the word belonged to a foreign language. "I've never been down."

A "Tonight" show staff member said: "There is no term describing a psychological state that Jay relates to. He's not in touch with his emotions at all."

Helen often chided Jay for his desire to be liked, saying he should stop with "that 'like' shit," as she called it. This all seemed very immature to Helen, who sometimes saw Jay as a big kid who had never really grown up.

Certainly Jay lived the life of a big kid, with his fondness for junk food and video games. Comics used to come to Jay's house after the clubs closed and play a tank game on Jay's Intellivision set far into the morning. The nocturnal play sessions continued even after Jay married Mavis Nicholson. He had met Mavis, a small, dark-haired, attractive, and intelligent woman, outside the ladies' room at the Comedy Store in 1975.

Though she was an aspiring comedy writer at the time they had almost nothing beyond comedy in common. She read ten to fifteen books a week; Jay did comedy and cars. But they hooked up. Mavis traveled the road with Jay for awhile; mostly they found they enjoyed their separate interests separately. For awhile, Mavis did professional astrology readings out of their home.

When they decided to marry in 1980, it was not a moment awash in romance. Jay told people he had talked a still somewhat reluctant Mavis into marriage when he realized it made sense because of his insurance policies. The wedding ceremony lasted less than ten minutes, and was held at Helen Kushnick's house. A single roll of wedding pictures was taken, but Jay later told friends that he and Mavis never bothered to develop it.

They agreed they would never have children. As his career took off, they settled into what Jay called "a fairly unique relationship." Though he never made "wife jokes," out of respect for Mavis, and often talked about Mavis with great affection—calling her his greatest supporter—Jay was not devoted to his wife in the conventional ways of most marriages. He and Mavis didn't go through life as an inseparable team. Jay spent much of his day working on his shows at NBC, then spent several hours each night working on his motorcycles and cars. About midnight Jimmy Brogan and occasionally some other comics would come over to Jay's house and help him work on his monologues. On Saturdays the cars took up almost the full day. On Sundays Jay almost always appeared in a comedy club. None of this ever bothered Mavis, Jay said. It wasn't exactly what most

Americans would call conventional or regular, but Jay and Mavis were both comfortable and happy with the relationship.

"If spending a day off working on cars was the kind of thing that bugged her," Jay said, "we wouldn't have gotten married."

To some who knew Helen Kushnick well, NBC's decision to hand her the reins of their most important television show was an unfathomable mistake. But Helen was not about to be denied. "Helen knew what she wanted, knew what she was after, and Helen was going to get it," one "Tonight" staff member who worked closely with her said. "She has the tenacity to go after what she wants. She had a style that was so offensive and grating that it was easier to give her what she wanted. More often than not people said, 'Just do it.' It's easier to just do it. And this went way up the corporate ladder at NBC." It was an attitude bred from intimidation, the staff member said.

This same staff member worked during the transition period from Carson to Leno. "The two camps grew to hate each other," the staffer said. Soon everything about the show had to be handled separately. "It was truly a monumental error to put Helen in charge of the show. Not because she didn't have some talent for it. She was thorough and organized, and you had to respect the intensity with which she worked. She's very smart and very focused—but very dangerous."

For the first few months after Carson's Carnegie Hall announcement and the subsequent naming of Leno to the job, nothing happened. Helen went about her planning, Carson went on with his shows, and Leno filled in when he was assigned. But NBC said and did nothing about the transition itself. Finally, after some prodding from the press relations department, NBC held some meetings to discuss the transition. One of the participants at the meeting said that NBC executives seemed not so much concerned about how Carson departed the scene as they were about lifting off Jay Leno successfully. Helen tried to make sure that's where the focus stayed. She always cited Jay's great numbers with younger viewers when he guest hosted. "That was her style," said the "Tonight" staff member. "Always keep the pressure on."

As Carson continued his last-hurrah season, emotions grew more intense on the show. But NBC succeeded in keeping the two staffs separated for the most part. A farewell tour of guests streamed through the "Tonight" show each night, each one getting to pay tribute to Carson. Helen took note of who was appearing, and like someone going to the mailbox every day to see if she had a valentine from that guy she couldn't stand, Helen watched and waited for Jay's invitation to arrive.

On the surface everything was smooth between Kushnick and NBC. But those directly involved in dealing with her began pointing out how rough she was being on anyone who didn't do things precisely her way. A lot of people were starting to resent being called incompetent.

Arsenio Hall began making noise about having to fight the "Tonight" show over guest bookings within weeks of Carson's announcement that he was leaving. Partly emotional, partly shrewd public relations man, Hall managed to set himself up, in the press at least, as a legitimate challenger to Jay Leno almost a year before Jay got the full-time job.

The truth was more complicated: Hall had actually been more of a threat to Carson, roaring onto the air in January 1989 and capturing a chunk of younger viewers who simply could not identify with a single element of the show Carson was still doing on NBC. Hall quickly grabbed the hip high ground; he booked music acts whose names the "Tonight" staff probably couldn't even pronounce correctly. He had an audience of frantic, whooping acolytes. His on-air clothes ranged from button-down cool to outrageous funk, from designer suits to raggedy overalls. His show started to work because it truly had a different sensibility for late night: It wasn't a talk show as much as a big, fun party, geared expressly for the young party crowd. Arsenio didn't break the color barrier in late-night as much as he broke the hip barrier.

Born in Cleveland, the son of a Baptist minister, Hall had spent his childhood watching Johnny Carson and pretending to be a talk-show host. He learned magic and played drums because that's what Carson had done. After quitting a sales job with Noxell to try stand-up, Hall worked comedy clubs in the Chicago area before being discovered by the singer Nancy Wilson. She brought Hall to L.A., where he bounced around for years looking to break into comedy or television or movies or anything. Paired with a bald-headed white comic named Thom Sharp for a short-lived summer series on ABC, Hall emerged briefly in late night as the sidekick for Alan Thicke on his ill-fated syndicated show in 1984. Nothing budged for Hall until the collapse of the Joan Rivers show on Fox in 1986. Stuck for a guest host one night after Joan had been fired, Fox executives called on Arsenio, who had been a successful guest with Joan on one of her last shows. Hall was just getting back to his car from the dry cleaners holding a freshly pressed suit when he heard the car phone ringing. His manager told him to get down to the Fox studio immediately. Hall turned on the ignition and drove off. He never looked back. He got to the studio, put on the suit, and went on the air. He was a hit.

For a fee of $1,000 a night, Hall took over the show for the last eleven weeks of Joan's contract, and the ratings built steadily. Fox, however, was already committed to a comedy news program, "The Wilton/North Report," as the replacement for Rivers at 11:00 P.M. weeknights. As the network looked at Arsenio's strong ratings, it decided it might have stumbled onto something. Fox initially offered Hall a show after "Wilton/North" at midnight. Then only two days after that show hit the air—accompanied by a loud, flopping noise—Fox came back with a better offer: Forget "Wilton-North." Hall could have the 11:00 P.M. slot, his own talk show, and $2 million a year. Now Arsenio could smell leverage. He told his manager he wanted an Oprah deal, modeled on the huge syndication package that had made daytime talk host Oprah Winfrey the richest show business celebrity in the world. What Hall wanted more than money, however, was control. Having decided his career had suffered when he was forced to adapt to somebody else's creative ideas, Hall wanted to own his show and be the executive producer. That was the deal breaker for Fox—and a huge mistake. In 1988 Paramount signed Hall to a deal that promised him $50,000 a week and a huge percentage of the profits in the show.

Hall was thirty-two when he launched his syndicated talk show, but his audience skewed much younger. He had a lock on the youth crowd, especially younger women. Within months Hall was a phenomenon, even if his overall ratings did not approach Carson's. Hall was a smart, insightful student of late-night television; he knew how to position himself and how to take advantage of every break. When the Sajak show was dead on arrival, Hall went around to CBS affiliates making deals to replace Sajak. He had found the niche in the Carson ratings armor: viewers born after Johnny went on the air in 1962. It could be transformed into a lucrative niche for Arsenio. Paramount began banking more than $50 million a year from "The Arsenio Hall Show," and the star's take exceeded $12 million a year. Hall was so hot, and Sajak so hopeless, that CBS tried to work its way into the deal. Howard Stringer, the CBS president, seeing how many CBS stations were going with Arsenio already, offered to buy into Paramount's deal as a partner. Paramount declined.

But by the time the transition from Carson to Leno started in 1991, Hall's meteor ride was already starting to burn up in the atmosphere. Like many acts that start off sizzling hot, Hall's was tough to sustain with the hip crowd, who never finds anything hip for the long term. Pressed by his fading position in late 1991, Hall decided to raise the ante: He went after Jay Leno like an attack dog. First he dropped hints about running off guests who two-timed his show with Leno's once it got on the air. But then he opened up with the heavy guns.

In an April cover-story interview in *Entertainment Weekly* magazine, under the headline "I'm Going to Kick Leno's Ass," Hall said, among other things, that it was an insult to Carson's legacy to say Leno was replacing him; that despite Jay's constant references to Arsenio as a friend, he was not Jay's friend; that he had earned his place in late-night, unlike Leno, who had a late-night silver spoon put in his mouth. Hall concluded by saying: "I'm going to treat him like we treated the kid on the high school basketball team who was the coach's son. He was there because he was anointed, too. We tried to kick his ass, and that's what I'm going to do: kick Jay's ass."

They were fighting words, but that only made them all the more bewildering for Jay Leno, a completely nonconfrontational personality. Like just about everyone else on the comedy circuit in the early 1980s, Leno had met and palled around with Arsenio. They had written jokes together and played endless video games together all night long at Jay's house. To Jay, that sounded like friendship, though Hall was not the only person who believed it was better described by a term like professional acquaintanceship.

But Jay would not have to worry much about Arsenio kicking his ass; he had his own hired gun to fight for him. Helen Kushnick had a plan for Arsenio Hall. Even before they went on the air, Helen had a letter drafted for the show's talent coordinators to send to people booked on the show. It told them in plain terms not to do any other shows if they expected to be booked on the "Tonight" show. Jimmy Brogan, among others on the staff, thought it was a mistake that would eventually get the show in trouble. He mentioned it to Jay, who simply said: "That's Helen's area. I do the jokes." Later, Helen held a meeting with her staff and made the purpose of the guest policy more specific. She gave them all a message: Let's get Arsenio Hall off the air. Now is the time. He's ready for the kill. Let's kill his show.

Like a Hall of Fame ballplayer making his final tour of the ballparks of America, Johnny Carson's last weeks on the "Tonight" show took on the aura of an ongoing tribute to an icon. Stars lined up to get one final turn on the couch next to Johnny. The farewell tour included all the stars who had become regulars on the show, along with many big names who had not appeared in years. One star who was honored with one of the very last audiences with the king was David Letterman, who appeared on the "Tonight" show for the last time only one week before Carson's finale. On the show, Letterman told Carson, "Thanks for my career," and he meant it. He always gave Carson the most credit for his success.

Conspicuous by his absence on the list of farewelltour invitees was Jay Leno. Jay had never been close to Johnny, had never even done very well as a guest with Johnny, and he certainly didn't owe the success of his career to sitting on the couch with Johnny Carson.

Still, Helen saw the Carson staff's decision to bypass

Jay as an unforgivable snub. To Helen it was obvious that they were sending a message by not booking Jay: They did not want Jay on the show. Helen had her own ideas about the best way for Johnny to bow out. Late in Johnny's last year on the air, she went to Peter Lassally with a plan for Carson's final act on his final show. She wanted Carson to leave his desk, take his microphone, walk to the adjacent studio where they were preparing for Jay's show, and hand over the microphone to Jay: "Passing the baton," she called it.

Ridiculous, Lassally called it. He told Helen that he absolutely would suggest no such thing to Johnny Carson. It was not within the realm of possibility. As with all the slights she felt from the old Carson guard, this one would stick in Helen's craw—and fester.

Carson's last show was set for Friday, May 22, 1992. That was to be a retrospective show, with highlights from the past and only the regular "Tonight" crew: Johnny, Ed, and Doc. There were to be no guests at all. The final regular "Tonight" show the preceding night was the true stunner, a combination of antic, hilarious comedy from Robin Williams and a surge of genuine sentiment from Bette Midler, who sang to Johnny and with him, creating one of the rarest of show business moments: an exhibition of warm, honest emotion.

David Letterman certainly felt the emotion that night and the next, when Johnny closed shop for good. Sitting home watching the last few minutes of the Johnny Carson era come to a close, Letterman felt a woeful depression overcoming him. Carson looked so good and still had such a mastery of the format that Letterman couldn't deal with the incongruity of Carson's truly leaving that stage forever. After the final show ended Letterman tried to sleep, but found he couldn't. He was up the whole night with an overwhelming feeling of sadness that lasted for weeks.

Emotion of a different kind had begun to engulf the relationship between Helen Kushnick and the NBC management in the days before Jay's premiere on the "Tonight" show. The tension seemed to have raised the temperature in every conversation she was having with Warren Littlefield, John Agoglia, Rick Ludwin, and any other NBC executive she came into contact with. Ludwin, who was on the set every day, was reporting back that the level of anxiety had increased. Littlefield got mostly secondhand reports, until Helen decided to press him directly about her plan for NBC to welcome Jay to the "Tonight" show.

Helen told Littlefield she wanted NBC to buy a two-page ad in the "Life" section of USA Today—and she wanted it to run on Friday, May 22. Helen had the design worked out. The ad would be a map highlighting every city in the country where Jay had appeared doing his stand-up act, and each city would be sending the same message of welcome to Jay. The Friday placement was vital to Helen because Jay's first day on the air, Monday the 25th, was Memorial Day and USA Today would not be printing on the holiday. Friday also made sense to Helen because it was the weekend edition of the newspaper, which was meant to stay around the whole weekend.

There was only one problem with this grand plan: NBC had already committed itself to buying a full-page ad that day as its send-off thank-you to Johnny Carson.

Littlefield politely explained to Helen that the newspaper was doing its own full page of stories in tribute to Carson, and NBC had bought the opposite page for its ad. "We're not going to crowd that with a 'welcome, Jay' ad," Littlefield told her. He added that Jay would get plenty of press, and all these things could happen on Tuesday.

But that wasn't fine with Helen, because Tuesday was Jay's second day in the job, not his first, and that simply didn't sit right. So Helen had another idea: What if she could get *USA Today* to print on Monday? she asked Warren. Would NBC buy the ad then?

Littlefield, a bit incredulous at what Helen thought her powers of persuasion might be, said sure. If she could get a whole newspaper staff to work a holiday weekend just to get her 'welcome, Jay' ad in, fine, go for it.

That was the last he heard of the ad crisis for awhile. But as the deadline for locking in an ad in *USA Today* approached, Helen made a last stab at getting what she wanted. Warren was driving to Burbank on the Ventura Freeway when his car phone rang. Helen's voice was at high pitch as soon as he picked up the line. She wasn't asking anymore. She was telling Warren: If she had to put the fucking ad in with her own money, it was going to get in *USA Today* on Friday, Carson ad or not.

Warren had used up his store of both politeness and patience on this issue. "No, it's not going in, Helen," Littlefield said, his own pitch rising to meet hers. "And it's not going to be your money and you're not doing it, because we won't allow it. We've thought about it, we've considered it, we've listened, and we have made a decision, and that decision is final."

Helen didn't back down. She told Warren that he had never been supportive of Jay anyway. Warren had opposed offering Jay his original contract with NBC, she said. She poured on the invective, the timbre of her voice rising with each charge she made against Warren, until it was all swearing and cursing at him and NBC— one long burst of screaming spewing out of the carphone speaker.

And Warren Littlefield, driving amid the morning rush-hour traffic on the Ventura Freeway, a man who lost his temper very rarely, and then almost always at home and not at work, waited, and held his breath deeper and deeper in his chest until Helen had finished. And then he exploded. "Hey, fuck you!" he screamed into the phone. "Fuck you and the horse you rode in on! You're wrong. We're not going to do this. I will not allow it. And you know what? You're out of your mind! I have been extremely supportive of Jay Leno. I have done everything in my power to see that this man is embraced by this network, supported by this network, and I resent hearing this from you. And enough. It's over. Done."

Kushnick put up no further protest. As Littlefield hung up, he was almost to the entrance of NBC's Burbank headquarters. He pulled into his parking lot, his breathing still shallow, his vocal cords raw from exertion. He looked at the clock on the dashboard and said to himself: "Holy shit! It's not nine yet. It's not even nine o'clock in the morning yet. And we haven't even premiered this show." Littlefield didn't want to exaggerate what had just happened, but he could see a bright red flag coming up over the "Tonight" show horizon.

• • •

NBC estimated that 50 million people watched Carson's last "Tonight" show, more viewers than had seen any previous late-night show in television history. Helen knew she and Jay weren't going to do as well on Jay's first night, but she was confident they would be strong, and in the long run they would easily justify NBC's faith in them. For the first show, she had lined up Billy Crystal, a surefire attraction only two months after another sensational performance as host of the Academy Awards show. Crystal happened to be another of Leno's old comedy crowd, so the chemistry promised to be perfect. The show would also be on the air live in the eastern and central time zones to accommodate NBC's schedule of NBA play-off games that night. Live shows had some risk, of course, but they also helped pump up the excitement.

If Jay Leno was excited he didn't show it. Mostly he seemed a little bored and impatient all that day. A guy who acknowledged that he had the attention span of a ten-year-old, Jay wanted to get on with it. The new staff had worked out whatever kinks were going to arise in two dry-run shows. It wasn't that Jay was really doing anything new, after all. This was just an extension of the work he'd been doing for five years, with some refinements to make the show, as Helen saw it, more hip and contemporary.

That afternoon, when Jimmy Brogan, Jay's writer and friend, stopped in to see if he was nervous, Jay said he just wanted to get it over with. He thought he might take a nap. Brogan was not totally amazed at how calm Jay was because he was always that way—the steadiest, most even temperament Brogan had ever seen. They talked a little while about the show that night, the mon-

ologue they had planned. Brogan had one more suggestion. He said he thought it would be appropriate at
some point early in the show to say something nice
about Johnny.

Jay answered impassively: That decision was the executive producer's to make and she had decided not to
do it.

Helen and Jay had already had this discussion. Helen
said that she was just taking the lead from Johnny. Carson didn't do anything to mention Jay in his final show,
so why was it necessary for them to do something for
him? And just in case Jay was about to have some mis-
givings, she reminded him of the way it always was at
the Comedy Store, where the weak comic who followed
the hot act would try to steal some of the departing
star's applause, by calling for one last round for the
great man they had just seen. As Helen saw it, Jay
wasn't going to be any kind of kiss-ass suck-up. Not for
anybody.

Two hours before airtime, the phone rang in Helen's
office. Bob Wright was on the line. This was no real
surprise: A wish of good luck from the boss just before
the network's great new venture with its new star was to
be expected. And Wright did want to wish them all
well. But he had something else on his mind.

"How are you going to open the show?" he asked
Kushnick. Helen said Jay would do his standard mono-
logue. "Well, what is Jay going to do to thank Johnny?"
Wright asked.

"We're not going to do anything," Helen said
bluntly. She simply didn't know how to do something
just to curry favor with the boss.

"I'd like to hear why," Wright said, just as bluntly.

Johnny Carson, after all, was not just NBC's former icon. He was Bob Wright's current friend.

Helen spun out a long explanation of how the new show was going to be different, how they didn't want to look as if they were beholden to Johnny's old audience. She brought up the Comedy Store analogy to Wright as well, saying Jay wasn't going to go out and look as if he was pandering to the audience that had just seen Johnny bid farewell.

"I think it's a terrible mistake," Wright said. To him the issue was clear and uncomplicated. There was only one way to handle it. It came down to simple politeness. It was just what people would do in their own homes. He tried to press Helen. "I would really appreciate it if you would go out and tell Jay to do something and to say, 'Thank you, I wouldn't be here but for Johnny.' Do a real connection. It's your show now, but you owe Carson and you owe the audience a real connection."

If this speech did anything at all to Helen Kushnick, it made her even more sure of herself. She said no, again. She was not going to ask Jay two hours before a live broadcast to insert something about Johnny Carson. That decision was over. Absolutely not, she told Bob Wright. Then she said good-bye.

As he hung up the phone in his Connecticut home, Wright turned to his wife and said, "This is the beginning of the end."

Back in Burbank Helen Kushnick was only wondering what Bob Wright was calling her for. What the hell did Bob Wright have to do with the "Tonight" show? She remained completely unimpressed with the entire NBC executive hierarchy.

About an hour later Helen called Wright back. She thought he might want a little more explanation. So she called back to say she had carefully considered everything he said and what he had asked for, and that she and Jay were still rejecting it.

For Wright the second call only made their position even worse. It was like telling him that they didn't take his suggestion lightly. They took it seriously—and still rejected it.

Wright never considered trying to order Jay to say something about Johnny. That wasn't his style of management anyway; he tended to look for consensus, not rule by fiat. But in this case he also felt that if a performer was told to do something he didn't want to do, he was likely to do it poorly. Wright didn't believe it would be the end of the world for Jay, though he was convinced it was an insensitive thing to do and would be read that way by both the audience and the press. But it certainly sealed his opinion of Helen Kushnick. From the very first day she put on a "Tonight" show as executive producer, Wright believed it was not a question of if but when: Helen Kushnick was heading for a meltdown.

The first "Tonight Show with Jay Leno" (Jay had steered clear of "starring Jay Leno" out of concern that he would look too presumptuous claiming a star title on his first day on the job) went off mostly as planned. Jay performed his monologue, firing off jokes at a withering pace. Then he introduced his new bandleader, Branford Marsalis, an accomplished jazz saxophonist who could work easily in other musical formats. Landing Branford had been Helen's proudest coup. It meant something to her to have the first black leader of the "Tonight" show band. Branford had put together a mix of talented jazz artists. NBC felt the band had the potential to be a hot act in their own right.

When Billy Crystal came out as Jay's very first guest ever, he pushed the show in a direction Jay was clearly trying to steer clear of: He sang a song to Jay, just as Bette Midler had sung one for Johnny four nights earlier. Crystal did an Ed McMahon joke, saying he'd seen Ed out on the street with a sign: "Will announce for food." Crystal made several other references to the Carson era, none of which Jay picked up on to say something generous about Johnny.

Wright would be proved right. In the reviews the next day, every critic would cite Jay's gaffe of not saying something about Carson and question how the show could have made such a poor choice.

But for Helen and Jay and most of the others on the new "Tonight" show, the evening soared on gossamer wings. Helen could charm even her rivals at times with her engaging enthusiasm. And she had never been more enthused than the night when it all really happened for them, when Jay Leno took over the "Tonight" show, which she herself was producing. People could question the opening she had approved—a batch of phony stage curtains opening as the names of the night's guests were posted, or the beach-scene backdrop she had placed behind Jay's desk, or the sometimes esoteric jazz that the band chose to play in the commercial breaks. But they had put their version, their vision of a new "Tonight" show on the air. They were off and running.

As the first show wound down to its close, Helen

Kushnick stood on the stage behind the cameras, waiting as the band played through the credits and Jay came out from behind the desk to shake hands with his guests. As soon as the tape stopped rolling, Kushnick walked near center stage, and as several of the show's crew members later reported to their old Carson allies, she was heard to say: "Fuck you, Johnny Carson."

6

GOOD COP, BAD COP

Even before Peter Lassally moved east to take his new job as executive producer of "Late Night with David Letterman," a job he was to share with the newly promoted Robert Morton, he had a lot of work to do trying to shake the mood of his despondent star. Lassally knew that for months after the announcement that Jay Leno would succeed Carson, Letterman was still shattered by disappointment and was increasingly depressed about his prospects for the future. Letterman kept telling Lassally that his market value had sunk to zero. When Lassally would try to laugh off that exaggeration, Letterman would point out that he didn't hear people coming to him offering new and exciting directions for his career. Dave kept telling Peter that he felt he was reduced to one of two choices: stay at 12:30 on NBC after his contract ended in April 1993, or quit the business. No matter what Lassally said to try to convince him otherwise, Letterman thought he was dead in the water.

On several earlier occasions, Dave had asked Lassally to move from his "Tonight" show job to New York to take over on "Late Night," but Peter felt such a commitment to Johnny Carson, after working for him for twenty-two years, that he promised to stay on until Johnny's last night on the air. But he spoke almost daily with Letterman by phone, and he knew that a huge percentage of Dave's despair was his penchant for self-denigration; no matter what was going on in his career, Dave always thought he was a disaster. This time the feeling clearly went deeper. He had had a lifelong goal, and when the time came for that dream to be fulfilled, Letterman had been rejected. As Lassally saw it, Letterman had to make a move as soon as possible to defy that rejection, to reestablish his career, or else he would be confirming the wrongheaded judgment of him by the NBC executives.

The answer, Lassally believed, was to find a true Hollywood killer to work for David Letterman. He had pulled Jake Bloom's name out of the air at the last minute, when Dave absolutely needed a legal threat to throw at the NBC executives in their June meeting. But that wasn't going to be enough to kickstart a new direction for Dave's career. Lassally knew Letterman needed a new manager, somebody more aggressive than Jack Rollins, or else a new agent. But those two words were still poison to Letterman. Lassally certainly didn't want to be his manager. He wasn't trained as a businessman; that wasn't a job he felt comfortable with. Years earlier Lassally had steered Dave to Marty Klein as his agent, paired with Rollins as manager, because of all the agents in Hollywood that Lassally knew, Klein was the most decent human being. Still, that chemistry had never worked. Klein's biggest move was to negotiate a movie deal for Letterman with Disney. But Dave never stopped thinking that the idea of making a movie was silly, and none in fact was ever made. Letterman wound up settling the contract with Disney and giving them a chunk of money back. So Lassally had no reason to believe that Letterman had built up a lot of confidence in Klein. But he had to find confidence somewhere. The very idea of moving his show or himself anywhere new was so scary to Letterman that whenever Lassally brought it up, Letterman would retreat back inside his shell.

But in his frequent calls from the West Coast, Lassally never stopped bringing up the need for Dave to get out of NBC. There was no other option, as far as Lassally was concerned. That was the point he kept hammering at Letterman; he had to go somewhere else because staying meant remaining the follow-up act to Jay Leno, a humiliation that Peter Lassally could not accept for David Letterman. He had enormous faith in Dave's talent, and not very much in Jay's. Lassally had worked with Jay for all the years he was guest host on the "Tonight" show, and he had concluded that Jay was simply a limited talent, too much the stand-up comic and not enough the broadcaster. And the Mr. Nice Guy image seemed cloying and unappealing to Lassally.

Late in the summer of 1991, Lassally pressed the issue with Letterman: "You must not follow Jay Leno," Lassally told him over the phone, "because you will hate yourself the rest of your life. It will drive you crazy. You will go home on the weekend and say, 'Why? Why am I, David Letterman, following Jay Leno?' You'll be unhappy and miserable the rest of your life." The process of persuasion was difficult and draining for Lassally, because Letterman's moods could be so blue that the constant effort to tell him that he shouldn't doubt himself so much, that he really was okay, could be utterly exhausting.

Carefully, in the months after NBC passed Dave over for Jay, Lassally started suggesting names of agents or managers who might be helpful to Letterman. Dave's reaction was invariably instantaneous: No way, they're all sleazes. Almost out of desperation, Lassally finally brought up a name he knew Letterman would recognize, a name that had so many inside-Hollywood connotations tied to it that he really didn't have much hope that Letterman would go for this one either. Lassally mentioned Mike Ovitz.

To his complete surprise, Letterman's spirit perked up immediately. "Now that kind of intrigues me," Letterman said. Michael Ovitz was an agent, yes—the chairman of Creative Artists Agency, which represented a roster of the biggest stars in Hollywood, including Tom Cruise, Sylvester Stallone, Sean Connery, and Kevin Costner. But he was also the acknowledged master of the show business power game. Having that level of power on the same team was a prospect even an anti–show business zealot could hardly resist.

"So would you have a meeting with Mike Ovitz?" Lassally asked Letterman.

"Yeah, I'd be kind of curious about that," Letterman said.

Lassally contacted Jay Maloney, a CAA agent he knew well. Lassally asked Maloney if he would find out if Ovitz would be interested in speaking with David Letterman about the possibility of signing with CAA.

Maloney agreed and called back with a message a short time later: Michael Ovitz had great interest in taking a meeting with David Letterman.

The two men did not really know each other. Letterman had once met Ovitz when he was a young agent with the William Morris Agency in the seventies. Ovitz had not followed the intricacies of Letterman's career. But CAA's empire had been built largely on Michael Ovitz's extraordinary ability to forge relationships with the biggest names in show business.

Michael Ovitz was fascinated with filmmaking from a very young age, when he would occasionally sneak into the RKO Studios lot near his home in the San Fernando Valley. Born in 1946, Ovitz grew up as a first-generation California kid. He went to Birmingham High School in Van Nuys, where he was elected class president. (The same class included future star Sally Field and future financier and felon Michael Milken.) Ovitz's parents sent him to UCLA to study premed. But medicine didn't have his heart. Ovitz sought out summer jobs as a tour guide at Fox and Universal studios. When college ended, Ovitz found himself in one of Hollywood's most famous career cradles: the mailroom at the William Morris Agency.

Within six months he was an agent. One of his first clients provided a bit of expertise in the world of television talk shows: Merv Griffin.

Ovitz quickly needed room to maneuver his outsized ambitions. In 1975, when he was only twenty-seven, Ovitz and four other agents split off from William Morris and started CAA. The key to the agency's high-speed growth was Ovitz's pursuit of a concept called packaging, in which one agency puts together the whole range of creative talents for a movie, from stars to writer to director. Ovitz began with writers, because he knew good stories always attracted stars and directors. Soon CAA was being talked about at the right tables in the right restaurants as the agency with the best vision for a changing Hollywood.

Ovitz himself was the key figure. He quickly gained a reputation for almost mesmerizing powers of persuasion and salesmanship. Always impeccable in his dress and irrepressible in his enthusiasm, Ovitz was tightly organized and unrelentingly intense. Compactly built, extremely fit, with strategically combed brown hair and a gap-toothed smile most reminiscent of a certain late-night talk host, Ovitz's physical presence was not striking until he added his ideas and his passion. Then Ovitz became so dynamic that even experienced businessmen came out of meetings with him slightly giddy from the ride. Ovitz delved deeply into oriental culture. At work, he became an early adherent of the Japanese philosophy of management, which emphasizes teamwork rather than competition; and in the gym, he became a black-belt practitioner of the self-defense art called aikido, which turns an aggressor's strength against him. Ovitz soon became the name most often whispered in Hollywood corridors of power—and not always with affection. He was seen as secretive and sometimes ruthless. But that image was tempered by his devotion to his wife of twenty years, Judy, and their three children. Movie deals often had to be scheduled around Little League games.

In the late 1980s CAA began to branch out, with Ovitz evolving into a more elevated breed of matchmaker. He brokered two of the most colossal Hollywood deals ever made, in both cases involving odd-couple marriages of Japanese electronics giants with movie studios. In 1989 he advised Sony on its $3.4 billion buy of Columbia Pictures, and the following year he was the middleman in the even bigger $7 billion purchase of MCA/Universal by Matsushita. Ovitz mixed other cultural crosscurrents in 1993 when he put together a plan for the French bank Crédit Lyonnais to salvage its investment in another studio, MGM. With the entertainment world about to erupt into hundreds of different technological directions, Ovitz positioned CAA as a player in everything from advertising, where he supervised CAA's production of a new campaign for Coca-Cola, to sports marketing, where he teamed with the athletic shoemaker Nike to produce sports for television. Ovitz also developed joint ventures with computer companies like Apple, software manufacturers like Microsoft, and even AT&T, all in the interest of keeping CAA on the cutting edge of every coming spin in the entertainment world.

Ovitz made enemies along with money for his company, and some said he stopped being interested in any deal that didn't further his image as a kingmaker. But most of his 700 or so clients had many millions of reasons to stand by their Hollywood samurai.

On a typical late summer morning in L.A., as David Letterman and Peter Lassally entered the spectacular three-story-high lobby of the I. M. Pei–designed CAA headquarters on the corner of Little Santa Monica and Wilshire boulevards in Beverly Hills, Dave was still skeptical. His dominant experience with the concept of agent remained as he put it: "a couple of nights in Pittsburgh with Tony Orlando, and let me call and maybe we can get you $500." Still, Letterman had to concede, this was a mighty impressive lobby.

They were escorted to Ovitz's long, narrow corner office on the third floor. Ovitz greeted them with a rush of warmth and enthusiasm. Letterman was a client Mike Ovitz wanted for his agency. As soon as they were comfortable, Ovitz revved up to high speed, talking his way into a presentation that was as much soliloquy as sales pitch.

Ovitz said he saw Letterman as an enormous star with geometric possibilities and he had drawn up what he told them was a complete architecture for Dave's future. CAA would deliver what Dave wanted, everything Dave wanted. Yes, there would be an 11:30 show for him, and there would be offers from each network. But the deal would be bigger than just that. Ovitz would be able to bid Dave around the entire television industry—networks, studios, syndicators, everybody. Dave would become a giant from this deal. It would all be open to Dave. And Peter? Peter would become a very big man in the business himself. What Dave should expect to achieve from this alliance was strategic, self-fulfilling growth in his career and his art, Ovitz told them. All these things would be delivered, because Dave was the biggest and the best. CAA would take care of everything.

It was virtuoso salesmanship, a performance so

charming, so dazzling, that even the two show business cynics who were bathed in it for one hour could not help but come away dripping with excitement. In the car, riding back to Lassally's beach house, they laughed like giddy schoolboys who had just witnessed the coolest show they'd ever seen. Letterman turned to Lassally and said: "That was too much!" And the two of them laughed out loud again. Back at Lassally's house, they sat on the deck and recounted what had happened for Peter's wife, Alice, and Dave kept saying over and over, "I've been to see the Godfather! I had a meeting with the Godfather!"

They both agreed it had been a dazzling performance by a master, but take away the hype and it was still Mike Ovitz promising the show business world at Dave's feet. If anybody could bring that off, Ovitz could. Finally Letterman asked the only question they really had to answer: "So what do you think? Should we go with him?"

Lassally said he was still a little unsure. "We can't know going in what signing with CAA would mean. But having Ovitz on our side would certainly make a statement to the industry. It would put the message out that you are looking for the next step in your career. And it would be awfully nice to have that power on our side. I can't tell you it would all be good, but there is something to that kind of power. I think we should take some time to think about it. Let's not make the decision right now."

But the dazzle didn't wear off. A few days later David Letterman called Michael Ovitz and told him he would like to make use of his services.

• • •

Ovitz's first duty was to spring David Letterman from his NBC contract. Lassally and Letterman wanted to be free to seek an 11:30 show somewhere else. But NBC's contract was more than a minor impediment. It was an unusually onerous contract, with a clause that allowed NBC the right to match any future offer for a full year, leaving open the potential for NBC to keep Letterman off the air entirely for a year after he left the network. Ovitz told colleagues he had never seen an artist abused and misrepresented so badly. Lee Gabler, the head of CAA's television department, thought the contract had clauses in it that a prisoner wouldn't have.

NBC also retained first negotiating position, which meant Letterman could not negotiate with any other party until NBC's first negotiating period lapsed in February 1993. That added up to seventeen months from the time Letterman signed on with CAA that no other network or syndication company could offer any concrete proposal to him for fear of being in breach of the NBC contract. Gabler could not think of how Ovitz was going to set Letterman free.

Ovitz, who saw Letterman as a human being who'd been badly beaten up, also felt he first had to build back Letterman's self-confidence. Neither job was going to be easy.

Some indirect approaches about Letterman were already being made. Howard Stringer, the president of CBS, began quietly cultivating a relationship with Robert Morton, who told him over several dinners how fed up the entire "Late Night" staff was with NBC. An ABC executive went even further, calling the "Late

Night" offices on September 24, 1991, with the message that ABC was ready to deal for Letterman as soon as he became available. The ABC executive said he was convinced that the two top executives at Capital Cities/ABC, Tom Murphy and Dan Burke, were ready to give Letterman the 11:30 time period, scrapping Ted Koppel and "Nightline." ABC had long been frustrated in its inability to get any kind of entertainment show launched after the half-hour news program. "We'll take Koppel off and go crazy," the ABC executive said.

Even though no one was allowed to discuss a deal for Letterman in any formal way, Ovitz believed he had to get the process moving. In the beginning of 1992 he started identifying the companies he thought would be the major contenders for Letterman; then he set down the goals he wanted from any offer for Letterman. For the next several months, Ovitz had conversations with NBC executives looking for a way to undo the contractual chains on Letterman. Mainly Ovitz tried to convince NBC that the network could enhance its good will with Dave by being conciliatory about the contract. That good will would eventually help bring the sides together for a deal, Ovitz argued. But there wasn't anything concrete in that for NBC. Not surprisingly, Ovitz made little headway in freeing Letterman from the entanglements of his NBC contract. But he did think of a way to increase the pressure on NBC to deal, and to get a sense of what kind of packages Letterman could expect from other suitors, while also supplying a jolt of confidence for the star. He worked out a plan for the networks, studios, and syndicators to come and pitch for Letterman.

The pitch meeting had long been a staple of Hollywood business. Every day creators of one kind or another—writers, stars, producers—pitched ideas to network or studio executives, hoping for a development deal. Ovitz, who knew a parade would form the day he said David Letterman was available, wanted to reverse the process: Letterman was to be wooed. Ovitz told the various interested parties that he would hold two days of pitch meetings for Letterman at the CAA offices in July.

CBS got a chance to express interest publicly a little early. On June 1, 1992, Letterman appeared at the annual George Foster Peabody Awards luncheon at the Waldorf-Astoria Hotel in Manhattan. Letterman had won a Peabody, among the most prestigious awards in broadcasting, for taking "one of TV's most conventional and least-inventive forms—the talk show—and infusing it with freshness and imagination." As Letterman stepped to the podium and began his acceptance speech, the CBS president, Howard Stringer, sitting on the left of the dais, far back from Letterman, could hardly believe his ears. Here was David Letterman looking for a joke to play off the fact that everyone in the ballroom was aware he was the unhappiest award winner NBC had ever had. His opening line was: "Is Howard Stringer in the house?" Stringer waited for the laughs to die down just enough for him to be heard before he came back with a booming "Yes!" But getting his own laughs was hardly all that Stringer intended to make of this opportunity. Stringer concluded that Morton had surely clued Letterman in to CBS's avid interest in him, and that the comment at the luncheon was not merely intended as a joke. So he quietly slid out of his seat as Letterman continued his thank-yous, dropped down off the dais, and slipped out into the hallway behind the ballroom, where he knew Letterman would emerge after his speech. He found Letterman a short time later, off in a corner looking sheepish, smoking one of his trademark cigars. Stringer rushed up to him.

Stringer said: "Listen, I'm delighted at what you said. I want you to know that everyone in the organization from Larry Tisch on down is eager to get you to CBS. I don't want to hassle you or harass you right now, but I want you to know we have a tremendous enthusiasm to have you, and anything I can do to make it possible I will do."

Letterman nodded politely and thanked Stringer. "I'm glad to hear that," he said in his shy way. "That's very helpful."

Stringer thought Letterman didn't look as if he wanted to continue the conversation, so he let it drop at that. But he had put CBS's toe in the water, and it didn't seem chilly at all. Howard Stringer was fully prepared to dive in.

At the same time, Letterman's incumbent bosses at NBC found themselves still flailing. Their efforts to cauterize the wounds inflicted on Letterman's psyche were limited. Warren Littlefield did take it upon himself to set up meetings with Dave to discuss some other options being dreamed up for him by his concerned and benevolent network—maybe some more prime-time exposure, the ill-fated "seamless late night." Littlefield talked with Letterman in New York several times, once for about an hour, just the two of them. Letterman asked if Warren had really flown into New York just to meet with him. Littlefield, who grew up just across the Hudson in Montclair, New Jersey, assured him that he was indeed in New York solely for the purpose of trying to explore these options with Dave. He wasn't even going to see his family, Warren told him.

Letterman felt flattered to a degree that Littlefield was making such an effort, but the more Littlefield talked, and the more he pitched, the more Letterman realized Warren didn't know a thing about him; he had no idea what Dave's interests were, and he was obviously not watching the show much. Letterman didn't have any basic animosity toward Littlefield; he figured he was probably a very nice guy. But Littlefield was simply not doing himself any good with his visits. Letterman came away from their meetings more certain than ever that his previous sentiments about NBC had been well founded: "I really am estranged here," he thought.

Littlefield eventually reached a similar conclusion: "If this isn't going to work, my response would be, 'So I should give up.'"

That was the message conveyed back to Bob Wright in New York: The situation with Letterman was hopeless. It was a conclusion Wright felt he could not accept for the company. A frustrated Wright ordered Littlefield and Agoglia to go and find other options, either to keep Letterman where he was, or to find a truly viable replacement for him. "We have too much at stake here," Wright told them. "For you just to say it's hopeless and then offer no options is not an acceptable alternative in my chair. So you go off and find the alternative and I will determine whether it's hopeless."

• • •

Helen Kushnick had her own ideas about how NBC could deal with David Letterman. She volunteered to expand the "Tonight" show back to ninety minutes, its original length, if that would help fill the hole when Dave went out the door. She called Littlefield with this helpful notion. Don't be concerned, she told him. If she had to stretch to ninety minutes, she could do it. Littlefield simply dodged answering the suggestion. Just in case word of her generous offer didn't reach the Letterman camp, Helen decided to make it public herself. She fed the story to the *Wall Street Journal*. Helen then added to this little bit of mischief by putting together a tape of material featuring the comic Paula Poundstone for NBC to look at. Helen viewed her as the female version of Jay Leno. Her point to NBC was clear: Paula would make a great complement to Jay if Letterman isn't there anymore. NBC never warmed to the Poundstone option.

Kushnick marched through her first weeks on the "Tonight" show like Sherman going through Georgia. The booking pressure never let up. When Helen thought that Lori Jonas, the press agent for both Jerry Seinfeld and Tim Allen, was playing games with the bookings of these two comics as some kind of publicity stunt, she whipped off a stinging note telling Jonas, "We choose not to play your game," and commanding that one of the comics be dropped. Later, another Jonas client, actress Sheila Kelley, had her "Tonight" appearance abruptly canceled, an act that Jonas interpreted as direct retribution, even though she had in no way been responsible for the conflict in the bookings of Seinfeld and Allen. It was one instance of dozens in the take-no-prisoners booking war Helen had declared. "It was an explosion five times a day," one of her staff members said. "How dare they? Who the hell are they? They think they're going to get on this show?" Press agents in town began to whisper among themselves about the ferocity of the booking rules coming from the "Tonight" show. Most of that ferocity was directed at keeping guests off "The Arsenio Hall Show" (and to a somewhat lesser extent "The Dennis Miller Show," another syndicated effort that was already sliding toward oblivion by the time Leno got the "Tonight" show). But there was another show in New York that Helen apparently saw as competition.

The "Tonight" show and "Late Night" had coexisted for ten years without serious conflicts over booking guests. There were rules, of course; the shows had established an informal two-week window. If an actress such as Sigourney Weaver appeared on the "Tonight" show, she would then not be booked on "Late Night" for at least two weeks. The agreement was loosely enforced and exceptions were sometimes requested and almost always granted. But double bookings were rare, mostly because the shows had such different styles and because relatively few guests crossed over frequently from one to the other. That changed when Jay arrived at the "Tonight" show. Helen intended to bring in the hot, young performers, especially in music, that the old "Tonight" show never booked.

Robert Morton had a long-standing, friendly relationship with Helen and Jay from all the years Jay had appeared so successfully on "Late Night." Morton thought that Helen had always been charming, gracious, and surprisingly easy to deal with. When Morton was named producer of the show six years earlier, Helen and Jay sent him a ceramic frog with a note that said, "To the little brown-nosed frog who became a prince." Morton had heard horror stories about Helen but he had never had any bad personal experience like that, and he refused to be influenced by other people's versions of events.

Before Peter Lassally arrived to join the show, Kushnick called Morton to warn him that Lassally was out to get him and that it wouldn't be long before he would stab Morty in the back. Morton's response was that he had known Peter a long time and would judge for himself. But he did have some concerns about how sharing the executive producer job was going to work. So did Lassally, mainly because Morton seemed to be friendly with Helen Kushnick, a woman he considered incompetent and dangerous. When he first arrived in New York, Lassally had Morton to dinner at his apartment and told him how concerned he was about Morty's relationship with Helen. Lassally said: "You haven't seen the side of Helen that we have seen on the West Coast." Morton said he understood what Helen was all about and not to worry.

Morton's first clue that he might be dealing with a different Helen Kushnick came when he sent a lovely tree for her new office, a gift for the show's premiere. He included a personal note of best wishes and good luck. A few weeks later he received a thank-you note from Helen: "Thank you for your beautiful gift. Your generous support is much appreciated." It was a form note.

Morton read the note and thought, What the hell is this? Not even a "Dear Morty." No "It's great to have friends like you." Just a form letter that looked as if it had been photocopied and sent out to anyone who sent a stupid little gift of congratulations. Morton began to have second thoughts about the depth of his friendship with Helen Kushnick.

In the weeks before Jay's premiere, Helen kept the show's bookings a strict secret. When the listings finally came out, the "Tonight" show had booked Roger Daltry, the lead singer of The Who, one week after he was to appear on "Late Night." Because "Late Night" had not kept its booking plans secret, Morton concluded that Kushnick had deliberately booked Daltry a week later. "Late Night" would still have him first, but this was surely a break from the past cooperation between the shows.

Then Morton and Lassally heard from Daltry's record company; Kushnick was putting pressure on them to get the singer to pull out of "Late Night," using the threat that other performers with the company might not get on the "Tonight" show. Morton and Lassally decided to fight, not because Daltry was a crucial guest, but because they didn't want a precedent being set. So Morton called Kushnick to explain—and he had his first taste of a Helen Kushnick he hadn't experienced before.

The conversation, at first pleasant, turned sharply as soon as Morton mentioned his intention to keep the Daltry booking. Kushnick told him he had no power at NBC to enforce that statement; his guy didn't even have a contract. Morton had no backing at the network, she said. She could put on whomever she wanted to put on. The network would never back his show over hers. The attacks got personal. Kushnick told Morton he didn't have any idea what was really going on with the network, and that she ought to talk to him about *his* next contract because he was making peanuts compared to her.

It was a revelation to Morton, who had never felt the blast of Kushnick's rage before. He didn't back down, and kept the Daltry booking—thanks to a bit of courage from the record company. But Morton no longer doubted any of the Helen horror stories. The episode helped shape a stronger working relationship between Morton and Lassally, and established clear battle lines between the two NBC shows.

It also meant that Helen had put a torch to one of Jay's most cherished relationships, his connection to "Late Night with David Letterman." In the space of a few weeks running the "Tonight" show, she had managed to isolate the show and Jay from PR agencies, record companies, and many other Hollywood power bases—and even from some people, like Morton and Letterman, whom Jay still considered friends. Helen, who said she never looked to be liked the way that Jay did, who believed that doing your job was all that mattered, was quickly becoming an object of intense dislike throughout the television industry. But Helen Kushnick could live with that. She had certainly lived with worse.

Helen Gorman Kushnick attacked life as though constantly surrounded by enemies. A child from a mostly Irish-American enclave in Harlem, Helen Gorman had toughness bred deep into her. She learned early in her career in show business that women were expected to play the game differently; but Helen never did. She had unquenchable stores of brass and sass and intensity.

Starting as a secretary, she moved up to the position of agent for International Creative Management in the early 1970s. Her specialty: holding on to clients who were thinking of leaving. When Helen was turned loose on them, they usually fell back into line. In 1973, during a contract dispute involving singer-dancer Ben Vereen, Helen got a phone call from Vereen's hard-nosed New York entertainment lawyer, Jerrold Kushnick. In her first conversation with her future husband, Helen told him to go fuck himself. Kushnick was impressed anyway. They had a phone relationship for awhile, then began seeing each other regularly, through Jerry was still married at the time. He left his wife and two teenaged daughters to move to Los Angeles, where Helen was based. The couple eventually married in 1979.

In 1974, Jerry Kushnick formed a management company beginning with comic Jimmie Walker. With Jimmie's help, the company, with Helen operating as a manager herself, added other performers like comic Elayne Boosler, dancer Debbie Allen, and for a time, David Letterman. Then in 1975, a twenty-five-year-old comic from Boston named Jay Leno was added to the roster of clients.

From the start, Helen put all her chips on Jay. She simply believed he was the comic spokesman of his generation. Jerry and Helen managed Jay together; Jerry made most of the club bookings, while Helen handled most of Jay's television work. It was all special care and handling; Helen put together Jay's schedule and took care of his personal affairs, including how he invested his money. She arranged his flights, gave him his travel money, advised him on wardrobe. Helen managed Jay's life as well as his career, and their relationship reflected that intense level of involvement. Jay came to depend on Helen; and soon she would have reason to depend on him.

In 1980 Helen, then thirty-five, gave birth to twins, Sara and Samuel Kushnick, at Cedars-Sinai Medical Center. Her joy was tempered by immediate concern for Samuel, whose health was fragile from the moment he was born. Both twins were premature, but Sara was quickly strong and healthy. Sammy had respiratory problems in the hospital, and even after he came home he was weak, plagued by ear infections and colds. His growth rate was slow, much slower than Sara's. Soon after the twins' second birthday, Sammy caught another cold, and this one lingered. Other infections sprang up. The Kushnicks were baffled; so were the doctors, who could only suggest that Sammy was suffering from some common childhood illness. But he got worse; the new symptoms included chronic diarrhea and high fevers. By October 1983, it was clear that Samuel Kushnick was dying, apparently of pneumonia. It was then that the Kushnicks learned that while Sammy had been in the neonatal unit three years earlier he had been transfused twenty times. The blood came from thirteen donors. One of them had AIDS.

Samuel Kushnick died October 13, 1983. The hospital administration refused to admit that Sammy had contracted AIDS from a transfusion. That set off a campaign by the Kushnicks to get Cedars-Sinai to search its records to see if any other children had been transfused with AIDS-contaminated blood during that period.

But the Kushnicks had another campaign to wage as well. Just before Sammy's death, the twins had begun preschool at the Temple Emmanuel in Beverly Hills. While the Kushnicks were still at Sammy's bedside in the days before he died, they were visited by the school principal and the temple's rabbi, who took time from the Kushnicks' bedside vigil to tell them they would have to keep Sara out of the school. The reason: panic by the other parents. It was still the early days of awareness of AIDS, and the other Temple Emmanuel parents were caught up in the hysteria over how the disease might be spread. At the same time the Kushnicks learned to their horror that Sara had also been transfused three years earlier in the neonatal unit, at least once by a donor whose blood had also been used for Sammy. Rocked to their souls, the Kushnicks had elaborate tests conducted on Sara; she was free of AIDS. But school officials would not be moved. When Jerry Kushnick threatened to send Sara to school anyway, he was told she would be locked in a room separate from the other children. Jerry Kushnick told them, "The God that is taking care of Sam is also an angry God, and He will bring down his wrath on you."

The Kushnicks' campaign to get Cedars-Sinai to release information about its contaminated blood supply received national attention. They were interviewed on "Donahue" and the ABC news magazine, "20/20." It took years and the formal intervention of the Centers for Disease Control, but the hospital's high incidence of contaminated blood was finally confirmed. In one more twist to the tragedy, the donor responsible for giving Sam AIDS was eventually located. He was a young gay man in West Hollywood who had often given blood to Cedars out of a sense of social commitment, long before the country was aware of the threat of AIDS. By the time Samuel Kushnick died, the donor had full-blown AIDS himself. When he learned that his blood had killed Sammy, he tried to commit suicide. Then his own family rejected him. He died, devastated and alone.

The Kushnicks never blamed the donor. While at war with the hospital and the Red Cross who administered the blood bank, Helen turned her rage into energy. She cofounded the American Foundation for AIDS Research, and brought as many show business names as she knew into the AIDS fight. Jay was right there, of course. When he made a deal for one of his favorite "Tonight" bits, "funny headlines and newspaper ads," to be turned into a book, he agreed that all proceeds would go to the foundation in the name of Samuel Kushnick.

But the Kushnicks were living a tragedy that had no sense of scale; already huge and overwhelming, it grew. Four years after losing Sammy, Helen Kushnick was diagnosed with breast cancer, which she successfully fought. Two years after that, Jerry Kushnick learned he had colon cancer. After a short, dreadful illness, Jerry Kushnick was near death. Jay Leno came for a last visit to his bedside, and Jerry asked Jay to take care of his wife and daughter after he was gone. The stalwart Jay, who had never wavered during all the long fights with hospitals and schools after Sammy's death, who always said he was willing to put his career on hold, whatever the Kushnicks needed, said of course he would; and he repeated the promise at Jerry's funeral.

A year later Helen's breast cancer recurred. She underwent a mastectomy, and her chemotherapy treatments continued throughout the long campaign to land Jay the "Tonight" show.

Through it all, Helen's style never changed. She never took her hand off the throttle. She didn't become beaten or bowed; she just became more determined, more driven, more ferociously focused than ever before.

What surprised many viewers, from NBC executives to television critics to fans, was that Jay Leno's early performances as the full-time, first-string host of the "Tonight" show seemed so out of tune, jumpy, so off from the reliably strong performances he turned in when he was Carson's guest host. Partly the explanation was simple: Jay had to hit the stage night after night now, instead of once a week. His monologues, formerly carefully honed from several nights of practice at a club, now were being written and delivered daily. The grind was on.

But more than that, Jay simply didn't seem as comfortable as he had, as natural as he once looked behind Johnny's desk. "He looked stiff, uncomfortable," one West Coast NBC executive said. "The interviewing was ragged. There wasn't a lot of spontaneity with the guests." Littlefield and Agoglia put it off to early jitters; Jay was just starting to find his own way in a familiar format. He needed time to make the show his own.

But the key NBC executives weren't really worried because, after all, the numbers were there. The numbers. Whenever questions were raised about Jay's early performance, somebody brought up the numbers. Most often Helen, if asked about some adjustments that might be made, would pull out the numbers and say, What for? The ratings were indeed solid, better than for a comparable period in Johnny's second-to-last year (his last year being considered an aberrant standard), and much better in terms of the younger viewers NBC wanted Jay to reach. And yet . . .

"I have a feeling that if NBC doesn't watch it, Jay Leno will turn into Merv Griffin on them." That was the assessment made by a major entertainment industry executive with long ties to network television. A president of programming with one of the biggest cable networks said, "I cannot watch Jay Leno. I cannot watch the guy. I cannot sit down and watch him anymore, he's so awful. What happened?" And one of the most influential comedy producers in television said, "It's a show that can't decide what it wants to be. I can't watch it. It has flop sweat on it."

Though she never heard those specific slams, many believed that Helen knew where the criticism was coming from, and saw a Hollywood conspiracy to undo what she and Jay had achieved. A "boys club," she called it. At various times the possible schemers included Michael Ovitz; Brandon Tartikoff; Bernie Brillstein and Brad Grey (managers of comics such as Dana Carvey and Garry Shandling); Tommy Mattola, head of Sony records; even, in more convoluted machinations, Warren Littlefield.

"It was Helen being vintage Helen," said one coworker. "She called it the Hollywood game. All the backstabbing that was going on. It's a better story when she's fighting the Hollywood establishment. But she wasn't fighting the Hollywood establishment. She was fighting herself."

Some of what Helen asked Jay to do seemed simply illogical, and helped to make Jay look awkward. On the first show, for example, she insisted that Jay finish his monologue, then go to his desk, then get up and walk over to talk to Branford Marsalis in the band area, then walk back to his desk. The rest of the staff told her this was silly and agreed that Jay could cut out his first walk to the desk. But that only set Helen off into a tirade of name-calling and demeaning criticism of anyone who raised the point. Jay did it Helen's way—and looked stiff and stilted.

The stiffness carried over into everything. It seemed as though Helen, in her quest to make Jay completely accessible to the broadest possible audience, had taken all the edges that had made Jay's comedy so razor-sharp and rounded them off, so that he came across soft and puffy. She put him in suits from Fred Hayman of Beverly Hills—classy, but somehow the wrong look for the tireless, blue-collar comic. Jay adopted a signature move for the end of his opening theme song (Johnny, after all, had made his golf swing famous). Jay's move was an exaggerated, stiff-legged sweep to the right followed by a theatrical pluck on an air guitar. Several staff members quickly came to dub the leg move the "Nazi three-step," and they thought the air-guitar business made Jay look hopelessly dorky. But he kept doing it night after night.

What most of the show's staff didn't understand was

how a terrific, gentle, giving guy like Jay Leno put up with the corrosive style of his manager—with never a peep of protest. Some came to believe Jay was some kind of wide-eyed innocent who went about his business oblivious to the cacophony that surrounded him. Others started to believe it was all part of a calculated strategy, a "good cop, bad cop" routine brought to the mean streets of show business. Arsenio Hall said he could never believe in Jay's complete innocence in the booking madness instituted by Helen. "I just can't buy the one-gunman theory," Hall said. One outsider who knew Helen and Jay well compared them to a married couple who had been together so long they were afraid to break apart. He saw Jay and Helen at a dinner in New York once where they seemed to be in a spat over everything. "I never could figure out what the guy was all about," this associate said. "Either Jay was aware of what Helen was doing and decided not to care about it, or else he wasn't aware of it at all. Sometimes I just saw a guy whose head is up his ass."

Those who believed Leno knew what was happening and simply put blinders on reasoned that he was well aware he was in a cutthroat business, so he needed somebody willing to cut throats while he was putting smiles on faces. And then there was Jay's obvious sense of gratitude for all Helen had done, and his sense of obligation to her after all she had been through.

Helen herself gave contradictory messages. While she would at times say Jay knew exactly what was going on, at other times she called him a sweet, simple guy who wanted to be liked, who knew only that Helen was serving him steaks, but never how she was slaughtering the cow.

It was Helen's slaughtering of Jay that most concerned the show's staff. They saw Jay's shaky performances as partly a function of how much Helen was intimidating him. "She was so vicious to him in public and in private that I assumed they had a relationship that I couldn't possibly understand," said an associate in Burbank who frequently came into close contact with the two. "She was abusive to him. She would tell him: 'Go write your fucking jokes. Get out of here and go write your fucking jokes. You don't get paid to think. I'll think.' " This berating would often go on in full view of people working on the stage, this associate said, and Jay's reaction was just as remarkable. "This is where I first noticed no change in facial color. He didn't flush with anger. He wasn't embarrassed. There was nothing. He was so used to it."

The relationship seemed so bizarre that this same observer concluded, "I don't think Jay saw the dynamics of the relationship at all. I don't know that he could take it from point A to point B and say, 'If she's doing this to me, she's doing it to others.' Denial is a very interesting phenomenon. If he grew up as a kid keying into denial, what does he know? He cannot know whatever he chooses not to know."

NBC's position was not much different from Jay's. The network's executives were apparently choosing not to know things they could have known. But at that time the entire network was reeling: Prime time had hit bottom. Problems sprang up everywhere. The Olympics were looming, and NBC's grandiose plan to pay for them, a package of supplemental pay-per-view coverage called the Triplecast, was a fiasco. Helen might be running the wackiest ship in late night, but NBC had other, more pressing problems to deal with. "An enormous amount of avoidance techniques were being employed," a senior NBC executive in Burbank said.

Still, as much as NBC tried to avoid it, the inevitable was gathering speed and hurtling down the track right at them.

7

PSYCHOLOGY 101

Jeff Sagansky and Rod Perth drove up to the gleaming, white-stone-and-glass, half-arc facade of CAA's headquarters on Wilshire Boulevard, and the first person they saw was David Letterman. He was walking from the garage across the sidewalk toward the front steps, in jeans, T-shirt, and blazer, holding an unlit cigar in his left hand. Sagansky and Perth, two senior CBS programming executives, feeling like a couple of kids who wanted to arrive less conspicuously, circled the block so Dave wouldn't see them drive up. It was Monday morning, July 27, 1992 and the CBS executives were scheduled to meet and pitch with Letterman and CAA.

Howard Stringer was already upstairs in the CAA conference room. He had interrupted his summer vacation to fly out the night before, at the specific request of Robert Morton, who had called over the weekend to tell him he'd see him in L.A. Stringer had said he wasn't going, but was instead sending his West Coast executives to make the pitch. Morton had jumped all over Stringer, assuring him that these pitch meetings were more than just an opportunity to show the network's colors. They were going to be extremely important, and he really thought Stringer, the man leading the CBS pursuit of David Letterman, ought to be there. As Stringer had understood it from CAA, this was just an early meeting. He didn't know who else was going to be there, from what other television entity. But Stringer took his cue from Morton. If Letterman thought it was crucial, then surely Stringer would be there. The CBS president hurriedly grabbed the one suit and shirt combination he had out in East Hampton and got to the airport. When he arrived in L.A., Stringer found he had brought no cuff links for his shirt. So here he stood, grinning and greeting in Michael Ovitz's conference room, wearing his traveling suit and shirt, with two tightly wound paper clips as cuff links.

Sagansky and Perth joined Stringer in the conference room and then the Letterman contingent entered: Dave, Peter Lassally, Robert Morton and from CAA, Lee Gabler, and Jay Maloney. Both the CBS executives and the Letterman crew were struck by the California ascetic style of the meeting: the Zen-like conference room, almost nothing to eat—no sweet rolls, no doughnuts, just a plate of watermelon. When Perth got up to take some melon, Letterman said, "Hey Rod, sit down. That's for Lucie Salhany." Dave expected to see Salhany, then head of Paramount Television, at another session later that day.

The tone of the meeting was loose and informal, and very quickly Howard Stringer's sense of humor had taken over. He had just flown overnight, with no prepared presentation, and here he was standing in front of this panel of people wearing his paper clips. The Welsh-born Stringer felt as if he were being interviewed for the university entrance exams at Oxford. But he swung into the pitch, unleashing his Welsh charm and eloquence. Most things that Stringer said simply *sounded* better than anybody else in television because of his classy accent and occasionally quaint Britishisms.

As Stringer had learned in a prepitch conversation with Gabler, more than a half-dozen pitches had been prepared for a two-day session. Nobody was there to negotiate; that was off-limits under Dave's NBC contract. They were all there to sell themselves and their companies. For Stringer that meant presenting a sense of why Letterman would fit in so beautifully at CBS, a network with such a rich history and tradition. He skirted over the fact that CBS had no history or tradition at all in late night. But he talked of the network's growing power in prime time and the strength of the CBS affiliate lineup. What he really wanted to show was the impressive style of the overall CBS organization, what strong executives it had, and its coherent programming strategy. He also decided the meeting was loose enough for him to take a few shots at the prospective competition. So he said Letterman could never be comfortable linked up with an unreliable situation like syndication: "Those companies are a place, not a home," Stringer said. ABC still had "Nightline," Stringer pointed out, and nothing had succeeded after "Nightline" because it was such a tough act to follow. And as for Fox, "You're much too decent a person to go with Fox," Stringer said.

He got laughs, but Letterman also had questions to ask—smart questions. Like how CBS would go about adding stations beyond the relative few that carried the network's lineup of late-night crime shows. Letterman wanted to know what it would mean to his audience to be at CBS instead of NBC. The CBS executives realized they were dealing with more than a star; they were dealing with an experienced, knowledgeable broadcaster.

The CBS meeting went on for about forty-five minutes. Stringer left feeling that it had been fun and worthwhile, if only because CBS got to give a broad picture of its strengths, and none of his people had said anything that would ruin the network's chances with Letterman. He also felt a vast sense of relief that Morton had picked up a phone and called him, because he heard the names of who was going to be in subsequent pitch meetings and it sounded like an all-star lineup of every heavy hitter in the business.

CBS was followed by the team from Fox, and it was headed by the biggest name of all, Rupert Murdoch, the international media mogul who owned Fox Inc. Murdoch was so giant a figure that Ovitz, who intentionally took none of the pitch meetings himself—wanting the pitchers to direct themselves to Letterman, not him—did duck into the conference room briefly to say hello to Rupert. Murdoch brought his full Fox Broadcasting team with him, including the president, Jamie Kellner, and the head of programming, Peter Chernin. One surprise addition to the Fox team was something of a personal touch: Stu Smiley, once Robert Morton's roommate in college and for a time one of Dave's managers, had become an executive at Fox. Fox emphasized the youth of its audience, its maverick style that meshed so well with Letterman's, and an advantage none of the other players could match: Fox could move Dave up even earlier than Jay; he could play as early as 11:00 P.M. on the Fox network.

When Columbia Television came in, its number two executive, Alan Levine, apologized profusely that the studio chairman, Peter Guber, couldn't make the meeting. But Brandon Tartikoff did; he came leading the Paramount presentation, pitching what he said would be the ideal combination: Arsenio and Dave. The Letterman guys just stared at Brandon; Lassally couldn't believe he expected them to take that seriously. "What do you mean they're a perfect match?" he asked Tartikoff. "They're two opposites." Lassally saw Arsenio as mostly flash and Dave as all substance. He also thought Arsenio's show was narrowly targeted, aimed at a hip, urban audience, and not grounded in comedy inventiveness, which was what Dave was all about. Tartikoff stressed what great entertainers both men were, but he was never going to win the Letterman guys over by putting Dave in the same strategy with Arsenio.

For the most part the syndicators were not warmly received. Letterman, who went into the pitch meetings with a strong affinity for network television, came out feeling even less inclined toward syndication. He saw the syndicators as blood-and-guts salesmen, not broadcasters. For the most part the entire Letterman contingent drew back almost instinctively from the approaches of the syndicators.

As good as Stringer had been, he didn't make the best impression in the pitch meetings. Everyone on the Letterman side was most impressed by Bob Iger of ABC. The president of the network's entertainment division and soon to become president of the network, Iger came completely alone, and the contrast to the other entourages of two and three and four was dramatic and effective. Iger just presented himself as a nice guy and his network as the ideal place for David Letterman. He made no promises about "Nightline," though weeks earlier the CAA people had dangled to Letterman the possibility that Ted Koppel might be ready to leave the network and how that might throw the 11:30 time period open. Iger said nothing about that. He said he wasn't sure what the network would do with late-night yet, but he wanted to sell ABC as the right place to be: It had the strongest stations and it had the young audience that fit Letterman's profile. Iger was low-key and soft-sell, and the furthest thing from stereotypical Hollywood. Perfect for David Letterman.

On their break from the pitch session, Letterman, Morton, and Lassally went over to Dunhill's, an L.A. cigar emporium, and sat in a humidor while Dave examined a vintage cigar that the owner said had once belonged to actor Yul Brynner. Peter Lassally, as always, contributed a sobering moment: He pointed out that Brynner had died of lung cancer. But nobody was in a sober mood. They all laughed at the absurdity of what they were witnessing: The captains of the television industry, all pitching their hearts out for David Letterman. The syndicators had mostly eliminated themselves. They laughed out loud at the silliness of the process.

But these were the top guys in all of television and they were certainly displaying an intense interest in David Letterman. Characteristically, Dave didn't see it that way. Every time either of the other men would point out how the biggest executives in the business were turning out just to talk to him, Dave would scoff. It was very entertaining, he agreed, but it had nothing to do with him. "This is all Ovitz," he said, "Ovitz creating a marketplace. It has nothing to do with us really. They're coming out for Ovitz."

After two days of courting, Ovitz had a good idea who the serious players were. So the pitch meetings had accomplished that much. But they had not restored Dave's confidence. Ovitz decided that David Letterman might be the most insecure star he'd ever dealt with.

The pitches continued with several other players in New York, all for syndicated deals. The most significant: the Walt Disney Company. Again the biggest of the big turned out; Michael Eisner, chairman of Disney, made the pitch himself. The Letterman team assembled at the Disney headquarters in New York, around the biggest conference table any of them had ever seen. The table was a relic from the days when the office space had been occupied by the Pepsi Company, and Joan Crawford, then running Pepsi, had the table built to the specifications of the existing room. Thus, it could never be removed without cutting it apart.

The Disney pitch, led by Eisner, was polished and classy; but Morton was even more impressed by a beautiful carved-glass ashtray placed on the conference table near Letterman. He could see Dave eyeing it admiringly throughout the meeting, apparently paying closer attention to the ashtray than he was to the guys from Disney. Here was Michael Eisner suggesting how they could all make millions together, and Morton started finding himself mesmerized by an ashtray. Promises were being made, dollar figures were floating up near the ceiling, and Morton was only barely aware of any of it. He was fixated on the ashtray.

When the meeting broke up and they all left the room, Morton made up an excuse about leaving something inside. He slipped back into the conference room, checked to make sure no one was looking, and dropped the ashtray into his briefcase. He lugged it outside, his bag now a good fifteen pounds heavier, and gave it to Dave later. It added a little more silliness to the adventure. "Here they were talking about paying us millions, and I'm stealing an ashtray," Morton said.

Before the summer was over, Ovitz would also lure two other heavy-walleted syndicators to the Letterman stakes. Chris-Craft television, owned by Herbert Siegel and hiring Fred Silverman, Dave's old NBC boss, as a consultant, jumped in with a proposal. Viacom, which owned cable networks like MTV and the rights to syndicated programs like "The Cosby Show," asked to be allowed to pitch even though Ovitz's original deadline had passed. He agreed. David Letterman was not yet out from under his burdensome NBC contract, but Michael Ovitz had filled the tent with potential customers. He knew if ever he could hold an outright auction, the numbers could get awfully interesting.

If Jay Leno had a best friend in the comedy business, it was probably Jerry Seinfeld. Seinfeld had been an early Jay crony, hanging out at his house around the video game machine after long nights in the clubs. Their styles were similar; Jerry was also an "observational" comic, emphasizing the idiocies of contemporary life. Tartikoff had singled out Seinfeld as a future possibility in late night, and had given him a development deal to hold him for the network. Seinfeld took that deal and developed a quirky, completely untraditional situation comedy called "Seinfeld," which was about Jerry, his fictional friends, and their self-absorbed lives in Manhattan. The series started slowly, with only a cult following for its decidedly offbeat approach, but by the time Jay got the "Tonight" show, "Seinfeld" was starting to take off. NBC could see the glimmerings of a hit.

In the summer of 1992, Jerry approached Jay with an idea. One of the running plots on his show concerned the fictional Jerry being approached by NBC to develop a comedy series. Jerry proposed a story in which he would come on the "Tonight" show and impress the NBC bosses. All it would entail was the use of the "Tonight" set for a day or two and a brief appearance from Jay. Jay thought it sounded great—and he said he'd run it by Helen.

Jay didn't get the reaction he expected. Helen said no, absolutely not. Jerry Seinfeld was the hottest star NBC had; he was also Jay's close friend. But Helen still said no. She told Jay that for the first year, they were just going to be on the "Tonight" show, nothing else. Doing something like this would look as if Jay were running all over town to get on other shows, and it would give him an air of desperation, Helen explained.

To others who wondered why Helen would turn down Seinfeld, she gave different answers. When an associate from New York called, Helen explained what the comic had proposed. It sounded great to this associate, who said so. But Helen said Carson would never do anything like that. "I said to her, 'What's the point, Helen? Carson was Carson. This is Jay Leno.' But it didn't make any difference. She hated Seinfeld. I never really knew why. But she would say he's not really a friend of Jay's."

That season NBC had scheduled "Seinfeld" against one of the hottest new comedies on television, ABC's "Home Improvement," which starred another comic, Tim Allen. Helen was convinced that Jay appealed to the Tim Allen audience, not the Jerry Seinfeld audience. Helen thought Seinfeld would pull Jay in the wrong direction, and, as she put it, she wasn't going to turn the "Tonight" show into Jerry Seinfeld's personal playground.

Another member of the "Tonight" staff heard about the dispute and asked Helen what the problem was with Jerry's request. "She said; 'I don't want to be associated with a show that's not hip. Jay is hip. And I don't want him to be on a not-hip show.' " Most of the press had by that time identified "Seinfeld" as probably the hippest show on television in ten years; and advertisers agreed, spending a premium to reach young adult viewers of "Seinfeld" who rarely watched any other shows.

On the "Tonight" staff, the "Seinfeld" argument presented a fascinating opportunity. They wanted to see if Jay would stand up for his friend. "But he never did that," the staff member said. "He never stood up to Helen, ever."

Jay thought Jerry would understand. So he told him that Helen didn't like the idea. It didn't make sense to

Jerry, who decided to call Helen himself. It was a revealing phone call for Jerry Seinfeld. When he got off the line from Helen, he immediately called Warren Littlefield.

"He was in a state of shock," Littlefield said. Helen had ripped into Seinfeld with such venom, such foul language, that Seinfeld could hardly speak. When he did, he told Littlefield that he had never been treated like that before in his life—and this would be the last time. He told Littlefield he was never going on the "Tonight" show again.

Littlefield saw Seinfeld twice more in the next few days, and each time, the phone call from Helen was the first thing he talked about. Littlefield decided to call Kushnick. "I have to tell you something," he said to her. "Jerry Seinfeld may not have a thirty share yet. But we think this guy is a huge, major asset. We care about him tremendously and we can't have this happen. We cannot have this happen."

That was enough to get Seinfeld back on the "Tonight" show's list of guests. Jerry patched up the situation with Jay. But Helen had ruled; Seinfeld didn't get to use the "Tonight" show in his series.

For Littlefield this episode was far worse than what he felt were Helen's loony efforts to get an ad in *USA Today*. This fight was over something completely illogical. And though Warren believed she could argue that she was within her rights as producer to say no, it was how she said no that sent her behavior over the line. She berated an NBC star.

Littlefield found himself sitting at his desk, asking himself how much of this was going on. Here was Jerry

Seinfeld, with whom he had a strong relationship, describing this offensive episode. What about all the people who came in and out of the "Tonight" show every day with whom he didn't have a phone relationship? What if Sylvester Stallone had an experience like that and said he'd never come back to that place again in his life? As Littlefield sat back and considered the entire incident with Seinfeld, he started to ask himself how far this all went—and the uncertainty of the answer made him shudder.

The word was around everywhere. Helen Kushnick was out of control. Acts were being canceled out of pique or because of the vendetta against Arsenio. NBC was hearing all the stories. And yet, even after the Seinfeld incident, nobody was doing anything about them.

In July, when the Democrats were holding their national convention in New York, Helen had an ambitious idea to have Jay milk some comedy out of the events of the convention every night. That meant the show would have to be done live for the East Coast at 11:30 P.M., which was 8:30 in Burbank, three hours later than the usual start time for the "Tonight" show taping. Helen had assigned Paula Poundstone to work the convention floor as a comedy reporter. She also arranged with NBC News to have anchorman Tom Brokaw come on for some brief banter with Jay. As Helen saw it, it was a way to solidify Jay's reputation as the leading political satirist on television.

But political conventions are unpredictable events that rarely run precisely on schedule. The Democrats did a good job the first night and NBC News got off the air near 11 P.M. That got the live version of the "To-night" show on the air close to its usual time. But on night two, the convention started to bog down. By the time the night's final speaker, Barbara Jordan, got to the podium, NBC knew the night would run at least a little late.

In Burbank, Helen Kushnick stood in the wings off-stage, watching Barbara Jordan speak, her face clenching tighter as the minutes drifted by. Standing around her, a few members of the staff warily observed her running commentary as Jordan spoke. Every time Jordan stopped for a breath, Helen would leap in and point out that she was pausing. Helen was screaming at the set: "Another pause, fade out right here!" she would shout.

A few minutes before eleven, Michael Gartner, the president of NBC News, got a call in the control room in New York. It was Helen Kushnick. She was stoked up and ready to fight.

"You promised you'd be off the air by eleven," Kushnick shouted at Gartner, the bile barely contained. "She's got to go off the air, right now. I've got a whole audience here waiting to see a show."

Gartner's response: "Well, I've got a black woman in a wheelchair making a speech."

The fight escalated. Kushnick spat out obscenities at Gartner. Then she said: "Well, I'm taking you off the air."

Gartner, who had his own reputation for flintiness, didn't flinch. "There's only one person who can take me off the air. That's Bob Wright. Here's his number; call him."

Kushnick bellowed a few more foul sentences at

Gartner and hung up. She didn't call Bob Wright. The speech stayed on. The "Tonight" show went on the air late in the East.

After the blowup in July, NBC tried to make the system work better during the Republican Convention in August. Mainly that consisted of Warren Littlefield and Rick Ludwin, the head of late-night programs, staying around late to make sure the transfer from NBC News was accomplished quickly. Gartner had a friendly relationship with Littlefield, whom he considered one of the good guys at NBC. But other NBC executives were pressuring Gartner to get the convention coverage off the air at the first opportunity. NBC had made a deal with PBS to share coverage, the latest in the streamlining moves made by the networks in the face of what they perceived as declining interest in the conventions as a television event. So NBC's commitment to the convention coverage seemed a lot looser than ever to many of the nonnews executives.

The first night of the Republican Convention, the "Tonight" show was again in place to go live in the East at 11:30. The Republicans generally ran their conventions on a tight schedule. But this night had an *x* factor: the closing speaker was Ronald Reagan, the former president of the United States. He was greeted by a tumultuous demonstration, and his speech was often interrupted for adulatory applause. It was soon obvious that the show was going to run late again.

Helen knew that Warren was in his office monitoring the situation. She called, screaming about getting Reagan off the air. Littlefield pointed out that they couldn't realistically cut off an ex-president in midspeech. Helen said the news division better sign off its coverage as soon as Reagan was finished or she was sending her audience home and NBC wouldn't have a show. Warren tried to calm her down, telling her the network was ready to act quickly as soon as the speech ended.

Reagan kept talking. The clock passed 11:00 P.M. In a fever, Kushnick dialed up the NBC News control room in Houston and demanded to speak to Gartner again. This time she had a different threat.

As soon as Gartner picked up the phone, he heard the shrill voice saying, "If you don't get this guy off the air, I'm not going to use Brokaw on the show tonight."

That was hardly a prospect to make Gartner quake. "I don't give a shit if Brokaw does your show or not," he told Kushnick. "But I'll tell you something. If you don't use him tonight, you're not using him another night. And let's get one other thing straight. I'm the president of NBC News, and you don't have anything to do with what I do."

Kushnick was emotional and threatening and just as profane as she had been the month before. But NBC News stayed with Ronald Reagan. In fact, for Warren Littlefield's taste, the news division stayed just a bit too long with its wrap-up after the speech concluded. But finally as the news coverage ended, Warren began to relax, thinking the crisis had passed. That was when Rick Ludwin walked into his office, a look on his face as though he'd been smacked across the bridge of his nose with a two-by-four.

"The audience has gone home," Ludwin said.

The dumbfounded Littlefield could only respond, "What do you mean?"

"Well, you know the seats?" Ludwin said. "They're empty. Got the picture?"

Littlefield still sat there looking at Ludwin across his desk with a vacant expression of shock on his face, saying, "I don't understand."

"The plane has left," Ludwin said. "You know, there's nobody there."

Helen Kushnick had just killed a scheduled NBC show, a show for which advertising had already been sold, a show the network had been promoting all night long. With the local newscasts already running in the East, the network had to scramble to rush a repeat on the air. Worse than all of that was the embarrassment of having the network held hostage to the wrath of one producer.

NBC could have fired Helen Kushnick after that night, citing a failure-to-perform clause in her contract. But again no one acted. On the East Coast, the amazement that a "Tonight" show had been killed on the whim of a producer was exceeded only by the amazement that nothing in particular seemed to be happening as a result of it. Bob Wright's level of tolerance was completely used up. He told Littlefield and Agoglia that this person was out of control. Warren told Wright that that was clear to everyone now. But he explained that Jay would be injured, perhaps beyond repair, if they tried to make a move on Helen right away. Littlefield said for the time being that it would be better to try to limp along.

One senior East Coast executive felt that Littlefield and Agoglia should know how Wright and others in the East really felt about the deteriorating "Tonight" show situation. So the executive called and told them how it was playing there: "You guys look pussy-whipped," the executive said. "You look like weenies in the show business community. This woman is behaving in a totally unacceptable way. When is the come-to-Jesus meeting? When is somebody going to grab her by the throat? You're not handling this, and you're making Wright have to think about it. He's getting drawn into this. You're going to get caught in a wringer with him."

And still the West Coast executives didn't act. One of Helen's staff members said that the NBC executives were simply intimidated by her. "She beat the shit out of them. She controlled them. They were afraid of her. She's a screamer and she's abusive; she's a fuck-you person. She was such a different woman than they were used to dealing with, and she was just tougher than those guys."

For Littlefield, the barrier to moving immediately on Helen was still Jay. What would Jay do if they tried to remove her? Warren couldn't be sure. He had not established strong personal ties to Jay, largely because Helen always got in the way. But he felt he needed to get through to Jay first, to convince him of how poorly she was serving him, before they could go after Helen. So he started calling Jay directly, gently prodding him about the growing problem with Helen. No matter how intolerable the Helen situation had become for him, and despite the impending loss of David Letterman, Warren Littlefield still wanted to preserve Jay Leno on the "Tonight" show. He gave no serious thought to solving both late-night problems by removing Jay and inserting Dave—for one simple reason. Warren had not stopped believing that Jay was the right choice for the job.

Late in August, with Helen still producing and the show still limping along, Bob Wright went to Los Angeles to attend the annual Emmy Awards telecast. After the ceremony, Wright attended a party at the star-infested Spago restaurant. He ran into Robert Morton there. Wright knew Morton had long experience in late-night television, so he asked him a question that had been on his mind for weeks. "What do you think of Jay?"

Morton got right to the point. "As long as you have that woman running the show, she's not going to handle talent very well and you're not going to have a good show," Morton said.

Wright nodded in resigned assent and said, "I know, and I'm going to have do this myself."

Ken Kragen never expected to wander across the "Tonight" show firing range. A longtime manager of country music stars, headed by Kenny Rogers, Kragen was low-key, well respected, and noncontroversial. He also just happened to be a guy who had no reason to allow himself to be pushed around.

In April, a month before Jay Leno took over the "Tonight" show, Kragen got a call from Bill Royce, one of the producers, who wanted to book a Kragen client, singer Trisha Yearwood, to an early date with Jay. Kragen consulted Yearwood's schedule and said she unfortunately wouldn't be coming to L.A. until October. Royce said he wanted to book her anyway, so they set a date of October 16. Kragen put it down in Yearwood's datebook.

Kragen had booked his artists on the "Tonight" show before, though not all that frequently. Kenny Rogers had done a date with Arsenio Hall a couple of years earlier, and he hadn't been booked back on the "Tonight" show since. Another of Kragen's singers, Travis Tritt, had once done an appearance when Jay was guest hosting, after Kragen felt he needed a TV appearance for Tritt to plug his new album. Kragen had specifically called Carson's producer, Fred de Cordova, and asked for a date, and Freddy had kindly booked him with Jay. The show had gone especially well, Kragen thought.

But since that appearance, Tritt had gravitated to Arsenio, simply believing his rock-oriented style of country music was more appropriate for Hall's show. Kragen booked Tritt for another date with Arsenio in September 1992. That date had been locked in the previous May. Again Tritt had an album coming out, so Kragen and the record company were pushing a major promotion campaign, which included large billboards all over L.A.

Soon after the billboards went up, Kragen started getting calls from the "Tonight" show. Both Royce and another "Tonight" producer, Debbie Vickers, called and asked if Kragen could deliver Travis Tritt in September. Kragen politely explained that he'd be happy to bring Travis on, but only after he had done his previously scheduled spot with Arsenio. They said that wasn't going to work for them. Even Fred de Cordova, now a "consultant" for Helen, called again, trying to get Kragen to break Tritt's appearance on "The Arsenio Hall Show."

Debbie Vickers also tried one more time, but Kragen hadn't changed his mind. Vickers then told him that

Kushnick was probably not going to take this well. She was right. Kragen's next phone call was from Helen herself, who lost no time starting in after him. "Arsenio's show is over with, he's in the toilet," Kragen heard Helen say. "His advertisers are deserting him; by the end of the year there won't even be an 'Arsenio Hall Show.' " An ever more belligerent Kushnick told Kragen he had to break the Tritt date on "Arsenio" if he ever wanted to book Travis Tritt on the "Tonight" show again.

Kragen, a calm person to begin with, let himself gear down and get even more tranquil. With no rancor at all in his voice, he simply told Kushnick that threats never worked with him. That seemed to flip a different switch in Helen. She lowered her own voice, and her tone became instantly pleasant. Suddenly she was explaining patiently how she and Jay had accommodated him a year earlier when he needed a TV date for Tritt. This would only be returning a favor, she said. Kragen found this tack reasonable, so reasonable that he said he would see what he could do about the "Arsenio" booking.

Naively, Kragen, who had not paid much attention to the increasingly bitter competition between the two late-night shows, went right ahead and called Sharon Olson, the booker at "Arsenio," relating in a straightforward way the story of Kushnick's request that he cancel the booking because he owed them a favor. The reaction from Olson was instantaneous: a litany of the horror stories of "Arsenio" guests dropping out of the show after being threatened with retaliation from the "Tonight" show, and how crazy this feud had become. Kragen listened and understood why the "Arsenio" show would be adamant about keeping a booking they had had first. He told Olson nothing more needed to be said. He would stand by his Tritt booking on "Arsenio."

Kragen called back and laid it out for Helen, trying to be as accommodating as he could under the circumstances, because he didn't want to torch his singers' relationships with the "Tonight" show. Kragen told Helen he couldn't get Tritt out of the "Arsenio" date but that Travis was going to be back in February to promote a movie he was doing with Kenny Rogers and Naomi Judd, and probably Kragen could deliver all three of them together for Jay.

"We don't do theme shows," Helen snapped. And then she unloaded on Kragen, telling him how it was going to be: Not only was Travis Tritt not going to do the "Tonight" show ever again, but she said, "You and I will be in this town for a long time and we'll see each other, and we're never going to talk again. It's your loss and the record company's." And then, with an audible slam, she hung up on him.

Even before he put down the phone, Kragen thought to himself, I have to go over there next month with Trisha Yearwood; boy, is *that* going to be uncomfortable. He didn't have to live long with that thought, however, because only thirty minutes later, the phone rang again. It was Debbie Vickers of the "Tonight" show. Vickers told Kragen she was sorry to have to tell him this, but that Trisha Yearwood's appearance had to be canceled. Vickers didn't sugarcoat the message. Though Helen would later say Yearwood had to be canceled to make room for another singer, George Strait, Vickers told

Kragen it was because Helen was simply furious about the Tritt booking. The clearest sign of that: No other date was offered to Trisha Yearwood.

And so Ken Kragen went public. He told a reporter from the *Los Angeles Times* his story of how his artists were being blackballed from the "Tonight" show. The paper had been hearing all sorts of horror stories about the booking wars in late night and had wanted to do a story about it. The reporter asked Kragen if he would go on the record. Kragen saw no reason not to.

The story, which ran on the front page of the newspaper's "Calendar" section, exploded all across the television industry the next morning. Kragen was the first artists' representative willing to go after Helen Kushnick, and it set off a frenzy of stories about her scorched-earth booking practices. Kragen himself was deluged with calls and letters from people who felt they had been victimized by Kushnick's tactics; they thanked Kragen for having the guts to take her on in the press.

Another group of grateful parties were the executives at NBC. For Littlefield it was "independent verification" from a source whose motives could not reasonably be questioned. (Kushnick would question them anyway.) Littlefield believed the Kragen charges would put to rest any effort by Kushnick to link subsequent actions by NBC to sexism.

The *L.A. Times* story about Kragen appeared on Tuesday, September 15. Littlefield, expecting action was coming soon, spent much of that week trying to shore up his relationship with Leno. Warren did not think it made sense to go after Helen with guns blazing, not with the doubts he still had about how Jay would react. The goal was to have Jay stay and Helen leave. In order to achieve this, Warren felt he had to lift the veil from Jay's eyes that prevented him from seeing how Helen was destroying his show. But Jay resisted; when Warren would suggest to him that Helen was wrecking the show, Jay would invariably return to the refuge of the ratings. "Aren't we getting the numbers?" he would ask Warren. And Littlefield would tell him: "Yes, but it doesn't matter. You're approaching disaster."

Neither Littlefield nor Agoglia believed they understood at all the true nature of the strange, interdependent relationship between Jay and Helen. But they both agreed that Helen and the uproar surrounding her handling of the "Tonight" show were eating up huge chunks of their time, dominating the business of the NBC entertainment division. During that week Warren spoke with Jay alone, and Helen and Jay together, and by Thursday he and Agoglia finally made the decision. They called Bob Wright and told him they were ready to fire Helen Kushnick. They still didn't know whether Jay would break with Helen, or back her and quit in sympathy; but they felt there was a good chance that Jay was clued in enough now to what had been going on that he wouldn't do something that self-destructive.

Helen never flinched from taking that approach. She took her case public on Friday morning, September 18, in a phone interview with Howard Stern on his national radio talk show. Helen contradicted Kragen's story and blamed the male conspiracy in Hollywood for undermining her efforts to run the "Tonight" show. The interview only outraged NBC further. Later in the day,

Helen had her lawyer, Ron Berg, send out a letter to Wright, with copies to every member of the General Electric board of directors, threatening to sue the network on the basis of sexual discrimination. NBC decided it couldn't wait any longer. Helen had to go.

But Jay was still holding out. He asked the NBC executives to draw up a proposal with acceptable terms for NBC on what Helen could and couldn't do. NBC came up with a list of conditions of employment. These included forbidding Helen to book guests and cancel them and to talk to the media. Littlefield was convinced this was a worthless stopgap because Helen could never have lived under any restrictions.

During a meeting held that afternoon, Agoglia and Littlefield witnessed as Helen changed from a cool, controlled, rational person to someone screaming and out of control in a matter of seconds. Agoglia started getting nervous as he saw Kushnick fold herself into a lotus position and start rocking. When she left, Littlefield told Leno that he had to make the break; he had to see that Helen needed help, that she couldn't stand up to this kind of pressure anymore.

By Saturday Warren was telling Jay over the phone that NBC's list of restrictions on Helen's activities wasn't even an issue now. "We're trying to put Band-Aids on a mortal wound," he said. "You're in denial, Jay. You've got to see this. The woman needs help. She desperately needs help, and whether she acknowledges that and wants to do anything about it, whether you want to do anything about it, that's not my job. That's just my opinion. But I'll tell you one thing: We're not continuing the show with this woman."

Littlefield and Agoglia went to Leno's house on Sunday night for a final confrontation. Littlefield, who had majored in psychology in college, dredged up some of that undergraduate expertise and told Jay that what he and John were staging was an "intervention." They had to break Jay of his "addiction" to Helen Kushnick, Warren said, starting to equate Jay's relationship with Helen to a chemical dependency. This was psychological dependency, as Littlefield saw it. Then he revved up the rhetoric.

"She is either going to take you down or you are going to separate from her," Warren said. "But she is not going to take me down. She is fired. She had to be fired. She's gone. She is not allowed back on the premises. She will have nothing to do with the show."

But Jay wasn't buying into this "intervention" talk easily. Even after all that had gone on, Jay still resisted. He had been with Helen for seventeen years; he knew that she had gotten him the show that every comic in America dreamed of getting, and besides, he was still carrying around that promise he had made to Jerry Kushnick on his deathbed.

Warren thought Jay was acting weirdly, passively commenting on much that was being said, dodging the ultimate question: Will you show up tomorrow after we fire Helen Kushnick? Jay just couldn't seem to say yes to the question.

Littlefield felt he had to press the ultimate button, the nuclear button as far as Leno was concerned. He said to Jay: "If you can't separate, then I think it's a mistake. I regret it, but we at NBC do have choices. And the choice we have is to tell David Letterman that it's time to take over the 'Tonight' show. And I have to tell you, Jay, I suspect that he and Peter Lassally would be in Burbank on twenty-four hours' notice."

That got Jay's attention. "Would you do that?" Jay asked.

Warren said, "We will absolutely do that. We will not hesitate to do it. That's how strongly we feel."

In reality, Littlefield didn't feel strongly at all about that alternative. He still wanted Leno, not Letterman, though that feeling was not shared by the full staff of people in Burbank who had endured the bedlam of the previous three months of a "Tonight" show under Helen and Jay. As one NBC Productions employee said to an NBC executive that weekend: "The really right move would be to fire Jay at the same time. They really should have known by now that it isn't working with Jay."

But that move was never in Warren Littlefield's plans. He had so much invested in Jay, he was willing to fight for him to the limit. Warren pressed Jay for a commitment that he would work Monday if Helen were let go—and Tuesday and Wednesday and the days after that. All Littlefield wanted to hear was some kind of commitment, some hint of assent from Jay.

Instead, Jay began asking over and over, "So you're going to fire me? You're going to fire me, right?" Every time Warren would say, "Well, Jay, we want *you* to stay, but not with Helen," Jay would come right back with, "So that means you're going to fire me? I'll be fired, right?" And then Jay would sort of dip his head and use body English as though trying to signal Littlefield and Agoglia that he was trying to convey something in code.

The NBC executives were totally bewildered. All they could think of was that Jay's winking and nodding about being fired must be for the benefit of his lawyer, Ron Berg, who was also Helen's lawyer. Jay seemed to be trying to set up some sort of odd legal justification for separating himself from Helen, as though he feared she would sue him, too. And then his response would be: I would have been fired otherwise. But Jay wasn't saying anything like that directly; he was just laying out these bizarre feints and clues. With much prodding, Littlefield eventually elicited a comment from Leno that indicated he was going to go off and work on his monologue because he had a show to do the next night. Littlefield pushed the point one more time: "And you will *not* do a show with Helen Kushnick." When Jay repeated, "Well, I have a show to do," that sold Littlefield. He concluded that Jay was ready to continue with the show—if only he didn't backslide when Helen called him after Littlefield and Agoglia went out the door.

Helen did call, of course. She and Jay were on the phone all weekend, many times with other members of the show's staff or outside executives and associates who knew both of them. All of these people were being drawn in, asked to describe their own opinions on whether Helen should go or stay. On some of these calls Jay asked others on the phone point-blank if they thought Helen was crazy. The questions put these people on the defensive, because they were never sure if Jay was still working with Helen and the answer was going to get right back to her. At least once that weekend Helen called a staff member herself and asked what the problem was with how she had been running the show.

When the staff member tried to dodge the question, Helen got Jay on the line and pulled him into the discussion, saying, See, this person has no problem with me.

"I tried to clarify what I said," the staff member said, "and then they started to go at each other. Then Sara is on the phone crying, saying Jay is hurting Mommy, and Helen at this point is flying back and forth between anger and a sort of childlike vulnerability at being rejected, looking for approval. I had to get off the phone. Later I heard that at some point Mavis stepped in and said, No more of this."

Dan Klores, a New York–based public relations executive, was also dragged into the drama that weekend. Klores, who had been working for Helen and Jay, felt himself tugged between these two clients—and realized he had to choose up sides. Helen had hired him to do publicity for Jay; she paid him and insisted that he deal with her directly, and not with Jay. But at this point Klores didn't see how Helen was going to survive this showdown. He decided to try to give Jay some advice; he thought Jay needed it desperately. Klores was another who tried to bring Jay to the light, get him to recognize what this woman was doing to him. But that weekend, Jay asked Klores to repeat for Ron Berg, his lawyer, the things he had been saying about the show being damaged by all that was going on. Klores complied, even though he knew his comments would be getting straight back to Helen.

During one of their own phone conversations that weekend, Jay even suggested that he and Helen go see a therapist together. Helen laughed at the idea, saying it was the NBC guys who needed help, not her—all you had to do was look at the programs they were putting in prime time to see that. But Jay suggesting therapy was in itself a shocker to associates who heard about it later. Therapy was an idea completely alien to a guy so disdainful of stress, emotional excess, and all forms of psychological mumbo jumbo. Jay would often lump therapy in with things like EST. But he was terribly torn between feelings of gratefulness for what Helen had done for his career and guilt for possibly adding to the misery that had descended on her life.

Still, Jay's mood turned darker during one of these conversations when Helen blurted out that she had indeed planted the story in the *New York Post* the year before, the story about NBC wanting to dump Carson that had stirred up so much bitterness. About this, Jay was finally appalled. Helen tried to tell him how it was done for his own good, how she had always acted in his best interests, but Jay rejected that excuse. He had called Johnny and sworn that his side had nothing to do with the *Post* story. Now he knew it was all Helen's doing, and he was ashamed and humiliated.

But the drama wasn't over. On Monday morning, when Helen arrived at her "Tonight" show office with Berg, she was handed an official letter of dismissal from John Agoglia. She scoffed, told him Jay wouldn't stand for it, and went about the business of producing that night's show. Somehow, through all the Sturm und Drang, Jay had managed to keep up his own routine. He and Jimmy Brogan had put together Monday's monologue as usual in the middle of the night at Jay's house.

Soon after he arrived that morning, Jay trooped up to the executive offices with Helen's letter of dismissal in hand and told Agoglia he couldn't agree with the firing. Then he walked out. NBC decided to let events play out. Agoglia and Littlefield considered sending armed guards to the "Tonight" offices to drag Kushnick out of the building, but then they thought better of that. That scene was too ugly to contemplate. Littlefield simply said to Agoglia: "She leaves the building of her own volition at some point at the end of the day, and then she's fired from the lot."

Ron Berg showed up to talk to Littlefield. He was still trying to negotiate something for Kushnick, but Littlefield simply cut him off, saying, "Time out. This is nonnegotiable. She's off the lot. She never returns. She walks out the door whenever she walks out the door, never to return."

A few scenes were left to play. Dan Klores got his termination letter, faxed into New York from Helen through Ron Berg. Boom, just like that. Fired. Klores decided to draw up a memo for Jay anyway, with ten ideas for changing the show after Helen left.

At midday, Bob Mazza, a replacement press agent Helen hired on the spot that Monday, announced that Jay would be releasing a statement. In his office, Littlefield was ready to explode with exasperation when he heard the news of a statement coming from Leno; but before he could, Jay called. He told Warren the statement would be coming out but that it had no bearing on the agreement they had reached. Everything he had said the night before was still in effect, Jay promised. "I'm moving forward with you. I'm doing the show.

Help me get through this. She's not the executive producer anymore. I'm doing the show."

Warren recoiled at the idea that Helen had enough hold over Jay still that she could manipulate a statement of support out of him, but he was relieved to hear Jay hadn't lost his senses completely and put his job on the line for her.

The brief statement seemed to contradict everything Jay was saying to the NBC executives: "I regret the actions of NBC today. I feel NBC's actions are unwarranted in light of the success of the show to date, and I continue to support Ms. Kushnick." The statement went out even as NBC executives were telling reporters to pay it little heed because Leno was still on board and would continue with the show.

Jay Leno, who had to go on a stage that evening and make 300 people laugh, sat amid chaos in his office all day. He had one arm out in each direction and was being pulled both ways at once. He was not going to give up his job, but he was still trying to avoid confrontation with Helen as she went down in flames. If he had hoped to skate by her one last day, it wasn't going to work.

She confronted him in her office. She was raging, pushing his buttons, screaming so loud that she could be heard by the rest of the staff outside. Finally they heard an enormous crashing sound. All day they had heard the sounds of Helen throwing things around the office, so they assumed she was now completely trashing the place. But Jay later said he had slammed down a glass mirror and shattered it on her desk in an effort to get Helen under control. In this last attempt to get him to stand by her, Helen came at Jay with her every emotion, eventually telling him he had to quit the "Tonight" show for Sara's sake. "Well, why is it for Sara's sake?" he asked her, though no rational answer to the question was even remotely possible.

Some of the other staff members were physically afraid of what Helen might do that day. By this point Helen had targeted one of the producers, Debbie Vickers, as a principal in the plot against her. Vickers was one of the few holdovers from the Carson days, but she had long since earned Jay's complete trust. Helen had screamed Vickers's name all day long Monday, how she never trusted Debbie, how Sara had told her Debbie was a snake. When it came time for Vickers to go out on stage and work the show with Jay, Kushnick approached her. She told her Jay was going to fire her in two days, and as Vickers walked onto the set to put Jay's notes for the night's interviews down on his desk, Kushnick continued after her, saying that Vickers was never going to get away with what she had done to her. In front of the camera crew and 300 of Jay's fans sitting in the audience, Helen Kushnick was screaming at the show's producer on the set. Finally the producer turned on her. The crew heard Vickers yell back at Kushnick: "When are you going to learn to take responsibility for your own actions? You are now being held accountable for your actions." Then Vickers escaped to the control room. A young production assistant was left with the responsibility of leading Jay through the show, though he stayed in constant contact by phone with Vickers in the control room.

Less than five minutes after the blowup between Kushnick and Vickers, the band hit the theme and Jay

Leno walked out onto the stage. He punched out another monologue, with all his usual authority. He interviewed his guests and got through the show with no outward signs of distress. Warren Littlefield watched the show unfold on the monitor in his office, thinking Jay had done a great show that night. Warren was in awe of Jay's ability to perform under such duress.

Helen left the NBC lot that night for the last time. As soon as she was off the premises, NBC had the studio guards post little photos of her at every entrance, with a message that this woman was banned from returning. The "Tonight" staff thought they looked like wanted posters.

When he arrived Tuesday morning, with Helen no longer a looming presence, Jay had changed his demeanor completely. At the noon staff meeting, which he previously had not attended, Jay gave a speech and apologized for all the madness that had gone on. He swore that a new day was starting, that everyone would now pull together. Jay took full responsibility for everything that had gone on, saying he should have known all that was happening, that terrible things had been done—things he didn't know about but should have.

Jay spent the next several weeks apologizing to almost everyone he assumed had been subjected to Helen's wrath. That included Johnny Carson, whom he called to admit that he'd been wrong to deny Helen was responsible for the *New York Post* story, and to apologize abjectly. Carson was generous to him, saying this was an incident to learn something from, that sometimes the people speaking for you are doing you a disservice.

Ken Kragen was generous as well when Jay called

him. Kragen told Jay that if Helen was a friend, he really ought to try to get her some kind of help, but he concluded that Jay didn't really want to hear that. Kragen decided that Helen and Jay's relationship came down to "abuser/abused."

The "Tonight" staff felt a pall lift from the show immediately. Some of them sensed, for a couple of days anyway, that Jay was still talking to Helen on the phone. When he would make some off-the-wall suggestions about the running order of the guests, or some other detail of the production, they guessed that the suggestions were coming from Helen. But before the week was out, Jay told several staff members that he had made a final break with Helen after one last call. In the call, Jay said, Helen had tried everything, from telling him she had a guaranteed $25 million deal for him that he surely couldn't walk away from, to leveling a threat to have her own daughter hold a press conference to tell the world what kind of person he really was if he didn't quit the show. Helen did threaten to sue him, he said, if he did not pay her $25,000 a week. Fearing legal entanglements, and worried about the fact that Helen still controlled all the stock he owned, Leno even made one $25,000 payment the first week after Helen was fired. After that, he said enough.

Later Jay said the revelation that she had planted the *Post* story was truly the last straw for him, because for all the insanity that had gone on, he had never felt he was lied to before. Their final conversation was so heated, Jay said, that he cursed Helen out, told her she had tried to ruin his career, and that he was never going to speak to her again.

Soon after Helen's departure, as Jay went about his campaign to pick up the pieces of the wreckage left in her wake, he tried to describe his motivation by referring to what he called his all-time favorite story: "A Christmas Carol."

"I always remembered the last line about nobody keeping Christmas better than Ebenezer Scrooge," Jay said. After all that had happened in his first three months in the job, Jay went about trying to keep the business of running a talk show better than anybody else: ending all the booking restrictions, rehiring people who'd been fired, putting up money for staff parties, apologizing for all offenses, righting all wrongs.

"I mean, I'd like to think the door is still open and eventually you can get into heaven somehow."

oward Stringer, who had taken the highly visible lead in CBS's courtship of David Letterman, thought he had found a perfect little memento to keep Letterman thinking kindly of him and his network. In a batch of historical photographs he was looking through, he just happened to see a shot from the Civil War in which a group of Union officers were standing outside a dilapidated-looking tent hospital. The caption identified the bearded, serious-looking man at the center as Dr. Jonathan Letterman, Army chief surgeon. To Stringer he looked incorrigibly grouchy. Attaching a note to a copy of the photo, Stringer immediately had it sent over to Letterman's office at NBC. The note said: "This man is so grouchy he must be a relative. If you all decide to come to CBS, I can promise you better accommodations than those in the photograph. You will leave the Civil War at NBC far behind."

The photo was just a small part of Stringer's campaign to win Letterman's heart. His mission was to show CBS to be not only a place where Dave could get the kind of business arrangement he wanted, but also a place that he would find warm, fuzzy, and comfortable, unlike the chilly atmosphere that pervaded his NBC bunker. For Stringer this was the artistic part of the job of talent relations, a part he was unusually skilled in— for a network corporate executive. But then Howard Stringer was an unusual network president, one who had actually been on the firing lines as a producer and director, one who had actually put a television show on the air.

The pursuit of David Letterman was in many ways a personal quest and challenge for Stringer, who had already helped stabilize what had once been the rockiest ship in television. To land Letterman would mean a chance to establish something CBS had never had through all its storied broadcast history: a late-night franchise. Stringer identified that goal early as worth almost any commitment CBS had to make to Letterman. "You do this in television all the time," Stringer said. "You gamble on talent. You put money up front. It's poker. You put your money on the cards you think are going to win for you." The truth was that Howard Stringer didn't really know how Letterman would do at 11:30, or on CBS. What he knew was Letterman was good, and good was worth having at CBS.

Almost no one at CBS knew anything more than that about David Letterman. Stringer himself had only met him twice: once at the Peabody lunch, the other time years earlier at a softball game between Letterman's show and the "CBS Evening News," played in a fittingly grand location: Yankee Stadium. There they had met at third base, where Letterman tagged Stringer out.

In his effort to get as close as he could to Dave,

Stringer continued to work his growing relationship with Robert Morton, who was, conveniently, a summer habitué of the Hamptons, as were Stringer and his wife, Dr. Jennifer Patterson, a dermatologist. Morty was only too happy to partake in a regular Saturday dinner at Howard's that summer. The food was good, and Howard was nothing if not excellent company.

In the fall Stringer was eager to keep up the CBS contact with the Letterman show, so he turned to one of the few people at CBS with a genuine connection to Dave: Connie Chung. Chung, one of CBS News's brightest stars, had been a favorite guest on the Letterman show from her days working at NBC News. They had real chemistry on the air: Dave teased Connie about her husband Maury Povich (whom he usually called "Murray"), her perky image, and her stylish clothes. In one of "Late Night's" most famous taped sketches, Dave had gone on a hilarious "shopping tour" with Connie, helping her select some new outfits for herself, as well as a gift for "Murray."

But the Dave-Connie relationship had cooled a bit since her departure from NBC in 1990. She wasn't close at hand in the NBC offices anymore. When Connie started "Face to Face," her prime-time magazine show at CBS, she wanted Dave to appear for an interview and profile, to help supply an early ratings boost. But Dave said no. Chung all but begged Dave to do it, to the point of being in tears, asking how Dave could say no after she'd been such a good friend to his show, after she'd done anything the show had asked, even the shopping tour bit. She was told it wasn't personal, that they were all still crazy about her, but that she had to understand that Dave simply didn't do TV interviews like the one she had in mind.

Even with that little contretemps, Connie was the best link to Letterman that CBS had, so she agreed to make a tape that would further the CBS effort while maybe giving Dave a few laughs. Stringer called Morton and told him, "Wait until you guys see what I'm sending over."

When the tape arrived, Morton took it to Peter Lassally's office and they brought Letterman in for a viewing. Then they popped it in the VCR.

On the tape, the plucky Chung was doing a hard sell for Letterman: "Hi, Dave," she said after a few scenes of their famous shopping tour. "Just trying to recapture some of those fabulous moments." She went on, "Dave, let me be blunt. Tell your people to back off and relax. Robert Morton doesn't have to spend any more weekends at Howard's place in East Hampton. I'm handling the deal now. David, I will take care of you. You know, David, there is no problem. Even Maury wants you to come to CBS." Then a picture of Povich appeared. Chung went on to say she would handle CBS chairman Laurence Tisch. "Carte blanche, Dave. You name it. Stuff CAA never even dreamed of. Are you ready? Okay, first, that GE Building thing really ticked you off, right? Well, I don't blame you." Then a picture of GE's headquarters appeared with a big *DAVE* written across the top. "That's right: the Dave Building. Next, an unprecedented prime-time bonus clause. Picture this, Dave. The 'CBS Evening News with Connie and Dave.' All right, 'David and Connie.' The all-new 'Circus of Stars' hosted by Dave. 'Murder Dave

Wrote.'" On it went until Chung wound up with her biggest promises. "One: Exclusive rights to Maury—er—Murray material for the lifetime of your contract. Two: You don't have to do an interview with me. Three: For one year, whenever Maury and I make love, I promise to say 'Dave! Oh Dave!'"

Letterman never saw that exciting exhortation. After just the first few moments of the tape, he had made a quick move for the door, saying, "I don't want to see any more." Morton and Lassally watched uncomfortably to the end, not blaming Connie so much as wondering about whoever helped put it together for her and how they could misunderstand the comic sensibilities of the Letterman show so badly.

Later Stringer fared much better when he sent over another tape, a more dignified effort with Charles Kuralt, the sonorous-voiced CBS newsman, narrating a history of CBS that included the great moments of Edward R. Murrow and the famous raid on NBC that brought Jack Benny to the network. Letterman looked at the Kuralt tape—all the way through—and picked up the intended message: CBS was a network with a rich, impressive history. The broadcaster in Letterman had enormous respect for that sense of history.

As for Jonathan Letterman, the Civil War doctor, he wound up on Peter Lassally's wall. Letterman looked at it just once and said: "Who cares?"

In September Stringer tried more hands-on wooing. He got tickets for Lassally and his wife and Morton and a girlfriend to attend the U.S. Open tennis tournament (long a CBS-covered event) in Flushing Meadow. They enjoyed the attention but even during a pleasant September afternoon at the tennis stadium, there were a lot more things to think about than which network had the best tennis tickets or the most storied history. For Morton and Lassally the complicated questions about money, time periods, and station lineups could all be boiled down to: What's best for Dave?

CBS was far from alone in the effort to curry favor at the Letterman shop. Other little gifts were arriving. One studio sent everybody hats. Bob Iger at ABC, tuned in to Dave's taste in auto racing, gave him a tape of the previous year's Indianapolis 500—as covered by ABC. ABC also had an even more potent ambassador than Connie Chung turn up to make its case: Ted Koppel, the anchor of "Nightline," a show Letterman had often said he admired, visited with Letterman in his office and tried to sell a Koppel/Letterman double-header as the ultimate late-night package. Letterman was flattered by the newsman's attention, but he also had some reason to be disappointed. At one point in the early soundings, ABC had dropped hints that Koppel might be fed up with his "Nightline" role and want out. That would have freed up 11:30, and the attractiveness of ABC's station lineup and its consistent appeal to younger viewers would have made the network the clear favorite to land Letterman. Letterman was not writing off the possibility of teaming with Koppel and going on ABC at midnight. But without 11:30 to offer, ABC's other attractions lost some luster.

Koppel's visit was part of a savvy campaign to protect his own 11:30 turf. He had made a kind of preemptive strike at that year's ABC affiliates convention in June when he tied his future commitment to "Nightline" directly to whatever decision the station managers of ABC's affiliates made about it. Koppel had been frustrated for some time by the growing tendency of ABC stations to delay "Nightline" a half hour in favor of some syndicated show like "Cheers" or "Entertainment Tonight." The news show's "live clearance level"—the percent of the country that broadcast the show immediately after the late local news—was at a low point: just 63 percent. "Nightline" had won every honor in television and was consistently praised as the most outstanding program in network news. More than that, the program became a ratings powerhouse any time a big story broke. Still, it was an easy target for an ABC station out to make a quick buck with a syndicated show.

But Koppel and his boss, Roone Arledge, the president of ABC News, saw an opportunity in Leno's entry as NBC's main man in late night. "Nightline" had a chance, if Leno proved less formidable than Carson, to increase its overall standing in the late-night ratings. And if Letterman chose to move into direct competition with Leno and split the available audience for entertainment programming, Arledge figured "Nightline" could begin to be the consistent leader in late night. So both men played a little hardball with the ABC affiliates. They said the program was at a crossroads; without more support from the affiliates, ABC News might decide to abandon "Nightline."

Koppel said that if more stations started delaying the program, "We'll be forced into a slow bleed to death." Though the program might continue to survive for a time in that weakened condition, Koppel added, he would choose not to be a part of it. "I did not work twelve years on this show to go through a slow dance of death. I will leave the program before I take part in that."

In effect, Koppel and Arledge were trying to reestablish "Nightline's" position by threatening to kill it. The idea that so prestigious a show could be forced off the air because too many ABC stations wanted to cash in on "Love Connection" was intended to seem outrageous and unacceptable. By taking the step when he did, Arledge also hoped to forestall any plan by a rival executive, Phil Beuth, president of early-morning and late-night programming for ABC, to get his hands on the 11:30 time slot in a bid for Letterman that would force "Nightline" all the way back to 12:30—or off the air entirely.

The Fox network had a potential complication as well. Before Letterman jumped into the open market, Fox had committed to a late-night talk show to star Chevy Chase. Chase, a graduate of another NBC late-night hit, "Saturday Night Live," had been promised an 11:00 P.M. time period as part of the inducement to lure him away from his movie career. But to get Letterman, Fox would almost surely have to give 11:00 P.M. to Dave. Fox toyed with the idea of moving Letterman up to 10:30, with Chase then set for 11:30, but that was going to raise objections from the many Fox stations that ran an hourlong newscast each night starting at 10:00. And just to add a little extra spice to this mix, Chase was also a client of Mike Ovitz and CAA.

CBS at least had no encumbrances. The network was filling late night with a patchwork of crime/action dramas that it called "Crime Time after Prime Time."

After Sajak melted away, Rod Perth had developed the idea as a sensible alternative to the programming available on NBC and ABC. In the wake of the Sajak fiasco, CBS needed to come up with something or risk being put permanently out of business in late night. The crime shows were produced on the cheap, shot in Europe in cooperation with European broadcasters who never had enough American action shows to please their audiences. Even cheap American action shows were far superior to the stuff the Europeans shot and called action shows.

For what it was, "Crime Time" had to be considered a modest success for CBS. The network made a few pennies on the package, thanks to the heavy foreign investment, and the ratings were passable. But the clearances were awful. Most CBS stations simply saw "Crime Time" as an invitation to preempt with syndicated shows.

That situation only figured to get worse if CBS didn't resolve a brewing confrontation with its affiliated stations over the issue of "compensation"—the cash payments that networks make to stations for carrying their programs. Larry Tisch, the CBS chairman, thought compensation was a preposterous, archaic notion, and moved to cut it drastically that May. Stringer believed at the time that the move was ill-advised and potentially a disaster if the stations retaliated against the network—as he expected they would. The certain targets: CBS's fragile morning news show and its barely breathing late-night lineup. Both could be undone by an affiliate revolt. And Stringer couldn't hope to win Letterman if he couldn't guarantee him a competitive lineup of stations. Before he could realistically bid for David Letterman, Stringer had to work within his own network to end the feud over compensation. Howard Stringer had confidence he could handle that; he'd survived bigger feuds inside CBS.

In the Byzantine chess game of network politics, Howard Stringer was a high achiever. He had risen to run a network from the most unlikely of bases: the network news division. But then he was also a British-born Vietnam veteran who wound up serving as the most quoted spokesman for one of the most American of institutions: network television.

Stringer, a native of Cardiff, Wales, with a degree in history from Oxford, landed in America in 1965 looking to be a journalist. He naively concluded that the fact that he was a permanent resident alien and not a citizen would protect him from the draft; it didn't. After he was drafted, Stringer could have opted to return to England, but then he could never have had a career in America. He had already landed an entry-level job at CBS. The idea of turning tail and running back to England, abandoning this adventure he'd set upon for himself, seemed unacceptably humbling. Stringer was also convinced he could talk and charm the Army out of drafting this likable Brit.

Not a chance. Stringer wound up serving in Vietnam for two years, where he managed to win a medal for meritorious achievement. He joined CBS News in 1968.

Stringer's career at CBS News was filigreed with successes, first as a director and producer of news specials and documentaries, then as executive producer of "CBS Reports" from 1976 to 1981, during that series's last great period as the leading source of news documentaries in America. Shows produced under Stringer, including "The Defense of America," "The Fire Next Door" (about urban decay), and "Teddy" (which undid Ted Kennedy's run for the presidency in 1980), won virtually every important prize given in television.

Stringer moved on to become executive producer of the "CBS Evening News with Dan Rather" beginning in 1981, steering that program to a period of dominance among the network evening newscasts. Like many others in the Machiavellian court that was CBS News in the 1980s, Stringer had compelling ambitions. But he also had wit, affability, and a gift for elegant corporate footwork. Physically he was a man of considerable size, as tall and broad as a defensive tackle in football, but not at all imposing-looking. The curly-haired, ruddy-cheeked, bespectacled Stringer was less bearlike than teddy bear–like.

With tenacious intelligence and charm, Stringer navigated his career clear of much of the chaos that enveloped CBS News in the eighties when two news presidents were fired in quick succession. He emerged as the news president himself in 1986. Stringer was then forced to preside over a period of frightful bloodletting of staff, bureau closings, and other draconian cutbacks. As always he managed it splendidly, perhaps too much so for some of his critics in the division who believed he was currying favor with the new CBS boss, Larry Tisch. Certainly Stringer presented himself impressively to Tisch, who then elevated him to president of the CBS broadcast group, the top job in the network, in 1988. It was not a position that news presidents, and onetime news producers, usually attained—or aspired to.

Stringer's tenure included some of the worst days in CBS history, with prime time in a shambles and staggering financial losses due to gross overexpenditures on sports rights. Some outside the network saw Stringer at first as the fancy-speaking front man for Tisch, whom many considered a know-nothing nonbroadcaster in the process of wrecking a grand institution. But Stringer never lost his light-footed grace. He remained steady, and eventually his leadership steadied CBS. Stringer put together a solid combination of executives under him, reshaping management in his collegial style. CBS rebounded in 1991, defying the early analysis of the Tisch regime. The network regained prominence in prime time and matched that success in daytime and children's programming.

To many, CBS still seemed locked into a hidebound strategy that had narrowed its interests only to broadcasting at the very time when technology was shattering every limitation on what might be available on a TV set. Yet Stringer remained capable of an eloquent defense of that mainstream approach. Under Stringer CBS might not look visionary, but it certainly looked well managed again.

Peter Lassally had agonized for weeks. Events were moving fast. The pitches had taken place; the other networks and the syndicators were scrambling to get their offers together for Letterman. If Ovitz could come through on finding an escape for Letterman from his entangling contract with NBC, he would soon be liberated from that network forever.

And that was the whole problem. Because in the quiet moments after the show had ended, or in long phone conversations on the weekends, Lassally would slowly pull the truth out of Letterman: He didn't want to go. Not to CBS or ABC or Fox or anywhere else. The thing he wanted, still wanted, was to walk out onto a stage as the host of the show he had watched when he was kid: the "Tonight" show. The dream was not dead.

Lassally talked it over with Morton: Should he do something to let NBC know how Letterman felt? And if he decided to do it, how would he do it? Couldn't an approach like that backfire in some way, with NBC only getting another chance to reject Dave? And whom at NBC could he really trust to understand the power of this dream and what an emotional thing this was for Letterman?

Lassally still had trouble believing that NBC could be completely satisfied with its choice of Jay Leno. As the new television season began that September, Jay's ratings had started to slide downward from their early heights. The network had just gone through the insanity with Helen Kushnick and the firestorm over her departure. Could they be having a hint of second thoughts? If there was even a shred of a chance that Dave could be brought back into the "Tonight" show picture, it had to be worth the risk.

So in mid-October, in one of their soft-spoken conversations in Dave's office after the show, Lassally put the question directly to him. He had to know, he told Dave. "If NBC would still offer you the 'Tonight' show, after everything that has happened, all the words, everything with Jay, would you say no?" They had been over this ground before, but Dave said it again. Of course he wouldn't say no.

"Under no circumstances would you say no?" Lassally asked, pressing the point so he would be able to add all the emphasis he felt necessary.

Dave said it the way Lassally wanted to hear it. Under no circumstances would he say no to an NBC offer to host the "Tonight" show.

When he got home later that night, Lassally carried the conversation with him. He was up most of the night talking it over with his wife, Alice. Then he made his decision. In the morning he would call Dick Ebersol.

Lassally had known Ebersol for almost twenty years, back to the days when a young, long-haired Ebersol had been hired to create and develop a new late-night show for NBC to use on Saturday nights in place of Carson reruns. That show was "Saturday Night Live." Ebersol had since bounced up through the network, and occasionally out of it. But his connections to late-night television ran deep. Aside from his initial association with "Saturday Night Live," Ebersol had created and produced the original "Friday Night Videos," which shared the weeknight 12:30 slot with Letterman for a time, as well as the Saturday night professional wrestling extravaganza that NBC used to great effect as the off-week replacement for "Saturday Night Live." Ebersol had been lured back to NBC to try and save "Saturday Night Live" in the early 1980s at a time when the show was on the brink of extinction. As executive producer of "SNL," he first helped raise Eddie Murphy to cult status, then filled the year after Murphy left with the huge creative talents of Billy Crystal and Martin Short. Two years later, Ebersol had conceived the newest (and truly latest) NBC late-night entry, the followup to Letterman, an ambitious, biography-style interview show called "Later" that featured the star of NBC Sports, Bob Costas. That became the successful postscript to the NBC late-night comedy lineup.

At the moment Ebersol was back inside the network, having taken over the sports division as president in 1989. As always rumors swirled about Dick, one of the slickest strategists and schmoozers in network television. Lassally had heard talk that Ebersol, fresh from impressing his NBC bosses with the production of the Barcelona Olympics, might be getting moved here or there to shore up one of NBC's problem areas. None of that was important to Lassally. All that was important was that he and Ebersol had a long history at NBC. Dick surely knew more about late-night programming than any other executive at NBC; and if anyone in the NBC hierarchy was likely to feel that the network was about to make a gigantic blunder in letting a talent like David Letterman go out the door, it was Dick Ebersol.

Lassally arrived at his office the next morning still not sure what he was going to accomplish with this plan, or if Ebersol was really the right contact. But he was determined to see it play out. Lassally picked up the phone and dialed Ebersol's extension.

After only a few pleasantries he told Dick he had something important to tell him, and that he had been up all night with Alice debating about whom they could reach out to.

"I don't know what promotions you're going to get, if you're going to get any, if you're going to leave NBC, or anything," Lassally told Ebersol. "I don't care which it is. You don't have to give me an answer. But before we leave here, I have to tell something to somebody at NBC, and I've selected you because I've known you a long time. We know something that nobody else in the world knows, no matter what the agents say about it. I finally got Dave to admit yesterday after the show that if NBC would offer him the 'Tonight' show, under no circumstances would he turn it down."

Ebersol listened without committing himself, as Lassally went on: "Dave would love to stay at NBC if he could get 11:30. I want someone at NBC to know that this is very meaningful to David Letterman. You cannot underestimate Dave's dream. Dave had a dream when he was a kid and he used to watch Johnny Carson; that's what he wanted to do. Someday he wanted to do what Johnny did. That dream is very deep-seated. That's never been out there. A lot of people think he would say no because he's been embarrassed and hurt."

The dream is so deep, Lassally said, that Letterman had long since decided that he could never do the "Tonight" show from New York as he did "Late Night." "Dave said: 'If I got the eleven-thirty show, I would want to do the show from Burbank. That's where Johnny Carson did it.' It was no decision for Dave."

Lassally then told Ebersol that he wanted him to carry a message: All this business about mistreatment in the past by NBC executives was meaningless; Dave would happily make a deal with NBC if he could still get the "Tonight" show. Dick could convey these points to Bob Wright or whomever Dick wanted to tell this news to—and he could add one more thing. "I want them to know," Lassally said, "that I will be more than happy to be a back channel for them to get directly to Dave."

Ebersol recognized the importance and the delicacy of the message Lassally had given him. Within an hour he was in Bob Wright's office telling him that David Letterman would not spurn a new approach from NBC out of bitterness over what had transpired in the past, and that if Wright chose to use it, there was a way for him to reach out directly to David Letterman.

A frustrated Michael Ovitz was having no success with NBC over David Letterman's contract. The network held all the cards. Letterman couldn't negotiate with any of the panting suitors surrounding him until NBC had exhausted its first negotiation period in February. Even then, if Letterman chose to make a deal with someone else, NBC had matching rights that could extend as long as a year. To Ovitz that meant NBC could keep Letterman off the air and possibly destroy his career.

Of course, in the process, the network would also detonate every hope of retaining Letterman. The best Ovitz could do was try to exploit NBC's need to maintain some semblance of positive relations with the star. That message had found some resonance with Bob Wright, who was still arguing that giving up all hope of retaining Letterman was an unacceptable strategy. John Agoglia knew the first negotiating right was worthless at this point, except in terms of delaying the inevitable.

The only time a first negotiating right made sense was when dealing with someone who wanted to make a deal with you. Agoglia had long since concluded that David Letterman did not fall under that description. "When the person professes—to his representatives and on the air—to hate your guts, I'm not quite sure what the legal terminology of a good negotiation means anymore," Agoglia said.

Wright's position was based on reason. He really wanted Letterman to stay at NBC, so if the only way to accomplish that ultimate goal was to show some flexibility, he was willing to try it—as long as there was something in it for NBC.

Ovitz kept making the point to NBC: Dave is fragile emotionally. He can't deal with this uncertainty about his future. Show some good faith and the situation will improve. Beyond that, Ovitz argued, it made no sense for NBC to try to wait until the last minute. Agoglia had to agree that NBC needed to get its own house in order. Besides, NBC had some protection; as long as it retained its matching rights, NBC could still trump whatever offers Letterman might be able to elicit elsewhere.

NBC constructed an escape for Letterman very much on its own terms. On October 30, in exchange for allowing Letterman the right to negotiate freely for his future employment, NBC agreed that it would extend the term of Letterman's existing contract from April 2, 1993, to June 25, 1993. The deal had one special attraction for NBC. The network had already sold advertising in "Late Night" through the end of June. If Letterman had left in April, NBC would have had to insert repeats for three months, forcing the network to return some of the advertising revenue it had already taken in. Now it could keep all the money.

What was most important to Wright, however, was that this part of the dispute was resolved rather amicably, leaving open the possibility that David Letterman, after hearing what was out there in the great big world beyond NBC, might decide there was no place like home.

Each of the Letterman bidders received a letter from Ovitz containing nine specific demands relating to the negotiation. The points included such items as salary for Dave, budget for the program, and rights of ownership. One point was the simplest, but clearly the most crucial: Under no circumstances would any bid be entertained for a show later than the 11:30 time period.

The demand seemed to affect only one bidder: ABC. The network had recommitted itself to "Nightline," so it had decided to formally propose a midnight start for Letterman, packaged with "Nightline." ABC's executives had thought such a tandem might lock in near 100 percent live clearances. But when CAA would not compromise on the 11:30 demand, Bob Iger informed Ovitz that ABC was passing on Letterman without even submitting a formal proposal.

That decision disappointed some on the Letterman side who had seen ABC as the likely first choice if everything else had been equal. Even ABC at midnight had some support. Bob Iger had made a lasting impact.

CAA set a mid-November date for initial bids. As the offers came in, CAA prepared a spreadsheet for Letterman and his associates. When they saw the numbers being offered to David Letterman, and the sheer magnitude of the deals, Lassally, Morton, and the others close to Letterman were stunned—and elated. Their unstinting faith in David Letterman as a major television star was being completely validated by virtually every important company in the television industry. It was only an initial round, but the figures were so staggering that the Letterman staff was caught up in the excitement.

That night Morton, Lassally, and a group of others decided to celebrate after the taping of the show with a dinner at San Domenico on Central Park South. The talk was all about Dave's prospects, of course, and the illustrious waiting list for his services. Many at the table had not been a part of the original pitch sessions in L.A., when the Hollywood heavy hitters had turned out in force for Dave. So Morton decided to tell them all a story of one of the many bizarre moments from those two heady days:

Peter and Morty and Dave had had dinner on Sunday, the night before the first session of pitches, at a Malibu restaurant called Granita. That warm summer night the three of them had sat at an outside table overlooking the Pacific, discussing what they might expect to hear in the morning. They were all excited but apprehensive. Then a waitress approached with some news: Warren Littlefield was in the restaurant.

The three of them had just been talking about how weird it felt to be in L.A., so near the NBC program executives while all this was going on. "We were plotting the assassination, and there he is," Morton told those listening to his story. Warren walked by the table to see them, he said. Without questioning for a moment why they might be there, Littlefield greeted them winningly and suggested they try the salmon. At that moment Warren's wife, Theresa, and their two children appeared. Warren's young son, Graham, walked over to the table and said to his father, "Daddy, is this the man who's been giving you all the trouble?" They had all laughed, of course, though Morton said he was convinced at the time that Graham had been fed the line—which he had delivered quite well. After a few more somewhat awkward exchanges at the table, Littlefield had left.

The table at San Domenico had just finished laughing at Morty's story and the overt digs at NBC when they looked up and saw a well-dressed group coming toward the table. It was John Agoglia, with several other NBC corporate executives in tow. By less than a minute, Agoglia had missed hearing them giggling like guilty kids about the Granita story. In New York for some NBC business, Agoglia seemed mildly surprised to have run into the Letterman group; but he made some small talk at their table before sitting down at his own table with his corporate NBC friends. Morton and Lassally began hatching an idea. They asked if the restaurant had a cake, but had to settle for a tray of cookies. At dessert time they had the cookies sent to Agoglia's table. As the waiter set the tray down, gesturing at the Letterman table for having provided it, Agoglia looked surprised, then looked down at the cookies. He threw his head back and laughed his hearty Brooklyn laugh, while shaking his head and waving to the Letterman table.

In the middle of the tray of cookies, the restaurant had written large in decorating icing: "11:30!"

Even before he knew the outcome of the bidding, John Agoglia had analyzed the prospects of his opposition. He put CBS down as the heavy favorite to win the bidding for several reasons, beginning with its ability to give Letterman the 11:30 position he most wanted. Agoglia believed he knew Letterman's psyche well enough to be certain he would lean to a network instead of a syndicator or Fox, a new network with more in common with the syndicators than with CBS. The syndicators would surely put together a package with the biggest bottom line, but Agoglia knew a lot of the money promised by the syndicators would not be guaranteed.

As Agoglia targeted CBS, he and other NBC executives began storing up ammunition. They expected that CBS would never be able to get past about 90 percent total clearances in late night, and maybe 30 percent or more of that would come at midnight or later. NBC began preparing a complete workup of every CBS station and how much time was left on their existing deals for syndicated shows at 11:30. If Letterman and CAA picked CBS, Agoglia was prepared to state flat out: Letterman will never be competitive on CBS.

Agoglia didn't expect to match CBS's money. He knew that the CBS executives would be able to bid higher than NBC because they would be offering the 11:30 time period, while NBC's offer would be for 12:30. The ad revenue available from 11:30 to 12:30 would naturally be considerably higher than what could

be brought in from 12:30 to 1:30, and CBS was likely
to be willing to hand more of it over to Letterman just
to get a late-night franchise started. Agoglia derisively
added another factor that might block any NBC bid to
keep Letterman: if Larry Tisch decided to open the
CBS vault again. NBC planned to slam any big-money
bid CBS might make for Letterman by making mocking comparisons to CBS's ill-fated $1 billion bid for
four years of rights to major-league baseball, a deal that
wound up losing CBS a staggering $500 million. The
move was blamed for driving the entire network into
two years of annual losses. Of course, it wouldn't matter
to Letterman if CBS seemed to be willing to lose another bundle. But Agoglia concluded it would soften
the PR blow to NBC from losing Letterman if NBC
executives could dump on CBS for winning him only
through more lunatic spending.

Bob Wright was in no way impressed by the fact that
CBS seemed to be going full bore in pursuit of Letterman. To him every CBS move had to be judged against
that baseball deal. What Wright knew was that CBS
hadn't made a nickel in late night in its history. The
network seemed to be willing to lose $30 million or $40
million a year without flinching. So he ruled out just
about anything CBS did. He was more impressed when
ABC showed such intense interest in Letterman because
he respected the ABC corporate leaders. And even Fox's
interest in Letterman had impact because Wright saw
Fox operating a system more like NBC's than CBS was.
But Fox, he reasoned, was out to get Letterman in order
to raise the entire image of Fox as a network. As Wright
sat back and watched the offers for Letterman pour in,

he did not immediately conclude that those company's programmers who were so hot for Letterman might know something his own programmers didn't; he just concluded they all had different agendas.

Wright was feeling pressure from two directions: The group on the East Coast that was arguing for keeping Letterman was finding more support among his New York executives at the same time his West Coast executives were pushing to reconfirm the choice of Leno on the "Tonight" show.

At the President's Council, the regular Tuesday meetings of NBC's top division managers, sentiment toward Letterman was being spoken out loud by Ebersol and others. They raised the issue of how potent a competitor Letterman would be for Leno. The West Coast executives, who attended by conference call, were increasingly challenged by Ebersol and other East Coast executives. What are you doing to solve the situation with Letterman? they asked the executives in Burbank. Littlefield and Agoglia said: We're working on it. John Rohrbeck, the head of the network's owned-and-operated stations—the man responsible for running the six stations that NBC owned—complained most vocally about the prospect of losing Letterman. He began assembling support in New York for keeping Letterman at all costs—even if the cost was Jay Leno. Rohrbeck made a powerful point: His division, the network's o-and-o stations, generated more profits than any other area of the company.

But Wright was also being pressured by Littlefield and others on the West Coast. Just push the button on Letterman, they said to Wright. Wright figured this suggestion was at least partly attributable to Leno's lobbying through Littlefield to get NBC to make an announcement: Good-bye David, good-bye and good luck, we're sticking with Jay Leno. Wright told Warren and the others he wasn't going to take that step. "I just can't do that," he said. When they said it was a question of loyalty to Jay, Wright told them, "No, it's a question of NBC. Jay is going to be there. He's got the show. He doesn't need our expressions of loyalty. That isn't going to get him one viewer. The issue is, What do we do if we lose this very important late-night personality? So show me the new plan."

But Wright didn't see a new plan coming together— and his temperature was going up through the sky. Littlefield and Agoglia assured Wright that they had lined up Dana Carvey, the newest star to emerge from "Saturday Night Live," as the next Letterman. He's there, they told Wright. The deal is set. But Wright pressed for details: Can we count on this? Is it finalized? Is it a done deal? Littlefield and Agoglia admitted it wasn't quite to that point yet.

It wasn't that Wright was ready to jettison Leno, however. He listened to Rohrbeck and others pressing for Letterman at any cost, and he decided to check what the cost would really be. In mid-November he pulled Rohrbeck and some other Letterman supporters aside and clued them in: The deal with Leno put NBC on the hook for a full payoff of the remainder of his two-year contract. It would cost NBC between $10 million and $11 million to settle up with Jay, Wright said.

Rohrbeck was undaunted. He told Wright that sounded like a big figure but it was short money, and it didn't matter. What mattered was the long term, he said—having the leading man in late night. But NBC was in the middle of a disastrous year for profits, a year when, even in network television, a figure like $10 million started to sound like real money.

Jay Leno's campaign to undo the damage of Helen Kushnick's reign over the "Tonight" show went on for weeks. He not only apologized to almost everyone he ran into, he also began to purge the show of Helenisms. If Helen liked it, Jay didn't. Except for the people; Jay was generous with everybody on the staff. The "staff member of the month" got a dinner at Spago—on Jay. Stars who called in asking about possible booking conflicts with Arsenio Hall were told anything was cool, just work out the best dates for each appearance. Jay began to apply a standard that Helen had never tolerated: He treated everyone well and let things work out for themselves.

Helen was not replaced. The show went without a formal executive producer. Jay worked with his two producers, Debbie Vickers and Bill Royce, to put together the show every night. The tension disappeared; Jay thought his own performance improved immediately, and that the performance of the show followed. Jay was managing himself now—"in that fool-for-a-client way, I suppose," he said—and functioning informally as his own executive producer.

And yet the pressure had only shifted; it had not been blown out to sea along with Hurricane Helen. Because now, the talk inside NBC was all about Dave. Jay's West Coast allies—Littlefield, Agoglia, and Rick Ludwin, the head of late-night programming—filled him in on the simmering pro-Dave movement building in New York. Clearly, Jay's performance in November was looking more and more crucial, because November is one of the three "sweeps" months of the television season, when the ratings for the widest number of television markets are taken and used for the next quarter's sales. After tailing off in the summer amid the chaos behind the scenes, Jay's ratings had stabilized in October. And as November began, the numbers started to climb again.

At the point of his one hundredth edition of the show, Jay made a pledge to his NBC bosses: "If I can't keep the ratings up on the show, I'll step aside. Don't worry about it." He even gave NBC a possible negotiating position to take to Letterman. "Look," he said. "I'm here for two years. If you don't like what I'm doing in two years, give it to David. I've got a contract. Live out the contract. If you're not happy, I can't stay on past when you want me to stay on."

Jay Leno was convinced the show had righted itself, that it was now running smoothly. He felt he could once again put his faith in the numbers.

The first time CAA narrowed down the bidders, most of the syndicators—Paramount, Warner, Columbia, Chris-Craft—didn't make the cut. Disney was still in, partly, the Letterman side thought, in deference to Ovitz's close relationship with Michael Eisner. But they also recognized that, of the syndicators, Disney was clearly the class act. Disney's money terms were way off, but CAA could put that down to early conservatism and Disney's well-known tightness with a buck.

David Letterman,
the daytime version
(courtesy of the
National Broadcasting
Company, Inc.)

RIGHT:
David Letterman,
shortly before the
debut of "Late Night"
in 1982
(courtesy of the
National Broadcasting
Company, Inc.)

BELOW:
A Stupid Pet Trick on
"Late Night"
(courtesy of the
National Broadcasting
Company, Inc.)

ABOVE:
A shaggier Jay with
Dave on "Late Night"
(courtesy of the
National Broadcasting
Company, Inc.)

RIGHT:
Bob Wright,
President of NBC
(courtesy of the
National Broadcasting
Company, Inc.)

RIGHT:
John Rohrbeck,
President, NBC
Television Stations,
and ardent
Letterman backer
(courtesy of the
National Broadcasting
Company, Inc.)

BELOW:
Dick Ebersol,
President, NBC
Sports, and the inside
connection to the
Letterman show
(courtesy of the
National Broadcasting
Company, Inc.)

ABOVE:
Jay Leno on the
"Tonight" set with Don
Ohlmeyer (center),
President of NBC
West Coast, and
Warren Littlefield,
President, NBC
Entertainment
(courtesy of the
National Broadcasting
Company, Inc.)

RIGHT:
Rod Perth, Vice
President of Late
Night for CBS
(courtesy of CBS)

Jay Leno and
Helen Kushnick
(courtesy of Wide World
Photos, Inc.)

ABOVE:
The "Tonight" show
getting wilder:
Jason Alexander
of "Seinfeld" is a
bound-and-gagged
guest of Jay's.
(courtesy of the
National Broadcasting
Company, Inc.)

RIGHT:
Jay Leno with former
"Tonight" show
executive producer,
Fred De Cordova, and
Warren Littlefield,
President, NBC
Entertainment
(courtesy of the
National Broadcasting
Company, Inc.)

Jay Leno and
friends:
From left: Warren
Littlefield, President,
NBC Entertainment;
Branford Marsalis,
bandleader; and John
Agoglia, President,
NBC Productions
(courtesy of the
National Broadcasting
Company, Inc.)

RIGHT:
Jimmy Brogan,
"Tonight" show writer
(courtesy of the
National Broadcasting
Company, Inc.)

BELOW:
Johnny Carson visits
David Letterman on
May 23, 1991, the
day he announced
he was quitting the
"Tonight" show. He
brought an extra
million for Dave.
(courtesy of the
National Broadcasting
Company, Inc.)

ABOVE:
Letterman with
Peter Lassally, his
executive producer,
and Johnny Carson,
in background, at a
party in Malibu in
1992. Johnny picked
up the tab.
(courtesy of Peter
Lassally)

RIGHT:
The man who made it
happen for David
Letterman—Michael Ovitz,
Chairman of Creative Artists Agency
(photograph by David Strick, Onyx)

RIGHT:
Lee Gabler, head
of the Television
Department for CAA
(Berliner Studios)

BELOW:
Steve Lafferty, lawyer
and Letterman
negotiator for CAA
(Berliner Studios)

RIGHT:
David Letterman
with CBS President
Howard Stringer at
his first press
conference for CBS,
January 1993
(courtesy of CBS)

BELOW:
Construction inside
the Ed Sullivan
Theater
(courtesy of CBS)

RIGHT:
Lorne Michaels, executive producer of "Saturday Night Live" and "Late Night with Conan O'Brien" (courtesy of the National Broadcasting Company, Inc.)

BELOW:
Conan O'Brien's first television appearance as new host of "Late Night" with Jay on the "Tonight" show (courtesy of the National Broadcasting Company, Inc.)

ABOVE:
The last shot of
David Letterman
on NBC: Riding off
to CBS
(courtesy of the
National Broadcasting
Company, Inc.)

CENTER:
Peter Lassally,
executive producer,
"Late Show with
David Letterman"
(courtesy of CBS)

RIGHT:
Robert Morton, co-
executive producer,
"Late Show with
David Letterman"
(courtesy of CBS)

Calvert De Forest,
aka Larry "Bud"
Melman, opens the
first "Late Show" with a
booming "This is–
CBS," 8/30/93.
(courtesy of Alan F.
Singer, CBS)

ABOVE:
NBC Anchorman Tom Brokaw makes a surprise appearance to claim NBC's "intellectual property" on the first "Late Show," 8/30/93.
(courtesy of CBS)

RIGHT:
Vice President Al Gore splits an ash tray with Dave on "Late Show"'s second week on the air, 9/8/93.
(courtesy of Alan F. Singer, CBS)

Viacom was still a maybe, through the sheer weight of cold cash. The Viacom terms were dizzying; they seemed to leave little or no room for the company to make money, because Letterman would be making so much. Viacom was guaranteeing Letterman $20 million a year in salary, against up to 70 percent of the profits from the show. Even a modest ratings success could have brought Letterman as much as $50 million a year. One CBS executive who discussed the deal with a top Viacom manager said the company had a grand marketing plan to rebuild itself as a presence in the syndication market, with a Letterman show in late night as the jewel in the crown. Viacom was willing to accept the show as a high-profile loss leader. But Viacom was still a syndication deal; so even at those prices, Viacom was barely a maybe.

Letterman had left little doubt about his skepticism about syndication. The syndicators could sign checks but they couldn't supply the answers he needed: Where would his show be placed? Would his promos run in the middle of some tawdry, melodramatic talk show or tabloid magazine? The CAA team knew from the start that Dave was only going to be comfortable with a network. Ovitz concluded that Dave wanted to have to listen to just one voice. And so the agency politely closed the books on Viacom. As for Disney, nobody was going to accuse that organization of being sleazy; but even Disney couldn't guarantee a lineup of stations that would make Letterman truly competitive with the "Tonight" show. It wasn't a network deal; it wasn't what David Letterman was used to. But the Disney Company was not going to go gently out of late night.

Michael Eisner, the Disney chairman, had been especially aggressive in the Letterman chase. On November 11, toward the end of the first negotiation period, during a National Conference of Christians and Jews dinner honoring Rupert Murdoch at the Beverly Hilton Hotel, Stringer spotted Eisner sitting next to CAA's Lee Gabler. Stringer could hear the Disney chairman loudly denigrating network television as a business about to go under and CBS in particular as a network with nothing but decrepit old viewers. Stringer jumped in immediately and defended the honor of his company, telling Gabler not to listen to that tired, old, antinetwork rant.

When Disney got the final word—that Mr. Letterman would be going elsewhere—Michael Eisner was upset. He called Ovitz to complain; he wrote Letterman a letter, even called Letterman himself, putting on a Hollywood full-court press to try to turn the decision around. Ovitz tried to appease Eisner while dispatching Gabler to deliver the harsher message: No matter what it tried, Disney wasn't getting David Letterman.

The Letterman side was mildly surprised at the fuss: Disney's offer wasn't even in the ballpark. It included a guarantee to Letterman of only $6.5 million a year in salary (a fraction of the other offers) and only a $53 million total two-year guarantee for the show's budget, prime-time specials, and other costs. By contrast, Warner's Telepictures, which never got to the later rounds, had guaranteed Letterman $8.3 million a year and a $109 million total guarantee for three years.

CAA was looking for huge guaranteed money in the packages, and for more than the most obvious reasons.

It still had to deal with NBC's right to match any offer, and NBC would not have flinched at putting up $6.5 million to keep Letterman at 12:30.

The two players left in the game were CBS and Fox—by no coincidence at all, the two network players. Fox had impressed the CAA negotiators. Jamie Kellner, the Fox president, had made a terrific case for Fox, Gabler thought, with his emphasis on how well Letterman would play to the core Fox audience. But CBS was the front-runner and everybody knew it. Ovitz knew Stringer and Tisch had no choice. They had to go all out for this deal. If the network's offer was intelligently assembled—and potent financially—it was going to win the first round of the Letterman sweepstakes.

CBS had already invested in some comprehensive research into how Letterman might play at 11:30 on CBS. In November the network's head of research, David Poltrack, began conducting regular telephone surveys of 2,000 people, some who had watched late-night television recently and others who hadn't. CBS offered the viewers four choices—Letterman, Leno, Arsenio Hall, or "Nightline"—and asked what they thought of each. In another custom research study, Poltrack put together 250 people who had not watched David Letterman and asked them to watch his show for one night. Ten different shows were included in the test period. After they'd seen Letterman, CBS asked these viewers whether they would watch him or the other shows.

In each case Letterman came out a strong winner. In the CBS tests Letterman's biggest competitor wasn't Leno but "Nightline." Poltrack checked back through various months of testing and detected a downward trend in Leno's popularity. He reported to Stringer that the test results showed Letterman's popularity was not just strong but broad, and much better with women than anyone had anticipated. More than that, it looked to Poltrack as though Jay Leno might be vulnerable, that his solid ratings might be more attributable to the consistent appeal of the "Tonight" show than to Leno's intrinsic popularity with viewers. The information wasn't going to make Stringer's pursuit of Letterman any more intense, because Stringer was going flat out as it was. But it certainly made him feel that the network had more evidence than his own programming instincts to justify a groundbreaking financial package for the late-night star.

Stringer spent hours on the phone with Ovitz, talking in more general terms about the values of CBS, and in person with Gabler, who conducted the specific negotiations. But Stringer never felt secure about CBS's position. He decided it was the most difficult negotiation he had ever been a part of. The variables were incalculable. When Stringer thought of Viacom and all that money, he also thought of things such as how they could try to sell Letterman on the virtues of cross-promotion on their cable channels, including MTV. When Stringer thought of Fox he thought of Rupert Murdoch tossing in movie deals that CBS simply couldn't match, because it wasn't part of a movie studio. About all Stringer could take comfort in was that he was negotiating for a person who was a broadcaster down to his loafers. Stringer never felt the deal would turn on money, partly because he could sense that Letterman was simply not the materialistic type, but mostly because this entire orchestration of escape from NBC could not have been about money. It had to be about more than that, Stringer thought. "It had to be about fulfillment and opportunity and a well-earned moment in the spotlight."

In the end, the CBS offer was not the biggest in terms of money; it was dwarfed by the Viacom offer, beaten by the Chris-Craft offer, and about the same as what Fox would have put up. Fox offered Letterman a guaranteed salary of $12 million a year, but that could have swelled by more than $3 million a year if he hit certain ratings figures. Fox's three-year deal included up to $10 million in bonus money for ratings performance. The three-year license fee guarantee from Fox was $84 million, or $28 million a year, with another $7.2 million set aside for prime-time specials.

When he discussed the merits of the deals, Ovitz emphasized that the CBS offer included "value-added" features, such as the chance to become, in essence, the on-air spokesman for the entire network, and the fact that CBS looked like the network that was starting to put it all together in prime time and elsewhere. Gabler believed CBS was truly hungry, and well on its way to recovering fully from its disaster of the late eighties. Besides that, Gabler concluded, Howard Stringer was a phenomenal executive.

Letterman had the Ed Murrow image stuck somewhere in the back of his mind, and that didn't hurt. Certainly at CBS the decision would be the cleanest: He would get his shot on a network at 11:30; it would be direct competition with the "Tonight" show, mano a mano with Jay Leno.

For some on the Letterman/CAA side, the selection of CBS was a nondecision. Syndication had never been part of the equation; Fox was a step into uncertainty. CBS won the game by default.

But it was not as though CBS hadn't put chips on the table. The network's three-year deal guaranteed Letterman a yearly salary of $12.5 million, with a bonus clause that could take it as high as $14.5 million a year. The bonus was to be calculated on the basis of how well Letterman scored with one specific audience: adults between the ages of eighteen and forty-nine—the main demographic on which advertisers buy television advertising time. If Letterman averaged a 3 rating with that group of viewers, he would get a bonus of $1 million. If he averaged a 3.5 rating, the bonus would be $1.5 million. If he reached a 4 rating with adults eighteen to forty-nine, he would get the full $2 million bonus.

In addition, CBS agreed to put up a total of $82 million as the budget fee for the show over three years, a fee that would cover all other salaries, costs of production, and the deal for use of the studio. The contract was for forty-six weeks of original programs in the first year, and forty-four weeks a year for the next two years. CBS also promised to pay a $7.2 million licensing fee for prime-time specials. CBS would also grant Letterman's production company, Worldwide Pants Inc., full ownership of the show, and the company would also get control of the production rights to a future backup show to run from 12:30 to 1:30.

When the decision was made, an effusive Lee Gabler

called Howard Stringer to let him know CBS had won the first round of the David Letterman sweepstakes. Stringer accepted the news with great enthusiasm and thanked Gabler extravagantly for his support. Certainly Howard Stringer felt good, but he was not elated. It was just the first stage, he knew, with the real challenge yet to come.

Nobody served champagne at CBS, though Stringer did dispatch more trinkets toward the Letterman offices. A Steuben glass eagle for Dave with a note: "If the eagle hasn't landed, at least it's in flight." Lassally and Morton got glass Steuben bulls.

As Stringer read the situation, CBS was still in a position to be the stalking horse, not the derby winner. For all the work he had put into landing David Letterman, the next stage would hinge on something completely out of his control: what NBC did. Larry Tisch said it plainly to Stringer: NBC is going to match. The mood at CBS was slightly negative about the chances of David Letterman ever turning up as the savior of CBS's late night.

Rod Perth, the head of late-night programming for CBS, wanted mightily to be the executive in charge of a late-night lineup headed by David Letterman; but he simply couldn't believe NBC would be stupid enough to let Dave go. His feeling, and it was shared by everyone from Jeff Sagansky, the head of CBS entertainment programming, to Stringer himself, was that NBC would bite the bullet and buy its way out of Jay Leno's contract; that Bob Wright and Warren Littlefield would look at Jay's performance, check their own research (which would surely show the same things CBS's had), figure in how much of Jay's strength was the hold-over popularity of the "Tonight" show, and conclude that Jay was a long-term problem at 11:30—especially if he ever had to go head-to-head with Letterman.

Stringer looked at all the publicity about the auction for Letterman—all the frenzied interest in him from top executives inhabiting every corner of the television industry, all of whom had decided this was a seriously undervalued star—and concluded NBC had to do something. It only made sense.

NBC had thirty business days to match the offer or lose David Letterman to CBS, a schedule that, because of the Christmas holidays, made the deadline January 15. NBC's public reaction, as articulated by Warren Little-field, was that CBS had proved to be consistent. "When Jay Leno hosted the 'Tonight' show, they went after him. When they couldn't have him they went after David Letterman. They didn't nurture, they didn't grow anything, they went after things that worked as opposed to creating any franchise of their own."

For Bob Wright the view of his West Coast execu-tives had proved to be equally consistent: They never fully believed David Letterman would ever leave NBC. "The West Coast view was just about money," Wright noted. It was self-serving, he said, because they never wanted to lose Letterman and they never thought they would when they picked Jay Leno. It was a way they could have both stars instead of one—as long as Letter-man didn't leave. "It was always hard for them to admit that the whole scheme didn't work," Wright said. "To lose one and have him compete against you. They weren't into that."

Agoglia had strong faith in his matching rights. But CAA had developed an idea of how to counter that as well. On December 7, when Lee Gabler drove the CBS deal over to John Agoglia's office, accompanied by the head of business affairs for CAA, Steve Lafferty, he wondered how Agoglia was going to react. Lafferty, and other lawyers for CAA and Letterman, had thoroughly vetted a special clause that had been inserted into the CBS offer. It was, in effect, a poison pill designed to thwart NBC if it decided simply to pay the fat salary and match CBS, keeping David Letterman right where he was, right where they intended to continue to hold him: at 12:30.

The CBS deal stipulated that the network would pay Letterman a penalty fee of an astounding $50 million if he did not get a show in the 11:30 time period. In other words, any deal presented by NBC had to guarantee Letterman the "Tonight" show time period or else pay him an extra $50 million. What CAA was attempting to do was ensure that no NBC deal could truly match the CBS offer if it did not give Dave an 11:30 show.

When Gabler and Lafferty arrived in Agoglia's office with the papers, Agoglia greeted them with his thin smile. Gabler was struck by how much Agoglia reminded him of the Cheshire cat. As Agoglia read the details of the CBS deal, he grew more and more dour. When he got to the penalty payment clause, he got downright testy. "Very cute, guys," he said. "But I'll tell you, we don't agree with this." The CAA lawyers were convinced they could make the penalty payment stick; Agoglia simply didn't take seriously the idea that time periods could become a contract issue that NBC had to match.

But the inclusion of the time period in the contract did tell Agoglia something: how important 11:30 had become in this fight over Letterman. It was an issue, he came to conclude, whose importance he may have underestimated. "I really may have misjudged the depth of desire for the 11:30 spot over anything else," Agoglia said.

NBC's initial response to Letterman's selection of CBS was much as expected. The network's executives denigrated CBS's ability to put together a truly national lineup of stations that would carry a Letterman show at 11:30. And they compared the extravagance of what CBS had offered Letterman to that network's folly with baseball. "It's the baseball deal all over again," a senior NBC executive said.

Howard Stringer laughed at the comparison, but it surely got under his skin. This was a talent deal, for a star who would appear five nights a week year-round, not a sports deal for a product that was worthwhile only in the month of October. It also cost a tiny fraction of the price CBS had paid for baseball. And David Letterman was no journeyman infielder. As Stringer saw him, he was a slugger of rare distinction, truly a wonder to behold in action.

"This may not be like the baseball deal," Stringer said. "But I feel like we got Ted Williams."

The word started coming back to Peter Lassally from his NBC contacts: There was movement; some people were speaking up for Letterman. It was still just talk, it seemed. But the names connected to it started carrying real credibility, Lassally thought. Amid all the talk from

CAA about CBS and how great the deal was, Lassally kept waiting for some word that NBC was still in there as a factor to be considered. He wasn't hearing that from Ovitz's people; but he was hearing it from his insiders at NBC.

Still, that meant Dave wasn't really hearing it from anybody. And Lassally felt time was too short to let it filter its way down to Dave. Soon after the CBS announcement, he and Morty met with Dave as usual after the taping of a show, dissected what worked and what hadn't, and settled into a discussion of what the future looked like.

Lassally decided it was time to bring Dave in on his quiet campaign inside NBC. "It's an outside chance," he told him, "But I think the 'Tonight' show is still possible."

Letterman's reaction was immediate dismissal, but Lassally pressed on. There are signs of movement, he told Letterman, hints of reconsideration. Lassally described how he had established a contact inside NBC, though he didn't want to use Ebersol's name. Now the contact had begun to assemble allies, Lassally said, executives who had never believed fully in the choice of Leno. They're in there arguing with Wright about how NBC can't afford to allow that choice to stand if it meant losing a talent like David Letterman, Lassally said. Lassally knew Dave didn't really want to hear all this because he didn't want to be let down again. But he told him anyway: There might still be a real fight for the "Tonight" show.

Letterman listened to this tale of second thoughts

and hints of movement and moles inside NBC, and shook his head all the way through it. "You know," he said, "there's just no point in considering this, boys, because I don't think it will ever happen."

9

THE EAST/WEST GAME

Every day somebody else talked to Bob Wright about David Letterman. The conversations reverberated all through the NBC floors of the GE Building, but nowhere as loudly as inside the chrome-and-glass executive offices on the fifty-second floor. Wright had less than a month to find a way to keep Letterman, and he could feel the options closing all around him. He had come to hate the thought of Letterman walking out the door at NBC, never to return. And the picture of him walking in the door at CBS made Wright almost apoplectic. The situation gnawed at his gut like nothing he had had to deal with in his six years at NBC.

Every meeting with his executive staff kicked up the familiar questions: Could NBC afford to lose Letterman? Would Letterman's style of comedy work at 11:30? Was Leno over his shaky period and would his show improve? Were Leno's strong ratings for real? And the biggest question of all: What would happen to NBC's forty-year dominance of late night if Letterman went head-to-head with Leno?

The dispute over which way to answer those questions was intensifying. Pier Mapes, NBC's head of affiliate relations and sales, told Wright that his two constituencies would start a revolution if the network overthrew Leno in favor of Letterman. But John Rohrbeck, the head of the owned-and-operated stations, argued strenuously that he was truly the number one affiliate since he was in charge of the stations NBC owned and he felt the decision to keep Leno instead of Letterman was putting the financial standing of NBC's biggest asset, its stations, at risk.

Wright decided to try to see if a special research study could clear away some of the smoke. In early December he told Eric Cardinal, the executive in charge of research in Burbank, to set up some competitive studies between Leno and Letterman. Cardinal was to ask a batch of viewers to watch each host over a period of time and make the assessment: Which guy do you like better?

But the research was going to take some time. As he waited, Wright was besieged by opinions. Beyond the established pro-Letterman forces, other influential NBC people began whispering Letterman's virtues in Bob Wright's ear. Tom Brokaw, the NBC anchorman and frequent Letterman guest, made it clear how fond he was of Dave's work. So did Lorne Michaels, who as the creator and executive producer of "Saturday Night Live" was highly regarded both for his acumen at late-night comedy and for his long experience at NBC. Michaels had developed a strong affection for Wright and he felt confident volunteering his views. And his views were based on a sense of self-preservation. Michaels thought the fate of the "Tonight" show tied in directly to the fate of "Saturday Night Live."

Michaels regarded the extraordinary clearance levels of both the "Tonight" show and "Saturday Night Live" as true aberrations in contemporary television. The "Tonight" show had held up for almost four decades and "SNL" for more than fifteen years largely on the strength of their near 100 percent live clearance rates on the network. "SNL" was still one of the hottest shows on television, with more viewers in the early 1990s than it had had in its original glory days of the mid-1970s. And its appeal to young viewers was unmatched in network television. But Michaels knew the show was fragile, a true throwback to a lost era of television: It was a live weekly show put on in a studio inside a venerable New York building, a show that required expensive sets to be built by expensive technicians every week. The show turned a huge profit for NBC, but much of that profit was generated by the ultra-high rates NBC could charge in the first half hour of the telecast, when the viewing was highest. Michaels knew how crucial his first half hour was, a period that was always vulnerable to preemption for a syndicated show by a station looking for a quick hit of extra revenue. Michaels was convinced that the powerhouse clearances of the "Tonight" show had protected "SNL" on Saturdays, because if stations started to delay the start of the "Tonight" show by a half hour during the week, they would surely be more disposed toward doing the same thing on Saturdays. Keeping "SNL" alive and healthy meant an enormous amount to Lorne Michaels personally.

Though he had expanded his career beyond television to include producing theatrical movies, and his *Wayne's World* had cashed in over $100 million at the box office, Michaels had a bedrock commitment to "SNL." He had left the show once, in the early 1980s, feeling burned-out. But the experience of being outside the show turned out to be much worse. He returned to "SNL" in 1985, following Ebersol, and set down roots as deep as they could go. Michaels intended to stay on "SNL" until the end of his career, or until it went off the air, or until the end of the network system of television—whichever came first. That gave him an intense personal interest in seeing that the "Tonight" show, the Atlas of late-night clearances, stayed as strong as possible; and that could only happen if the show had the best host possible. Lorne Michaels told Bob Wright that David Letterman was the best late-night star since Johnny Carson.

But if more voices in the East were speaking out for Letterman, the chorus coming from the West Coast was near unanimous: Burbank was Leno country. Those who had been involved in the original decision to choose Leno over Letterman, Warren Littlefield and John Agoglia, had no reason to reconsider at this point. They were rooting heavily for Jay's ratings to continue to improve; that would validate their programming instincts. For Littlefield that validation was especially critical because the NBC prime-time lineup was showing few signs of resurrection at this point. The usual Hollywood rumblings that accompanied the scent of failure started to include Littlefield's name. The November sweeps would make or break him, the rumors went; Wright had to be out looking for a new programmer. Littlefield kept true to his nature: He lowered his head and did his job. But he sure wasn't about to stop backing Jay. After what they'd been through with the separation from Helen, Warren saw their relationship as forged by fire.

For Agoglia, retaining Leno meant holding on to a vital piece of power. As the head of NBC Productions (NBCP), the network's in-house production company, Agoglia now had some direct control over the "Tonight" show, which he never had when the show was owned by Carson. Now the ownership had reverted to NBCP, and would remain there if Leno kept the job. Letterman's deal with CBS gave him ownership of his show; John Agoglia had no reason to want to see the "Tonight" show plundered from his personal fiefdom again.

But as ardently as Littlefield and Agoglia supported Jay, they were surpassed by Rick Ludwin, the head of the network's late-night division. When Ludwin and the head of production for NBCP, Gary Considine, would stop in New York to meet with the Letterman producers, Morton and Lassally would take turns browbeating them over the decision to choose Jay over Dave. It was partly sincere, but partly pure entertainment as the Letterman producers jumped around the room, screaming, yelling, telling the NBC executives how foolish they were, how Letterman towered over Jay in terms of sheer talent. Considine laughed at the display, feigning that the assault was killing him. But Ludwin got defensive and terribly offended that they would pick on Jay that way.

Morton was convinced that Ludwin, who earlier in his career had worked on "The Mike Douglas Show," considered himself the father of the new "Tonight" show, and with Helen Kushnick out, was now able to fill some of the duties of executive producer. If it had been offered, he believed Ludwin would have grabbed the job.

But Ludwin's devotion to Jay was only part of his overall dedication to all his late-night children. One of the producers who worked under Ludwin said: "Rick lives for late night; it's his whole life." Ludwin didn't have a family; he wasn't married. He put everything he had into his work.

He was no less vigilant about "Late Night with David Letterman." Ludwin taped every one of Dave's shows and watched them the next day—without fail. He was a huge fan of Letterman's, often telling people he was Dave's biggest fan. But he had never got close to the show. Partly it was the distance between Burbank and New York—both physically and philosophically. But mainly it was a matter of personalities. Ludwin, who always looked preppy and somewhat square with his neatly trimmed hair, wire-rim glasses, and blue blazers, didn't mesh with the more renegade sensibilities of the Letterman show. Of course, the fact that he was so clearly one of "them"—an NBC executive—played a significant role in that. Ludwin tried to break through and develop some kind of relationship at "Late Night," but it never worked out. He wasn't bitter about it; he simply accepted the situation for what it was, and gave himself "credit for attendance." That was a standard Ludwin phrase; network executives often had to be satisfied with credit for attendance.

But clearly Rick Ludwin was getting credit for a lot more than that from Jay Leno. Jay's warm, welcoming style lightened Ludwin's day. Ludwin had essentially the same kind of regular, nice-guy personal style that Jay had. Jay was right there every day in Burbank, being pleasant, listening to suggestions, fulfilling every network request for promos or guest bookings or tickets for so-and-so's Aunt Gladys and Uncle Ed, perfectly willing to bring Rick into the running of the show. Nobody at NBC had more reason than Rick Ludwin to be eager to do the dirty work in the pits for Team Leno.

The Leno team kept up its own drumbeat in Bob Wright's ear; Jay is going to win, they told him day after day. Forget about what was being written in the press about Jay being stodgy and not as freewheeling and funny as he used to be. The media, as the pro-Leno forces saw it, were part of the enemy. Most of them were based in New York anyway—Letterman country—and newspaper writers never had the same taste as the people. Trust the everyday people, the West Coast executives told Wright. They're voting differently from the press.

And remember, they said, that David Letterman has only done a 12:30 show, a truly late-night, edgy, not everyday-people-friendly show. Littlefield and Agoglia had that image of the nasty Dave branded into their memories. They argued for Jay as the broad-based comedian who could play to the big crowd at the earlier hour, where Dave simply couldn't.

Wright was not at all sure of that, not if he could believe what he was hearing from Dick Ebersol, who was his contact into the Letterman show. In phone calls, Lassally had been filling Ebersol in on Dave's intentions. Dave recognized the need to adjust the show for 11:30, Lassally told Ebersol. He'll keep the key ingredients of "Late Night," Lassally said, but will add more mainstream guests. And he'll be able to get more of those guests if he's based in Burbank.

After hearing that message, Wright told the pro-Leno executives that Letterman could change his approach for 11:30. But Littlefield and Agoglia dismissed the possibility. Dave's not capable of a change that drastic, they told Wright. And then they pointed to the numbers: Jay is doing fine, they said over and over. Look at the numbers. Jay will hold up. Jay is going to win.

"You don't understand," Wright told them. "It isn't a question of who wins. We lose. When you have two entertainers going after essentially the same audience and the same show and the same time period, you both lose."

Wright had a hard time getting that message through. What he heard back was: At worst the audiences for the time period would grow; Jay would win, Letterman would do okay, and NBC wouldn't be hurt. "That's a hell of a risk to take," Wright responded. "If we don't have to take that risk, I would rather not, thank you. We already have plenty of risks in prime time. We don't have to test a theory to see whether 11:30 can withstand two big stars going against the same audience, when we've been there by ourselves for thirty years. That isn't a risk high on my list of risks."

The answer obviously was to try to keep both men. But to find a way for Letterman to coexist with Leno meant finding a way for him to live happily without the

"Tonight" show. Wright felt he could make a strong case to Dave about how he was going to be taking on an enormous risk in shifting to 11:30, where he would surely have to make changes in his show. This was a risk that he could avoid if he stayed with NBC. Wright was prepared to offer Letterman all kinds of options beyond staying in his 12:30 show. NBC could provide much more exposure in prime time, or any other part of the day Dave might want to invade. Dave could test his strength with wider audiences at no real risk, because he'd keep his 12:30 base of operations. Wright had even asked the research department to look into what effect it would have on the late local news on the NBC affiliates if the network ran a Letterman show at 10:00 P.M. each weeknight. Wright was considering offering Dave a weeknight show across the board at 10:00 P.M. as a possible fallback if that was the only way they could keep him at NBC.

All of these options seemed promising to Wright, but he could get nowhere with them. He had no direct contact with Letterman. He spoke only to Ovitz, and Ovitz simply wasn't listening, Wright felt. He spun out the options in phone conversations with Ovitz, but Wright came away from most of them sensing that Ovitz was always cutting him off at the pass. Every time Wright reached out, he ran into a wall that he believed Ovitz and others around Letterman had constructed to keep NBC out of the deal. All Ovitz could offer Wright in the way of a formula to keep David Letterman was zillions of dollars up front and an eviction notice for Jay Leno.

Wright suspected that Ovitz had invested something

of his own personal reputation in the negotiation, that Ovitz wanted to show the world how CAA could take this big television guy and move him over to CBS. As Wright read it, all Ovitz and the other CAA guys wanted to talk about was how great their package with CBS was. "Our issue is not that package," Wright said. "That's a blip in our life. Our issue is retaining David Letterman."

Finally he told Ovitz: "You're asking us to do things we can't do." Bob Wright concluded he wasn't getting anywhere dealing with Mike Ovitz.

Peter Lassally was having his own difficulty getting a message through to Mike Ovitz. With the CBS deal secured, a deal that Ovitz clearly felt met the criteria he set for Letterman before the negotiations began, Ovitz seemed satisfied. The days passed toward the deadline and nothing seemed to be forthcoming from NBC.

But Lassally felt Ovitz needed to know just how badly Dave still wanted the "Tonight" show. He and Morton thought that message had been communicated to Ovitz, but apparently he still did not fully appreciate the depth of Dave's desire. They were wrong. Ovitz knew all about Letterman's undiminished desire to take over the "Tonight" show. From the beginning Ovitz believed Dave had really come to him wanting Ovitz to get the "Tonight" show back for him. But Ovitz had moved away from NBC very early on, though he had never told that to Letterman. Lassally wanted CAA to know that he was hearing real stirrings of interest from inside NBC, suggestions that it still might happen, that the network still might see the light about Letterman.

But he realized the only way for that point to get through effectively was for Dave to make it himself.

After some further prodding from Lassally, Letterman spoke to Ovitz directly. In a phone call to Ovitz, Dave said the words himself, simply and without complication: "Mike, I've had one dream in my life. All I want is the 'Tonight' show." Ovitz, believing that Letterman was blinded by his childhood dream, made the inarguable points about why it made little sense: The "Tonight" show was now damaged goods; Dave had so little to gain by taking over a diminished franchise. But Dave was Mike's client, and his client was telling him what he really wanted him to do for him.

And then Mike Ovitz knew that this long, intense, exciting negotiation would not be truly complete until David Letterman had an offer from NBC for the "Tonight" show.

Bob Wright was still waiting for his West Coast team to supply him the option he needed to make the gnawing in his gut about Letterman go away: the Dana Carvey option. NBC had announced in July that it had signed Carvey to what it called a "long-term" deal that made him exclusive to NBC. His name surfaced almost immediately in industry rumors as the likely choice to replace Letterman in the 12:30 slot, rumors that NBC did not waste any energy denying. As the hopes to hold on to Letterman grew dimmer, Littlefield played the Carvey card, telling Wright that the star was lined up to step into Dave's late-night sneakers.

But almost from the time the rumors started, other NBC executives who knew the Carvey situation well told Wright that the star wasn't going to accept a late-night show, not with his movie career soaring, and especially not a show to follow Jay Leno. Carvey had told people that he idolized Letterman and would probably consider doing a show following Dave, but he would inevitably be cool to the idea of trying to follow Dave's act as the host of "Late Night" after Jay's "Tonight" show.

In mid-December the Carvey subplot twisted off in a new direction. A leak to the press from people close to Carvey generated a story that NBC's deal with him might not be what the network thought it was. Carvey's agent, Brad Grey, disputed the idea that Carvey's deal with NBC was long-term at all, saying it ended "after January." Suddenly NBC didn't even have a secure contract with the star supposedly lined up to replace Letterman. Worse than that, the press accounts of the botched deal included a rumor that Stringer was negotiating with Grey to bring Carvey to CBS for its own 12:30 show to follow Letterman.

Stringer denied that part of the rumor, and NBC tried to dismiss the entire story as a publicity stunt. But Wright, feeling even more acid filling up his already suffering midsection, started asking Littlefield and Agoglia much tougher questions about how firmly they had secured their option to take over for a departed Letterman. To Wright it seemed as if that part of the late-night transaction weren't happening at all. The exasperated Wright said to his West Coast executives: "After all this, after ten years on the air, this is going to come down to whether *I* can convince Letterman to stay. That seems to be the company strategy."

The frustrations seemed endless: Wright couldn't get anything going with Ovitz; the option supposedly being supplied by his West Coast team was turning to dust on him; all anyone wanted to tell him about Leno was that the "Tonight" show would somehow hang on to first place in the ratings. The NBC president had few clicks left on the remote control. But at least he knew one channel was still open. Wright contacted Peter Lassally.

It was a conversation Lassally had been waiting for. But when Bob Wright got on the phone, he seemed to be looking for someone, anyone, to negotiate with. "What if we build something in prime time for Dave?" Wright asked Lassally. "We could try to expand Dave's exposure to different parts of the schedule." Lassally knew he was in no position to negotiate for Dave, and he didn't want to make assumptions for him or Ovitz. He told Wright he couldn't be sure what Dave would think of any of Wright's proposals. Finally he said to Wright, "Well, why don't you have a meeting with him directly?"

There was nothing Bob Wright wanted more. But time was extremely tight. They set a date just a couple of days away.

Lassally had heard enough from his NBC contacts about how Wright was desperate not to lose Letterman, that a deal was truly doable, that he felt the meeting he had set up between Letterman and Wright was the most positive step so far in the campaign to steal back the "Tonight" show. But Lassally knew he should run the idea of the meeting by Ovitz.

When Lassally reached him in his CAA office and

told him the news of the meeting, Ovitz expressed immediate reservations that quickly shifted to strong disapproval. The client shouldn't be meeting with the dealmaker, Ovitz said. CAA should do Letterman's talking to Bob Wright. He asked Lassally to cancel the meeting, at least until Ovitz and Dave could talk about it.

The next day Lassally sheepishly called Wright and made up an excuse for why Letterman couldn't make their scheduled meeting. "Dave's just not going to be available tomorrow," he said. Wright immediately looked on his calendar for another date, as Lassally dodged and weaved and tried not to commit. They made a tentative date for Monday, December 21, with Lassally cautioning Wright that Monday was the day Dave often had to leave the office to go tape a remote comedy bit.

When Lassally and Morton talked it over with Letterman, they weighed all the factors, including CAA's understandable opposition to Dave's meeting directly with NBC's top decision maker. But Dave agreed when his producers made the point that in this case Bob Wright was more than that; he was also the guy who had been Dave's boss for six years. "This is your boss. You've got to see him. He wants to talk to you," Morton said. They decided to buck Ovitz on this point.

In a conference call with Ovitz, Letterman explained his reasoning, why he felt he should sit down and talk with Wright. Ovitz calmly explained his concerns that Dave might say something that was not consistent with what his representatives at CAA were telling Wright. But Dave pressed the point: It was the right thing to do to talk to his boss, and he was going to do it. Ovitz said he understood, and only asked for Dave's assurance that he would not get into anything that constituted a negotiation. Then Lassally contacted Wright's office and let him know the Monday meeting was on.

The week before the meeting with Letterman, Bob Wright expected to be fortified by the information gathered in the special research study he had commissioned. Both the Letterman camp, represented by Rohrbeck and Ebersol, and the Leno camp, represented by Littlefield and Agoglia, were avid for ammunition to apply to their cause, so the research study was a hotly anticipated item. Ebersol and Rohrbeck were tipped early by the New York research department that the raw results of the study were in. They jumped on the phone immediately. The reseachers gave the NBC executives the raw interpretation of the results—and to the Letterman backers, it sounded like good news. Even accepting the predictable fuzziness in this kind of speculative research, they believed the results showed Letterman would win a head-to-head test with Leno. More specifically, the study showed that negative reaction to Letterman, which NBC had picked up in earlier research, had significantly decreased. They wasted no time in barging into Wright's office with the news.

The NBC study had elements of the research that CBS was conducting about the same time, but it was not exactly the same. It was phone-based research with viewers in cable television homes who were asked to watch the two stars and make a choice.

But the West Coast executives had not yet weighed

in with their spin on the research numbers. When they did, they provided a read on the results that made the outcome completely confusing—or so Bob Wright thought. He found the research data as confusing as the executive-level discussion had been.

Wright concluded that the research could say whatever one wanted it to say, because the questions being asked were too speculative: "Who would you rather watch at 11:30?" implies both guys are available at 11:30, which was not then a reality. And it did not answer the question of whether the David Letterman that viewers were seeing in his 12:30 mode would be the same Letterman at 11:30. The pro-Leno spinners had an available defense for any argument that the numbers showed real strength for Letterman, saying Letterman's results had to be affected by all the press coverage of his big CBS contract. There was also the possibility, said Robert Niles, an NBC senior vice president with a background in research, that Letterman's strong support might be partly attributable to what always happens in attitudinal research: People choose answers based on attitude rather than what they would really watch. They give the answer they think is preferred instead of giving their own preference. Taking into account all the publicity Letterman was getting, his showing really wasn't all that great, the Leno executives argued.

After all that smog had been blown across the numbers, Wright's vision was just as blurry as it had been before the research arrived. But John Rohrbeck was infuriated. He told some colleagues that he believed the research was being deliberately muddied up, and that it was poorly conceived to begin with. He asked Wright if he could quickly throw something else together, something from the Frank Magid Company, one of the most widely used television analysts in the country. Rohrbeck had used Magid as a consultant when he managed KNBC, the NBC station in Los Angeles. Wright agreed to put up $100,000 for whatever hurry-up research Magid could provide.

In the meantime, with only days before he was to sit down with Letterman, Wright decided to look for help from some unscientific consultants. He started calling people whose opinions he valued. Brandon Tartikoff told Wright that he believed Letterman was better than Leno, but he questioned whether he was enough better to justify the price that NBC would now have to pay to keep him. One colleague outside the network whom Wright called was more blunt: "You can't deal with David," this colleague said. "Don't lose sleep over this. It was bound to happen at some point; it just happened under your watch. Take it in stride."

On Sunday, just a day before his scheduled meeting with Letterman, Wright made another call, one he had previously resisted making. He called his friend Johnny Carson.

Carson had become fond of Bob Wright; their wives had grown close and the four of them even scheduled vacation trips together. But Carson had no interest in stepping into the middle of the situation NBC had got itself into. When he had been at NBC, there on the scene, no one had asked him to give his opinion on who should follow him on the "Tonight" show. Now Bob was calling, asking what Johnny thought he should do with this Leno-Letterman dilemma.

"Bob, why are you asking me now?" Carson said.

"Isn't this a fait accompli? Doesn't Jay already have the job?"

Wright said of course he did, but added: "We made a mistake. I should have asked you before."

Johnny politely declined the invitation to cast a vote on who should get the "Tonight" show at this late date. "I'm not volunteering now," Johnny said. But he did have one very strong opinion: "It's going to be a shame if you lose David, Bob."

On that point, Carson was preaching to the converted. All of Wright's instincts as a businessman, and just as a regular viewer of television, told him that Letterman was a unique talent, the kind who could get people talking in the office the next day about what they had seen the night before. In very small circles at NBC, among the people he trusted with his private thoughts, Bob Wright had said it time and time again: If only this had been his decision all along, he would have picked David Letterman.

But now that a different decision had been made and was long in effect, it was going to be wrenching and hideously expensive for Bob Wright to undo.

Even when the pressure on Bob Wright was excruciating, he didn't show it. Panic was not in his nature—he had dealt with a string of crises in his six years at NBC, and seldom lost his veneer of cool control. An extremely fit man of forty-nine, Wright surprised a lot of people who saw him as a bland corporate creature of the General Electric Company. He dressed with executive style but also with a touch of color and dash; he even seemed to go bald stylishly.

Wright had come to NBC as a total outsider, the "GE plastic" man who had started his GE career in the plastics division. The clash in corporate cultures was instantly jarring, as Wright seemed intentionally to ruffle every feather in the peacock after he was named president in September 1986. NBC had been riding high on a pile of profits of more than $500 million a year, thanks to its completely dominating prime-time lineup. But Wright walked in the door sensing trouble, announcing that the company had to change or be engulfed by the revolution about to splinter the industry into hundreds of much smaller slices. Soon rows of holdover NBC executives began heading for the exits, some in disgust over the new direction Wright declared for the company.

Gradually, however, Wright won over many of his initial detractors, at least on a personal level. He clearly had a talent for relationships; some of the biggest NBC names grew fond of him, including Carson, Bill Cosby, and Lorne Michaels. Wright, a native of Hempstead, Long Island, and graduate of Holy Cross College, had a Jesuit-trained mind, went to church on Sundays, was devoted to his wife, Suzanne, and their three children, and exhibited an unexpected sense of playfulness about his position.

Critics inside NBC accused Wright of being a non-broadcaster, because his training at GE was in the financial services division, and before that, in the cable business as president of Cox Cable. They also said he was no more than a yes-man for GE chairman Jack Welch. Wright had a truly close relationship with Welch; they were neighbors in Connecticut and sometimes vacationed together. But he resented the implication that GE was micromanaging NBC and that he was serving as no more than the on-the-job foreman. Wright saw himself as a forward thinker in a business encumbered by some calcified traditions. He had also begun to assemble a core of executives, including Ebersol in sports and Ed Scanlon in personnel, who were intensely loyal to him on a personal basis. If Wright had led the network into some mistakes, it was at least partly out of the need for change. And the changes, he believed, had positioned NBC much more advantageously to deal with the unpredictable media future. Even his sharpest critics did not doubt Wright had keen intelligence and perception into the big picture of industry.

But the facts were stark; NBC's performance had been in a free fall since the day GE and Wright arrived. Absolutely nothing about NBC was in better shape at that point, except for its nonbroadcasting interests. Wright picked up a reputation as someone more interested in making good deals than making good television shows. The cable channels that NBC invested in were seen as distractions that kept Wright from focusing on the erosion all around him. NBC executives who liked Wright enormously on a personal level couldn't help but question his management skills as the network's position deteriorated in almost every area—daytime shows, its Saturday morning lineup, news programs, and worst of all, its prime-time shows. At the close of 1992, NBC, once the house of hits in prime time, was sinking faster than a sandcastle that misjudged the tide.

. . .

As he prepared to look for a solution with David Letterman, Bob Wright heard from one other interested party: Jay Leno called.

Leno was getting his information from his West Coast allies. They provided all the assurances they could that Jay was secure, but they described Wright as a wild card. He would not accede to their request for a straight-out statement of irreversible support for Jay. Wright was in New York surrounded by the Letterman cabal, they told Leno. Littlefield and Agoglia had met with Leno and told him how much they supported him. But they conceded it was going to be Bob Wright's call. All they could report to Leno about what Wright was saying was that NBC was committed to him at 11:30—for now.

Leno was perplexed and anxious. Things had seemed to be going so well. His ratings, down as low as a 4.2 in the summer, had climbed back up to a 4.9. He felt suddenly unappreciated. He was committed to working forty-eight weeks a year, five nights a week. Letterman was doing a show only forty-two weeks a year, and he only produced four original shows a week.

Jay had seen his staff come together in the aftermath of all the craziness of the three months under Helen. Now they had to put up with this sudden uncertainty, the fear that a New York executive might pull their jobs out from under them.

But Jay didn't have a manager to intercede on his behalf anymore. Soon after Helen was fired, he had rehired one of the many victims of Helen's rage, Dan Klores. Jay had read Dan's ten-part memo on how to improve the show, which Dan had faxed to him even after having been fired by Helen. Now Jay wanted Dan and his ideas back on his team. Once back with Jay, he was having more impact. Jay was clearly coming to trust both Dan Klores and the account executive Klores had assigned to him, Hayley Sumner. When Jay discussed with them the mixed messages he was getting from inside NBC, the PR executives started to push Jay to take some action. Sumner, who visited Leno often in Burbank, never stopped urging him to be aggressive. So did Klores. "You have to make it clear to them," Klores told Leno over the phone, "there's going to be a problem with you if they keep up this thing with Letterman."

Jay heard from his supporters in Burbank that Bob Wright was about to meet with Dave. As he often did when he wanted to solve a problem, whether with a critic he felt had rapped him unfairly or someone in the industry who had raised an issue about him, Jay picked up the phone himself. He called Bob Wright.

As always Jay was mild-mannered and polite. He asked Wright if he could explain the situation. All Wright could tell him was he supported him, that he was happy with his performance, but that this was a tricky situation. He told Leno he simply was not sure yet what the network would do.

Jay made a pledge that he would win the competition with Dave. "I'll win by a lot or by a tenth of a point, and if I don't I'll go," Leno told Wright. But Wright explained that winning wasn't the issue. "My issue is whether there will be enough audience there to sustain the kind of support you need to support these two shows." He explained that his concern was that CBS would, in its typical fashion, go out and destroy the time period. It would be another baseball deal. They would make a huge mess out of NBC's perfect late-night world.

Leno thanked Wright for speaking with him and for his candor, but he ended the conversation feeling even more strongly that Bob Wright was on the fence—and that his future at the "Tonight" show was in true jeopardy.

On the afternoon of December 21, Bob Wright walked into the warren of offices on the fourteenth floor that housed the "Late Night" staff. Without a show to do on Mondays, it was always quieter down there. In the late afternoon of the shortest day of the year, all the windows were dim with the faint daylight. Wright came alone. He ran into Robert Morton in the hall and greeted him warmly. Then Wright dropped by Peter Lassally's office. He told Peter he would prefer that he not sit in on this meeting with Dave. "I really would like this to be just the two of us," Wright said. Lassally thought that was appropriate. And then Wright went off to Dave's big corner office, the same office where Dave had orchestrated his walkout on Warren Littlefield and John Agoglia eighteen months earlier.

Letterman had no agenda this time, other than to listen to whatever Bob Wright had come to say. He welcomed Wright pleasantly but seriously. Letterman had worked for Bob Wright for six of his ten years at "Late Night," but he did not know the man at all. Much had happened between Dave and NBC, and Dave and GE, and Dave had never felt any sense of humanity coming down from above. But Bob Wright had turned up prepared to talk to Letterman as a man with a problem so troubling that he hardly knew how to approach dealing with it. It wasn't NBC or GE talking, it was the guy Dave worked for—a decent guy in the midst of a real dilemma—and Dave found himself connecting with Bob Wright.

Wright asked in a very straightforward way for Letterman's help. Not because he was worried that the business he worked for was going to suffer terrible financial losses if he left for CBS, but because Letterman had made himself a part of the NBC family and Wright really wanted to find a way for him to stay.

"Is there anything we can do to keep you here?" Wright asked.

In his guts Letterman wanted to say yes. He wanted so badly to stay at NBC. He truly liked it at NBC, despite all the pettiness and the second-class treatment and even the crushing snub when the "Tonight" show went to Leno. He loved the building, and the way the other NBC shows were close by, and especially the NBC late-night tradition, which had such an intoxicating effect on those who had become a part of it. But Letterman had to tell Wright the reality of his position. "I don't really think there is," Letterman said softly. "I don't want to mislead you. I have to say I don't think there is."

Of course, there was one thing NBC could do and Letterman had to get it out on the table. "You know," he said. "I would stay, but your 11:30 show is taken. And so beyond that I can't stay."

Letterman did not hammer Wright with a demand

that he offer him the "Tonight" show. The perfect solution might have been to have Wright declare that NBC had acknowledged its terrible blunder and was redressing it immediately by removing Jay and installing Dave. But Letterman didn't expect to hear that. He could tell that Wright was tormented and wrestling with the frustration of the situation, and he respected him for the effort.

And Bob Wright tried. He moved the discussion away from the 11:30 issue as best he could, toward the assurances he could offer that the network truly did appreciate Letterman's talents. Wright knew damage had been done, that talent relations in Letterman's case had been destructive instead of supportive, and he wanted to assess just how bad the damage was. Wright could sense from Letterman's sympathetic tone that he was eliciting a favorable response to his fence-mending. So he tried to move on to an exploration of what NBC could still do for David Letterman.

"There are things we can put on the table," Wright told him, "to improve your career, your image." But the packages that Wright had in mind for Letterman, with all their prime-time exposure and other opportunities to appear all over the network—while retaining his 12:30 base—missed the point. Letterman had never looked for more prime-time appearances; it made him nervous to have to try and compete in prime time even once a year with an anniversary special. He saw himself as a late-night performer, a specialist.

And so Letterman kept coming back to his desire to move to 11:30—not to be petulant, but simply because that was what this whole, long waltz around the floor had been about. Dave felt he had to go to 11:30 now because it was time, time to play in that bigger arena, the biggest arena in his chosen field. He didn't belong in prime time or anywhere else on the network; and he certainly didn't belong at 12:30 anymore. He had done that; now it was time to move up. He belonged at 11:30.

And then Letterman told Wright just how carefully he had thought about the move to 11:30, how he recognized that being on an hour earlier would require some subtle adjustment in his performance. It was exactly the thing that Wright had wondered about himself, the thing some of the NBC West Coast executives had said Letterman would never be able to do. But the explanation certainly sounded impressively lucid to Bob Wright.

"I know I can't do my show at 11:30," Letterman told him. "I have to change the show and I am completely able to do that, and I want to do that. And I would only do the 11:30 show if I could change it." Letterman laid out his philosophy of smoothing out the edginess from his 12:30 show: using more mainstream guests, doing a more traditional monologue, adding more class to both his own look and the show's. The flexibility that Letterman was displaying, the savvy, the confidence that he could drop part of one audience and add part of another, left Bob Wright a total believer that Letterman would be able to pull it off.

Wright heard what Letterman was saying about his need to be at 11:30, and how he would change his act to accommodate that time period, and it all was pretty convincing. As the hourlong conversation came to an end, Bob Wright started to feel his heart sink. It was never more clear that there was only one thing that was going to keep David Letterman at NBC.

As he left, Wright didn't promise Letterman he would deliver what Dave wanted; but he didn't tell him it wasn't going to happen, either.

Dave didn't know if anything positive had been accomplished, but he certainly felt good. It had been a warm, surprisingly emotional exchange. Letterman saw Wright as a guy not all that different from himself, a guy with a distressing problem who was behaving about the way Dave felt he himself would have behaved. This wasn't a cold-fish executive from GE at all; there was real humanity there, Letterman thought. He was touched and very impressed by Bob Wright.

Sitting nervously in his office, Peter Lassally could not imagine how this talk could be taking so long. He could not help wondering how it was going, what Wright might be telling Dave, how Dave was handling himself. Lassally was simply glad it was happening; surely it meant that NBC was planning to do something to keep Dave.

When Wright left Letterman's office he walked directly down the hall to Lassally's. "Got a minute?" he said, as he closed the door behind him. Lassally said sure, and motioned for Wright to sit.

"I had a very nice talk with Dave," Wright began. "It was a really good conversation." And then, after a pause, he said, "What do *you* think I should do?" Peter Lassally could not have asked for a more direct invitation. If Bob Wright wanted to hear what he thought, he would tell him what he thought. This was Lassally's opportunity to go to bat for his boy, and he wasn't going to hold anything back.

First he told Wright that he should know just how meaningful the "Tonight" show had been in David Letterman's life. How much of a dream it was, how far back it went, all the way to Dave's childhood when he watched Johnny Carson on the show. He explained how Dave had steered his career in this direction and what patience he showed, how gracefully he had tried to handle the idea of being in position to succeed Johnny. Much of this had already been fed to Wright, Lassally knew, by his allies among the other NBC executives. But it surely wouldn't hurt for Wright to hear it again.

But then Lassally related the dilemma Wright faced to his own professional experience, his forty years in working with talk shows on radio and television. He explained how that experience had made him realize just how big a talent David Letterman was—especially when compared to Jay Leno.

"I know what works and what doesn't work," Lassally told Wright. "Whatever people are telling you at NBC, Jay Leno is a very limited talent."

Wright nodded and said, "I know."

"I don't care what producer you're going to bring in," Lassally said. "Jay Leno will never get any better than he is today. If you think he's going to learn and he's going to improve, from my experience I can tell you, this is as good as he's going to get."

Again Wright quietly said, "You're right. I know."

Lassally could hardly believe he was getting no resistance. Nothing but total agreement was coming back at

him. He had one last point to make: the main difference, the crucial difference he had always seen in Dave
Letterman and Jay Leno. "Jay's not made for this," he
said. "He's not a broadcaster. Dave is a broadcaster."

Wright told Lassally he agreed with him again. The
points seemed to raise no protest from Wright whatso-
ever. Every critical word out of Peter Lassally's mouth,
Bob Wright took in and said, "I know. You're right."

For Lassally this development was nothing short of
astounding. Wright's reaction seemed so totally in assent that Lassally could feel a surge of excitement building inside him. As soon as the twenty-minute meeting
with Wright ended, Lassally bolted from his office and
down the hall to confer with Dave. As they compared
notes Morty joined them. Dave related how well he and
Bob had gotten along, but predictably he took no optimism at all away from the meeting. Lassally, however,
was totally up from his own conversation with Wright.
He told Dave and Morty how incredibly well it had
gone and how he had given Wright every reason to
question Jay and support Dave—without once hearing
Wright say he was wrong. "I'm convinced this man left
that room saying, 'That's the decision. Stand clear.' "

In his mind Peter Lassally was sure: The decision had
been made at the very top of the network. Dave was
going to get the call to replace Jay.

The next day, Bob Wright made a series of phone
calls to several of the New York executives who had
been supporting Letterman. He described his meeting
with Dave the night before, how well it had gone, and
how it was going to affect his decisions. The Letterman
supporters all came away from the calls with the same

impression. What Dave had said, what Peter had said, it all meshed with Bob's own gut feeling about what was best for NBC's late night. Wright was telling them he saw no other way out for NBC other than to go with Letterman. But it's going to be very difficult, he said.

Bob Wright had no idea how difficult it was going to get.

On Tuesday morning in Burbank, the news of Wright's meeting had reached Jay Leno. He wasn't sure what to make of it, other than the fact that he knew it wasn't likely to be good for him. Here he was, still having trouble getting anything out of Bob Wright, any words of encouragement at all, and Wright goes and meets with Dave one-on-one for an hour. Leno called Dan Klores when he arrived at the "Tonight" office and went through his whole litany of disbelief again. He couldn't believe what was happening at NBC in New York. They had a host who had come in, replaced a legend, and was doing well. Advertisers were happy with the ratings, affiliates were thrilled; the guys in Burbank, the guys supposed to know about entertainment programming, were completely supportive. But the big bosses in New York were thinking about overruling them. It was crazy, Leno said.

Klores agreed and gently suggested it was time for Jay to do something about it. Maybe call some affiliates, mount some support. The problem, Dan knew, was that the NBC people in Burbank had to be careful about what lengths they went to in supporting Jay; they had their own backs to protect. If New York was going in a different direction, it made no sense to start sticking necks out for Jay.

But Klores knew from talking to Susan Binford, the head of press relations for NBC on the West Coast, that the frustration level was rising among the executives there.

Binford, as strong a professional as any publicity executive working in television, had been involved in the transition from Leno to Carson and all the fractiousness with Helen Kushnick. She had hoped the upheaval at the "Tonight" show was over with. But now she told Klores that she sensed that the momentum was shifting away from Leno. That concerned her deeply because she guessed that a decision to choose Dave over Jay would trigger a bloodbath in Burbank. Leno, she knew, would be out the door the day of the announcement.

When Binford went down to Jay's office for a visit that week, she saw the boxes placed around the room with Jay's few personal effects loaded up in them. To Binford, the message was clear: Jay had already packed up his things and cleaned out his office to make it quick and easy. He told her point-blank: The minute that decision comes down, I'm out the door; I just won't show up that night. Binford knew Jay had delivered the same message to his allies in Burbank, who had relayed it to New York, just to lay one more brick on the pile of predicament sitting on Bob Wright's shoulders. It was another consequence he had to consider before pushing the button on this action.

But Jay wasn't likely to be alone in the rush for the exits. One of Binford's main duties was to keep Warren Littlefield and John Agoglia as clean as possible in the press, and she knew their reputations were mortgaged to Jay. If Jay went down, she thought Littlefield and Agoglia would be dead men. Warren would be so damaged he almost would have to quit, she concluded. She didn't know about Agoglia. Nor about herself; but it crossed her mind that she herself might have to go. Then there was Rick Ludwin, the whole "Tonight" staff, the band. It would be a massacre.

Personally Binford backed Jay for many of the same reasons as the others in Burbank: He had been steadfast and responsive; he had pulled through when he had to break with Helen. He had stepped up and done the job. He was squeaky-clean personally. And the performance was there; the strong ratings proved it.

Binford found herself feeling annoyed from the moment she walked in the building in the morning to the moment she left at night. She had rarely been so infuriated. New York had meddled in a set situation, and now, no matter what happened, NBC had a mess on its hands. She acknowledged that the company had to protect an asset like David Letterman as best it could, but it seemed like the latest of late decisions to wake up suddenly and realize: We can't afford to lose this guy. By this point nothing besides the big prize was going to satisfy Letterman, she concluded, and the same had become true for Leno. There might have been a time earlier in the process when a different offer, a shot in prime time, something else, might have been workable with Jay. Now, as Binford assessed it, Jay was looking at every glass as being half-empty. Anything NBC suggested was going to strike him as just a way to nudge him toward the door.

Real damage had been done already, as far as Binford was concerned. After all this, how could Littlefield and Agoglia still have credibility with the Hollywood community they had to make deals with? They seemed to have no power at all. That was the saddest part for Binford herself: What Warren and John thought on this issue didn't seem to count for much.

Binford wanted to take some action, but she felt constrained by concern that she might find herself on the wrong side of the official NBC corporate position. She also didn't want anything Jay might do for himself to be interpreted as a campaign by the Burbank executives to pull it out for Leno. Then it would surely have no impact. So Binford avoided talking to Jay directly about the situation. She chatted with him in the mornings about the ratings, referred him to anything that came up in the press clips that day. But she had to make it clear to Jay that she had to step back from any advocacy position—though she told him she would always be in touch with Dan Klores.

Binford got on the phone with Klores to give her assessment of where things were going. Klores thought Binford was the smartest person he dealt with at NBC. She had a sense of humor about the craziness of this business, and the smarts to think it all through. To Klores, Jay seemed like a sheltered guy, a little naive. He was smart intellectually, Klores thought, but he didn't think Jay was blessed with the kind of street smarts he needed to deal with the cut-and-slash side of the business. Klores, whose accent sounded as though it had its roots in an argument over stickball in Bensonhurst, put a lot of stock in street smarts. He could picture Jay walking down the street at 12:30 A.M. in Chinatown with four threatening kids coming his way, and Jay wouldn't even think of crossing the street.

In the wake of Letterman's positive meeting with

Wright, Klores felt Jay needed to go on an all-out offensive. When Binford called to check in with him, Klores told her the plan. Binford, who had been advising a certain degree of caution to that point, had a much stronger reaction this time: "Dan, do it!"

Klores called Jay. He got the usual response: Jay sounded more forlorn than truly upset. Klores had had enough of that.

"Stop whining," Klores told him. "Get a little angry, for God's sake. It's okay. Do it. You'll feel better."

Jay acknowledged that he was angry, but Klores felt he had to truly stoke him up. He told him the meeting with Letterman just proved that "wrong-way Wright was at it again." Jay had a case to make for himself, Klores said. Wright wasn't giving Jay any signal that his work was appreciated. "You're getting a real fucking here," he told him. Look at those ratings: a 6 rating in one recent overnight figure from the big cities. The advertisers loved those numbers, and the affiliates knew what a solid job he was doing for them.

Jay pointed out that the affiliate managers he had talked to were completely supportive. One, Jim Waterbury from Waterloo, Iowa, thought the show was doing so well he wondered if NBC could run it twice, once in prime time.

That's great, Klores said, telling him that was the kind of stuff they needed to get out. "Wright is sitting on the fence now hoping the fairy godmother comes along and saves him," Klores said. "You've got to come out and talk about your feelings." But Klores wondered if that was possible for Jay, who kept his emotions so astonishingly, maddeningly under check.

Klores's plan was an all-out assault: first a big shot across NBC's bow in the press, then a whole lot of calls to affiliates to stir them up. Maybe an advertiser or two could endorse Jay publicly. "You're a guy whose done a good job," Klores said. "You've worked your ass off. You've got to talk about it. And it's okay if you sound angry. The overwhelming point is that NBC is treating you shabbily."

Leno was uncertain, because he didn't know how it would play. Would it only make the NBC guys in New York more determined to be rid of him if he challenged them this way?

But he was certainly angry about how unfair it was. And one image came to mind that had some real impact on him. It was the last scene from the Robert Redford movie *Three Days of the Condor*. The hero, a loyal, true-blue American spy on the run from assassins—unsure who are his friends and who are his enemies, but certain that right is on his side—decides to take the only action he can think of that will ensure that the world knows what's going on, what's been happening to him: He calls the *New York Times*.

When Klores suggested to Leno that he call the *Times*, Jay finally saw the real wisdom in this plan. He could make his case; the affiliates would read it and come to his defense. NBC would see what a strong constituency backs Jay Leno. He told Klores to set up the phone call.

On the morning of Wednesday, December 23, two days after Bob Wright's crucial meeting with David Letterman, Jay Leno was the lead story in the *New York Times* culture pages. In the interview, Jay expressed his "surprise and disappointment" with how he was being treated by the NBC executives. He made his points about how happy the affiliates and advertisers were and asked, "Am I crazy? I feel like a guy who has bought a car from somebody, painted it, fixed it up and made it look nice, and then the guy comes back and says he promised to sell it to his brother-in-law."

Leno specifically ruled out switching places with Letterman. "I'm not going to do some little happy hour from Omaha at 12:30," he said. Instead, if Dave got the job, he said, he would "of course" go to CBS. Not that he had anything against Dave personally. As always, Leno acknowledged his great debt to Letterman for boosting his career when he was a frequent guest on "Late Night" in the mid-eighties. "I wouldn't have this job if not for Dave," Leno said. "Dave is worth whatever somebody wants to pay him. Anything I can do toward keeping him at NBC, I'd do. Dave is truly a star and terrific, and this is a terrible position NBC is in. But fragging your own soldier doesn't make any sense to me."

Leno made his points strongly, but he still sounded more hurt than angry, more incredulous that his good work was going unappreciated. He confirmed the split inside the NBC executive ranks, with the West Coast backing him and the East Coast apparently going for Letterman. "NBC's West Coast executives have said everything is okay," Leno said. "But the East Coast people won't say that." He added that he had talked with Bob Wright, who did not give him the assurances he wanted. "He said they don't know what they're doing yet," Leno said. "I appreciate the candor, but it does disappoint me. NBC is like a guy with two girlfriends who doesn't know which one he's going to marry on January 15. And the longer you wait, the madder they both get."

Leno said he had received a lot of input from NBC research about what worked on the show and what didn't, and he was trying to be responsive to that. For example, he was adding more comedy to the show. The bottom line, Leno said, was that the show was clearly working. The numbers proved it. "If you're saying business is business, this just doesn't seem like good marketing to me." Among other things, he said, NBC's public dithering was bound to hurt him even if they now decided to keep him on the "Tonight" show, because NBC was letting the world know they had doubts about him. "I just want to be judged by my performance," Jay said, restating his pledge that "if I'm not doing well, I ought to be out." Leno concluded by saying he really didn't think NBC would do this to him. But he wasn't absolutely sure, and "that's the annoying part."

If not quite the righteous anger that Dan Klores had wanted, Jay had at least gone public with how annoying it was to be in this shaky position. Jay had gone on the offensive; he had taken his fight to the press—and he was not going to stop there. The next step was to call the many NBC affiliates he knew well, whom he had helped by providing promos or anything else whenever they asked. Once he felt free to express his feelings, Jay was going to express them to anyone who would listen.

In New York, most of the executive group was preparing for their escape for the Christmas holidays; many of them, including Bob Wright, headed to the Rockies for their families' annual skiing trip. Wright had other plans as well. He knew he would be sharing the slopes in Aspen with an important contact—Michael Ovitz. They had agreed to get together one day during the holidays to talk about a new proposal for David Letterman.

Some of the other New York executives who were backing Letterman began to get a bit nervous as Leno's PR campaign started rolling in the press. They hoped that Wright would get together with Ovitz fast and get a deal done before some of the added pressure from Jay's campaign with the press and the affiliates started to erode Wright's resolve.

At 6:45 on Christmas Eve, Mike Ovitz was in his Aspen condo with his family, getting ready for dinner after an exhilarating day of skiing. They had only just arrived; nothing had happened with Wright, and the two men hadn't even set a day yet for their meeting. Ovitz didn't have Letterman or any other business on his mind. Nothing ever happened on Christmas weekend; everyone was away, everything shut down, even in Hollywood.

So when the phone rang, Ovitz immediately thought of trouble. When he heard it was David Letterman on the line, his concern grew. In the back of his mind, he wondered if Letterman had heard something he hadn't heard from NBC.

But when he got on the line, Letterman greeted him so affectionately that Ovitz knew this wasn't about a crisis. It was about something else.

"I'm just sitting here at home," Letterman told him, and Ovitz immediately calculated that it was 8:45 in Connecticut, rather late on Christmas Eve, and Dave was home. He hoped he wasn't stewing but relaxing. He sounded relaxed.

"I'm here in front of the fire," Letterman said. "And I decided I wanted to tell you something. I just wanted you to know that I never felt so good in my life. Things are going so well for me. I feel secure and well protected. And I think I have you to thank for it. I just wanted to call and tell you that."

Ovitz had represented many of the most glamorous and powerful stars in the world. He had been thanked in person by scores of them and even, occasionally, on the stage on Oscar night. But he never stopped appreciating the sentiments; and from David Letterman, a star he hadn't even known before they started this adventure together, the words were especially affecting.

Ovitz thanked Dave and told him they would be talking soon. They wished each other a happy holiday and hung up.

For all the reasons that Rick Ludwin had for supporting Jay Leno over David Letterman, he made his case most passionately on the different ways the two stars responded to the needs of the network. Ludwin had had personal experience with those differences. In one episode, Ludwin had encountered a vivid example of Letterman's treatment of NBC executives that he would never forget, chiefly because of what it did, not to him, but to another NBC executive.

Sissy Biggers had been with "Late Night" for its entire run on the air. She was the network executive assigned to the show, which meant she sat in on the tapings and once in a great while raised a question about some word that was said or some piece of material that crossed a boundary of taste. Biggers was also responsible for "Saturday Night Live," but that was just once a week in the TV season; "Late Night" was a year-round assignment. For the most part it was a year-round joy for Biggers, who loved working with the show. It meant staying somewhat late in New York every day instead of getting home to her husband and two little daughters. But Biggers had a deep commitment to Letterman. She sat each night on the "back deck," as the last row of seats in the control room was called, showboating with everyone and marveling at the incredible Letterman talent.

In the early years of the show's run, Biggers was responsible for putting together the parties that followed each year's anniversary special. She took great pride in trying to top herself party after party. Dave came to the parties, usually reluctantly, and every year Biggers would look forward to the kind word he always had for her. It was social; it was outside the pressure of the nightly grind; and Sissy Biggers cherished that nice moment with Dave.

In February 1992 the anniversary show was something truly special—a celebration of Dave's tenth year on the air. Even in the midst of his deep estrangement from NBC—and this was before any of the pitch meetings, when Letterman was still feeling scarred by the rejection of not getting the "Tonight" show—this was an huge network event, set to be one of NBC's biggest draws in the February sweeps month. The big show was set for Radio City Music Hall, where Dave would do two tapings on a Saturday night, with the broadcast show, to air the following Thursday, a mix of the best moments from each taping.

The parties had been removed from Biggers's direct jurisdiction by this time; NBC Productions thought they had gotten much too costly and now handled the budget for them itself. They were, of course, much smaller than they had been when under her direction. And the invitations were left to the Letterman people.

Several weeks before the event, Jack Rollins, Dave's manager, who was then also the executive producer of the show, stopped Sissy one night to tell her that the tenth anniversary party was being held after the second taping at Michael's Restaurant, and that she should bring along her husband. Rollins also told Sissy to let Rick Ludwin know about the party. Ludwin came into town shortly after that, and Sissy told Rick there would be a party at Michael's. Both Biggers and Ludwin subsequently got goofy photocopied invitations from Rollins's office.

The Friday before the taping of the anniversary special, Biggers got a call in her office from Jack Rollins. He clearly sounded uneasy as Biggers greeted him on the phone.

"Sissy, it's Rollins," he said. "Um, I really don't know any other way to say this, so I'll just come right out and say it. Um, I'm going to have to uninvite you to the anniversary party."

Biggers's breath was caught short; she was stunned to silence by the impact of what Rollins had just said.

"I'm really sorry," Rollins said. "But I was going over

the invitation list with Dave and, well, when I got to the NBC people, he felt it was really inappropriate for you and Rick to be coming to the party, that the party is really for the people who really work on the show."

The people who really work on the show. The words cut through Biggers like a propeller blade. And the pain went deeper when Rollins went on to add that "only Rosemary Keenan would be coming to the party." Keenan also worked for NBC. She was the publicist assigned to "Late Night," whom everyone on the show liked enormously. Rosemary was on a lower rung at NBC than Sissy, but she had passed Dave's test of "people who really work on the show." Sissy hadn't. She had been put into the same classification as Rick Ludwin—the NBC enemy.

Biggers knew how she was supposed to react: She was supposed to be polite and professional. She was that kind of person; she was brought up that way. "I see, Jack," she said. "I understand this is putting you in an awkward position. I will let Rick know. Thank you for telling me." And she hung up the phone.

It was a devastating slap in the face for Sissy Biggers, who had cared so much about Letterman's show, tried so hard to see that he was happy, paid the price of being in New York late each night, of being a mother away from two daughters under five years old. But she had paid it happily, because she believed so strongly in David Letterman.

She cried all the way home on the train.

The next day, when Ludwin got to town, he tried to comfort Biggers, telling her he could understand why they would do this to him, but he just couldn't accept the fact that they would do it to her. He spent the day telling her over and over, "Me, yes. You, I don't understand."

That night Bob Wright turned up with his wife, Suzanne, and went to the first taping of Letterman's special. He found Dave's assistant, Laurie Diamond, and asked her innocently if there was going to be a party afterward. Diamond realized Wright did not know anything about the showdown over NBC invitations and that she was thus completely on the spot with the president of NBC. Diamond did the only thing she could; she said she had to check with Dave. Letterman, caught up in the pressure of doing two shows at Radio City, just told her to go ahead and invite him. So Bob Wright and Rosemary Keenan would represent NBC at the tenth anniversary party of "Late Night with David Letterman."

In between Letterman shows, Wright walked over to studio 8H in 30 Rockefeller Plaza to take in that night's edition of "Saturday Night Live" and he ran into Rick Ludwin. Wright, again innocently, asked if he'd see him over at the Letterman party. Ludwin then told him the story of how he and Sissy Biggers had been disinvited by the Letterman people.

After the party snub, Ludwin would always have an incident he could pull out of his pocket to demonstrate just what NBC had to deal with in David Letterman.

For Biggers the episode provided carte blanche not to give a damn about David Letterman anymore. But she never really felt that way. She never stopped waiting for Laurie Diamond to call up and say "Dave wants to see you," so she could hear him apologize. Then she could be polite and professional, the way she was brought up to be, and say, "Oh, stop it, Dave. It's fine."

Even though they shared a hill in Aspen, Mike Ovitz and Bob Wright did not have their face-to-face meeting until the first of the year, the last weekend they were together in Colorado. There had just been too much going on earlier, with so many other people in the industry in town for the holidays—all the parties and the other social occasions with business associates and friends that had to be attended.

During the whole period, Jay Leno's campaign for his job raged on. He granted other interviews. *USA Today* had a story on the subject for three days running. The *Miami Herald* ran a story that suggested the matter might not be resolved until after the top NBC executives attended a GE retreat at Boca Raton in the second week of January. On December 31, the *Los Angeles Times* led its "Calendar" section with a story about the near-unanimous affiliate support for Jay Leno. In an informal poll of station managers, all said Jay was doing just great. Most of them echoed with startling precision the arguments Leno himself had made: He was broader-based than Letterman; he had improved the young demographics in the time period; the numbers were there.

And Jay was even using the heavy press coverage of the cold shoulder he was getting from NBC management to excellent use on the air, mocking NBC for their indecision. In one monologue joke, he revealed that NBC really stood for "Never Believe your Contract." Jay's feistiness reminded a lot of viewers of shots they had heard another late-night host taking at NBC. But they were playing very well for Jay, and only adding to his increasingly potent case on his own behalf.

At various vacation spots the NBC executives on Letterman's side exchanged worried phone calls all week about the impact this PR bombardment might be having on Bob Wright. They also began asking who else might be talking to Wright and what they might be saying. They suspected that he was still undecided enough about what to do that the latest information he had might be the information he took to the meeting with Ovitz.

Their suspicions were confirmed soon after the meeting. Ovitz placed a call to Peter Lassally and Robert Morton in New York. They had eagerly awaited this call, hoping it would bring the news that Wright had asked Ovitz what it would take to get Dave to drop the CBS offer and sign on for the "Tonight" show.

But Ovitz said no, he didn't have a deal offer from NBC yet, but he did have something different to report. He told Lassally and Morton that Wright had brought along a shopping list of sorts, made up of complaints about Dave's response to various requests by NBC and its executives. It was all about how Dave was generally uncooperative; how he fought over every little thing, even the promos and the guests; how NBC needed to be able to book guests from its shows on the "Tonight" show, and they simply couldn't have Dave resisting or then agreeing only to go on the air and pick on somebody that NBC needed to promote. And, one thing Ovitz said Wright really wanted to know: How can NBC be sure Dave will really sell the show and be a team player when he still does things like excluding entry to his anniversary party to NBC executives?

Lassally stared down at the phone in stunned silence. He didn't know whether to scream or laugh out loud. Refused NBC executives entry to a party? Lassally knew exactly the incident that Ovitz was talking about because he had spoken with both Ludwin and Biggers about it at the time. He had even told Dave that this was a terrible thing to do, that he was wrong to treat people like that and should apologize. But *this* was what Bob Wright was discussing with Mike Ovitz in their desperate, almost last-minute negotiations on the slopes in Aspen? Lassally was simply dumbfounded.

"I can't believe this was brought up as a major issue," Lassally said to Ovitz.

Ovitz did not sound as mortified by it as Lassally and Morton were. They were almost coming out of their skins. Ovitz sounded as though it were an issue that had come up and had to be addressed before he could go forward with anything with NBC. It was Bob Wright saying there can't be any more stuff like that party thing with Rick Ludwin if Dave is going to get the "Tonight" show.

All Ovitz could do at the time was assure Wright that with Lassally now on board—Lassally, the voice of reason—those kinds of things wouldn't be happening anymore.

Peter Lassally wanted to dismiss the incident as too silly for consideration. But after he talked with some of his NBC contacts, he knew that Wright had indeed gone to Mike Ovitz and made an issue out of Dave's snubbing Rick Ludwin at the party. The Letterman backers could only conclude that the Leno supporters in the West had gotten to Wright before the Aspen meeting and run all this stuff by him as a way to confuse the issue again.

For Lassally this was incredibly deflating news. Not only had Bob Wright not come to Ovitz in Aspen with a firm offer for David Letterman, he had come there with a laundry list of complaints about him. Instead of courting Letterman, Wright had all but insulted him. Lassally had hoped to return from vacation and hear from Mike Ovitz that a deal for the "Tonight" show was nearly wrapped up. Instead, he was hearing that a deal might be more distant now than it had been just two weeks earlier, when Bob Wright left the "Late Night" offices nodding in agreement that Dave should have the show. Far from being wrapped up, everything he and Dave had hoped for seemed about to unravel— thanks to the most ludicrously insignificant of threads: a party invitation.

10

CHOOSE YOUR PARTNERS

When he got back to Los Angeles from Aspen on Monday, January 4, Michael Ovitz, a patient, confident man, told his associates at CAA that he believed NBC would be delivering an offer for David Letterman sometime that week.

While it was true that Bob Wright had spent time at their meeting in Aspen exploring Letterman's reputation for being difficult, seeking reassurances that Dave would be cooperative with NBC if it took the enormous step of removing Jay Leno and giving Dave the "Tonight" show, Ovitz came away from the meeting feeling that Wright was inclined to try to make something happen with Dave. Wright had surely been pleasant to Ovitz and thoughtful about the difficulties of finding a combination to the lockbox NBC found itself in. Ovitz had told him, "I've been dealing with talent for 25 years. When talent is rejected it requires special handling. You can't give the show to Jay and then say nothing to Dave about it. That just isn't done." Wright said he understood. But nothing definitive had been settled.

Wright clearly still had reservations, as did Ovitz. The circumstances guaranteed that this deal could not be clean; no one was likely to escape unscathed if NBC decided to overturn its now eighteen-month-old decision to give Leno the "Tonight" show franchise. The question Wright was wrestling with was the same one that preoccupied Ovitz and his colleagues at CAA: How is it going to look if David Letterman suddenly replaces Jay Leno? Ovitz was simply petrified by the prospect of the story being interpreted as a display of arrogant power by Letterman: "Dave buries Jay Leno with his demand for the 'Tonight' show." To have Dave perceived in the press as destroying his old friend Jay and driving him out of television for a year or two, or however long, was not just the opposite of a "value-added" deal; it was potentially a public relations disaster. Ovitz knew the press could be extremely unforgiving of stars who took on the image of bullies. He could envision how well it would sell newspapers if they promised details of the "Leno-Letterman war." The press would have a field day with something like that, Ovitz thought. And he knew that Letterman himself was uncomfortable at the prospect of that outcome; Dave didn't want the fulfillment of his dream to be accomplished only over the bleeding body of Jay Leno. Letterman said it explicitly: "I wouldn't want somebody angling to get my ass out of a job. I wouldn't want the job that way."

So the issues were extremely delicate, and Ovitz came back from Aspen weighing them carefully. There was a way for Dave to get the "Tonight" show without accepting the blame for shoving Jay out of his chair. But it would entail NBC accepting the blame itself. The network, after all, still had specific language in Dave's contract that allowed it the opportunity to match any offer. If an NBC deal for Dave could be fairly described as a direct match with CBS's, then the interpretation would simply be that David Letterman had no option: He legally had to accept the NBC deal. But CBS was the unknown factor there; the network had negotiated in good faith and made a spectacular offer. If Dave accepted a proposal from NBC that truly did not reach the financial levels of the CBS deal, what might happen then? Nobody thought CBS would sue, because Howard Stringer and the network's other executives would surely recognize that the only relevant issue in a talent deal like this is: Where does the client really want to be? But would CBS feel it had been dealt with unfairly? And how would that affect the press and public reaction to the Letterman takeover of the "Tonight" show?

Ovitz had been considering all of that, along with his own steadfast conclusion: CBS made more sense, and always had from Day One.

Ovitz felt especially good about one thing: The situation was working out precisely as he had predicted it would when David Letterman walked into his office in August 1991. He had been told he would get an array of offers from all over the industry to choose from and that they would include proposals from every network, including NBC. With less than two weeks to go before the NBC deadline, only the NBC offer had still not arrived; but Ovitz was fully confident it would. Bob Wright had indicated to him as they left Aspen after New Year's weekend that he still wasn't sure exactly what he was going to do about Letterman, but, yes, he was going to do something.

Wright just needed a little more time. In the next several days he would be consulting with all his important executives in the same place: a meeting for the top managers of the General Electric Company held every year at the Boca Raton Resort Hotel in Florida.

The General Electric Company held two management meetings every year. One, the Partners' Meeting, was always scheduled for the first week in October, and dealt with issues of concern to GE's worldwide operation. NBC, one small division of the industrial super-conglomerate, only sent five or six executives—the heads of its divisions and Bob Wright—to the Partners' Meeting. The other meeting, always set for the first week of January in Boca Raton, was much broader, with the 500 top managers of the company invited. NBC's representation grew to include most of its senior vice presidents.

As they prepared for the meeting, the NBC executives on either side of the Leno-Letterman battle marshaled their arguments, anticipating one last confrontation over the late-night decision. The Boca meeting, which was designed to discuss the company's large-scale business agenda for the coming year, was not an ideal place for a problem of singular focus to NBC. It certainly would not be on the official GE agenda. But the NBC executives knew they would all be in the same place at the same time, and could easily set up a meeting late at night, after the official business of the day had been concluded.

On Monday evening, before the first official function, the GE welcoming dinner, Bob Wright invited two executives to the lounge for drinks. Wright was fresh from his meeting with Ovitz and still on a quest to determine the best course for NBC. He wanted to talk to Pier Mapes, the network division president in charge of affiliate relations and sales, and Betty Hudson, the senior vice president of corporate communications and his top PR executive. Hudson had always impressed Wright with her trenchant comments about programming whenever new NBC pilots were screened for reaction from the full executive body. He valued her opinion as a nonprogramming executive with a sensitivity to how matters would play in the press.

Over drinks, Wright told Mapes and Hudson that he wanted to hear what they had to say because he didn't believe they were as invested personally in the Leno-Letterman outcome as many of the other executives. He went through a long, tortured explanation of where the situation stood and how it had reached this point. For the first time the other two executives heard confirmation that Leno had been formally in place to succeed Carson because he had signed a contract with NBC just days before Johnny's official announcement to resign. They realized that that deal, signed because of NBC's fear that Leno would jump to CBS, had set all these subsequent events in motion.

Wright took note of the beating NBC had been taking in the press for mishandling Letterman in the first go-round. Now, he said, all they could do was put blinders on and find a solution. If some way could be found, even at this absolute last minute, to keep both guys at NBC, the network could wipe out every bad late-night moment of the past two years. Wright revealed that he was hearing regularly from Ovitz that there was a way to keep this alive, that there was still hope. The door isn't shut, Wright told Hudson and Mapes. They presumed Wright was getting some message from Ovitz that Letterman might be willing to compromise on his demand for 11:30, though Wright didn't say so. For reasons that came down to loyalty for Hudson and keeping the affiliates happy for Mapes, both executives supported Leno.

Later that night, after the welcoming dinner, the NBC group that had arrived by that point met in a small business suite overlooking the Atlantic. Because he had to take care of some entertainment division business, Warren Littlefield was still back in L.A., due to fly in the next morning. They hooked him in to the meeting by conference call. He sat in his office in Burbank along with Rick Ludwin and joined the discussion on a speakerphone. In the suite in Boca Raton were Wright, Hudson, Mapes, Rohrbeck, Ebersol, Rick Cotton, the general counsel for NBC, Agoglia, and several other executives. The discussion began with Wright asking what the guys on the West Coast wanted to say. Littlefield very succinctly made his points: Jay's our guy; we believe in him. And he added that over the long haul Jay would be a more stable personality than Letterman.

Ludwin jumped in to say that the Dana Carvey thing was looking good, which set off a violent disagreement between him and Dick Ebersol, who argued that anyone who would say that didn't know anything about the reality of the Carvey situation. Ebersol said that they ought to pick up the phone and immediately call Lorne Michaels, who would tell them that Carvey, if he's going to do late-night television at all, would only do a show behind Letterman, not Leno.

After that hot moment cooled down, the argument shifted to the persistent disagreement over which host would truly command the biggest—and the youngest—late-night audience. Rohrbeck had received his research study from the Magid Company just that week, and for the Letterman executives it was another round of ammunition. They described it as clearly stating that Letterman would be the favorite in the late-night competition if all other things, such as clearances and starting times, were equal—which, of course, they would be for Dave if he got the "Tonight" show on NBC.

But Wright felt the research was still unconvincing. It was as though one study said one thing and the other said the opposite, and they just seemed to cancel each other out. That night's discussion ended without a resolution of any kind, but the executives agreed to meet again late Wednesday night, after the formal GE sessions ended. Then they would have a long meeting, Littlefield would be on hand, and the whole late-night issue could be totally thrashed out.

Inside CBS, the state of uncertainty had created a dizzy feeling of trepidation and excitement. Howard Stringer went through his days oscillating back and forth between confidence and pessimism. All through the holidays and into the first week of January, Stringer found himself suspended on tenterhooks, vulnerable to whichever way the rumor breezes were blowing that day. He knew that NBC was mounting a serious effort to keep Letterman. That, he expected. But when he talked to Ovitz and Lee Gabler at CAA, they never wavered in their calm stroking of his jangled nerves: Stay cool, they kept saying. You're going to get him. It's going to be okay.

Stringer appreciated the words and all their kindness. That same month, he and Jennifer adopted a baby boy, their first child, whom they named David (not after Letterman, Stringer announced; he wasn't going that far in his wooing). Ovitz and Gabler sent their congratulations. But the reassurances from CAA didn't reduce Stringer's anxiety, because he knew Bob Wright always had the last card to play, and so all the reassurances in the world didn't mean a damn thing. Stringer tried to buoy his own spirits by putting himself in the position of the guys he had come to know at the Letterman show, Peter Lassally and Robert Morton. And Stringer thought: "If I were the Letterman guys, I would not want him to go to the 'Tonight' show under these circumstances." Stringer comforted himself by replaying how badly NBC had bungled its relationship with Letterman. Stringer had never seen such a cataclysmic failure of talent relations in his entire television career. That had to have had some impact on Letterman, Stringer thought.

But he knew he must be prepared for the worst. And in as upbeat a way as he could, Stringer tried to consider his options. From the start, Stringer had felt that CBS was in an ideal position. First he had gone after Leno, and that had forced NBC's hand: They had to give Jay a contract to keep him at NBC, but that contract set in place the alienation of David Letterman. Stringer didn't have a strategy from the beginning to win Letterman in that fashion, but it seemed to be working out that way.

At the start of the negotiations for Letterman, Stringer considered ABC to be CBS's main rival, but only if that network was willing to give up on "Nightline." Had that happened, Stringer would have been ready with a CBS News version of "Nightline" within twenty-four hours. Now, with NBC dithering about whether to keep Letterman and jettison Leno, Stringer contemplated another possibility: turning around and handing the CBS late-night slot to Jay.

That scenario appealed to Stringer at first as a decent consolation for losing Letterman, because he could see advantages in positioning Leno as the unjustly aggrieved star. That might work out. Stringer pictured himself taking the battered Jay under his ample wing, relaunching him as the hardworking star who had been unfairly squeezed out in the power play at NBC.

Certainly Leno believed he could still turn to CBS. That was one of the threats he made public in his late-December interviews in the *New York Times* and elsewhere: He wouldn't simply accept some sort of demotion at NBC; he would go immediately to CBS. Jay never added, "If they'll still have me," because he had reason to believe CBS most definitely would. By that time Jay had had indications of CBS's ongoing interest.

The Leno option was viable enough at CBS that Rod Perth, the CBS executive in charge of late night and the one who had first made contact with Jay when CBS made its run at him two years earlier, suggested to Stringer that it might be wise to keep a line out to Leno, just keep a dialogue going. Stringer told him to go to it.

So Rod Perth called Jay Leno in the midst of the final uncertainty at NBC. Perth put the call in the context of the casual friendship they had struck up over motorcycles. "I'm really sorry you're being put through all this," he told Jay.

Jay responded in his usual "aw shucks, I understand" sort of way. He was so patient and understanding that Perth found himself wishing for Jay's sake that the comic could come on a little stronger, at least be irritated enough to say: "This sucks, doesn't it? It's really bullshit and I'm fed up with it." But that wasn't Jay's way.

Perth didn't make any promises that Leno could count on a CBS offer, explaining that for obvious reasons the network had gone after Letterman and still hoped to get him. "But if it doesn't happen," Perth told him, "sit tight."

Those words made Leno confident that he was still sitting pretty with CBS, confident enough that he could overtly threaten to jump to that network, taking his formidable ratings with him, if NBC were foolish enough to throw him over for Letterman.

Inside CBS, George Schweitzer, the executive in charge of promotion for the network, felt the situation was cloudy enough that he needed to consider the Leno alternative as the final days of Letterman's NBC contract dwindled down. Schweitzer found himself doing mental flip-flops about which outcome was better and which was worse for CBS. For Schweitzer it was like a game of mental Ping-Pong, thinking through the promotion campaigns. "Okay, say we don't get Letterman," Schweitzer thought, his conclusions shaping themselves almost identically to the arguments going on inside NBC. "We get Leno instead. How do we sell him? How do we position him? So he's the underdog, he's the good guy. He'll do a lot more. He'll be out there. He'll do a lot more for you. But he doesn't have the comic edge. He doesn't have the image of the guy who's more electric." Like everyone else at CBS, Schweitzer was certain the network would be better off with Letterman, but he had to be ready if CBS wound up with Leno.

Howard Stringer did not want the backup considera-tion of Leno to reach anything close to a serious stage, however, because he had begun to have strong reserva-tions about whether Jay could walk away unmarked after being ejected from the "Tonight" show in mid-flight. The question of whether Jay would carry around a "damaged goods" label became much more troubling. And besides all that, Stringer never wanted it to get out that he was sitting back like a Roman emperor waiting to pronounce as champion whichever gladiator came out of the ring. In thinking practically about helping CBS in late night, Stringer didn't want to appear cyni-cal. He also didn't want the Letterman people thinking he didn't care if Dave chose CBS or not. At this point Howard Stringer, who had thought out all the benefits a talent like Letterman could bring to CBS, burned with the desire to be able to stand up in front of a room full of reporters and make the announcement that David Letterman was coming to the network of Ed Murrow and Jack Benny.

• • •

Jay Leno had always felt he worked best under pressure. In his own image of himself, he was a tricky, resourceful guy who got where he was on willpower, hard work, determination, and a willingness to stick out his ample jaw, even if it meant somebody occasionally knocked his block off. Once unleashed by the urging of his PR man, Dan Klores, Leno had turned the save-Jay campaign into an all-encompassing PR onslaught. The affiliates were energized, giving interviews to all their local papers about their support for Jay. The audiences on the show were primed to roar every night when he took shots at NBC; even the guest interviews were clicking better as guests had fun with the craziness surrounding Jay. Leno seemed to drop Letterman's name whenever he could, telling stories about what he and his good comedy friends had done at some point in their careers and always including Dave in that group. When he was telling the audience one night about the goofy gifts he and Jerry Seinfeld and other comedy friends had given another comic, Larry Jacobsen, for his wedding, Jay dropped in how his friend Dave had sent the happy couple a set of snow tires and a pile of meat.

Leno wasn't sitting back and letting his fate play out; he was taking action, fighting back, and that felt good. Jay felt as though he were on a roller coaster and the ride felt bumpy but exhilarating. As his Burbank allies prepared for the Boca Raton meeting, they congratulated him on how well he was handling the situation, especially on the air. Littlefield said, "Look, the world is reading about it and talking about it. You're in the eye of the storm, so you're taking some shots at us. You know what? That's fine."

Jay had concerns, of course. He thought about his writers and other staff members, many of whom had quit other jobs and moved their families out to L.A. to work on his show. Some had bought houses; Jay himself guaranteed home loans for some of them. He cringed at the prospect that his fate might put all these people under financially.

But he also thought about Helen Kushnick. If NBC dropped him now, Jay knew, Helen was going to be going around saying she was right, that the NBC guys and the other members of the Hollywood boys club had been out to get her and Jay all along, and without her there to outthink and outtough them, they had made it happen. Jay thought enduring a vindicated Helen would be the worst thing of all.

So it wasn't all fun. There was a daily battering of doubts. But Jay knew he could take the blows. "I'm not particularly strong," he liked to say. "I can just get hit a lot. I can get hit all day long. And you can keep on hitting me." The fighter that Leno most admired was the legendary Jake LaMotta, made mythic by Robert De Niro in the film *Raging Bull*, because Jake could get hit so much and keep on coming at you.

As the Letterman deadline approached, Jay was ready to keep on coming at NBC. Working his phones, Jay tried to dig up useful information every day, something he might be able to use. Most of his calls started with the phrase: "So what do you hear?" And what Jay learned made him realize he had to keep on the offensive, not let up. His allies told him how hard Wright was working to find a way to keep Letterman, how uncertain they still were about the outcome, and how important the meeting in Boca was likely to be.

David Letterman had gotten a similar message about
the importance of the Boca meeting from his executive
producers, Peter Lassally and Robert Morton. Their
contacts inside the NBC hierarchy were telling them
much the same thing: The deal isn't over; it's going to
be argued out at the GE conference. Lassally was hearing that things were shifting every day: Bob Wright was
struggling to make the final decision; the East Coast was
battling with the West Coast. When Letterman heard
all this, it sounded to him like a Mafia meeting with the
various families struggling for power. And it struck him
how silly this had all become. All this over a television
show—though in his heart he knew the television show
in question was anything but silly to him. And he
couldn't help himself: He was caught up in the excitement. It was like a tight football game with the clock
winding down. Letterman found it unbelievably tense
and exciting to be in the middle of it.

Ovitz was providing reassuring words whenever
Dave needed them. Something seemed to be cooking
with NBC, he said. Still Letterman resisted the urge to
get his hopes up. As he analyzed it, NBC had every reason to hesitate over this decision. It seemed like a knot
much too tangled to untie at this point, after so much
had been done, so much had transpired. How could
NBC go back into it now and make it all come out
straight and clean?

For Morton and Lassally the question of an NBC
offer still came down to: How will it be engineered?
Knowing that a perception already existed of David
Letterman as a spoiled, arrogant star, they shuddered at
the thought of fighting a defensive action against the

PR campaign Jay Leno would mount if he lost the "Tonight" show to Dave. Every press story Jay did from that point on, they guessed, would be dominated by accounts of how the nice guy had been assassinated by the mean guy. So they were into engineering the assassination as carefully as possible—with no blood on Letterman's hands. Morton worked his contacts in the press as best he could, emphasizing the NBC contract stipulations and how that contract, and not what David Letterman had demanded, would determine what happened. But that was a hard version to sell, because the story simply read better as star versus star.

Overall the two producers expected the decision to come down to dollars and cents. This was GE they were dealing with, after all, and a bunch of NBC executives who were making every decision with their heads twisted around to watch their own backs. To commit to Letterman now would require an enormous outlay of money, not only to match the pile CBS was promising to shell out, but also to pay off Leno's contract. The deal could be worth $14.5 million in the first year to Letterman, plus another $10 million or so to Leno. Would GE *ever* authorize NBC to spend that kind of money on one guy? The idea struck the Letterman producers as almost too absurd to contemplate.

And they concluded that nobody could make the call to spend that much without thinking long-term, because it only made sense as a long-term investment. That's how they had pushed it to Ludwin and the others: Think down the road. Johnny Carson had owned the time period for thirty years. Take Letterman, they said, and he'll tower over any competition that comes along for at least another ten years, maybe twenty. But they were sure that argument would never fly with the NBC executives like Warren Littlefield, whose prime-time schedule was so shot through with holes that he had to worry about where he'd be in ten weeks, never mind ten years.

A friend of Lassally's had told him that all network heads of programming are short-term thinkers, just by the nature of the job. They have to worry about prime time every week, and every sweeps month, and every development season, and every new fall schedule. They don't think about the next ten years, or even the next five. All that instant pressure was amplified for the programmer of a network with trouble in prime time.

Morton and Lassally also worried about the nature of the commitment to CBS: What exactly did the contract promise CBS, and what had Mike Ovitz promised? That issue had the potential to get messy if NBC didn't come up with something that fit the legal definition of a match. The Letterman side still wanted NBC to come through, but they all had strong reasons to insist it be a deal that came substantially close to the ante that CBS had tossed on the table. Like all the others, they looked south, toward Boca Raton, and waited for the smoke to rise.

After taping his show on the night of Wednesday, January 6, Jay Leno dashed down to his dressing room to get out of his suit and back into jeans and a workshirt, his offstage uniform. The postmortem for the night's show, usually quick, was especially perfunctory this night. Jay heard the staff talking as he changed. One of the producers observed that Rick Ludwin wasn't there, as he usually was. Another staff member explained that Rick had said earlier that he had to take part in a conference call with Boca later that night. He had gone back to his office until he got word that the conference call was going to start. Then, Rick had explained, he and Eric Cardinal, the head of research for NBC on the West Coast, would meet up in Warren Littlefield's office to take the call on the speakerphone.

As soon as Jay had changed clothes, he told Jimmy Brogan that he'd see him as usual back at the house later. Brogan, Jay's good friend and a writer on the show, always came to Jay's about midnight to help put together the next night's monologue. Jay then told the other writers and producers gathered in his dressing room that he was taking off right away, so they could all split early. Saying some quick "see you tomorrows," Jay grabbed his shoulder bag and bolted.

The "Tonight" show dressing room was one floor below ground level in Burbank. Leno dashed up the stairs, out into the broad hallway behind the stage, and then outside, down the ramp toward the alley between the studio building and the main NBC office building. At a little past 6:30, the January evening was still warm in the valley, the sun having set only an hour earlier. Jay didn't need a jacket. He reached the black Chevy pickup he had parked that morning in the "Tonight" host spot located right at the end of the ramp, pausing only a moment to pull something out of his bag before he tossed it into the truck's cab. Then he turned and headed across the alley toward the two glass doors that amounted to the back entrance of the NBC headquarters building in the Burbank complex. Jay pushed through the doors and into a short hallway that led to the elevators on the right. A few feet ahead were two more doors and the main security desk for the building.

Jay was carrying a notebook under his arm. As he entered the back entrance, he didn't bother with the elevator, but turned sharply and took the stairs, making sure not to catch the eye of the guard behind the desk. He climbed the stairs quickly, up to the second floor, where the NBC entertainment division executives had their offices. Most of the office doors were closed. It was getting close to 7:00 P.M. and the place seemed completely cleared out. Jay didn't pause to look for anybody. He moved quietly down the long hall toward the big heavy glass doors that blocked the entrance to the executive suite of offices at the end of the corridor. On the doors, etched into the glass in gold lettering, were the names: WARREN LITTLEFIELD and JOHN AGOGLIA.

Jay paused at the doors only long enough to scan the outer offices. The two desks behind the doors were unoccupied. The room looked empty and dark. Jay pushed his way in. Warren's office, Jay knew, was off to his left; John Agoglia's was to the right, past the area where John's secretary sat. Jay moved almost on tiptoes to his right, past the desks of Warren's assistant and secretary and into the room where John Agoglia's assistant and secretary worked. Jay knew where he was going. He slipped past the secretary's desk toward a door at the back of the room. Jay tried it; it opened.

The room behind it was small, dark, and crowded like a closet; it contained a photocopying machine, fax machines, a shredder, and all sorts of supplies stacked in boxes. Pushed up against the wall was a small desk where guests of the executives could come and sit to use a phone in private. Jay carefully pulled the door closed behind him, making sure it was securely shut. Then he eased himself down into the chair and arranged his notebook on the desk in front of him. He pulled a pen out of his pocket. His setup was complete. He had the phone in front of him to tell him when the conference call from Boca Raton was coming in; now all he had to do was sit in the dim light in this cramped closet of an office—and wait.

The official good-bye dinner for the GE group who was leaving the next morning ran later than expected that Wednesday night, so the NBC executives eager to get into the Letterman-Leno debate one last time were forced to wait until well past 10:00 P.M. Finally they began to gather in a much less accommodating business suite than they had for their Monday night meeting. This one had no windows, bad lighting, no air-conditioning to speak of, a beat-up wood table in the middle of the room, and a small cache of warm Coca-Colas to drink. It was going to be a long, hot night.

Things got going about 10:30. Littlefield had contacted Ludwin back in Burbank and told him the conference call was about to start, so he should order in some pizza and call Eric Cardinal. They could sit around the speakerphone in Warren's office and wait for the call. In the session in Boca were Littlefield, Agoglia, Rohrbeck, Ebersol, Hudson, Mapes, Cotton, Warren Jensen, the chief financial officer for NBC, and Bob Wright.

As the meeting began, several people asked Agoglia if he had heard anything from Ovitz that day. Agoglia had nothing new to report. Bob Wright then asked a few people to give their opinions of how they thought the network should go on late night. Various people began offering their perspectives on the two stars. The debate fell along familiar lines: Jay got points for his agreeable attitude; Dave got points for sheer talent. Leno still had the ratings on his side, however, while the Letterman backers had only their opinion that, head-to-head, Dave would overmatch Jay, especially in terms of pulling in the crucial younger viewers. Over a speakerphone from Burbank, Ludwin was extolling Jay's improving performance and his increasingly cooperative attitude.

That raised objections from Ebersol and Rohrbeck, who questioned many of the choices Jay was making on his nightly show. Speaking partly to the others in the room and partly directly to Ludwin in the speakerphone, Ebersol, referring to twenty years' experience as a late-night producer, hit especially hard on the selection of musical acts and how they were placed in the show. How did this square, he wanted to know, with Jay as the totally agreeable prince of a guy, willing to cooperate with every suggestion, when he had been told repeatedly not to place musical guests in the first half of the show? Music tastes had become so stratified, with so many different styles broken down into so many groups of people, that few or no acts could ever hope to please all of the viewers at the same time—particularly when a viewer had a choice to turn off the set and go to bed. And yet, Ebersol and others pointed out, here was Jay on a recent night bringing on Neil Young as his opening guest, as though Young was a booking coup. This was in defiance of all the research, which said that people tune in late-night shows to see comedy, comedy, and more comedy. And what did Letterman give them? Comedy. An opening with a couple of jokes, an inventive comedy bit before the first commercial, and then the "Top Ten List," a third comedy segment before even one guest was brought out. And that first guest was *never* a musical act and was always someone that Dave worked for more comedy, Ebersol said.

While they were at it, the pro-Letterman group wanted to know why Jay Leno had a band playing forty seconds of esoteric jazz after his monologue, bringing down the audience's readiness to laugh right after Jay had done seven minutes of jokes. How was this going to affect the show, they asked, when the greatest competitor in comedy is on another channel doing something funny in those forty seconds? And what about this announcer, Edd Hall? Why couldn't Jay have a sidekick on the couch, someone he could connect with and bounce jokes off?

In Burbank Rick Ludwin would not tolerate this kind of criticism of his star. He defended Edd Hall, saying with an edge in his tone over the speakerphone that if anybody had to sit on the couch with Jay, Edd certainly could. As for comedy, Jay had begun to work his "celebrity in a sack" routine to good advantage. And, Ludwin said, Jay's opening monologue was the best seven minutes of comedy on television. Rick Ludwin was vociferous in his all-out defense of Jay Leno.

The meeting spun off into a more clinical discussion of the state of the Leno show and what its potential might be. Why couldn't there be another comedy segment after midnight? someone asked. Sometimes after the first guest the show gets crashingly dull. Everybody agreed the monologue was the best part of the show, but even there Jay was criticized for his hokey air-guitar gesture and big leg kick as the band finished the theme song. Those affectations made him look like a bad Las Vegas act, one executive said. Next, the music was dissected, with some of the executives agreeing it was too rarefied for the contemporary mass audience, and others wondering why Marsalis always looked as though he regretted in some way being in the studio. Jay's interviewing was the most widely slammed part of the show. He still looked stiff and distracted, several critics said, as if he weren't really listening to the guest but was instead checking his notes to see if he could find any funnier questions. Maybe they should hire him an interviewing coach, one executive suggested.

Back in Burbank, outside the office where Rick Ludwin and Eric Cardinal were engaged in this loud argument over the speakerphone, Jay Leno sat in his gloomy closet, listening in very intently, scribbling notes on his notepad. The whole thing struck him as wildly funny; he felt like Huck Finn overhearing the mourners at his own funeral.

Jay didn't feel insulted by the criticism he was hearing. He told himself nothing could insult him, because it was all just product and nothing personal. To him the questions were all about what's wrong with the product. Jay could deal with that. The experience reminded Leno of something he did when he was first breaking into the clubs as a comic. After he finished his spot in the Comedy Store or wherever, Leno would sometimes go to the men's room, get in a stall, lock the door, and then sit on the toilet with his feet up so it appeared that nobody was there. Then he could listen to the comments of those who had just heard his act: What'd you think of that last guy? Jay liked the unself-conscious reviews, if not the accommodations.

In the suite in Boca Raton, Bob Wright turned to Betty Hudson to offer some comments for the group. He knew where she stood, of course, from the session over drinks on Monday night. But he wanted her ideas out for wider discussion. Hudson had given the situation a lot of thought. She had formed a strong opinion. Hudson told the meeting that she saw this question as one that would demonstrate what NBC stood for as a company. The company's loyalty to an employee who had served it well was now the issue, she said.

"Against the criteria of success that we established at the time he got the job, Jay is achieving success," Hudson added. "Could it be a better show? Probably. Would it be better with more time? I guess we'll find out maybe. But we said to the whole world this is our guy. And we put him on the air. And maybe some of the problems are our doing and maybe some are his. But for us to suddenly decide to throw out the loyal dog and put in the guy who has been saying in any forum he can find that he can't stand us, he is sick to death of us, what would that be saying about us? And against the public perception that we are opportunistic, venal shits, against that, what about the next guy you want to make a deal with? You think he or she is going to say: 'I can certainly depend on NBC to stand by its people?' "

And then Hudson said the situation in her mind carried certain parallels to another NBC talent relationship disaster, one that ended up giving NBC an extended scorching in the press and almost destroyed another of its franchise shows. Hudson said this deal reminded her of Pauley/Norville.

It was like opening up a giant scab that everyone had stopped paying attention to and hoped had somehow healed. In the summer of 1989, a move to juice up the increasingly stodgy "Today" show by adding a young, attractive news reader named Deborah Norville had gone humiliatingly wrong for NBC. Norville had been perceived by the press and public as an interloper and threat to the popular cohost of the program, Jane Pauley. Eventually Pauley quit the show, Norville did replace her, and the show went into an immediate tailspin that it only pulled out of after Norville departed and was replaced by a far more popular female host, Katie Couric.

When Hudson invoked the specter of Pauley/Norville, it summoned up images of NBC depicted as callous to its longtime stars, disrespectful of substance, and always looking for something a little sexier and glitzier.

But that imagery truly outraged one of the Letterman supporters, Dick Ebersol, who had been one of the key decision makers three years earlier when Deborah Norville was added to the "Today" show. "Wait a minute," Ebersol said, stopping Hudson as soon as the names were uttered. "How is this Pauley/Norville all over again? You mean to tell me that Letterman, who's been here for ten years, whom you shafted by the way this decision was made in the first place, is Norville and Jay is Pauley? How does that work?"

Hudson said that was how the public would see it,

but to Ebersol there was no way in the world it would be seen that way. He said one segment of the audience might be upset, but another would be pleased no matter which way NBC decided. "You are not going to have the whole world pissed off at you," Ebersol said, "like I did in the 'Today' show mess."

Ebersol and the other Letterman backers argued that this decision should come down to what was the better show over the long haul, what works and what doesn't, and that all the other issues should be tossed out.

But the Leno supporters said the issue of what the host will do and won't do for his network was very much a major consideration. Ludwin, Littlefield, and Agoglia brought back their arguments about Letterman's unwillingness to cooperate. He'll stiff us, they said. He won't go out and do the hard work to help the network. The Letterman backers asked how they could possibly say this with such certainty when Letterman had never been asked to function as host of the network's primary late-night show before.

On and on the argument went, with Bob Wright maintaining a scrupulously neutral position, never tipping his hand, just asking for opinions around the table.

One opinion came from outside the basic NBC group. Jack Welch, finished with the other GE meetings, happened to pass by in the hall in the midst of one heated exchange. He and Dennis Dammerman, the chief financial officer for GE, ducked into the meeting for a short time. Welch listened for a few minutes, then contributed just a few thoughts. He was not a regular late-night viewer, so he wouldn't presume to make a call based on taste in comedy. His essential point was that, as always, he would support the best long-term business deal. However, he said, if the decision seemed to come down to a tie from all angles, he would cast his vote on the side of loyalty.

Jay Leno had hung in there through some tough times, and that made a case for his loyalty. David Letterman's loyalty was being questioned all over the room by the executives who saw him as either nasty or impossible to deal with.

But Littlefield made a more telling point, as least as the Letterman backers saw it. He asked a question about Letterman's stability, based on how he sometimes acted even when there was no crisis to speak of. The tales of Letterman's locking himself in his office after a show, berating himself, and cutting himself off totally from communication with the outside world were well known inside NBC. Now Littlefield and Agoglia wondered out loud: What happens if something goes wrong on the show and we lose contact with this guy? What if something goes wrong for a month? And it always could, of course. There could be technical problems; the lighting could be bad, the camera focus could be off. It was suggested that this could be risky territory in trying to deal with a personality like Letterman.

And the money issue came up. They discussed what might happen if NBC bit the bullet and offered the show to Letterman. What would it really cost? How far did the network have to go to match CBS? And what about Leno? He had told the *New York Times* he would immediately quit to go to CBS if Letterman got the show. If he did, wouldn't NBC be out from under the penalty payment of between $10 million and $11 million it was obligated to pay Leno to settle out his two-year contract? If he didn't quit, would he settle for some smaller increment of the penalty: $3 million, or maybe $6.5 million, his full current salary for another year?

The meeting limped on past midnight. Voices grew softer as they grew tired. Despite all the words the issue still seemed unresolved because Bob Wright had said nothing about which way he was leaning. The voting was clearly heavily on Leno's side. But Wright hadn't heard what he wanted to hear. He wanted to hear how he could keep his whole late-night franchise together, not who was better or who would win. To Wright it seemed that the people backing Letterman liked Jay personally and wanted to see him stay if possible. But to Wright many of the people supporting Leno had not bothered thinking about what it might take to keep Letterman as well. Wright still made the point: "The issue isn't black-and-white. Black-and-white, we lose." Wright knew he would soon be talking to Mike Ovitz, and he had promised him he would come up with some formula for keeping David Letterman.

The group in the suite, exhausted by the argument and hot from the crowded, close room, began to break up. They signed off over the speakerphone with the two executives back in Warren's office in Burbank. Ludwin and Cardinal said their good-byes and punched the line dead.

In the next office, Jay Leno was so edgy and excited he had to hold in his urge to leap up and run out of there. He had sat in his tiny room with the photocopier and shredder and listened in on the entire conference in Boca Raton. He had taken notes on all of it, and now he had specific quotes from specific people on what they thought of him and his show. Best of all, he knew exactly who was for him and who was against him, and what all the arguments were. It had been intense and sort of thrilling, Jay concluded, like the Hardy Boys hiding in a cave to figure out a mystery. Jay was proud of himself. He had taken some action—and he had pulled it off. Staying quiet, breathing softly throughout the meeting, he had heard it all as Ludwin and Cardinal listened to the talk over Warren's speakerphone. At one point the thought had crossed his mind: What if somebody opens the door and finds me in here? But in a second he had laughed that off. "What are they going to do?" he thought, suppressing another laugh. "Fire me?"

Jay sat still and quiet right where he was for several long minutes after the call ended. He wanted to be absolutely sure that Ludwin and Cardinal were out the door and gone. He sat there looking over the notes he'd made as best he could in the near-dark of his little hiding place. After what seemed like half an hour—though he realized it was probably a lot shorter than that—Leno decided he could leave. He carefully gathered up his notes, pulled his chair out quietly, and listened at the door. He heard nothing, so he slowly opened the door and peeked out. The offices seemed deserted. Out he came, the host of the "Tonight" show, emerging from his listening post in the shadows.

As he did, a janitor was just walking in through the glass doors of the executive suite. He spotted Leno slinking through John Agoglia's secretary's office, and he said, "Hi."

"Hi," Jay answered, muttering quickly that he "just

needed to get some stuff up here," while he kept moving right past the janitor, being polite with a "have a nice night, see you," and then strolling out the door, down the hall, down the stairs, a quick left turn, and finally outside, in the alley, near the truck, into the truck, and pulling away. Just like that. A neat, nearly flawless spying operation.

Jay Leno laughed himself silly all the way home.

Jay told Mavis all about it when he got home, and they cracked up together at his sheer brazenness. When Jimmy Brogan arrived about midnight to start work on Thursday night's monologue, Jay told him the story of the closet and included the encounter with the janitor. All the while Jay was laughing, though, Brogan had to wonder if Jay had put himself at more risk than he seemed to realize. It was a wild and strangely thrilling night for Leno. He said, "I know everything. I know who likes us, who doesn't like us. I heard John Agoglia talk about the contract. I heard Dick Ebersol say why he likes Letterman. I heard Wright say he still doesn't know what he's going to do. I heard John Rohrbeck say Dave would beat us in the big cities. I heard it all!" As Leno described it, it sounded like a kid's prank: listening in on the stairs as the adults revealed their secrets.

The next day Leno couldn't resist playing with his inside information. When he saw Rick Ludwin, he cornered him and said, "So John Rohrbeck's a big Letterman fan, huh?" Ludwin tried to bluff his way through it, saying that that wasn't necessarily true, that there were people supporting both sides. So Leno told Ludwin he knew what Rohrbeck had said about him, and threw a few of Rohrbeck's lines out just to see Ludwin's face go ashen in disbelief. He also mentioned that whatever happened he would never just quit this job—and, by the way, he certainly wouldn't settle for a payout of his salary, making sure to mention the exact figures that had been thrown out as what he might be willing to accept as a settlement. He didn't tell Ludwin how he knew what he knew.

Mostly Jay wanted to reach Warren Littlefield, but the meetings had resumed in Boca Raton and Warren wasn't available. Jay kept calling back all day, trying to catch Warren in his room. Much later in the evening he called and tracked Warren down to one of the meeting rooms. He found out he had just missed him; Warren had told people he had to jump back to his room for a minute.

Jay made a supposition, and waited just a minute or two before dialing Littlefield's room again.

Warren wanted to make use of the first little break in the long day and evening of meetings. He got back to his room, tossed some of his material on his bed, and headed straight for the bathroom. Just as he sat down, the phone rang. There was an extension near the toilet in the bathroom.

"Hi Warren, how're you doing?" Leno said.

"Okay Jay, how are you doing?" Warren said pleasantly, not really surprised at a call from Jay.

"So Warren," Jay continued, "you probably just had a long day of meetings and you walked back to your room to take a little break, probably, you know, throw your stuff down, and you walk into the bathroom just to relieve yourself, and God, what do you know? Here it is, I'm on the phone."

At this point, Warren Littlefield started looking into

the mirrors for a hidden camera. "Jay!" he said in total amazement.

But Jay, knowing he'd hit it big time on his supposition, just kept rolling. "I gotta tell you, Warren. I sure hope that GE protects its nuclear weapons better than they protect their late-night secrets."

Littlefield laughed nervously and asked Jay what he could possibly mean.

"Well, that was quite a meeting you had last night," Jay said, leading into a series of direct quotes of what each individual had had to say at the previous night's meeting. Warren knew he'd heard the words said exactly that way the night before—this was no paraphrase or reconstruction of a conversation. This was *exact* wording.

"Holy shit, Jay," the stunned Littlefield said. "Where the hell do you get your information?"

"Well, I may look dumb," Leno said, "but you know, I am Italian. We know how to get information." Jay was having a field day with poor Warren, thanking him for comments he had made, asking about other comments, laying out the sides in the arguments precisely.

Littlefield was totally blown away. By this point he was looking under the toilet for microphones. Shaken, he started fumbling for words, telling Jay the thing wasn't over yet, he should hang in; but he should definitely *not* talk about what he had heard in the meeting with anyone else. Jay thanked him again and hung up.

In his office in Burbank, Leno burst into laughter. He couldn't believe how perfectly he had hit it with Warren in the john.

But in Boca, Warren Littlefield was in a panic. He

didn't go back to his meetings. Instead he sat in his room and tried to figure out who had leaked this to Jay Leno—and how they did it. Jay knew everything. When Warren checked in with his office, his assistant, Patty, started listing the messages he had received. She told him of some calls made about a potential deal—and Warren suddenly told her to stop talking. "We can't be sure the lines in this hotel are protected," he said to his bewildered assistant.

Later Littlefield called home. Theresa wanted to go over the events of the day with him, especially about how the late-night story was totally dominating all the news, in the papers, on the radio, on television. It was all anyone was talking about: Jay Leno, David Letterman, and you guys in Boca. "And so what's going on?" she asked.

Warren told her he couldn't discuss it. Theresa was taken aback. What did he mean he couldn't discuss it? Warren told her he thought his phones had been tapped. "Warren," she said. "You work for NBC, not the CIA."

"Listen," Warren said. "I've never been paranoid about anything. But I just can't discuss this. I don't know what's being listened to."

After he hung up, Littlefield tried to sort it out. How had Jay found out all that? Who was talking to Jay? It was a career-risking move as Littlefield saw it. He didn't know who to talk to about it, so he chewed it over for awhile, and as he did, he started getting more and more paranoid. Much later that night, he finally decided he had to talk to someone about it, so he called Betty Hudson in her room.

Betty was already in bed when the phone rang. She

had just turned out the light, so she sat up in the dark and picked up the receiver. When Warren said hello, she could tell right away he was shaken up.

"Betty, we've got a big problem," he said. He was speaking very low, as though afraid he might be overheard. "I don't know what's going on. I just hung up with Jay. We have a leak of such proportions. Jay knows everything. He knows who said what to whom. It was more than just somebody called him and told him about the meeting. It was like a recorded tape being played back."

Both of them thought of Ludwin, with his intense loyalty to Jay. But Littlefield could hardly believe an executive he trusted like Rick would put his career in jeopardy by giving all this privileged information over to one of the subjects of the meeting. Warren knew he would have to call Ludwin about it. In the meantime all he knew was that he was going to keep anything important about NBC and its decisions completely to himself until he figured this thing out.

At dinner on Thursday night in Boca Raton, the NBC group talked passingly about the late-night question, but not in anything like the depth of Wednesday night. The next day, Friday, they all finished their meetings in Boca with some discussion about what would be on the agenda during NBC's own management meetings to be held in the Westchester County business retreat in Crotonville, New York, the following month. One concept they were working on was replacing the President's Council meetings with something called the "Executive Programming Council," in which a small group representing NBC's entertainment, news, and sports divisions would get together for a conference call every Monday morning to spill everything active in the network out on the table for quick discussion.

After most of the NBC executives headed for the airport, Wright convened a much smaller group one last time in the hotel business suite for some final thrashing out of late night. A group of the eight highest-ranking NBC executives gathered for about twenty-five minutes and made some final plans. Wright told them he had made a decision: He was going to take a run at keeping Letterman. In not very specific terms, he gave John Agoglia some instructions: Go back to California and make the best deal you can with CAA. The executives knew that Wright had been talking with Mike Ovitz regularly. They assumed Ovitz and Wright would continue talking and that the framework of an offer was going to come together. Wright and Agoglia would be in constant touch. None of the other NBC executives was sure exactly what Bob Wright had going with Ovitz and how the deal would be structured. But something clearly was about to happen. Despite all the talk for Leno throughout the Boca Raton meetings, and the clear majority of NBC executives who had spoken up for Jay, Bob Wright had looked long-term and concluded he could not allow David Letterman to walk out the door. He had stepped up to the decision. He was going to make an offer to David Letterman that included his taking over the "Tonight" show.

That evening, just after 6:30, David Letterman was back in his office with his top staff members, going through the usual postmortem of the show they had just completed. A call came through: It was Mike Ovitz at CAA in Los Angeles. Dave excused himself and took the call.

At 7:20 P.M. the main members of the Letterman staff heard the news. One hour earlier, David Letterman had officially been offered the job as host of the "Tonight" show. The excitement went up and through everyone in the room as if the floor had been suddenly electrified. But what about the terms? The terms, as explained by Ovitz, were strange, a bit vague, and more than a little maddening.

NBC was offering a deal that would give Letterman a "Tonight" show with a budget no more than 5 percent bigger than what Leno currently had—so they knew they would not be doing a very expensive show. Letterman himself would be paid a fee that was described as somewhere between his present salary of about $7 million a year and the $12.5 million base salary in the CBS deal.

Immediately, those in the room familiar with the terms of the contracts knew that NBC was in no way offering to match the CBS deal; they were coming in with an entirely separate offer on their own terms.

NBC was promising a three- to four-year guarantee, which was fine. But then came the truly unexpected twist: The deal would not go into effect until May 1994. It was January 8, 1993, at that moment. NBC was offering David Letterman the "Tonight" show after a seventeen-month waiting period.

The May date, as everyone knew, coincided with the end of Jay Leno's current contract. So the implication was clear: NBC wanted to avoid paying off Jay. He could stay until the end of his deal, with Letterman sitting on his shoulder waiting to step in, or he could quit and forfeit his $10 million penalty payment.

Ovitz was not simply presenting the NBC offer. He couched all the details in terms of "CBS is offering this, NBC is offering that." But he did say the magic words: NBC will give Dave the "Tonight" show.

The others in the room could see the flame of excitement ablaze in Letterman's eyes as Ovitz said the words. But Ovitz went on, following the details of the offer immediately with his analysis—and his recommendations.

With CBS, you have to figure out how they are going to handle the affiliate situation, Ovitz said. CBS could not guarantee anywhere near the full affiliate lineup that NBC could in the first year, but Ovitz pointed out that CBS had momentum in prime time for the first time in six or seven years, and clearly that momentum was almost certain to carry over into better relationships with its affiliates. Next, Ovitz said, there is the downside to the "Tonight" show. Leno had reached about a 4.9 rating, Ovitz said. If Dave were to take over the show and fall below that figure, it would be immediately perceived as real trouble. That was something to consider seriously, Ovitz pointed out. The CBS situation was just the opposite, he said. Its late-night lineup was only doing about a 2.7 rating. If Dave could reach a 3.9 rating on CBS, CAA could go back in and renegotiate his contract, because he would already be a big winner at the network. Another issue was ownership, Ovitz said. With CBS, Dave would own his show; NBC was going to retain ownership of the "Tonight" show. And with

CBS, Dave's company would also control the 12:30 time period. That led to the overall issue of goodwill. CBS had poured it out by the bucketful in pursuing Dave. NBC had never expended much in the way of goodwill on David Letterman. And finally, Ovitz reminded Letterman and the others, you want to beat NBC's pants off.

For all those reasons the recommendation from CAA was clear: Dave should go with CBS.

Letterman heard him say that, but in truth he had not heard too much after the part about having the "Tonight" show. The dream was alive and there for him to grab.

Peter Lassally had been stopped in his tracks by the bizarre requirement that Dave wait until a year from the next May before he got a shot at the show. He jumped in to make two points: "This gives Jay an extra year and something more to make a hit out of his show," he said. "And if he is a hit, NBC's going to weasel out of the deal with us. And even if Jay is not a hit and we take over, you, Dave, will be the villain who threw Jay Leno out of that time slot."

They discussed how the May date was clearly designed either to force Jay's hand by making him quit, or to give NBC another seventeen months' worth of both stars in late night. In either case, Letterman was absorbing all the risk. If Jay felt forced to quit, there was the likelihood of a major public relations fiasco. If Dave held on while Jay did the show as a lame duck, Dave had to face all the possibilities of something unpredictable happening to him or to Jay in that long period of time.

They went over some of the economics. Since Jay's deal was apparently part of the framework for the offer, they looked at what it would mean. Jay was making over $6 million in salary in the first year of his deal, set to go to $7 million in the second year. The show's budget was at $23 million in the first year, $24 million in the second year. Figuring that they could go up no more than 5 percent, the show's budget wasn't going to reach the $27 million–plus set out by the CBS deal until the last year of a four-year deal.

Everyone tried to guess what NBC was up to with this offer. Was this a sly tactic to save GE a barrel of cash, dreamed up to take Letterman's temperature for Jack Welch? This was where Dave was vulnerable; he wanted the "Tonight" show so badly. So how far would he go toward taking a lesser deal to get a shot at it? Or was this just NBC's answer to undoing the tangled late-night knot? Promise Dave the job; let Jay know, and if he chooses to go to CBS, so be it. Why should NBC have to pay both guys a bundle if it was only going to retain one of them? The consensus started to build that this was an offer for the "Tonight" show, yes, but a convoluted, gimmicky one that had very little to recommend it.

But one key vote seemed to be going against that consensus. David Letterman still had that dreamy look in his eyes. He had heard Ovitz recommend strongly that he go to CBS. But that jarred so strongly with the thrill he was feeling at that moment that he couldn't even begin to say the words: Okay, it's CBS.

For Letterman the moment was one of pure astonishment. He had heard Peter Lassally telling him for weeks that something was happening at NBC, that there was still a chance the "Tonight" show would come around again. But he never truly believed; he wouldn't allow himself to believe. It clashed so violently with his assumptions about the General Electric Company and how the guys who ran a conglomerate like that worked. Letterman figured these were guys who chewed up puny decisions like this and spit them out their noses. But now, to see it actually unfolding this way, where the "Tonight" show was truly being offered to him, struck Letterman as some kind of miracle.

"I can't make this decision," he told Ovitz. "It's every race driver's dream to drive a Ferrari." No one had to ask which late-night show equated with a Ferrari. "You're asking me to give that up," Letterman said.

Ovitz told Dave that they needed to come to a decision. The weekend had started. The offer was out there. They had to respond.

"I appreciate what you're saying and I understand," Letterman said. "But I just can't make this decision. I need to see how my stomach is going to feel for a couple of days."

"There is one thing I can do now," Ovitz said, putting the idea together on the spot. "I can buy some time. I'll get Agoglia in here on Saturday and Sunday and have him start drawing up a contract."

The idea made Letterman howl. It was just so perfect. He howled with laughter and shouted back to Ovitz on the phone, "Yes, get him in there! Get Agoglia in there! I don't want to be the only one whose weekend is ruined. Get Agoglia in there."

Sure, it was an ugly thought, an unpleasant, cruel notion, to have John Agoglia dragging his ass out to CAA on a weekend to negotiate a contract that may not ever come to anything, knowing that as one of Leno's biggest boosters, he didn't even want Letterman anyway. But it made David Letterman laugh with naughty glee. It was just such a hoot: Let Agoglia go in there and spend some of his weekend working on a contract, Letterman thought, while I sit at home in hell trying to decide what I'm going to do.

On Saturday morning Lee Gabler arrived first at the CAA offices. While waiting for the others he flipped on the Buffalo-Pittsburgh play-off game, propped his feet up on the desk, and relaxed. He would be leading the CAA negotiation with John Agoglia. This was not a meeting Mike Ovitz was going to take.

About noon Steve Lafferty, the head of business affairs for CAA, showed up with Jim Jackoway, a young lawyer who had first represented Peter Lassally and then had taken over as Letterman's show business attorney. The three men had known something had been brewing between Wright and Ovitz for some time, and had been preparing some ideas for the offer they expected to receive from NBC. What they knew from the offer that Ovitz communicated to Letterman the night before was that it was still in the vague stage, certainly nowhere near the point where they would have to call Howard Stringer. What the men on the CAA side concluded was that their client wanted an offer for the "Tonight" show and they were there to get the best offer they could out of NBC.

Shortly after noon John Agoglia arrived. He was accompanied by Leslie Maskin, a senior vice president for business affairs for NBC and also an attorney. Many lawyers who had negotiated with John Agoglia felt he was extremely self-conscious about the fact that he himself was not an attorney and had to deal with attorneys on the other side of negotiations all the time.

The football game was zapped off and the group sat down around a table in Gabler's office. Agoglia first explained that NBC was not relinquishing any of its positions with regard to matching rights. Then he laid out the terms of the NBC proposal, which were much the same as what David Letterman had heard from Mike Ovitz the night before. NBC was offering Letterman the "Tonight" show to start at a date no later than May 1994. The "no later than" was totally a function of how Jay Leno was going to react, Agoglia explained. NBC was looking to protect itself, he added. The network had to be concerned with losing advertisers: Should Dave move up to 11:30 immediately, NBC wouldn't have a show to offer at 12:30. This was why they wanted Dave to hang in at 12:30 for awhile. But, of course, if Jay followed up on his threat to quit, Dave would get the show much sooner.

The five participants then speculated on what Jay might do if this deal were accepted, with some of the lawyers suggesting how they would advise Leno were he their client. They all agreed that whomever Jay got to advise him would surely tell him not to quit, because he would be forgoing the huge penalty payment if he did.

The negotiation continued with Agoglia discussing how NBC could offer Letterman's company, Worldwide Pants, a production service arrangement in lieu of taking ownership of the show. NBC didn't want to sign away the rights to the show, but it would grant rights to Worldwide Pants in the production service agreement that would include most of the advantages it would get from outright ownership. What NBC was proposing did not seem unreasonable to anyone on the CAA side. Gabler saw no deal breaker in the ownership issue. Nor was the salary offer for Dave substantially short of the CBS arrangement, he felt.

But the parameters of the deal remained a bit vague. One of the CAA team thought that the promise of hosting the "Tonight" show, as it was presented orally by Agoglia, contained a lot of flexibility. He wondered if the deal would have left it open for NBC to split the job somehow after May of '94, giving Letterman the job for twenty or twenty-five weeks instead of full-time. That and many other questions needed to be answered.

The two sides broke several times during the three-hour-long meeting so that calls could be made for updates with the main players, Wright and Ovitz. When they got back in the room, the CAA side had more questions. Gabler made the point that CAA would need to see some of this give-and-take over the terms of the offer put down in writing so that questions could be framed better—and for the simple reason that if Letterman was going to reject CBS, he was going to need something written down that he could hold in his hand before he took that step. The CAA side asked Agoglia if he could distill the main terms to writing and fax them the proposal on Sunday. He agreed.

Gabler and the others were somewhat surprised that

John Agoglia had been the one to carry the offer, given how they well knew of his strong resistance to making a deal with Letterman from Day One. Gabler thought Agoglia's demeanor was typical: businesslike but icy cold. He seemed at best halfhearted about the offer. But they knew it was coming from Bob Wright, not John Agoglia, and Wright had the only heart that counted.

The substance of the offer on Saturday had not changed much from what Ovitz had communicated to Letterman the night before. So Dave's decision was not made easier in the least. At home in Connecticut that weekend, Letterman made and received dozens of calls. He spoke with his longtime director, Hal Gurnee, one of the steadiest veteran hands on the show. He talked to Jude Brennan, a "Late Night" producer, whose counsel he also respected. He spoke most frequently, of course, with Robert Morton and Peter Lassally, his executive producers, who had ridden the whole, long, choppy voyage with him. All these voices were unanimous: The NBC deal was half-baked, inadequate, lousy. How did this prove that NBC really wanted David Letterman? For all sorts of reasons it didn't match up with what CBS had put on the table.

For Morton, who had a better relationship with the press than anyone else on the show, the outcome of this last-call approach from NBC was fraught with all sorts of danger. He was jumpy because he saw Dave being lured into a situation where he would consider some offer and then NBC would reject him again and the headline would be: "Strike Two, Dave: Letterman Loses Again." Morton considered leaking the news of the NBC offer to the papers so NBC could never say it didn't come scratching around Letterman's door at the last minute, ready to dump Jay Leno. Personally, he thought the NBC offer was his worst nightmare for Dave: a horrible offer that would lead to denunciations of Dave in the press for pushing his old friend Jay in front of a train. He could foresee Jay going around the country giving every interview he could line up and bemoaning the fact that his good friend Dave had taken his job away. When he spoke with Dave that weekend, Morty was completely sympathetic to Dave's desire to get the "Tonight" show; he had wanted the show almost as much as Dave had. What producer in television wouldn't want a shot at doing the "Tonight" show? But he couldn't see taking it on these terms. He told Dave he was voting no.

Peter Lassally was more upset than anyone else by the NBC offer—because he had fought so hard to get it for Dave. But he thought the offer was dreadful, ridiculous, insulting, and embarrassing. It was a bogus offer, Lassally thought, not an offer you give a guy who had made millions for your company. How could they ask Dave to wait until May 1994 to get the job when CBS had a deal ready to go for the summer of 1993? How was this a match of the CBS offer? And yet because he knew Dave so well, he knew how badly Dave wanted to say yes, so that he could have the show he always wanted, even on these third-rate terms. Lassally's greatest fear was that after all this, after the thrill of having most of the television industry at Dave's feet begging to win him over, after the elation at the CBS deal, it was going to be another Dave disaster. It was going to be Dave not listening to the people around him again, or them not getting something right for Dave. Only this time Peter knew he himself was part of the picture, and still Dave was about to step into another disaster. The idea was frightening to Lassally.

And so he called Dave at home that Saturday and argued the points with him. There was no upside, he told Dave. "It's damaged goods," Lassally said. "You're not taking over for Johnny Carson. You're taking over for a show that no longer has any class. That's not worth anything; that's not any kind of victory. We can start from scratch at CBS and it will be your victory and it will be your show and not you're taking over for this damaged show."

Dave trusted Lassally, so his words could not be dismissed. But all Dave kept saying was "I don't know, I don't know."

When Ovitz called he had many of the same arguments about the absence of an upside at NBC. He also pointed out how unimpressive the NBC offer was. "This is indicative of what your future life will be like there," Ovitz said. But he emphasized the positive aspects of the CBS deal: the ownership, the opportunity to produce a companion show at 12:30, the chance to build his own franchise, and to be the spokesman for the network. "CBS is like a train coming out of the station," Ovitz said, suggesting that it was the right time to jump aboard. But he knew that Dave remained terribly conflicted. He urged Dave to keep thinking and wait for the developments the following day, when Agoglia had promised to put some details on paper.

That night Dave was telling himself the others were probably right: It had to be CBS. That was what made sense for him. It had to be CBS. But he asked one more opinion, one that obviously counted heavily with him. He asked his girlfriend, Regina Lasko, what she thought he should do.

Regina, who worked at NBC herself and who had been through all the ups and downs of Dave's interaction with the network as their personal relationship grew through the late 1980s and early 1990s, had witnessed up close the tough days with Dave in June of 1991. When NBC spurned him that first time, when they made Jay Leno the host of the "Tonight" show, Regina watched it break Dave's heart. She had seen him a wreck for weeks with the sorrow of missing out on the biggest dream of his life. So now she said what she thought he wanted to hear.

"I know what this means to you," Regina told him, urging him to go for the "Tonight" show. "And I really don't think anybody has gotten that fond of the guy who's hosting it now."

On Sunday, the Letterman representatives went to their respective offices to wait for the details of the NBC offer to be faxed in from John Agoglia. They had prepared some refinements of the positions as they understood them, trying to be sure that in the process of negotiating with NBC, no other previous agreement could be jeopardized. The basic point of the Sunday exchange by fax was to get something concrete in writing for Ovitz and Letterman to look at and to close up some details that the CAA side found too ambiguous in the original proposal. No one knew exactly where the exercise was heading, but it seemed to be heading toward a real attempt at an agreement.

With all the CAA guys waiting for the fax to ring,

they decided to hook up by conference call. Nothing was happening yet. So they put in a call to Agoglia, who got on the conference call with Lee Gabler and Steve Lafferty in their CAA offices and Jim Jackoway in his law office. They began by talking about some of the adjustments that Agoglia had made, following up on questions that had been raised the previous afternoon. To the Letterman side, it seemed that, given the parameters of the offer NBC apparently wanted to make, Agoglia had come substantially close to what he'd been asked to deliver. Except for one thing: It wasn't in writing.

And it wasn't going to be. After they had talked through some more details, Agoglia got to the substance of the NBC proposal. He read it through in detail over the phone. When the Letterman people, who had been taking notes, threw out a few more questions, Agoglia cut them off. He told them that they really had it all by that point, that they knew what was available, what was out there, and they could massage this along from there. You know where we are, Agoglia told them. You know how to try to make this work, and there isn't going to be anything sent. Nothing is going to be faxed.

The CAA team did not object to that position. They had waited several hours for this fax to come in, and now Agoglia was saying, no, nothing in writing. They concluded that Agoglia felt NBC was in a delicate position, what with Jay Leno's fate hanging in the balance in these talks, and that the network wanted to preserve a level of deniability. NBC could not feel secure about that deniability if they knew somewhere out there a piece of paper on NBC letterhead documented that the network had offered Jay Leno's job to David Letterman in an explicit, term-by-term offer. Frankly the CAA executives didn't mind helping NBC out to spare them possible further embarrassment with Jay, because they themselves didn't want CBS to get word of this and think they were about to be cut out.

Without paper, the offer was what it was: a promise of the "Tonight" show down the road. The promise at least seemed solid. The Letterman negotiators came away from the Sunday conference call convinced NBC had made a substantial commitment to give Letterman the job at some point in the future; they simply hadn't put it in writing.

The Sunday negotiations did nothing to change the equations, or the uncertainty. Letterman, who was being informed of the developments almost hourly, had not been handed a Get Out of Jail Free card; he had no new information to make his agonizing decision easier. It was going to come down to just how strong the dream still was.

The sentiment opposing the NBC proposal was unanimous from the staff members of the show and Dave's agents at CAA. Ovitz and his CAA partners pointed out that even taking into account what Dave wanted emotionally, what was being offered by NBC was not really going to satisfy those emotions. He would get to do a television job for NBC in Burbank—eventually—but it certainly wasn't a job that would make him the successor to Johnny Carson. Was NBC really offering him Johnny Carson's job? No, they were offering him Jay's former job, and they weren't even doing that for some period of time. Unfortunately, they told Letterman, it was too late to get Johnny's job. It was not available now or ever anymore. It was forever changed and gone.

But Dave had come to a point where he couldn't deal with all that rational analysis. "I can't say no," he said.

When Lassally talked to Dave that evening after the meeting with Agoglia, he knew that there was now a very good chance David Letterman was going to accept the NBC offer—against the advice of everyone around him. He was going to say yes. Dave's conviction was clearly growing. He didn't care what everyone else was saying. "I want the show," he said to Peter.

Lassally was in a panic. He had brought Letterman to this point where he was about to jump back into NBC, into a position Lassally now considered disastrous for his career, and somehow Lassally had to pull him back from the edge before he leaped. His own influence seemed to be waning; so did Morty's and even Ovitz's. They were powerless against the dream. Lassally needed reinforcements. He knew that the list of people who could have any real influence over David Letterman was exceedingly limited. But he could certainly think of at least one name.

Johnny Carson had been reading the papers; he knew that NBC was up against a deadline to keep David Letterman and that the top NBC executives had been meeting in Boca Raton amid much speculation over what they would do. Johnny had nothing but good feelings about Dave; he considered him a true entertainer, someone with style and attitude, all of which made him invaluable on television. He also just liked the guy. But Johnny had no ill will toward Jay Leno, whom he considered a very nice young man, and he was very good friends with Bob Wright. When Wright had called three weeks earlier looking for advice about what do with the Letterman/Leno situation, Johnny had said he wasn't jumping into the middle of that dispute at that late date, though he urged Wright to find a way to keep Letterman.

Now Peter Lassally was on a different mission. He called Carson at his Malibu home and filled him in on NBC's last-minute offer, the differences between what NBC and CBS were proposing, and why it was so wrong for Dave to throw away everything CBS was offering for the inferior, specious deal being put forward by NBC. Lassally told Johnny only a few details, including the fact that ownership would not be involved. He never even got into the money. He just communicated that it was a half-assed, unworthy offer. He asked Johnny if he'd talk to Dave about it.

Carson reacted as Lassally expected. He agreed that the offer sounded weak. But this wasn't an easy spot for him. He didn't like to get involved in sticky deals like this. There was no upside for him. Lassally pressed him, stressing what a crucial moment this was in Dave's career, and how much Dave respected Johnny. Johnny said he'd think about it.

When Lassally got back to Letterman, the star hadn't changed his intentions. He was leaning strongly toward taking the NBC offer. Lassally called Carson back. Johnny was still thinking about it. Then he called a third time, and finally, after a tough fight, Johnny said he would talk to Dave about the deal. "But I don't want to volunteer," he said. Dave would have to call him.

Lassally thought he had to have an alternative if Dave felt too uptight to call Johnny about something this personal. The only other name he could think of was Grant Tinker, the former chairman of NBC, the leader in the network's great glory days, who had been in charge of NBC when Dave started his late-night show. Lassally knew that Dave respected Tinker, as did he. So he called Tinker and filled him in on what was going on. Tinker agreed that NBC was playing games with Letterman. Lassally asked the former chairman if he would tell Dave that, and Tinker, without hesitation, said of course he was prepared to talk to Dave if he wanted to call.

Then Lassally went back to Letterman. Call Johnny, Lassally told him. Ask him what you should do. Dave was reluctant. Then call Grant Tinker, Lassally said. He thinks it would be a mistake to take this deal. And he gave Dave the number.

That was too much for Letterman, who started to believe that Lassally was loading the deck, searching out people who would counsel him to turn NBC down. This was an effort to spoil his dream, Letterman thought, to muddy the facts as he understood them. He would never question Peter's loyalty or that his motives were good. He was sure Grant Tinker would be sincere. But he simply didn't want to hear it. It was just torture for Letterman because he felt as if he might have blown one opportunity to get the "Tonight" show, and yet here it was, back again. "Am I dumb enough to blow it again?" he thought.

"Why are you doing this to me?" he snapped at Lassally. "Don't you understand? I don't care. I cannot lose the 'Tonight' show twice, once to Jay Leno and once because I'm not accepting the second chance."

Lassally said he really did understand Dave's feelings. "But *you* have to understand," he said. "The conditions are not right."

Letterman had never been so conflicted in his life. He knew he had to tell Ovitz which way he was going. He had very little time left. He was running out of new ways to analyze it. But he still needed help.

So he called Johnny Carson.

Carson took the call and listened for awhile to Letterman and the jam he was in, then he asked if he could think awhile about it and call Dave back.

All the other votes were in; the impact of all those recommendations that he reject NBC and pick CBS was slowly eroding some of Letterman's holdout emotions. It was getting late on Sunday night and Dave was starting to waver. Then Johnny called back.

"You have to do what's best for your career," Carson told Letterman. "Do what's in your heart." The problem for Letterman, of course, was that in this instance those two sentiments didn't precisely coincide. He asked Carson what he really wanted to know: "What would you do if you were in this situation, Johnny?"

Carson didn't dodge the question. "I'd probably walk," he said. "I'm not telling you to do that, David. But if you're asking me what I'd do if I had been treated like that, I would probably walk."

Letterman was always terribly nervous when he spoke to Carson, and he had rarely in his life been as nervous as he was at this moment. So Carson's words didn't completely register. What he came away from the conversation with was the same message he had heard from everyone else: Go to CBS. Even Johnny wasn't saying the "Tonight" show was everything. If anybody knew a little bit of what this was all about, it had to be Johnny.

It was time to make his decision. Letterman had started to see how imbalanced the two offers were: The CBS deal was just so much better. It had to be CBS. And he knew he had to put away the dream. It was there for him to grab, but he had to put it away.

When it all calmed down, Letterman made one more call that night. He dialed the Indianapolis number and got his mother on the phone.

"Mom," he said, "NBC has offered me the 'Tonight' show, but I think I'm going to go to CBS."

"Well," said David Letterman's mother. "I just hope you know what you're doing."

When NBC heard nothing in reply to its offer that Sunday night, a bit of fear set in. No one wanted this deal to leak to the press, and certainly no one wanted to be used by the other side for a public relations coup. By the next morning, even as CAA was ready to inform NBC that David Letterman had rejected the offer, John Agoglia called Steve Lafferty at his CAA office and told him NBC was withdrawing the offer.

That morning David Letterman came into the "Late Night" offices and found Peter Lassally. Dave was bent nearly in half with the weight of second thoughts. "I think I've made another huge mistake," Letterman said, over and over. "I've made a huge mistake. I took my dream as a kid and fucked it up once, and now I've fucked it up again." For Lassally, it was, as it so often was with Dave, a back-and-forth, up-and-down experience. It was to be expected that he would be overcome with buyer's remorse.

Then Letterman talked to Ovitz again. And Ovitz told Letterman a story about how he went out and bought a house—and he really couldn't afford the house, and so he was miserable in it for the first month, for the first two months. His kids were miserable, they were all miserable. And then he said: "I'm still in that house. It's the best house I ever lived in. It's the best thing I ever did in my life. Don't look back," Ovitz said. "Just keep going."

And David Letterman decided you can either be brave or pretend to be brave, but it's pretty much the same thing.

11

THE SECOND FRONT

I n New York, David Letterman had hours and hours of anguish all day Monday over the decision he had made to surrender his dream of hosting the "Tonight" show; but those around him knew that was Letterman's nature. He would replay the decision again and again, the same way he replayed the tape of his show every night, checking every nuance, rethinking every line, kicking himself over every lost opportunity. But in the end the show was going to air. And Letterman's decision to go to CBS was going to stand.

In Los Angeles that same Monday, Jay Leno felt a surge of relief. He had gotten a call from Bob Wright telling him that he should relax, things were going to work out. It immediately struck Jay's comedy instincts: He was supposed to celebrate because he was getting a job he already had. "It was a question of hey, either you're going to be fired or else you're going to be the guy to lead us into the next century!"

Jay's nature was *not* to replay shows or events in his life—especially bad ones. He always tried to stay buoyant, look forward, not back. This was show business, he told himself, and he was coming to expect the hard knocks and inanities that went with this line of work. Not that Jay could totally shrug off the way he'd been kicked around. In the aftermath, Jay saw it as another sobering show business experience. "Show business is a bit like guys that say, 'You know, that hooker really likes me,' " Jay said. "When you've been in it twenty years and you've gone through things, you get slapped down a few times. After a while you don't mind getting hit anymore. It's just part of the business. But it does take a part out that doesn't come back. It's a bit like: You'd do anything for the woman but love her again. There is some of that in there. You lose a piece of heart."

Just after noon Pacific time that Monday, in the middle of a lunch he was sharing with a tableful of newspaper reporters at the Loews Hotel in Santa Monica, Howard Stringer got a message to call Michael Ovitz. Stringer, who was in L.A. to address reporters taking part in a press tour to publicize upcoming CBS shows, had been fending off questions about the Letterman deal all morning. He excused himself from the table and went to the nearest pay phone, where he heard the word from Ovitz: The last-minute NBC effort looked as though it had fallen through. NBC had not relinquished its rights yet, and so nothing could be announced. But the network's negotiators were already talking about coordinating times with CAA so NBC could hold a press conference with Jay that Thursday, the 14th—one day before the official Letterman deadline expired. Ovitz was suggesting that CBS hold its own press conference in New York the same day.

Stringer hadn't planned on that, but he was agreeable. He was in the mood to be agreeable with anything Mike Ovitz said. What Stringer was hearing was that it was all but certain CBS had Letterman—and he was trying to figure out how to stand at a public pay phone in the middle of a hotel lobby teeming with reporters and resist the urge to bellow: "Yes!"

Later that day Stringer met with other CBS executives in his room at the hotel and discussed the network's plans for the official Letterman announcement Thursday. The only thing NBC seemed interested in negotiating with CAA now, he told them, was the timing of the press conferences; they wanted to go first. CAA had said that would be okay. Some of the CBS executives were concerned that NBC might use the press conference to trash CBS or put down Letterman. But Stringer told them not to worry, because both he and Ovitz knew that NBC had made a serious run at Letterman. "If they get ornery about this," Stringer told his executives, "we can say that NBC was out there just days ago making offers to keep Letterman and dump their own guy."

For the NBC executives who had supported keeping Letterman, the news that Monday of the collapse of the negotiations brought frustration—and questions. From what they were hearing inside the company, John Agoglia might not have gone as far as his charge from Wright allowed him to in his negotiations with CAA. As they understood it, Wright would have allowed Agoglia to move up the "no later than" starting date for Letterman on the "Tonight" show from May of 1994 to December of 1993. Had Agoglia really been flexible in his offers? More than that, they asked: Why was Agoglia, known to be as committed a Letterman foe as there was inside NBC, the man charged by Bob Wright to go out and reel in Dave at the last minute? Why couldn't Wright have designated a different negotiator for this delicate deal? Maybe Rick Cotton, the general counsel—or anyone who could have gone to the table without the baggage of hostility the Letterman supporters felt that Agoglia brought because of past dealings with Dave.

But they also wondered about what had happened on the Letterman side, because they had heard the word that was spreading from the NBC negotiators: that NBC couldn't get anywhere that weekend because of opposition from those around Dave who stood to gain much more financially from a deal with CBS than from an offer to stay at NBC.

Agoglia had made the same point to Bob Wright. Agoglia's take was based on his own long experience as a Hollywood negotiator. When looking to scope out why a negotiation takes the turns it takes, he said, "My answer is: Always follow the trail of the dollar bills." The NBC executives looked at Mike Ovitz and saw an agenda: What was in it for Ovitz to keep Dave at NBC? But they looked at the others close to Letterman and saw the real impediment to holding on to Letterman. The CBS deal, Agoglia and the others concluded, was going to pay Letterman's key staff members so much more money that, as Agoglia put it, "there was no incentive for his people to convince him to stay. It was like: 'Hey, Dave, look at CBS.'"

Littlefield and Agoglia speculated specifically about

Peter Lassally and Robert Morton and what the CBS deal was allegedly going to be worth to them. "Think what this means to them," Littlefield said. "Doubling their incomes." And Agoglia added, "More than doubling." They suggested that the top production salary on the show would grow from about $1 million a year at NBC to about $2.5 million in the new CBS deal.

What made NBC even more convinced that Peter Lassally was a prime obstacle to the network's bid to keep Letterman was the presence at the CAA offices, during what Agoglia came to call "the Lost Weekend," of Jim Jackoway, the attorney for Lassally. Bob Wright made it clear in his own postmortem of what had gone wrong with NBC's last-minute offer that "lawyers for all kinds of third parties entered the picture."

What Agoglia and Wright apparently didn't realize at the time was that Jackoway was present at CAA that weekend as David Letterman's lawyer, not as Peter Lassally's lawyer. Jackoway had quietly replaced Jake Bloom that fall when Letterman and Lassally decided Dave should have someone with more television experience, someone who could almost function as an in-house lawyer. Jackoway had extensive experience in the television business and was prepared to devote a large percentage of his time to Letterman's interests. Bloom was one of Hollywood's most highly regarded lawyers, but he was mainly a top-echelon film industry attorney.

Morton and Lassally knew that NBC was blaming them for the failure of the effort to win back Letterman, but they scoffed at the idea that it was self-aggrandizement that motivated them to steer Dave to CBS. Lassally had helped instigate the campaign inside

NBC to match the CBS offer. Nothing would have satisfied him more personally than to march back into the offices in Burbank in triumph with Dave at his side. Lassally and his wife longed to move back to their Los Angeles home. All that was possible only with an NBC deal. As for Morton, he said he had a dream as well, a producer's dream: to run the "Tonight" show. As a single guy he already felt he had more money than he would ever need. His motivation, he said, was what would be best for David Letterman.

Morton and Lassally also became the targets when NBC needed to point a finger at someone for leaking the story of its last-minute offer to Letterman. Early that week, as questions from the press started coming in about what had happened over the weekend between NBC and CAA, John Agoglia and the other NBC executives took a vehement position: They said they had made no offer to David Letterman that would give him the 11:30 time period. No offer, no "shading" of an offer, they said. They had never in any discussion offered 11:30 to Letterman, they said. Never had they put a financial package together for him; never at any time in the course of any NBC action did they make an offer to David Letterman for the "Tonight" show.

Agoglia and others at NBC raised questions about who was behind the leak that NBC had offered 11:30 to Letterman. One NBC executive made reference to "a number of people around Letterman who ingratiate themselves to him and tell him who his enemies are." These people were floating the story of an offer to Dave, the NBC side suggested, because they didn't want it to look as if Dave had been rejected again.

Lassally and Morton, however, had been warned by CAA to keep away from the press with this story. Neither producer initiated any calls to reporters about the offer to Letterman and the weekend debate over whether to accept it.

Those who had been personally involved in the tense negotiations the weekend before at the CAA offices were not surprised to read NBC's adamant denials. The CAA negotiators understood that NBC was in an awkward position. The press coverage in repeated stories over several weeks, most suggesting that the network was considering removing Jay Leno and installing David Letterman, had already done untold damage to Jay's image. With the Letterman dalliance finally finished, NBC was about to tell the world that Jay Leno was their late-night champion and always had been. The PR campaign to bolster Jay was about to begin. Stories about the closeness of the last-minute encounter with Letterman would only undermine that campaign. The CAA side understood all that. Still, one member of the Letterman team said bluntly of the NBC denials: John Agoglia did not tell the whole story.

Agoglia's position in the aftermath of the negotiations was that he was in a room with David Letterman's representatives, and so scenarios were discussed that he believed those people wanted to hear; he explored every avenue to keep Letterman, he said, with all kinds of different configurations. But none would have dug the ground out from under Jay Leno, he noted. When put on the spot as to whether any NBC proposal in all these configurations would have given Letterman a shot at the "Tonight" show, Agoglia said: "Maybe if we had canceled Jay, David would get a shot at it."

But the CAA representatives said that they would never have negotiated a deal for Letterman that didn't completely guarantee him the show—and that's what was on the table in the offer John Agoglia presented to them.

By the time these stories were breaking, Agoglia and Littlefield had problems beyond dealing with all the recriminations about the offer the network made to keep Letterman. That Monday, as soon as they knew the 12:30 slot was definitely going to be available, NBC made formal its offer to Dana Carvey to take over "Late Night." As much as they had talked about Carvey to Bob Wright as their ace host in the hole, they had not been able to offer him the show formally because of the proposal still on the table at CAA to keep Letterman there until as late as May 1994.

The Carvey alternative had been consistently held out to Wright as the West Coast's answer to a 12:30 vacancy. This continued even though Carvey's manager, Brad Grey, had fired a warning shot across NBC's bow the previous December when he told the *New York Times* that the network did not have the long-term contract with Carvey that it had announced it had. When rumors surfaced at the same time that Carvey might also be negotiating with CBS for its own 12:30 slot following the new Letterman show, NBC took it as Grey pulling a negotiating stunt.

Every time Carvey's name had been mentioned as NBC's savior at 12:30, network executives close to Carvey said the comedian would never do a show behind Leno. One member of "SNL" explained the confusion by saying, "What the West Coast guys don't realize is that Dana is a comedian. He wants to see people smile.

So he tells them something to make them smile, and then when they're gone he says: 'Get me out of this.' "

By midday Monday, January 11, NBC had formalized its offer to Dana Carvey in a call to Brad Grey: Dana could have the 12:30 show starting sometime that summer after Letterman's exit on June 25. It was certainly an offer welcomed by Grey, an ambitious, hotshot young talent manager. Grey had built an impressive stable of comedy stars with Bernie Brillstein at the agency that was now named Brillstein/Grey. The list included Garry Shandling, Mike Meyers, Dennis Miller, and George Wendt. In a twist destined to have unpleasant repercussions for NBC, Grey also represented Lorne Michaels, the executive producer of NBC's "Saturday Night Live." That meant Grey was well aware that in Michaels's last contract Lorne had won a clause that gave him "first look" rights to create a show for the 12:30 time period if Letterman ever left it vacant. Grey felt Letterman's move to CBS—opening both the 12:30 spot on NBC and creating the need for a show to come at 12:30 on CBS—would throw the late-night market into flux. And he knew Brillstein/Grey was especially well positioned to ride in with the new tide.

Grey had told the NBC executives all along that the late-night hosting job was something Dana Carvey would consider when it was offered to him. He never doused their hopes, nor built them up. But the NBC West Coast executives, especially Littlefield, who felt he had a close relationship with Carvey, believed they were getting strong indications of interest from Dana.

They were wrong. Almost as soon as the offer was formally delivered to Grey, the answer came back. Carvey said no. Grey found NBC's immediate expressions of dismay a little out of place. After all, he told them, Dana at no time said he would for sure take the job if it were offered to him. If NBC was getting that message, it was the wrong message, Grey said. When NBC howled something about being taken advantage of, Grey was nonplussed. How could he and Dana Carvey take advantage of the General Electric Company, for God's sake?

Certainly Warren Littlefield believed he had gotten assurances that Dana could be counted on. Suddenly, the after-Letterman option that he and John Agoglia thought was solid had evaporated into mist. NBC had just gone through the catastrophe of losing the second-biggest star in the history of late-night television, and now the network had nothing, absolutely nothing, in hand to replace him. It was Bob Wright's worst nightmare coming true. When he heard the news about Carvey, a picture formed in Wright's imagination: David Letterman's boat sailing over to CBS and Dana Carvey sailing out into the Pacific.

Among the executives inside NBC who had aggressively supported Leno in the face-off against the Letterman backers, questions were now raised, especially about John Agoglia and his negotiating tactics. "Knowing all the fragility of the late-night situation," one senior executive said, "and then not to have locked up Dana, how could that happen? Not just this year. I mean a year and a half ago he should have locked him up."

One producer who frequently negotiated with Agoglia said he wasn't surprised the Carvey deal was never really a deal, because Agoglia often played it so cute in negotiations, trying to give the network the edge, always keeping certain options open, making sure there was an out. A longtime, close NBC associate said, "Agoglia has a lot of bluster and then when you ask to see the bill of sale, it's questionable."

With Carvey taking a pass, Littlefield had no name to announce as the replacement for Letterman at the Leno press conference, which was scheduled to take place just three days later. It was going to be: Jay didn't get fired, and no, we have no idea what we're going to do at 12:30. Sue Binford, the head of public relations for NBC on the West Coast, knew that had the makings of yet another debacle for NBC in the press. "You cannot go out there Thursday and say Jay's here, David's gone, and we'll figure the rest out later," Binford told Littlefield. "It would be okay if you just had a creative name to throw out there. You've got to figure out how to get Lorne."

Lorne Michaels had such a prestigious name in late night that saying he would be the executive producer of a new late-night entry might be enough to bring off the notion that all was well at NBC. There was just one problem with the Lorne option: Agoglia hadn't locked him up either. Michaels's first-look deal on a new late-night show left it to his discretion to add another show; he could say no, I'd rather not. No one at NBC had any idea whether Michaels would go for this idea—or how much it was going to cost the network to twist his arm.

"It was just amazing," one senior NBC executive said. "To have made that many mistakes in a row."

Tuesday night, Bob Wright, now sucked back into the pressurized late-night spin cycle, called Michaels himself. Bob and Lorne, though seemingly an odd match on the surface—the hip comedy producer and the buttoned-down GE corporate man—really had found much in common. They were about the same age, and as Lorne fell into a more domestically oriented life with his wife, Alice, the two men had found they had more similar lifestyles and interests. Michaels had come to like Wright as a human being and to respect some of his programming instincts. In fact, he'd wished Bob had followed his instincts more closely and closed the deal for Letterman.

When Wright called that Tuesday night, Lorne was sick with a knockout cold. He was hard-pressed to deal with Wright's shock over Carvey's rejection of the NBC offer. "How could this happen?" Wright asked Michaels. But if he had asked Lorne earlier, he would have heard how unlikely it ever was that Dana would take the spot after Leno. Now here was Wright asking Michaels to step in and save the situation for NBC by allowing his name to be tossed out as the genius who would create anticipation instead of chaos in the transition from Letterman to whomever on "Late Night."

Michaels was certainly aware that he had the first-look option on 12:30. With the Letterman issue aflame inside the NBC offices for months, he could hardly have failed to consider what it might mean for him if Dave went out the door. But Michaels had asked for that clause in his last contract only because he wanted to protect the overall late-night franchise, which he felt was the key to ensuring that "Saturday

Night Live" would continue to thrive at NBC. As far as genuine ideas for the show, Michaels had none at that moment. He told Wright he would have to think about whether he really wanted any announcement that he was to be involved in starting up another late-night show.

By Thursday morning the news had been confirmed everywhere. Jay Leno was keeping the "Tonight" show; David Letterman would be his competitor on CBS starting in August. The media had been invited to the dueling press conferences, with NBC's starting first in the Loews Hotel in Santa Monica, followed immediately by CBS's at their Black Rock headquarters building on West 52d Street in Manhattan.

That morning NBC still had no answer from Lorne Michaels. The network's executives had been practically on their knees the night before, pleading with Michaels over the phone to allow Warren Littlefield just to say his name in connection with a 12:30 show at the press conference the next day. With only about three and a half hours to spare, Michaels relented. He still had no signed deal with NBC to be executive producer of a new 12:30 show, but for Bob Wright's sake, he was willing to allow his name to be uttered—only in a specific context. Lorne dictated the exact language that Warren had to use at the press conference. Littlefield could say that Michaels, the Emmy Award–winning executive producer and creator of "Saturday Night Live," would be "overseeing the development and production of a new comedy hour that will be following the 'Tonight' show with Jay Leno."

With an enormous gasp of relief, NBC's West Coast executives prepared for their grand introduction of Jay Leno as the once and future host of the "Tonight" show.

Lee Gabler had flown to New York to represent CAA at the Letterman press conference scheduled for that evening after the taping of "Late Night." Gabler found Letterman a bit more agitated—and in need of hand-holding—than usual.

The first Letterman had heard of a press conference was that day when he got to NBC to start work on his show. He thought CBS would issue a press release and everyone would leave him alone. Then he heard that Ovitz had forced Stringer to make it a press conference. It wasn't simply that Letterman was reluctant to answer questions about his decision; it was that he was just plain scared. Dave didn't feel as though he had won anything. He knew NBC was having its own press conference right before his, and that only added to the anxiety. The burden would be on him to go over to CBS and tell everybody how happy and delighted he was to be there. Letterman really didn't want to do anything to upset anyone at CBS, because they had showed him so much good faith and had made such a generous offer. But he was still a complete wreck inside. He had just seen the chance at the "Tonight" show go away and he was still mourning the loss. All he really wanted to do after the show was go home and shut the door behind him. He didn't want anything to do with a press conference.

Both press conferences were to be covered that day as though news of enormous national import was taking place: CNN sent crews to cover the events live. Other camera crews from every local television station in New York and L.A., and from "Entertainment Tonight" and other nationally syndicated news magazine shows, all converged on both sites.

At the Loews Hotel, the large conference room was packed with more than 200 members of the press at about 4:00 P.M. Pacific time when Susan Binford stepped to the stage NBC had set up. She told the crowd that NBC was committed to ending its press conference by 5:05 P.M., when the Letterman conference would be piped in to the reporters on the West Coast. The NBC press conference had been a scheduled event on NBC's portion of the January press tour for television reporters. It was not originally designed to cover late night but rather to give Warren Littlefield a chance to address any questions about prime time or anything else involving NBC's entertainment division. NBC had already planned on a gimmick to give Littlefield a boost as he met the press: Binford introduced the cast of NBC's hottest comedy series, "Seinfeld," to put the group in a positive mood for Littlefield.

Jerry Seinfeld and his cast members made cracks about being the only thing working on NBC—and that they were prepared to take over every division of the network themselves. Then Seinfeld, who joked that he would be hosting every show in late night, introduced Littlefield as "the man we're all behind."

Warren wasted no time. He said everyone was there to learn what was going to happen in late night, and lifting his voice to an excited pitch, he said, "The answer is that the host of the 'Tonight' show will continue to be: Mr. Jay Leno!"

Amid applause from the NBC staff members all around the room, Jay roared into the press conference riding a huge, red Harley-Davidson. He was beaming a broad smile, his aquamarine eyes dancing. When he got to the stage, he shook Warren's hand and they shared a laugh. They looked like two guys who had shared a foxhole, weathered a bombardment, and now felt the light-headed joy of coming through unscathed. When he got the mike, Jay hit the crowd with his tested, bulletproof opening line: "Welcome to NBC: It stands for Never Believe your Contract." After that surefire laugh, Jay took note of the live coverage on CNN and asked, "You know what this means? This means Saddam Hussein now has an opinion on this. He's in a bunker going, 'I like Dave, but yet the other guy, I don't know. It's very confusing.' "

Jay continued to have fun at his own and NBC's expense. "You know, Bill Clinton said we will be living in an age of lowered expectations. You people are all here. I *have* the job! What we're celebrating here is: I *haven't* been fired! Okay? Understand that? I already have the job. *I'm not being fired!* Hey, Leno, let's get him down here! Hey, he didn't get fired! Boy, that's great! Good for you!"

In a break from the laughs, Littlefield added that NBC had tried hard to keep both late-night stars, but that in the end David Letterman was only interested in being on at 11:30. "And quite frankly," he said, "we have a terrific host in Jay Leno on the 'Tonight' show."

Jay thanked Warren and said, "Again these words are all new to me, if I look a little surprised. It's the first time I've heard a lot of this, so please indulge me briefly if you will."

Then Warren said it was important to thank David for his eleven years at NBC and to wish him well. "But, you know, in the eight months that Jay Leno has been occupying his new chair, what he has shown to all of us at NBC is just how terrific he is hosting the 'Tonight' show. And we can all see why he will be doing that for a long, long time to come."

"Pending current renegotiations," Leno joked.

After the carefully worded but enthusiastic announcement that Lorne Michaels had agreed to develop the show to follow Jay, Littlefield opened the floor to questions. But before that began Jay said a few kind words about Dave himself, and how he wouldn't have the job at all except for Dave and the exposure he have given Jay on "Late Night." Jay said he and Dave had never had any ego problems and that when he took over the "Tonight" show, Dave was extremely gracious, bringing Jay onto the show so they could shake hands and Dave could congratulate him on the air. "Throughout these whole negotiations this has not been a case of somebody trying to screw somebody else," Jay said. "It's a matter of, hey, it's an important job and everybody would like to have it. I'm glad I got it."

A reporter asked Jay if he felt secure. "In the way that Saddam Hussein feels secure, yes," Jay said. "I think I have a bunker." Jay said people he met on the street had been greeting him sympathetically, as though the "Tonight" show had fallen into third place and wasn't doing well. He pointed out how well the show was really doing in the numbers. New advertisers were coming on, he said. Then, though no one at the conference had said the show was struggling, Jay went on to suggest people look back at when Dave started and some of the things that were said, or even back to when Johnny started. "But do I feel secure? I'm a comedian. I don't know how secure you can be. You do a one-nighter, you get paid, you go home. And that's sort of the way it is. Yeah, I feel secure. I pick up the paper every week, the numbers are real good. That's all we need to know."

Leno jumped all over a question about whether he felt bitter. "No, I don't feel bitter. Please. Not for this kind of dough, please." When that got a big laugh, he rolled on: "You switch places, huh? No, really, please. I mean, I'll call you a moron and then give you my check and see if you can handle it, all right?"

A little later a reporter asked if Jay would have felt better if it hadn't taken a month for NBC to endorse him. "Yeah, okay," he said. "But come on. I mean, nobody lied to me here. This was not a case of Bob Wright calling me up and going, 'We love you, baby, you're great,' and then calling Dave up, 'No, we love you, you got the job.' I mean, a month ago people said, 'Look, David Letterman is a huge asset to this company. He's made a tremendous amount of money for this company. And we don't know what to do,'" Jay said. "Would I have liked them to have decided on the spot? Yeah. But I mean, that's life, you know. Come on."

Jay said he had heard the official word only the day before in a phone call from Warren. He explained how he had called sixty to seventy affiliate managers in the preceding weeks to sound them out about the program, and he found out how much they liked what they'd seen.

When asked if he was concerned about stories that

had NBC ready to "screw you out of" the penalty payments in the contract by getting him to quit, he said simply: "How do I feel about that? I don't know. Did it work?"

Jay said he was looking forward to the competition with Dave. "I think it will be great fun," he said. "This is what makes you better." As Binford shooed him and his Harley out of the room—and to the waiting helicopter set to take him back to Burbank to begin taping a show in less than an hour—Jay turned back to the reporters and said: "All right, thanks, you guys. And I'll see you in the fall when the war begins again: the late-night battle!"

After Jay left, Littlefield told the reporters categorically that NBC did not offer the 11:30 time period to David Letterman. He said it was "absolutely not true" that NBC could have prevented the outcome by handling Letterman better and "stroking" him before Leno got the "Tonight" job. "One thing was consistent," Warren said. "Dave wanted to be on at 11:30. Anything else was window dressing."

About Dana Carvey, Littlefield said the star had many things on his plate to consider, including feature films. And even with the flat rejection of NBC's offer for the show earlier the same week, and the consistent message from some people close to Carvey that he simply wouldn't do a late-night show after Leno, Warren said, "There is no deal that has fallen through. That is very much still an option for Dana."

When asked to predict how Jay would fare against Letterman, Littlefield said he didn't want to be in the prediction business but he tied the decision on Leno to his own security in his job, noting that "my job is performance-oriented." As for the Leno decision, "we feel very, very good about Jay, about the show, the quality of the show, and clearly about the results, how well we are doing," Littlefield said. "Time will tell just how bright we are and how strong a decision we made."

NBC had piped the press conference in live by satellite to its offices in New York. David Letterman sat in one of those offices after the taping of his show that Thursday night, dreading his own press conference to come at CBS. Jay had been on for about twenty minutes or so when the Letterman group assembled for the short walk along Sixth Avenue to CBS. As he put his jacket on, Letterman could hear Jay's voice on the monitor wrapping up. He was just saying, "Thanks, you guys. And I'll see you in the fall when the war begins again: the late-night battle."

Letterman all but groaned out loud. He thought: "What am I getting into here? 'When the war begins.' Oh God, leave me alone."

Most of Letterman's top staff members joined him for the walk to CBS. They went outside into the brisk January evening, a phalanx of supporters surrounding the shaky Letterman. Lassally knew that Letterman didn't want to do this press conference and only wished for it to be over. But he knew Dave, and how his mind worked. He was confident he would get it all together. And he personally had no doubts at all at that moment that they were making no mistake in taking their future two blocks up Sixth Avenue.

Inside the elevator heading for the nineteenth floor

of Black Rock, Letterman stood behind his producer Jude Brennan and his director Hal Gurnee and said, "We're just going from one bizarre circumstance to another. I'm sorry, but this is about the strangest thing I've ever been through." But then they were there, outside a room that looked like some official chamber in Washington where a horde of reporters was about to get a briefing on the Gulf war.

Every important executive at CBS lined the walls, reporters filled every chair, and dozens of others sat all around the floor. A wall of television cameras were aligned on a small platform across the back of the room, pointing lenses forward like a video firing squad. The CBS chairman, Larry Tisch, was beaming almost impishly. As the Letterman group entered, they were directed to chairs arranged on the stage: Robert Morton on Dave's left, Peter Lassally on his right. Tisch grabbed a chair in the middle. Photographers began snapping Letterman madly as soon as he entered, shutters firing off explosively, sounding like a rocket assault. "How late is Photomat open?" Letterman said into the din. As he looked around the room, he noticed the thick blue carpet on the floor and what looked like soundproofing on the walls. He thought: "There's too much carpeting; the walls are carpeted. You're not going to get any laughs in this room. I'm screwed."

Howard Stringer stepped forward to the microphone and made some introductions of the Letterman staff members, the other CBS executives in the room, and, of course, Larry Tisch. He began by thanking Michael Ovitz and Lee Gabler of CAA for "a negotiation of matchless skill and great integrity." Then he talked about the goals CBS had in order to renew itself, and how late night had always been the "empty piece of the jigsaw puzzle that's glared at us over the decades." David Letterman had been the man to fill that space, Stringer said, comparing him to one of his own reference points, the British comedy tradition of "Beyond the Fringe." Stringer said he had watched Letterman himself for years and thought "he would be a signature for this network, the likes of which we haven't seen in years. Because he's smart and thoughtful, because he's original, because he's daring, and he's fun." He said it was a great moment for CBS and he added that it was also worth remembering "that a long time ago Mr. Paley put up the cash for Jack Benny, at a big turning point for this network, and Larry Tisch has just done the same thing, with considerable enthusiasm and total resolution, to bring David Letterman to this network and turn another facet of its history into something special."

Larry Tisch got up to say a few words, about how delighted he was to welcome "this great star" to CBS. He complimented Stringer for having the vision to bring Letterman to the network.

Finally David Letterman got up from his chair and stared out into the mass of news people and equipment in front of him. And playing off one of his most frequent references, he shouted: "I never dated Amy Fisher! I fixed her car! I helped her with her homework! I never laid a hand on Amy Fisher!"

And he had them; every reporter in the room was his. The laughs were bouncing off the carpet and all around the room like racquet balls.

Letterman said he was happy to be coming to CBS, and thanked the network for its patience and the generosity of its offer. "This deal would have put a smile on Jack Benny's face—even in the condition he's in now," Letterman said. Then he agreed to take questions from the rows of reporters arrayed in front of him. "And then when we're finished," Letterman said, "Colin Powell will come out and update you on the bombing."

Letterman sprinkled his answers with pungent cracks, but he also answered the questions honestly, detailing his uncertainty about whether the show would stay in New York, his intention to bring most of his staff with him to CBS, his conclusion that NBC had behaved "honorably and as gentlemen" throughout the process. "I have nothing but great thoughts about my eleven years at NBC," Letterman said, adding that if asked what he was going to miss most about NBC, he would have to say, "the back rubs from Irving R. Levine. The man is a master, yet there's a certain gentleness to him that I find incomparable."

Asked about the coming competition with Jay, Letterman said he felt confident his team would do all right. "We should not have too much difficulty being competitive. I mean, we've been doing it for eleven years."

When one reporter suggested that the bitter and angry David Letterman was a much funnier David Letterman, the star responded in mock rage: "Well, come up here and let's settle this now!" Then he took on the question straight. "I've never considered myself to be a bitter person. When Johnny Carson retired and I was not given the job as host of the 'Tonight' show, I was disappointed. But to my way of thinking it was not bitter. But you know there are many, many other things to make fun of in the world," he said to the reporter. "Like, you know, beginning with your tie, for example."

Asked if he thought General Electric made the best managers for a television network, Letterman dodged by answering, "I don't know about that, but have you tried their toaster ovens? They're not a bad product."

Letterman also refused to discuss what had been negotiated with NBC over the previous weekend, except to say the talks went up to "pretty much the last contractual moment."

Asked what rights to his work NBC might own beyond the "Late Night" title, Letterman said, "They own the rights to my old ice-dancing routine."

The persistent question of whether his viewers would follow him to 11:30 came up, and Letterman seemed truly amazed. "It's kind of insulting," he said. "It suggests that people who watch my show don't understand the complexities of the remote control." And later when someone suggested that his humor was so hip it should be on later at night, he said, "I don't know. You people seem to be keeping up."

Letterman worked in some kind words about Bob Wright, whom, he said, he had grown to respect, and especially about Johnny Carson. "I don't know of a person in comedy or television who didn't sort of grow up with Johnny Carson as a role model. It's one of the reasons people leave home and come to New York or go to California to get into comedy or show business." Letterman even revealed that he had spoken to Carson the previous Sunday, though he did not even hint at the significance of that phone call. He said instead that of all the people who had been helpful and supportive in his career, the most important figure had been Johnny Carson. "The man has been encouraging and helpful to me in ways that he doesn't know I know about," Letterman said. "I will never be able to repay the kindness to the man."

The reporters had not applauded when Letterman was introduced, but after a half hour of big laughs and straight answers, they cheered him as he left. In his usual way, Letterman left the CBS conference room feeling he had done miserably. No one else thought so. Stringer and Tisch were euphoric, with Stringer immediately concluding he had made a can't-miss deal for CBS. Peter Lassally beamed with pride; he thought his boy had been absolutely perfect. Ovitz phoned in his congratulations. And pretty soon even David Letterman realized it had been fun. By the time he read the raves in the papers the next morning, he knew his backers hadn't just been blowing complimentary kisses at him. He knew he had killed again in a stand-up when he needed it most.

Though Jay Leno and Warren Littlefield had linked their futures together through two trials of fire, first with Helen Kushnick and then with the threat from Letterman, Littlefield still had not cleared up with Leno exactly how he had broken through NBC's security and learned everything that happened in Boca Raton. Jay had promised he would tell Warren after all the Letterman stuff was over. All Jay told him right away was that he had not gotten the information from Rick Ludwin. That relieved Littlefield, who had suspected Ludwin only because the late-night division head had argued for Jay so long and so fervently.

In late January, Jay finally felt it was safe to tell Warren his secret. He described for Warren how he had come up to the executive office suite, squeezed himself into the closet-like guest office with the photocopier and shredder, waited for the phone line to light up so he knew the conference call was coming in from Boca, and then listened in to every word being said to the other executives on Warren's speakerphone. He told Warren how he took notes on everything that was said, waited quietly until everyone else had gone, and then walked out into the night.

As for hitting him exactly as he got to the bathroom, Jay explained how that was mostly luck, knowing Warren had left a meeting to head back to his room, then timing it so that he caught him just right.

Littlefield didn't know quite how to react to this revelation. Here he had been in Boca Raton sitting with his pants around his ankles, listening to this verbatim account of a private meeting delivered by one of the subjects of that private meeting. Warren felt violated. But on the other hand, Jay was so jolly in the retelling, so enthused about his coup and how valuable it had been for his cause at a time when nobody at NBC seemed willing to tell him anything, that Littlefield found himself starting to admire Jay. This was a guy with his back against the wall, Warren thought, a guy who, with a stiff wind, could have been king or could have been a pauper. And he had figured out how to identify where he stood. Littlefield didn't think Jay's spying affected the outcome of NBC's decision making. But it certainly kept him close to the game.

Littlefield also thought about how Leno had gone out every night during this most volatile period of his career and put on a "Tonight" show every night, a show that by Warren's estimation Jay was simply nailing night after night. And then Warren started feeling flat-out amazed. "Superman could not do this," Warren told himself. And Jay had also just dumped his executive producer, the closest professional associate in his life, who was still calling occasionally and trying to climb back into his life.

And so Warren Littlefield got past his feelings of personal violation and vulnerability, and started to feel incredible appreciation for Jay's sense of humor, his resiliency, and his sheer gutsiness. And he said to himself: "Street-fighting man. This is a street-fighting man." And more than anything else that had transpired, the Jay-in-the-closet story convinced Warren Littlefield of one thing: "Bank on this guy."

As late night preoccupied most of the NBC executives throughout the fall and early winter, other pieces of the network's entertainment business were rusting away. NBC was dogged by bad decisions and worse luck in prime time. Few of the fall shows had worked, and worst of all, the network's crown jewel, its eleven-year-old hit sitcom, "Cheers," announced in December that it would not be back for a twelfth season. Littlefield had already lined up a deal with the show's producers and studio, Paramount, but it all came undone because the comedy's star, Ted Danson, decided he was in midlife crisis. He was leaving his wife; he was starting an affair with Whoopi Goldberg and walking away from the more than $10 million a year he was making to star in "Cheers." The news hit the reeling NBC network like a vicious low blow. One year after its other pillar from the eighties, "The Cosby Show," had shut down, "Cheers" was going off the air as well. At that moment "Cheers" was the only NBC show consistently finishing among the top ten weekly series in prime time. What more could happen to the beleaguered Warren Littlefield?

In early February he found out. Without his knowledge, Bob Wright had been looking for a new executive to help run the entertainment division. Finally Wright settled on Don Ohlmeyer, the owner of a successful independent production company that mainly produced sports programs. Ohlmeyer himself had had a long career as one of the most ambitious and most creative producers of sports programs ever to work in network television. After a long career at ABC Sports, highlighted by a stint as the best producer "Monday Night Football" ever had, Ohlmeyer had moved on to NBC, where he became executive producer of the sports division. From there he had spun off into independent production, building a powerhouse company called Ohlmeyer Communications. He packaged many sports events and created others, including, most profitably, a unique golf format called "The Skins Game." But when Ohlmeyer dabbled in entertainment he occasionally hit a home run as well, as he did with "Special Bulletin," an Emmy Award–winning movie about a nuclear accident.

Other entertainment projects had not worked out as well. And Ohlmeyer's only attempt at producing a weekly series, an examination of true-life medical dramas called "Lifestories"—a favorite project of Ohlmeyer's close friend Brandon Tartikoff—had not been a success.

Still, Ohlmeyer was a big, blustery figure with friends throughout the television business (he had also been known to play golf with Jack Welch), and had a reputation for putting a lot of muscle on big problems. Bob Wright had big problems and he needed muscle. Ohlmeyer was hired as NBC President, West Coast, an invented title that basically put Ohlmeyer in charge of everything and everyone in Burbank, including John Agoglia and Warren Littlefield. Both men were told their roles wouldn't change. But outside NBC it was surely read as a demotion, especially for Littlefield. Don Ohlmeyer would now be the top guy that the other top guys in Hollywood called first when they needed to make contact with NBC.

After some initial rage, Littlefield made the ego adjustment he needed to make in order to work under the new system. He had proved before, during the long years under Tartikoff, that he could be resilient himself. Still, it was a blow. It reinforced the image of some in the Hollywood community that Warren Littlefield was a great number two executive who could not quite cut it as a number one. That perception rankled Littlefield, who felt he had as much program savvy as anyone in television. But after Don Ohlmeyer arrived, unfair or not, it was a perception he had to live with.

• • •

Letterman and Leno had started out in the comedy clubs, so NBC's search for a new late-night host predictably started there. Over the course of several months, Lorne Michaels solicited names and saw acts, trying to stumble into something magical. In reality, his heart was hardly in it. Michaels had never gone after conventional stand-ups to fill spots on "Saturday Night Live." As he conceptualized the new late-night show, he sought something different within what he knew was necessarily a limited format. The economics more than tradition dictated that there be one host, a small band, a desk, some chairs, and three guests a night who could talk engagingly if not always amusingly. As Michaels reviewed the available comics, he believed he saw a consistent tone of what he called "light hostility" in every act. As he pictured these guys sitting at a desk talking to guests, all Lorne could foresee was the comic constantly bursting out of the host, and then a battle ensuing: Who could score the most comic points, the guest or the host? Michaels was uncomfortable with that kind of television, and he sensed that most viewers would be, too, even at one o'clock in the morning.

Still, he tried to keep an open mind as NBC rounded up the usual comic suspects. As this process went on, Michaels started to put together a production team for the show. He knew he wanted to include Jeff Ross, who had worked for Michaels producing another comedy series, "Kids in the Hall," featuring a Canadian comedy troupe of unusual inventiveness. They had first played in HBO specials and then in a weekend series for CBS. Lorne figured he himself would help put together the format for the new NBC show, get it off its feet the first several weeks, and then drift back to his consuming duties as executive producer of "Saturday Night Live." He would still consult on the new 12:30 show and retain the title of executive producer, but Ross would run the show day-to-day as the on-site executive producer.

The show would then need writers and a producer, of course, and Michaels thought immediately of a young writer who had impressed him during a three-year stint on "Saturday Night Live" that ended in 1991. He was best remembered for co-writing a sketch about a nude beach that dropped in the word "penis" fifty or sixty times—a sketch that put "SNL" back in the news again for its outrageousness. Michaels knew the writer had gone on to work for the Fox animated hit "The Simpsons," but if he could get clear of that commitment, Lorne wanted him brought on as the producer of the new 12:30 show. His name was Conan O'Brien.

The twenty-nine-year-old Conan O'Brien was indeed ready to move on beyond "The Simpsons," but his plans for his career did not precisely parallel Lorne Michaels's plans for him. O'Brien's previous performing experience was confined to work as an extra on "Saturday Night Live," some improvisational stage comedy with a Los Angeles–based troupe called the Groundlings, and a few appearances in industrial films on behalf of a company selling musical instruments; still, he decided he wanted to be a star.

The real basis for this desire was difficult to trace because O'Brien had mostly built a résumé common to other top-level comedy writers in television. He was out of the Harvard *Lampoon*, the hub for the underground railroad that for years had been supplying comedy writers to television shows—principally "Late Night with David Letterman," whose offices constituted a kind of unofficial Harvard Club. At Harvard, O'Brien had carved out a bit of history for himself by being twice elected president of the *Lampoon*, a feat not duplicated since 1912, when a certain Robert Benchley had earned the distinction. O'Brien's style was a bit different from Benchley's, as evidenced by the penis sketch. Conan had a distinct television bent. His first submission to the *Lampoon* was a parody of the CBS sitcom "One Day at a Time."

O'Brien was raised in a big Irish family in Brookline, Massachusetts. Both parents were professionals: His father, Thomas, was a doctor and his mother, Ruth, a lawyer. Conan had three brothers and two sisters. And though he grew to be as tall as a basketball forward, O'Brien looked more ungainly than athletic. He was skinny, unmuscled, and his posture wasn't great. In high school he played on the debate team, not the basketball team. O'Brien also looked like an Irish-American poster boy, with a flamboyant shock of hair the color of Manhattan clam chowder and skin tattooed with freckles.

Coming out of Harvard in 1985, O'Brien headed immediately for Hollywood. He and a partner, Greg Daniels, got jobs writing for HBO's satirical news series, "Not Necessarily the News." In 1987 he got his first taste of late-night TV in a writing job for the instantaneous Fox flop, "The Wilton/North Report." He emerged undamaged on the writing staff of "Saturday

Night Live," where he met Michaels. O'Brien pestered Lorne to use him in sketches, entreaties the executive producer resisted. The best Conan could do was a few crowd-member bits, asking questions at mock press conferences.

But he didn't relinquish his dream of moving out in front of the camera; he just didn't do anything about it. He never dropped in at the Comedy Store or other clubs to try out routines. He didn't go to workshops or acting classes. Conan confined his performing tendencies to spontaneous show-off sessions with the other writers on "The Simpsons." At that he was successful, however, keeping the room of exhausted writers amused with his antics. Matt Groening, the cartoonist-creator of "The Simpsons," saw this as a real indication of performing talent. "He can keep a roomful of seething, self-hating, resentful comedy writers laughing for minutes on end," Groening said. He described O'Brien's method as pushing the bit he was playing well past his viewers' endurance until they reached the point of submission to laughter. "He does a lot of shtick and runs around the room. It first makes you laugh, then gets annoying, then exasperating, and then comes full circle and makes you fall out of your chair."

At the start of 1993 O'Brien hired a new agent, Gavin Pallone, of United Talent and told him of his desire to perform, not write. Pallone eventually told Michaels that Conan didn't want the producing job on the new 12:30 show; he wanted to be considered for the hosting job.

It was late March and NBC had made a promise to its affiliates that it would have the name of the replacement for Letterman by April 15. Some inside NBC thought it was foolish to set a date, because it only increased the pressure to hire some host nobody was fully satisfied with. But NBC felt the affiliates needed to be reassured so they wouldn't go off looking for syndicated shows to preempt its regular programming at 12:30. Michaels had winnowed the comics he had seen down to a few, and NBC had a few others it wanted to see. All of them were assembled for a one-night stand/audition at the Improv comedy club in L.A. The list included Paul Provenza, who was Leno's preferred choice for the job, and other young comics like Drew Carey, Jon Stewart, and Rick Reynolds.

Michaels sat in the audience and watched the performances that night with some of his staff, along with Ohlmeyer and Littlefield. Each comic did his best ten minutes or so. Everybody laughed; Michaels thought one or two of the comics showed a hint of spark; but nobody was overwhelmingly impressed. The new David Letterman did not emerge.

After the comedy showcase failed to make a strong case for anybody, Michaels began thinking more seriously about Conan. He was young and Lorne wanted young; he wanted to be able to sell the new host as the spokesman for the under-thirty-five generation, who would make up the bulk of the 12:30 audience. Conan was also a pleasant personality. People warmed to him quickly and almost everyone he met spoke well of him. He had a certain comic spontaneity, if no real performing skills. Lorne began to talk himself into the notion that Conan's lack of stand-up experience could be a plus as well as a minus; he hadn't learned the habit of looking to nail people with the quick put-down. Lorne had had two exceptionally good experiences in the past with comedy writers who wanted to shift to performing: Steve Martin and Chevy Chase. When Lorne started asking people who had worked with Conan what they thought of the idea of him as host of the show, Michaels got surprisingly affirmative answers. Everybody seemed to like Conan.

So he mentioned the idea to Littlefield. He pitched it in terms of Conan filling the role of comic for the new generation. As Michaels put it, "Conan may not be that funny to people of the forty-plus generation. But he will be the first post–baby boom host."

Littlefield had some obvious reservations. It was such a crucial job for NBC to fill, with competition sure to come from CBS in a show following Letterman. But Michaels was clearly enthused by the notion of pulling this unknown talent out of his hat. He had done it before with complete unknowns on "Saturday Night Live," and Littlefield had, after all, labeled Lorne "the master of midnight" in the January press conference. Littlefield agreed to test O'Brien out. He arranged what amounted to a screen test, with Conan O'Brien to sit at the desk on the set of the "Tonight" show, auditioning to be the 12:30 host.

On the evening of April 13, Conan O'Brien, in a blazer over jeans, walked out onto the stage of the "Tonight" show, where he had never before been in his entire life. In front of a hand-picked test audience made up mostly of friends and NBC employees, he stood at center stage and, looking rather sheepish, explained how he was an unknown with no performing experience trying to host a television show for the first time: "Let me explain why I'm here. This is the result of a drunken wager between Lorne Michaels and Don Ohl-meyer." Most of his jokes had to do with how silly this whole notion was. Conan said "uh" a lot and giggled occasionally into the camera. He just had a few jokes that he and Rob Smigel, a writing partner from "Satur-day Night Live," had thrown together that afternoon. Conan looked nervous, but surely not as nervous as he should have looked under the circumstances. His jokes weren't much, and his delivery was close to awful. But he projected a nice-young-man quality that had a cer-tain winning charm.

At the desk he was only slightly less awkward, but he calmed down when his first guest, actress Mimi Rogers, appeared. It was as though the human contact gave him some outlet for his nerves. Rogers was giggly and friendly. O'Brien noted that he didn't get to talk to many attractive women. He said he lived upstairs from a model and that the extent of their relationship was his leering at her. His ad-libs weren't much, except for one line: When Rogers talked about posing for *Playboy* and said she had done it in a "classy way," Conan replied: "So you're wearing a top hat and reading *The New Yorker*?" Later Jason Alexander of "Seinfeld" came out and bantered for a few minutes. Conan kept saying how much he liked it up there on camera. But once, he said, "You sit here and become an asshole," as if oblivious to the fact that he was supposed to be simulating a net-work television appearance.

But Conan did not ooze out of the chair into a pud-dle of sweat; he projected the likability that Michaels expected from him. And Lorne, who watched the performance on satellite in New York, was totally pleased. So was Don Ohlmeyer, who watched live in L.A. He got on the phone with Michaels after the audition was completed, and they both felt they had seen the same thing: Conan was likable—very raw, but with moments of brilliance. The two men had clearly watched the performance with the stardust of hope in their eyes.

Warren Littlefield watched the taping and saw more of the raw than the brilliant. He was concerned enough about the thought that this untested comedy writer would be the successor to David Letterman that he wasted no time taking some action. Without saying anything to Lorne Michaels, Littlefield put in a phone call the next morning to Brad Grey.

Grey represented Michaels, so the fact that Littlefield was calling didn't surprise Grey in the least. He was in the process of finishing up negotiations with NBC over Lorne's deal for the 12:30 show, which had still not been completed. But the subject of the call stopped Grey in his tracks. Littlefield wasn't calling about Lorne's deal; he was calling about the availability of another Grey client, Garry Shandling.

That Shandling's name would pop up in the consideration of a late-night host was completely logical. Shandling had once been in contention to be the successor to Carson; he once split the guest-hosting chores with Leno. Now his career was ablaze thanks to the wide praise his latest project, a comedy on HBO, was attracting. In "The Larry Sanders Show," Shandling was mocking all the conventions of the late-night talk show so brilliantly that many of those in the business, including Letterman, thought they were watching their own lives on camera. "Larry Sanders" was so effective HBO had run repeats of its first season as an 11:00 P.M. late-night entry of its own—with great success.

Grey told Warren, "I don't know the answer to that question, but I will certainly be happy to discuss it with Garry." For Grey this was a provocative phone call at an intriguing moment: In the middle of closing a deal for one client, he was being pitched about another. Grey knew at once that if NBC hoped to land Shandling, they were going to have to offer him a substantial contract.

As soon as Grey hung up the phone with Littlefield, he dialed up Lorne in New York. He asked Michaels if this approach to Garry was part of what he had going with NBC. The stunned Michaels said no, he knew absolutely nothing about it; but he sure wanted to find out. Michaels called Bob Wright and told him, "You're the one who called me to get me into this thing. What is this all about?" Wright told him he would have to find out.

The Shandling overture grew more serious in the next few days. NBC went past its April 15 deadline of notifying its affiliates of the new host. Conan was put on hold. NBC considered signing him as the backup to Bob Costas for the 1:30 A.M. show, as a way perhaps to get Conan over the kinks of never having performed before. Meanwhile they pursued Shandling.

That prospect cheered some executives inside NBC who saw Shandling as a potential coup for the network, an announcement that would instantly reestablish NBC's late-night credentials for all those who doubted them in the wake of Letterman's departure. But Michaels was genuinely offended. He had allowed his name to be used to save NBC embarrassment the day they'd lost Letterman. Now NBC was pinning its hopes on a new star, not on its old star producer.

The deal was getting closer. NBC was discussing an offer of $5 million a year for Shandling. But timing was an issue. NBC wanted him to start in August, right at the end of his commitment to "Larry Sanders" for the season. Shandling, who wanted to bring a totally fresh concept to the late-night area, wanted to wait until January to launch the show.

But there were other complications. Some close associates of Shandling suggested that he, like Carvey, was reluctant to do a show following Leno. And then NBC heard the faint rumblings of CBS and Howard Stringer tiptoeing around Shandling themselves. On April 22, one of the show business trade papers, *The Hollywood Reporter*, printed a story that said NBC had formally offered the show to Shandling. NBC brought out its vehemence again, denying the story in an unusually detailed press release. Ohlmeyer in particular began to suspect Brad Grey's motives. He believed Grey had people out planting the stories that NBC was offering the show to Shandling, a move that did not indicate to Ohlmeyer that Grey was ready to sign the comic with NBC. He began to wonder if Grey was using NBC to force a bid out of CBS for its 12:30 show, or if Grey just wanted to puff up his client in the press before they grandly announced they were turning NBC down. In either case, NBC would end up embarrassed.

A week later, on Monday, April 26, Grey announced

that Shandling was turning down the NBC offer. The network angrily denied ever having made an offer to Shandling. Ohlmeyer said the network had never had a "creative meeting" with Garry, and so there could never have been a formal offer on the table. Ohlmeyer said he had always been arguing for Conan, because NBC had research that showed Conan, with zero name recognition, was only .2 of a rating point behind Shandling when viewers were asked if they would watch a show starring either man. Ohlmeyer also felt that the first night Shandling came on NBC, he would be doing at least 90 percent as well in the ratings as he would ever do, while there was "a chance for a big upside with Conan."

Brad Grey did not back down. He said NBC had made a firm $5 million-a-year offer for Garry Shandling, which Shandling mulled over for a week and then turned down. The outcome was the same in any event: NBC didn't have Garry Shandling. That afternoon NBC made its own announcement: The new host of its 12:30 A.M. show would be the unknown comedy writer, Conan O'Brien.

The press reaction to the O'Brien announcement was surprisingly favorable. To the press it was intriguing: the kid from nowhere getting a shot at big-time television—as though NBC had picked somebody out of the audience at one of the shows and told him he would be a star. It was such a flight of fancy, it caught people's imaginations. The fact that Lorne Michaels would be the executive producer of the show, guiding this new face, gave the notion a shred of credibility. Even before anyone knew if he could be good on television, Conan O'Brien was a good story.

That night, NBC insisted Conan be introduced to America by Jay Leno on the stage of the "Tonight" show, even though Michaels thought it was a dumb idea. Jay brought Conan on right after his monologue, but Conan, looking faintly like a man pulled in from the street and told he'd just won $20 million in the lottery, was at a loss for words. He grinned and said he was "just thrilled" several times. Just nerves, the optimistic NBC executives said to themselves after Conan's unveiling on the "Tonight" show.

One week later, on Monday, May 3, Conan turned up in New York for his own press conference. NBC staged it in the elegant Rainbow Room on the sixty-fifth floor of the GE Building. Amid generous servings of wine and canapés, about two hundred members of the press swarmed on the scene, waiting to hear the first bons mots from the new Letterman. When O'Brien strode in, flanked by Michaels and backed up by Ohlmeyer and Littlefield, he was surrounded by a dizzying circle of photographers who screamed "Conan" from every side, as though he had already entered the pantheon of show business stars identifiable by first name only—like Clint or Dustin or Roseanne.

But if all the lights, cameras, and action fazed the man in the middle of the swirl, he didn't show it. Freshly turned thirty, Conan seemed to enjoy his first moment as a public spectacle. He fielded questions for about a half hour, filling in some blanks in his personal résumé (he cleared up any confusion about his height, saying he was six feet four), describing his intentions for the show by saying he would most like to do a show that his three brothers would think was funny, and trying to display wit when the opportunity arose. When someone asked how it felt to get such a prominent job as a "relative unknown," Conan said in mock outrage: "Sir, I am a complete unknown!" Later he said that his fame was already spreading. He was being stopped on the street by people saying: "You're that marginally talented guy, aren't you?"

Michaels stood to one side, examining the proceeding as would a sociology professor studying an unusual show business phenomenon. In a brief opening statement, Littlefield had celebrated Michaels as a "great discoverer" on a par with Columbus and Magellan. At that moment he looked more like Stanley, wondering if this person in front of him might possibly be Livingstone. Lorne said he hoped Conan would succeed based on his talent for being "playful and intelligent."

As Conan left the room, with some reporters beguiled by his gentle humor and winning charm and others still wondering if NBC had a lick of sense left in the network, Warren Littlefield said to another NBC executive, "This could work."

12
CLASH BY NIGHT

The Asian-American family was packed into the tan Nissan Sentra as it pulled into the Exxon station in Burbank, near the entrance to the Pasadena Freeway: two adult women in the front seat, four children in the back. One of the women climbed out and walked to the pumps. As she dragged down the hose for self-service regular, she looked across the service station island and saw the enormous sky-blue vehicle draw up to the pumps on the other side, a car like nothing she had ever seen before in her life. As though watching a whale cresting the surface of the ocean, her eyes grew wide with wonder at the sight, even before she recognized the figure emerging from the driver's side of the car. When she saw it was Jay Leno, host of the "Tonight" show, she smiled hugely and began gesticulating wildly to the others in the car. "Jay Leno!" she yelled to them, knocking at the back window, "Jay Leno! Jay Leno!"

Jay acknowledged her with a friendly wave and a "hiya, how're you doing?" as he walked behind the massive car and stuck the premium hose into the tank. As he pumped the gas he waved at the others in the car, saying, "Hiya, you guys. Nice to see you." The woman stepped over to him gingerly, as though unsure if she could interrupt the delicate operation of filling this blue monster with gas. She said hello. Jay reached out his free hand and shook hers. She giggled with excitement and got back in her car. Everyone inside it waved energetically to Leno as they pulled away. Jay waved back again, warmly. Then he stepped on the running board and plopped himself behind the wheel of his pristine, precisely restored 1930 Duesenberg and drove off, across the avenue toward the freeway entrace, then down the ramp and into the teeming traffic heading toward the hills of Pasadena.

It was a spectacular Saturday afternoon, and Jay Leno was taking the prize of his automotive collection out for a spin on his day off. Leno had spent most of the day as he spent every Saturday when he wasn't booked somewhere on the road: working on his cars and motorcycles in the modified airplane hangar he owned adjacent to the Burbank airport. The hangar was arranged like a car dealer's showroom, with the fruits of Leno's success as a comic: more than forty bikes and about half as many cars, all of which had been worked on by him and the mechanics he employed. That day two mechanics and Jay had worked on a 1951 Vincent Black Shadow motorcycle, tuning the engine to perfection as a younger assistant applied special wax dozens of times and polished the black hood that closed over the rear tire. The work and the camaraderie with the mechanics seemed to relax Leno like nothing else in his life. Under the bike tightening a screw, Jay had looked focused and serene in his grease-spotted coveralls, as though listening intensely to a musical instrument, while one bare-chested mechanic gently revved the motorcycle's engine.

Now on the freeway, Leno could feel the wind racing under the elegant canvas-cloth roof that was unfolded and attached by polished bamboo braces from just behind the backseat to the windshield of the otherwise windowless car. He steered the Duesenberg like a battleship with wheels, its leviathan hood stretching out in front of him like a prow. The speedometer in the opulent mahogany dashboard edged toward eighty.

Heads jerked and spun inside every car the Duesenberg passed, the other drivers and passengers as stunned by this sight as if the starship Enterprise had taken to the Pasadena Freeway. They craned their necks up to see who might be behind the wheel of this apparition, and what they saw was the familiar, friendly face of Jay Leno. So they waved, and honked their horns; one passenger even pulled a camera out of a purse in the backseat and held it up to the window. Jay slowed just enough to stay even with the tiny Honda, waving pleasantly as the fan snapped away.

Jay had spent $350,000 to restore this museum piece to a state where he could periodically set it free to roar down an open road. He knew the car's story: how a previous owner had used it to commit suicide in his garage and how a surviving brother had let it rot for forty years rather than use it after that. The story didn't really give Jay pause; but the circumstances of the past eighteen months of his own life surely did. As his now-flawless machine flew by the Chevys and Mazdas and Buicks sixty years younger, Jay Leno sat in the afternoon breeze and looked down the road ahead of him. It still wasn't easy to get away from where he had just been.

• • •

Friends had begun to notice how little joy Jay seemed to be getting out of his life. "I just don't think fun is anywhere in his life," one friend said, with real concern for him. Though Jay was still tightly reserved with his feelings and his innermost thoughts, these friends detected more self-evaluation from Jay than they ever had before. He seemed to be often replaying all that had taken place in the battle for the "Tonight" show, as though looking for a way to make it different, or at least less uncomfortable than it had turned out.

"Dave never had it in his contract that he would get the job," Jay said in one of his detailed explanations of how the situation had played out. "I think what you had there was David, an extremely honorable person and a decent person, and I think he thought if he put anything in the newspapers, it would look like a slight push-Johnny-out. I mean, in retrospect I realize that's probably what it is, and what he did is probably what I should have done. I mean, I think everything was handled totally wrong from my point of view and my side. I think that where all the hurt and anger on the other side came from is that David chose to do the right thing, the honorable thing, and he got slapped down for it."

Months after Helen Kushnick's departure, the aftershocks were still rolling through Jay's life. Jay felt as though everything he did were being filtered by the experience with Helen. Here he was, a man who had consistently presented himself in his comedy—and his life—as the nice guy, the good guy, and he was suddenly being targeted as a schemer, part of Helen's reign of terror. "Now I'm the bad guy," he said. "It's so odd for me to wind up being the bad guy in a situation."

Jay, who was generous with time and advice to every comic he had ever worked with, was now hearing himself put down on the comedy grapevine as only marginally talented and undeserving of being Carson's successor. Jay, who was open and accessible to journalists in a way unmatched by any other major star in show business, was getting ripped regularly in the papers. He professed an ability to shrug it off; but those closest to him knew it was unfair—and that it hurt.

Jay vacillated between taking full responsibility for all that had happened under Helen and defending himself because he really didn't know all that had gone on. "Helen wouldn't argue. She'd yell. It was a nightmare, a nightmare," Jay said. "It's hard to believe it all took place in a three-month period." Jay said he had always looked past the excesses of Helen's behavior earlier in his career, "because she was there for me when nobody else was." But as he asked himself why it had all come crashing down, he said, "I guess absolute power corrupts absolutely."

In the wake of Helen's exit, Jay himself had assumed last-say power over the show, and set out to prove that he could be a success without any ugly backstage maneuverings. Now, he said, "there's no problem on the show that can't be fixed. There has not been one raised voice since Helen left, not one confrontational situation." In his effort to purge every aspect of Helen's influence and impact from his life, Jay sounded to some of those around him a bit like the born-again sinner driven to cast out the demons that had pulled him in the wrong direction. Every gift Helen ever gave him, he said, he had thrown away; every picture of her, every piece of memorabilia, all gone. And included in that broad sweep: every one of the shows they had done together.

"Those first three months of shows will never be rerun," Jay said, taking his mea culpas as far as they could go. "That's the deal I made with NBC. The shows Helen produced will never, ever be rerun. NBC can't throw them away, I guess, but I've thrown away my copies of them. As far as I'm concerned, my anniversary show isn't in May, it's September 21—the first show I did without her."

The power of the emotion he felt toward Helen was unusual for him, and it clearly was not in perspective yet. With some reluctance, Jay acknowledged that Helen had devoted herself to his career and that it might be true that he would never have gotten the "Tonight" show without her. But he said, "I never wanted it this way. If I knew this was being done for me in order to get me the show, all the dirty dealings, all that sleazy Hollywood stuff, I would never have wanted it."

He decided he was like a guy who's been in prison, and all he wanted to do now was forget about it and get on with his life.

As David Letterman wound down toward his final shows on NBC, he felt a surprising degree of nostalgia—or at least it might have been surprising to some at NBC who never understood how much he cared about the place. Letterman was worried enough about the emotion getting to him that he packed up most of the personal things from his NBC office three months early and had them stored for transfer to CBS. Letterman knew the leave-taking was going to be tough on him, not only because he was a nester by instinct, but also because being at NBC had always held special significance for him. It was the center of all the late-night comedy tradition in television, and that tradition had always had strong resonance in Letterman's life. "I felt early on in my career that NBC would be the place I would go to," Letterman said.

But the show was going on. In one of the odder television transition periods, Letterman did his show every night on NBC from January through June, even as he started planning his CBS show and often referred to the move to CBS on the air. His loyalties were truly divided. As CBS began its effort to woo its affiliated stations to add the new Letterman show to their late-night lineup, Letterman was pressed into service. On an off week from the show that March, Letterman made the rounds of a few CBS stations to press some flesh and politick for the cause of clearing his show. When he visited St. Louis he did a guest spot with the weather anchor, cut some promotions, and schmoozed with the general manager. In an interview with Eric Mink of the *St. Louis Post-Dispatch*, Letterman said, "This project is a huge gamble for everyone, and I will not be comfortable with myself unless I am able to say at the end of the night: 'I've done everything I can do to help this thing along.' If later I find out for some reason there's a problem in St. Louis and I didn't come, I'll think, 'Jesus, why didn't I?' "

A few days after Letterman returned from St. Louis, Peter Lassally received a letter from Don Ohlmeyer. The always aggressive Ohlmeyer was not about to allow

Letterman such free rein while still in the employ of NBC. He pointed out in the letter that Letterman was still being paid by NBC, and it seemed less than professional to be out in a market doing promos for a CBS station while he was still on the air on the NBC station in that market. He also noticed that Dave seemed to be having more and more guests from CBS on the show. The initial response to Ohlmeyer from some members of the Letterman staff: Screw him. But Dave didn't visit any more CBS affiliates while he was still an NBC employee.

Letterman had other preoccupations anyway. Now that he had agreed to join CBS, he and the top people on his staff were wrestling with the problem of where exactly at CBS he was going to do the show. With the "Tonight" show there would have been no question; Dave would have done the show from Burbank. But CBS had no obvious place for Dave to set down his roots. At CBS there was no classy broadcasting hub like Rockefeller Plaza, with its rich television tradition. CBS produced its New York–based shows out of a sprawling, characterless broadcast center on West 57th Street in Manhattan. Howard Stringer knew the limitations of that facility, and he also knew that Letterman had some affinity for Los Angeles, where he had first built his career and where he maintained a residence and many interests. Dave, in another odd parallel to Jay, was also a car enthusiast and also had an airplane hangar full of vintage vehicles and extravagant sports cars—only Dave's was at the Santa Monica airport.

But Stringer believed strongly that New York, in all its gore and glitz and glory, was a full-time player in

David Letterman's comedy. Stringer also had deep personal loyalty to the city he had made his home for almost thirty years. He wanted CBS's Letterman show to stay in New York. And Stringer had an idea about where it could find a home.

Even before he finalized the deal with Letterman, Stringer began thinking about how CBS could replace the broadcast tradition and the New York ambience that came with working out of a studio in Rockefeller Center. He thought of one place the show could move that might bring with it some of those elements. And once he had the idea, he couldn't let go of it: David Letterman at the old Ed Sullivan Theater on Broadway. For Stringer it seemed like some kind of broadcast destiny.

To many on the Letterman staff, the idea seemed more like broadcast folly. The initial reaction was strongly negative: Dave was so accustomed to working in a *television* studio; he was a broadcaster, not a stage-trained actor. It seemed too grand, too out of scale and showy, too much a contrast to the basement club-room atmosphere of the 12:30 show on NBC. When Stringer suggested a tour of the theater, the Letterman staff went along with reluctance; they thought they were being nice to Howard.

Dave himself had an open mind. The idea of California was attractive, for the weather and the easier access to big-name show business guests. But he also knew New York had proved to be an endless source of comedy ideas. And much of his staff had put down deep roots in the city.

The Sullivan Theater had fallen into wretched disrepair. It was occasionally rented out for specials or industrial shows, but most of the time it was another dark, decaying New York building. Dave thought it had a bit of nice theatrical feeling to it, but overall it simply seemed too big. He thought the relationships on the stage would be completely out of whack; he would be too far from the audience and from Paul Shaffer and the band. And while the stage seemed enormous, it didn't seem as if much of it could really be used.

Most of the rest of the staff was even less impressed—with one exception. Director Hal Gurnee, who had always had the best visual eye on the staff, envisioned real creative possibilities working in an old theater. He liked the idea right away.

Robert Morton's reaction was more typical. "David Letterman is not a proscenium performer," Morton said. "You can't put him on a stage. He needs to be around a working studio, somewhere that is rich with material." Letterman had always made advantageous use of the adjacency of his show to NBC's other New York programs. Letterman liked to break into news shows in progress or bring on the anchors as last-minute guests. Up at the Sullivan Theater, the show would be isolated, Morton felt, severely limiting the opportunities for interaction with other programs.

So the Letterman staff pressed Stringer to find studio space inside the broadcast center on West 57th, an idea Stringer thought was disastrous. The CBS broadcast center was a labyrinth of halls and offices and studios, so confusing and alienating that visitors often took wrong turns and wound up lost. The place seemed to have the fewest windows of any building in New York City, and it was already uncomfortably overcrowded. Even if a suitable studio could be found in the center, there was nowhere near enough office space for the writers, producers, and other staff. As an alternative, the Letterman staff examined the possibility of locating the office across 57th in a separate CBS building. They paced off the available office space and worked on the logistics: How would Dave get across the street every night to do the show without causing a commotion?

In the midst of these considerations, Letterman, Morton, and Lassally went west to take a look at the CBS studios in Television City in Los Angeles. Their eyes were knocked out by CBS's state-of-the-art facility there. The studio would be bigger, the office space was fresh and comfortable, and the offices even had windows. Morton began wondering if Letterman could get at least as much mileage out of lampooning the inanities of the show business world as he had out of poking fun at New York. Certainly Peter Lassally, who had made Los Angeles his home for more than twenty years, wanted to go back.

Letterman began thinking about the implications of uprooting his entire staff. "Oh man," he said to himself, "this is going to be awful."

The pressure on the decision was stoked up several notches when David Dinkins, the mayor of New York, jumped in to say that Letterman's continued presence was of utmost importance to the city. In several interviews, Dinkins pledged to take any steps necessary to keep Dave in New York, including, the mayor said, "doing back-flips off my eyebrows" if that would be enough to convince Letterman to stay.

But Howard Stringer had a vision of just what the Ed Sullivan Theater could be: a big marquee right smack on Broadway permanently announcing the presence of the David Letterman show, a line of avid fans out in the street waiting to get in, new excitement in the city—even, in Stringer's wildest fantasy, something that could be read as a rebirth and revitalization of the fabric of the city. With the Letterman staff leaning toward L.A., Stringer urged them to reconsider the Sullivan Theater.

Stringer promised CBS would buy the building and fix it up to whatever specifications Letterman and his staff would want. An office building was already attached to the theater, so he could have all the new offices right there. It was on Broadway, right in the heart of midtown Manhattan; whatever connection they needed to the CBS news shows being shot at the broadcast center could be worked out somehow, Stringer said.

As Letterman evaluated it, doing what Stringer wanted would at least mean no one had to be uprooted. And if it wasn't working, California would still be there in a year. Finally David Letterman said yes, he'd try it at the Ed Sullivan Theater.

Howard Stringer's vision of new, exciting television for New York City was intact. Now all he had to do was try to steal a theater for David Letterman before the current owner realized it had become the centerpiece in the plan to keep the star in New York.

Months before the final show on NBC, Letterman and his staff began thinking about what they wanted to be able to bring with them to CBS. NBC had been extremely vague about what ownership rights the network was going to claim. The only public statement about it was Warren Littlefield's comment during his press conference with Jay in January, when he said NBC certainly would retain the title "Late Night." Otherwise, he said, the network had not yet decided what part of Letterman's material it was going to preclude him from taking to CBS.

In early May, Jim Jackoway, the attorney for Letterman and the show, began framing a letter to NBC spelling out all the elements of the show Letterman wanted to retain. In the letter Jackoway said they wanted to continue using some fictional characters they had created, starting with Larry Bud Melman, the gnomelike character, played by an obscure New York actor named Calvert De Forest, who had been raised to the status of cult figure on the show. Jackoway told NBC that Paul Shaffer's group wanted to continue using the name World's Most Dangerous Band. He even asked if they could take Dave's old wardrobe and the microphone from his desk. Dave, who had once built a microphone with his Tinker Toy set as a boy, was especially attached to the mike he used on "Late Night." As for the show's most famous routines and comedy concepts, including the nightly Top Ten list, the letter said explicitly that the show planned to continue using all of those.

John Agoglia responded to the letter by telling the Letterman staff that NBC wasn't ceding the rights to anything that had been created for the show. NBC would respond, Agoglia said, in a letter that would be delivered after Mr. Letterman's final appearance on NBC. The Letterman crew thought that it was childish to be held hostage that way—but that it was typical of the show's relationship with NBC. They knew they had one last fight with NBC and John Agoglia on their hands.

Letterman wound down toward his last show with a minimum of nostalgia. Dave insisted the last show not be some sort of farewell festival of memories, for several reasons. That had just been done a year earlier by Carson, and Dave wasn't about to try to compete with such an emotional parting. Dave also knew that NBC wasn't about to celebrate his final show right before he started competing against them by pouring out the promotion for a Letterman finale. But mainly Letterman felt that this exit should not be treated as the end of something, but only as a transition to something new.

"It's not like I'm retiring," Letterman said. "I do have another job to go to." Most of the emphasis Letterman and his staff were putting out to the press in the show's final weeks was on how similar his CBS show would be to his NBC show. They had already settled on a new name, and it was designed explicitly to demonstrate just how much things would remain the same. Instead of "Late Night with David Letterman," viewers would be treated to "Late Show with David Letterman."

Dave did consent to having some clips from his eleven years of "Late Night" used on the last couple of weeks of the show. But that wasn't entirely for nostalgic reasons. Since those shows were owned by NBC, Dave realized he would soon be losing access to all that work, all his classic comedy bits. So he thought they ought to trot some of them out one last time while they still had some control over the material.

The only thing that really came together to make the

finale an event was a booking pulled off by Lassally. He wanted to find something, one element that would make the last NBC show special—as much for Dave as for the viewers. Lassally knew there was one star Dave had never been able to book, though he had always wanted to. Without telling Dave what he was up to, Peter made some phone calls. It turned out to be surprisingly easy. Bruce Springsteen said of course he would do the show, as long as his appearance could be kept a total secret.

All Dave said before the finale was that the show had come up with a "wonderful surprise," a guest, he said, who was "someone in my life who has meant a great deal and someone who had never been booked on the show before."

The press speculation centered on Johnny Carson (he'd been on the show before), Dave's mom (she'd been on, too), Joey Buttafuoco (he'd only meant a lot in Dave's jokes, not in his life), and the woman who made frequent headlines—and frequently found herself arrested—by breaking into Dave's Connecticut home and pretending she was his wife.

Tom Hanks was the lead guest that night and he had stored up some hilarious stories about his days as a bellhop. Dave kept the secret right to the end of the show and then, with genuine excitement and gratitude, he introduced Springsteen, who in one of Dave's favorite descriptions, "blew the roof off the joint" one last time with "Glory Days." Letterman did one last Top Ten list for NBC: "Top Ten Real Reasons I'm Leaving NBC." The list included: "I've stolen as many GE bulbs as I can fit in my garage"; "Tired of being sexually harassed by Bryant Gumbel"; "Can't convince them to do another Triplecast"; and "CBS had the best Amy Fisher movie."

The show, and David Letterman's NBC career, ended with a shot from his eighth anniversary special in which Dave rode off the stage on a white charger.

They held a party on the stage after the audience had left. Lassally told Dave he had to make an appearance, despite the star's deep-rooted resistance to such social occasions. Dave agreed, and surprised Lassally by being gracious to everyone, even standing for pictures with every member of the staff and crew who wanted a memento of the night. It was a night full of emotion, but no real sadness. Lassally thought Dave looked content and even happy as he graciously thanked everyone for all they had done for him and the show. He seemed a man who knew he was taking a step in his life he had long needed to take. And as Peter Lassally stood off to the side and watched, he was delighted and proud of his talented, accomplished, deservedly celebrated professional son.

Warren Littlefield didn't feel like Jay's dad; he was only three years younger than Jay, after all. But he certainly believed in him, enough to stick his professional neck out to save him. Warren was convinced that Jay would continue to produce strong ratings, even after Dave went on the air. Still, Warren never stopped being a television entertainment executive, and as he watched Jay's show, he detected certain flaws he felt should be addressed—especially before Letterman came on the air. The two-month period between the end of June and the end of August was the time for adjustments in the "Tonight" show. After that, anything that was done would surely be read as reaction to whatever Dave was doing.

Littlefield didn't say it, but other NBC executives, who were scrutinizing Jay's performance more closely than ever, felt one main change was needed in Jay's material. As one senior NBC program executive put it: "The guy needs a shit detector." Littlefield agreed to the extent of suggesting that perhaps it was time for Jay to consider adding a true executive producer. Helen Kushnick had been out for almost a year. The show could use an experienced production hand who could also take some of the decision-making workload off Jay. Quietly Warren began exploring the possibility of bringing in Don Misher, who for a generation had been one of the top variety producers in television. Warren had been impressed with Misher's sure-handed balancing of a very delicate assignment NBC had asked him to take on earlier that spring: trying to get together a big special for Bob Hope's ninetieth birthday. The show was in near chaos when Misher took over and turned it into something of a triumph. Littlefield knew Misher usually worked on a free-lance basis, but he thought the producer might be getting ready to tie himself to something more permanent. When he made some inquiries he was happy to learn Misher was interested.

Unfortunately, Jay wasn't. Leno didn't see it as more ammunition for the fight to come with Dave; he saw it as implicit criticism that the show wasn't quite working—or at least he suspected the press would interpret it that way. Jay felt the press was already out to bury him.

A special edition of the "Tonight" show that NBC had him do to mark the end of the run of "Cheers," on location from the Boston bar the series was based on, had turned into a fiasco. The "Cheers" cast had sat around the bar drinking all evening, and many were pie-eyed by the time the show started. Most of the bits Jay had planned had to be scrapped, and he could barely get the "Cheers" cast through the interviews. The show was ragged and nearly out of control. Then Jay had made things worse in an interview with a Boston paper, offering some critical remarks about the cast. Jay later said the reporter had used the remarks even though Jay had asked that they be kept off the record. After that episode, the last thing Jay wanted to do was supply the press with another reason to question how well he was doing as host. When Warren raised the notion of Misher, Jay simply said, no. "If the ratings were bad, okay. I need the help. We've got a problem. But we don't need the help right now."

Jay also thought he should be loyal to his two producers, Bill Royce and Debbie Vickers, who he felt had been extremely loyal to him during the dark days with Helen. He told Warren he didn't want Don Misher. Warren backed off.

But the concerns about the direction of the show ran even deeper in some circles at the network headquarters in New York and Burbank. After months of watching Jay on the air, some executives were raising questions about his comedy range. For these in-house critics, Leno seemed so attuned to the setup-line/punch-line style of pure stand-up comedy that many other things he tried after the monologue looked either poorly conceived or lamely executed. From some writers on the staff, the executives picked up the information that Jay resisted attempts at conceptual humor. "The stuff that might be a little weird," one executive said, "the more Letterman-type stuff, Jay doesn't get. He wants the joke. He has to see the joke."

In April Jay tried a sketch called "The Crying Game," which was a one-joke idea based on the then-hit movie. The premise was that the old TV game show "The Dating Game" would have a lineup of three "bachelorettes," one of whom was quite obviously a guy in drag. The contestant, who was never identified as being on the show's staff or being picked out of the audience, clearly got the point right away, making it look as if he were in on the joke. But, as the nearly silent audience indicated, there weren't any jokes, just the kind of silly questions always asked on "The Dating Game." Worst of all, Jay was all but left out of the sketch, standing on the sidelines as the "host" of the game. The piece was roundly excoriated by the NBC staff members who saw it.

Others said it was somewhat typical: The show's material simply seemed weak, too weak to serve Jay well. And NBC executives with all that experience watching Letterman knew Jay would soon be up against some very strong comedy material on CBS. Jay openly said he devoted "ninety percent of my effort" to the monologue, which he considered not only his own signature, but also the traditional signature of the "Tonight" show. Some Burbank executives felt that even the monologue needed better writing. They believed that Jay recycled too many premises during the week and sometimes went on too long with a monologue that used weak jokes, when a shorter, punchier routine would have played far better. They granted Jay's strength in delivering the monologue, but they questioned why he couldn't spread his effort out a little more evenly.

One problem, it was suggested to the NBC executives, was that Jay didn't have a head writer, and so he accepted too much material that someone else might reject before it got to him. Jay, again citing loyalty to writers already on his staff, and questioning the need for change when the numbers indicated things were working just fine, resisted the appointment of a head writer just as he had the appointment of a new executive producer.

Forget the head writer, some of Jay's harshest critics at NBC said: Jay himself is the problem. These critics said Jay frequently failed to maximize the comedy material. They reported that the writers were frustrated at times because Jay didn't present the material as written. He had a habit of messing up the premises for some material so that the jokes that followed couldn't possibly pay off fully. The complainers cited one night when Jay was in the audience and was playing off Bill Clinton's penchant for making up excuses for things that had happened. The idea was to get some of the best excuses from audience members. The card in front of Jay said that he should ask the audience members to give the situation and then give the excuse used to get out of the situation. But in one instance Jay got the audience member's name and then just asked, "What's your excuse?" He forgot to ask for the situation that set up the excuse.

It was not an isolated incident. Some of the writers whispered to some Burbank executives that all comedy material beyond the monologue had to be simplified so that Jay wouldn't get an element twisted and undo the joke. Nobody said this to be cruel. Almost everyone liked Jay for his sweetness and vulnerability; and no one questioned his willingness to do whatever it took to make the show work. But the tougher critics in Burbank and New York did question Jay's instincts for any comedy that wasn't the kind he had been trained to do so well: stand-up monologue. Certainly, these internal critics said, Jay never seemed to improve the joke by his delivery or to add to it by doing a funny take into the camera the way Carson had—the way Letterman did.

Still, it was the interview segments that were of most concern to NBC. What no one could completely understand was why the affable, likable Jay that they all encountered in the office, in the hall, or at certain events seemed so mechanical with people when he was on the air. Partly his attention span, which he himself acknowledged was distressingly short at times, seemed responsible. But others said Jay just didn't seem to have a wide enough range of interests to conduct really satisfying interviews.

Certainly he wanted to do better, as always. And this time he was willing to go along with an NBC suggestion. The network wanted to bring in some experts from the Frank Magid Company, the nation's leading media consultants. They were asked to evaluate Jay's technique and give him some help. The Magid people looked at tapes of the show and made notes. Then they met with Jay and went over some ideas with him in a long, two-hour session. They didn't want to resort to the familiar critique that Jay simply didn't listen well enough; Jay had heard that point a dozen times over. Instead they tried to stress the point that he never seemed to be in present time while he was interviewing someone. Instead he always seemed to be rushing on, going to the next thing. He always seemed to be getting ahead of himself. What it came down to was not being focused. They hammered the points to Jay: Stay focused, pay attention, stay in present time with your guests. You're there for an hour, you're not going anywhere, and you might as well apply yourself. There's no reason to space out. And if possible, Jay ought to share more of himself—things from his own life—with the guest. That would not only make the exchange livelier, it would also help the viewers warm up to him more.

The only problem with these suggestions, some of those worried about the show concluded, was that Jay was a guy who seemed to have a lot of trouble making meaningful conversation, because he apparently had not had a lot of them earlier in his life.

None of these problems seemed insurmountable to the NBC executives overseeing the show. Jay was obviously giving the audience what they wanted for the most part; the numbers proved that. Still, the staff was told to work out the kinks in July and August, because come September, the heat was going be turned up high.

The week after Letterman closed up shop on "Late Night," he was still in his office at NBC. Lassally and Morton had worked out a deal with some more sympathetic executives at NBC so that the show could stay temporarily in its old offices while CBS worked frantically, around the clock, at the Ed Sullivan Theater to get their new offices finished. Dave had stopped going over to the theater to look around. Every time he went in it seemed all he could see were choking clouds of dust and hundreds of workers and artisans banging, drilling, and producing such chaos that he had to flee in a state of depression.

That state would soon deepen. The long-awaited letter from John Agoglia arrived early that week. In legal terms it was a demand letter. Citing provisions in Dave's employment agreement, NBC was saying that it reserved all rights to *all* elements of the show. All, as in every single thing they had ever done on "Late Night." The same letter was sent to CBS. The implication was clear: Don't tread on us—or we'll sue your ass.

The Letterman side wasted no time. Jim Jackoway framed a letter in response, which stipulated that the show was well aware of its rights and obligations and that the new CBS show would not infringe on any rights that NBC had.

In truth, what had been decided was that the items specifically requested in the original letter—Larry Bud Melman and all other fictional characters the show had created, as well as the World's Most Dangerous Band— would be abandoned. NBC had a legal right to keep those elements, the Letterman legal team concluded. But they still had no expectation that NBC would attempt to block the show from using generic comedy bits such as the Top Ten list. That seemed beyond silly.

NBC's executives, led by Ohlmeyer, quickly disabused them of that expectation. Speaking to reporters in July, Ohlmeyer began emphasizing that NBC not only had the right, it also had the obligation to protect what he called the network's "intellectual property." His comments were later backed up by Bob Wright in a press conference in California.

NBC's position attracted widespread derision in the press: Was the network seriously going to claim that a Top Ten list and "Stupid Pet Tricks" were "intellectual property?" But the derision missed the point. What Ohlmeyer wanted to argue was that Letterman could not go to CBS and do a show that was "substantially the same" as the one he had done for NBC—as he and his staff members had been saying all spring was their intention. Ohlmeyer implied that the Letterman people had started this dispute by trying to convince viewers they would be seeing the exact same show. But NBC owned that show, Ohlmeyer said, and still intended to go out and sell it in the syndication or cable TV market. Ohlmeyer, who had built his career on the skillful presentation of competitions and contests, clearly didn't mind putting up his dukes on this issue. He never said NBC would sue if David Letterman put a Top Ten list on his CBS show. What he said was that if the new show looked like a carbon copy of the old one, NBC would be obliged to protect its property.

When Letterman met the press himself a few days after Ohlmeyer held a press conference in Los Angeles, he didn't pass on the opportunity to perforate Ohlmeyer with a fusillade of wit. He said, "The name of the new show, which is a setback for us automatically, was going to be 'Late Night with Don Ohlmeyer,' so we can't do that." Then he added, "One of two things will happen. We'll just do all of the stuff that we want to do and that will be fine. Or we'll do all the stuff that we want to do and they'll sue us and that will be fine. By the way, if that comes to trial, get a seat down front."

Despite the public bravado, Letterman was in what he called a "blue panic" behind the scenes when it looked as though NBC were going to sue him—which may have been part of NBC's motivation. Letterman was genuinely worried. "What the hell are we going to do?" he asked his staff.

What the staff decided to do was to take every legal precaution. A special litigator was hired and told to prepare the case. They came to expect legal action by NBC on the Friday of the first week on the air—after enough time had elapsed for NBC to make some sort of claim that they were doing the same show. The legal staff concluded there was no real chance for NBC to win an injunction, but they were fully prepared for NBC to try.

Meanwhile the writers, producers, and the star went about the business of planning a new show in a new place. With some lingering trepidation, they moved into their new home at the Sullivan Theater the second week in July. The transformation was nothing short of amazing. CBS, having spent $4 million to acquire the theater, poured another $4 million into its restoration. The costs soared because the theater was declared a landmark building by the local historical society; that mandated that certain original elements, such as some stunningly ornate molding, be fully restored. The CBS effort, led by an administrative senior vice president named Ed Grebow, encountered further unexpected difficulties including the discovery of a stream running under the building and the necessity of exterminating a colony of rats the size of wolverines. Somehow Grebow kept the enormous effort moving, and had the offices ready for Letterman and crew—with air-conditioning in working order to stifle a sizzling New York July—almost precisely on schedule.

Letterman was truly amazed. He didn't see how anyone could get a building fixed up that quickly, especially in New York, where nothing was ever finished on time for any amount of money. After just one day of feeling a bit strange in a new office, Letterman fell in love with the place. It was new, fresh, clean, with big windows overlooking 54th Street and Broadway. Letterman quickly grew intrigued by the whole place; the columns, the beams, the piping, the corridors below ground level that were almost like catacombs. He loved everything about it.

But the work wasn't coming very easily. From the moment they closed up shop at NBC, it seemed that every pent-up and put-off illness descended on the entire staff. Producer Jude Brennan started getting migraines; people started going lame from running. Letterman himself developed a summer cold that afflicted him for weeks. Everyone seemed to be falling apart physically. But nobody took vacation. The launch of the new show loomed like the opening of a Broadway show—which in one sense was exactly what it was.

Letterman himself did not feel exhilarated at that point; instead he felt an overwhelming sense of responsibility and obligation. He tortured Morton and Lassally about production items; Rob Burnett, the head writer, about the comedy material; and everyone else about every other detail: guest bookings, camera positions, and CBS's on-air promotions. He was fitful about every aspect of the project. There was never a sense of "I can hardly wait." It was all a sense of "We have to do it, we have to do it, we have to do it."

They were out of NBC; they were into CBS, and David Letterman still hadn't stopped feeling he was in the middle of the most bizarre period of his life.

For the Fox network, late-night had become the black hole in an otherwise rosy success story. Chevy Chase was supposed to end all that. Lucie Salhany, the new head of Fox Broadcasting, had already fashioned one late-night success when she brought Arsenio Hall to Paramount. She made fitting the late-night piece into the Fox puzzle an immediate priority. Salhany put on the full-throttle effort to recruit Chase, who had used his breakout year as a performer on "Saturday Night Live" to build a film career, starring in a long string of comedies. Only a few, mainly his "National Lampoon Vacation" films, had been truly successful. Many others, including *Oh Heavenly Dog*, had been loud flops. But Chase was inarguably a star, and he had proved once that he could make a mark on television.

Salhany was seduced by one other factor: Chase had a truly outstanding Q-score. The Q-rating, produced every spring by a Long Island–based company called Marketing Evaluations Inc., had long been used by network programmers as a casting device. It measured a performer's level of recognition and popularity. But the Q-ratings were based on certain categories, and they did not indicate how a performer would score outside his category. Chevy was in a group labeled "Comedy Actors and Comedians." He was ranked an exceptionally good fifth place in that group, trailing only Bill Cosby, Tim Allen, the star of the top-rated sitcom "Home Improvement," Robin Williams, and Dana Carvey. Chase was even ahead of Billy Crystal.

Chevy's Q-score of 39 was well ahead of both Letterman and Leno, who could do no better than a 16. But they were in a different category, "Hosts, Announcers, DJ's." The Q-score really could not predict how Chase would fare against the competition in that category. It also could not give any indication whether Chevy could actually do the job of hosting a comedy/talk show.

Doubts about that extended through most of the television industry. Chevy had been off TV for so long, and he had never demonstrated the skills that made previous hosts successful: He didn't do stand-up at all, he had never shown he could bring out the best in somebody during an interview, and he had never especially exhibited a taste for long hours and grueling weekly work. Chevy's one foray into this sort of thing, a shot at guest hosting the "Tonight" show in November 1986, was something of a disaster. His monologue fell flat and he seemed to be trying to top every line tossed out by his guests, who happened that night to include one Jay Leno. Still, television viewers remembered him from that first great season on "Saturday Night Live," and he had that great Q-score. Fox wanted Chevy.

Chase's reasons for wanting the job weren't hard to fathom either. Late night was one of the biggest paydays any performer could hope for. Fox's offer came in at about $9 million a year. Chevy signed on.

For months before Fox mounted the show, speculation was rampant that Chevy would never go through with it. People who knew him well couldn't see him in the role. They didn't expect him to have the energy for it, nor the willingness to banter amiably night after night. The group with that opinion did not include his agent, Michael Ovitz, who said Chevy had become a fully rounded human being with his recent devotion to family life. (Chase had a wife and three young daughters.) Ovitz predicted success for Chevy's show. And as the summer progressed, a writing and production team was put in place. Fox even leased an old theater and named it after Chevy. Chase did the publicity rounds. He admitted he was scared about the prospect, especially with all the hype that was now surrounding the late-night competition. But Chevy said he worked best with his back against the wall.

In New York Conan O'Brien had no Q-score to rely on. All he had was his winning personality and the underdog factor. Americans always rooted for the underdog, and the idea that a star could emerge from total obscurity had the kind of delightful storybook quality that people seemed to eat up. Even without a Q-rating Conan was popular.

Conan's executive producer, Lorne Michaels, was in the midst of the hardest summer of his life. He was readying his film *Coneheads* for release at the same time *Wayne's World 2* was beginning production—without a finished script. "Saturday Night Live" needed reinforcements what with Dana Carvey and several top writers gone. And then there was Conan. Michaels knew his latest protégé needed work. Conan had to get accustomed to working with writers to develop material, to finding whatever comedy a guest had to give. He had to get accustomed just to being on camera. A set had to be built back in Dave's old studio. A band had to be hired. It was like building a house with a pile of wood and nails and no blueprint. Michaels wanted to get a show up and running as early as possible because he knew Conan would need a lot of practice before he dared take on the public.

One other late-night opening remained unfilled. CBS had its own 12:30 show waiting for the right star. The network's battle to win clearances from its affiliated stations made it certain that the 12:30 show couldn't be launched anytime soon. Stations had been pushing their syndicated shows back to 12:30 to make room for Dave. They would not be willing to clear a network 12:30 show for some time—at least until they knew how Letterman was going to fare at 11:30.

In mid-July CBS made a run at Garry Shandling anyway. At the time of the close encounter with NBC in the spring, CBS had entered the picture late, holding out to Shandling the promise of taking the show after Letterman instead of the show after Leno. But CBS didn't go through with a true offer then, thinking it might only have been brought in to juice up NBC's bid. At one point in the summer, Shandling seemed close to making a deal with CBS, but then he backed away. His "Larry Sanders Show" on HBO had won Emmy nominations. Shandling was getting offers to do movies. He was intrigued with the idea of becoming a comedy actor rather than a stand-up. And CBS started to wonder about the mix with Letterman anyway. Would they be too close in style? In August Shandling's manager, Brad Grey, finally pulled Garry out of consideration for CBS's 12:30 show, signing up instead for an extended deal to do "Larry Sanders" for HBO.

David Letterman was on the cover of *Time* magazine the week before his CBS show was to prèmiere. He was also on the cover of *TV Guide*, along with Jay, Chevy, Conan, and Arsenio. The frenzy over the late-night war, the one Letterman said he would rather be exempted from, reached its peak that week. Every newspaper was writing about it. Executives from every side of the industry—networks, studios, advertising agencies—were prognosticating the outcome. The consensus: Jay would continue to win in terms of overall household ratings, but Dave would lead among the more important younger viewers. CBS had sold out its initial batch of advertising in the Letterman show, asking the same $30,000 per thirty-second unit that NBC was getting for the "Tonight" show. CBS guaranteed advertisers a 4.1 rating, with NBC setting a 4.7 figure for Leno.

The 4.1 guarantee for Letterman was questioned by some who wondered if Dave could attain that figure with the much lower levels of clearances on the CBS stations than Leno had on NBC. The "Tonight" show was still put on the air immediately after the late local news on NBC stations covering 99 percent of the country. CBS's head of affiliate relations, Tony Malara, had called in every one of his chits and still Letterman's clearance level on CBS stations was under 70 percent.

That meant in more than 30 percent of the country, Jay would go on a half hour earlier—an enormous advantage. In one of the country's biggest television markets, Washington, D.C., Letterman would be delayed until after Arsenio Hall, a full hour after Jay had started on NBC.

That advantage accounted for the conviction that Leno would hold off Letterman at least for their first season of head-to-head competition. Of course, some people at NBC didn't foresee Leno having any real difficulty maintaining the network's unbroken forty-year string of late-night dominance. Warren Littlefield, in the weeks before the competition commenced, looked forward and pronounced that Letterman would be "a worthy opponent" only initially because of the hype that was attending his defection to CBS. "But a long-term worthy opponent?" Warren asked. "The question is, How broad-based of an audience does he have? It was curious to me to see the press acclaim Dave's big final show and the level of audience response. And the interesting thing is, it was like a one-night surge. For the quarter he was down from the prior year. The trend has been going down. Jay just finished his best quarter since he took over the show. Those are the trends."

Inside CBS, there was a quiet confidence that had nothing to do with the recent ratings trends at NBC. At CBS the confidence was based on just one thing: Dave was better than Jay. Rod Perth, the head of late-night programs for CBS, said of NBC's decision to keep Jay instead of Dave: "If they're proved right, I don't understand television." In Perth's estimation, having watched Jay do the "Tonight" show for more than a year, "Jay can't handle it. I don't think he's handled it for a long time now." Letterman, on the other hand, had already impressed Perth and everyone else at CBS with his clear-eyed vision of what was right for him and for late-night comedy. "He's demanding, exacting—I think he has a clear understanding of what works for him and what doesn't," Perth said.

But Perth was not ready to forecast an instant sweep to the top for Letterman, leaving NBC out of business in late night. Nobody expected that. But CBS was concerned that all the positive press surrounding Letterman would create the presumption that he was going to drive Leno right off the air. "We're scared to death about how it's going to be reported," Perth said. "We know we'll start with this huge initial rating the first week and then it will drop off. We want to make certain everybody knows we don't expect to knock them off the perch over the short term. We're taking a very cautious, low-key approach to it. What people don't understand is the lineup, the distribution mechanism at NBC, is so powerful."

The combatants themselves took their usual disparate approaches to the imminent heavyweight showdown. For Jay Leno, all the noise and hype was energizing. The anticipation seemed to have rejuvenated Jay. "It's very exciting," he said at an NBC press conference about a month before Letterman's premiere. "Let the games begin. I think this is great fun. I think late night is suddenly the most exciting part of television. Twenty years ago it was eight o'clock and nine o'clock and the sitcoms. Now I think it's exciting. This is *live* television. It's happening live at CBS; it's happening live on the

'Tonight' show. It's happening live in syndication. It's happening live on Fox. I think it's great," Jay said. "It's millionaires arguing at late night, battling for audiences. I just love it. It's hysterical."

For Letterman the hype got to be just a little too overwhelming. He and his staff had made an issue of getting the proper promotional push; then when the CBS promos started airing in bulk, it seemed like overkill to Dave. Everywhere he tuned in for a time, he seemed to see his face. He was floored at the thought that his decision to jump to CBS could be front-page news in the *New York Times*. The day after the story appeared, he got a call from his sister, who works for the *St. Petersburg Times*. She said in amazement: "Do you know your picture is on the front page of the *New York Times*?" Letterman told her he thought it was just nuts. Then came *Time, TV Guide*, and every other newspaper in the country.

A week before the show went on the air, Letterman was in Chinatown having dinner. Two elderly Chinese people spotted him and came over. "Why you go to Channel Two?" they asked. Letterman was flabbergasted. How could even they know? They could barely speak English and they knew what was happening with him. He concluded, "It was all those silly, fucking promos—dah-dah-dah-dah, night and day and day and night. It was insane."

Howard Stringer felt the pressure of the coming competition that he had helped so significantly to set up. He was slightly unnerved, as he put it, but totally excited. "I barely know there's a fall prime-time season going on," Stringer said. He was gratefully surprised that no last-minute crises seemed to have arisen. He had returned a week early from his summer home in the Hamptons anticipating some howl of horror to emanate from the corner of Broadway and 53rd. But when he called over to the Letterman offices, he found everything had suddenly become tranquil. The wave of attention that was engulfing CBS about the Letterman debut, all centering on the rebuilt Ed Sullivan Theater, confirmed for Stringer his conviction that this was the kind of nationally attended event that could only take place on network television. "This is all about keeping the broadcast networks alive," Stringer said. "It's about brand identity and public image and everything else. This is exciting."

Then he thought about the long road he had been down in wooing and winning David Letterman, and all the times something else might have happened, something that would have denied CBS its part in the excitement of the Letterman opening night. "If I had had to pick up Jay Leno after NBC had dropped him," Stringer said, "I can't imagine we would be going through all this buildup to his opening at the Ed Sullivan Theater."

On the afternoon of August 19, less than two weeks before opening night for "Late Show with David Letterman," Peter Lassally was working in his twelfth-floor office when he had a totally unexpected visitor: He looked up from his desk to see the sunny, grinning face of Jay Leno. Jay had talked and charmed his way past the security desk and slipped up in the elevator. He used the same charm on the receptionist and got right into Lassally's office. Peter greeted him warmly, though he was a bit put out at being surprised that way. Jay had no way of knowing how busy he might have been and what he might have been working on—maybe something that Jay Leno shouldn't know he was working on. It just seemed awfully odd to Lassally that the competitor had dropped in to visit the opponent right before the big game. But that was Jay's way: Defuse the competitive tension with a wave of pleasantries. Jay chatted amiably about all that was going on, a little about Conan, a little about Chevy. As they talked, Peter's assistant, Julie Bean, got word to Susan Shreyar, Robert Morton's assistant, that Jay had just walked in.

When Susan let him know Jay was in the house, Morton figured he'd be next for a visit. So he decided to get ready. On the wall across the room from his desk, Morty always posted index cards with guest bookings. He had several months of names already filled in, though many nights still had open spots. Expecting to hear Jay bounding down the hall any second, Morty grabbed a few blank cards and began scribbling out bogus bookings. He quickly filled out ten cards and stuck them up to replace names for shows during Letterman's first two weeks on the air. He posted Madonna; he posted Frank Sinatra, with the notation "two songs"; he posted Woody Allen. But after Morton got all that done, Jay still didn't show up. Morty couldn't wait any longer to be in on this; he bolted down the hall toward Lassally's office. As he reached the door, he could hear Jay Leno's voice, chatting away. Morty then took a beat and burst into the office himself, saying with great excitement to Lassally, "Peter, we got Jackie Onassis for the first show!"

Leno laughed and said, "You asshole." Then he

greeted Morty with an enthusiastic hug. The three of them talked for awhile, with Jay mostly pacing around the office. Lassally and Morton thought Jay might ask to speak with Dave—though he almost never did, either in person or on the phone. Despite how often he cited his friendship with Dave, Jay mostly talked to Peter and Morty. He rarely even tried to contact Dave, saying, with accuracy, that Dave was usually reluctant to come to the phone.

Lassally was struck again by what a weird scene this was and what a truly unusual personality Jay Leno had. Later, after Jay had gone, he and Morty talked about the little visit and decided that Jay was probably going to find a way to get it into the papers that he had stopped off in Dave's new offices. They were completely unsurprised when the item turned up in the television columns of the New York papers a day later.

The afternoon of David Letterman's debut on CBS, crowds milled around the corner of Broadway and 53rd for hours. The chosen few with ticket vouchers had lined up hours early. There was a party atmosphere in the street, with many of the fans holding up little Dave faces made from paper plates. One fan from Minnesota turned up with a bust of Letterman's head made out of butter and placed on a plate with hunks of bread for easy dipping. A couple of enterprising hucksters pushing wedding wear turned up in wedding gown and tux and tried to talk their way into the theater. They were bounced. Almost a dozen microwave trucks lined the sidewalk across Broadway from the big blue marquee that read "Late Show with David Letterman." Many of the camera crews from CBS affiliates were there to report back to their early-evening newscasts the scene of the big New York premiere. Stations as nearby as Philadelphia and as far away as Phoenix had reporters on the scene.

CBS had arranged a private party at McGee's Pub, a modest neighborhood bar that was part of the theater building itself—and so a new tenant of Larry Tisch. Tisch himself turned up, along with Stringer, Perth, Jeff Sagansky, the president of CBS Entertainment, and a whole cadre of CBS management. Ed Grebow had set up the bar with television monitors so the invited guests could watch the show live as Dave taped it. Dave was keeping to his rule against stocking the audience with VIPs. They made him uncomfortable during a performance. He preferred an audience of regular folks. Tisch had asked if he could watch the show from the control room, but no one there needed more pressure on this night. So Stringer convinced the CBS chairman to join him inside McGee's.

Mike Ovitz turned up with his 13-year-old son Chris. He ducked into the bar briefly to say hello to Tisch and Stringer, but then ducked back out again just as quickly. Ovitz *did* sit in the control room.

Letterman had tried the stage out in two practice shows in front of audiences the week before. They had loaded up the first show with some special bits, including a ghost appearance by Ed Sullivan himself. They also had several jokes prepared to play off NBC's legal threats about protecting its "intellectual property." But the lawyers weren't treating the threat as a joke; they had met with the writers and had carefully gone over what they had decided would be legally defensible. NBC's main point seemed to be that the new show had better not be so close to the old one that it would be confusing for viewers—that would lead to a suit.

So "Late Show with David Letterman" opened its first show very deliberately with the image of a huge CBS eye, from which Calvert De Forest, no longer Larry Bud Melman, popped out with a booming message: "This is . . . CBS!" Paul Shaffer's band was introduced as the "CBS Orchestra." Letterman came out to a standing ovation, smiling like a man about to hand out cigars with an "It's a Boy!" on the label. He was quite purposefully different-looking, and not just because he had a new flashy set in a grandly refurbished theater. Dave himself was perfectly turned out in a double-breasted blue suit, custom-tailored at Barney's, and a smashingly elegant diamond-patterned tie. No more blazers with loafers and white socks. From his first moment on the air for CBS, this was the new Letterman, the grown-up Letterman, the 11:35 Letterman.

In the middle of the monologue, a quite noticeably longer monologue than Dave had ever done on "Late Night," the show tweaked NBC's nose with a vengeance in a walk-on by anchorman Tom Brokaw, who marched over to the cue cards, grabbed a joke, declared it NBC's "intellectual property," and walked off. Paul Newman did a cameo appearance in the audience. He simply asked, "Where the hell are the singing cats?" The Top Ten list had a new high-tech introduction, with graphics and numbers spinning around like the halftime stats on "Monday Night Football." Again there was a method to the window dressing: No one could say this Top Ten list looked anything like the old one. Dave did one of his trademark remote pieces on tape, some hilarious interviews with the colorful folk of New Jersey. His first guest, as he had been eleven years earlier on "Late Night," was Bill Murray. Murray, in an over-the-top performance, spray-painted Dave's name on his new desk. And Dave did summon up the ghost of Ed Sullivan.

Letterman was swathed in laughs and affection from the audience all night. He would receive ecstatic rave reviews in the papers for his first CBS performance. But, true to his nature, he left the stage that night displeased. It wasn't perfect; it wasn't exactly what he wanted. After the show Letterman gathered with the CBS management up on the stage and sheepishly accepted congratulations for a moment before disappearing upstairs. When Ovitz came up to his office to congratulate him in person, Dave told him the show had been a disaster. Ovitz was slightly stunned; he thought the show was a smash, and said so. As people milled all around him in his office, Letterman shied away, taking refuge from all the adults in suits by striking up a conversation with the only kid in a suit—Chris Ovitz. They talked about sports. At one point, without suspending the conversation for a second, he reached into a humidor, and said to Chris, "Cigar?" The kid had never heard anything funnier in his life.

Later, a thrilled Stringer called. Lassally took the call, listened for a moment to Stringer's effusive enthusiasm, and then put him on hold. He asked Dave if he wanted to speak with Howard. Dave couldn't bring himself to listen to compliments at that moment—as he almost never could in the first minutes after a show. He always found it uncomfortable talking to "outsiders" right after a performance. "No, I can't talk now," Dave said. Lassally asked Stringer to call back later.

Howard did call a little later from the CBS celebration party. He told his star how great he was, how perfect the opening had been, and how the theater was surely a wonderful home. Letterman thanked Stringer for his kind words, even though he still wished he could have the first show back. He just knew he could make it great with just one more crack at it.

A week later Chevy Chase would wish for a second chance as well, but no one would think he was being overly self-critical. Chase came on with an opening show so excruciatingly awful that it became an instant television classic—of the wrong kind. With an opening that simulated vomiting and a mawkish display of mutual congratulations with his onetime costar Goldie Hawn, Chase lost all credibility as a talk-show host in just one night. Only masochism and massive investment induced Fox to keep Chevy on the air for six weeks.

Chevy's humiliating flop provided helpful protective cover for Conan O'Brien, who made his own debut one week later. Michaels had done all he could to smooth the ragged edges of Conan's first hours as a television star. They had squeezed in eleven practice shows to get Conan accustomed to standing and talking in front of an audience. Even then Michaels felt as though they could have used three more weeks of practice.

The premiere show opened with a superbly produced

little video of Conan heading to work on his first day, laughing at everyone's advice about getting nervous. The piece ended with O'Brien in his dressing room, standing on a chair with a noose around his neck. Conan met the live audience for the first time in a high-strung and high-pitched state. Much of what he did seemed manic and forced. But he got through the show without coming unglued; and his appeal with people seemed to come through on camera. One of his guests that first night, Tony Randall, said after the show that the new star was so appealing, Conan didn't have to be funny—words that Conan didn't exactly want to hear. But the mostly kind reviews the next day, almost all of which pointed out how much better Conan was than Chevy, emphasized the same point. It seemed that a nice young man, if not quite a star, had been born.

Later, at the opening night party, Conan was relieved and charged up—and then he was overwhelmingly lonely. There was no one else who could feel exactly as he felt at that moment, having made this improbable dream a reality, or at least the start of a reality.

David Letterman's show became the talk of the television industry before the end of his first week on the air. It wasn't just that he was drawing monster ratings; it was the show itself. The hype got viewers to tune in. Letterman himself got them talking about what they had seen. He had done what he told Bob Wright he would do: He had subtly reinvented himself for the larger audience available an hour earlier. With his sophisticated suits, his obvious enthusiasm for his new surroundings, his increased warmth toward his guests—

especially his women guests—David Letterman was sending out the signal: He had moved to 11:35, and he was there to win. Letterman put it circumspectly but unflinchingly: "It would be very gratifying if we could prevail."

NBC had lined up its arguments to dismiss Letterman's early ratings—temporary, not as good as they should be, not really hurting Jay anyway. But NBC was fighting with credibility as much as with Letterman. The press reaction was nearly unanimous: Letterman was a great star with a great show. For NBC to deny that was futile, so nobody really tried. Instead there was some talk about Letterman being—as Pier Mapes, the network president in charge of affiliate relations and advertising sales, put it—"a flash in the pan."

But the weeks went on, and Letterman won night after night. More than winning the overall ratings, he clobbered the "Tonight" show in the important demographic contest. Dave dominated in all viewers below the age of fifty. Leno's audience was getting smaller and older. Its makeup, in a bit of truly unexpected irony, was beginning to match that of Carson's most recent audience. The preponderance of older viewers had been one of the main reasons why NBC had wanted to nudge Johnny aside in favor of Jay.

The Letterman show was accomplishing this startling success, Robert Morton was fond of saying, "with one arm tied behind our backs." The difference in clearances was almost never mentioned because Letterman was winning so decisively anyway; but it was still there. The "Tonight" show had a 30 percent advantage in getting on the air earlier. That should have given Jay a big edge. But Dave was erasing it night after night. People wanted to watch David Letterman. The broad-based audience wasn't finding him edgy, or nasty, or off-putting. They were finding him appealing—and funny.

Jay himself stayed calm, as always. He watched the numbers carefully, just as he had before, and he thought he would be all right. It was a marathon, he reminded people, not a sprint.

"Dave is awfully strong," Jay said after the first few weeks, acknowledging, in his gracious mode, that "Dave is awfully good." Jay watched Dave just about every night and picked up immediately on how he was doing a longer monologue. That might help, Jay felt, because, in as modest a way as possible, he gave himself credit for winning the battle of the monologues. "We touch on more subjects, I think," Jay said. "We're doing okay," he concluded.

But after Dave's arrival on the scene, Jay found himself even more often the target of cruel cracks in the press. In pieces that declared Dave the outright winner of their late-night clash, Jay's show was frequently put down for being stodgy and unimaginative. Typical of the nasty digs being tossed at Jay in the media was a cartoon in *The New Yorker* just two weeks after Letterman went on the air. The full-page cartoon labeled itself "Items from the Jay Leno Fan Club" and included a cap that said, "Jay Leno does *not* try too hard!"; a button that said, "Jay Leno: He's not *that* bad!"; and a T-shirt that read, "I, for one, do not find Jay Leno *painfully embarrassing* to watch!" Much of the anti-Jay commentary crossed the line into unfairness. Jay, after all, was still drawing a respectable audience every night, and his show was in no way the embarrassment that Chevy Chase's had been. But nothing like that had ever been written about the previous host of the "Tonight" show. Never in thirty years on the air. But then never in thirty years had Johnny Carson lost month after month in the ratings.

Fair or not, the assessment was having impact. It was quickly entering the cultural consciousness. Letterman was cool; Leno was square. Dave was hot; Jay was not. Letterman and CBS were winning; Leno and NBC were losing.

The empire of the night was under siege.

13

WHAT HAVE YOU DONE FOR ME LATELY?

In September 1993 Jack Welch sat in an NBC conference room surrounded by about twenty-five of the network's top executives. The GE chairman always attended the NBC quarterly review meetings. The meeting, as always, was being run by Bob Wright, the NBC president, who asked for reports from his division heads. The entertainment division executives were tied in by speakerphone from Burbank. The review included all of the network's recent activities, with a heavy emphasis on the prime-time season that started that month. The executives talked about what they hoped to achieve with their new shows and their expectations for the overall performance of the network in the fourth quarter.

Jack Welch listened to the conversation around him with his customary scaring intensity. A finely chiseled block of a man, with thinning gray hair and steely blue eyes, Welch's style was as blunt and straight as his posture. He ran a $60 billion-a-year company, which relegated NBC to the status of modest, if incredibly visible, investment. He did not pretend to be an expert in television programming, but he often had opinions, and he was not the type to be timid about expressing them.

As Warren Littlefield ran down the prospects for the fall programming over the speakerphone, Welch didn't hear a certain subject being discussed that he felt ought to be discussed. So he brought it up himself.

"When are we going to talk about late night?" Welch blurted out.

No one at NBC had missed the implications of David Letterman's quick, impressive success in the ratings over at CBS. He was beating the "Tonight" show like a drum, night after night after night. The early results of the competition seemed definitive, with Letterman especially dominating the younger viewers that mattered most in television. NBC wasn't even bothering to try to contradict the conclusions being drawn in the press anymore: that Dave was already established as late-night's leading man. The recognition of that was so widespread that the subject wasn't even being discussed formally inside NBC.

Except by Jack Welch. He wanted the issue addressed. Put on the spot, Warren Littlefield, a stand-up guy himself in the face of direct confrontation, jumped to respond to Welch's challenge. "We can talk about late night anytime you want, Jack," Warren said.

Jack wanted to discuss it right then and there. He had something he wanted to say; he had made his own evaluation of what had transpired, and it was time to get it off his chest.

"All I want to say about the late-night situation is this," Welch said. "Ebersol, Rohrbeck, and—" Welch hesitated for the briefest moment before continuing,

"—Wright were right. And Warren, you and Agoglia and—" again the slightest pause "—Welch were wrong."

The group of executives on each coast knew that Jack Welch was putting the question of who was responsible for the decision to choose Jay Leno over David Letterman out on the table to ensure it did not fester inside NBC. By including himself on the wrong side of the decision, he softened the blow for Littlefield and Agoglia, the executives most exposed on the firing line for choosing Jay over Dave. Welch didn't deal in recriminations; he wasn't that type of corporate executive. Nor was he going to play games with the facts. The decision had been made. It looked as if those who had backed David Letterman had been correct in their assessment that he was a stronger television star than Jay Leno. It was time for NBC to acknowledge that truth and move on.

As Welch later put it: "Letterman has clearly been a success. Jay is doing well, but it really isn't sampling anymore."

With the last comment Welch was echoing Warren Littlefield's own realistic assessment as the ratings settled into a normal pattern and Letterman regularly won the nightly competition—despite his 30 percent handicap in clearances. Warren had looked at the numbers for the first ten weeks of competition and said that Dave's edge couldn't be dismissed by NBC anymore as merely an indication that the audience was trying him out.

Welch said the real decision to pick Leno over Letterman had been made back in 1991, not in January 1993, during the last-minute reconsideration. "It was a decision made more than two years ago," Welch said. "NBC made it. Obviously we'd be a lot happier if the ratings were reversed. But they're not."

As he had said in the meeting in Boca Raton, Welch himself had come down on the side of loyalty—and loyalty was Jay. "The decision we made, which was a commitment to Jay, we kept. Then we moved forward. And I supported that totally. So I'm part of that support system. I was part of that decision."

Like others at NBC, Welch had questioned whether Letterman would be able to alter his style to adapt to the earlier time period. That question had been answered very quickly; Letterman had fine-tuned the act perfectly. His CBS show, virtually every NBC executive conceded, was being executed brilliantly.

Bob Wright was among the least surprised. "Dave has come out and done basically what I thought he would do," Wright said. "Maybe to the surprise of some other people—not as much of a surprise to me." Like Welch and most of the other NBC executives, Wright remained supportive of Jay. He didn't want to say anything to undercut the network's effort to prop up the "Tonight" franchise as best it could. But Wright's close friends knew that as the Letterman show took off, sweeping up the best ratings in late night, all the best comments in the press, and the best part of the late-night advertising budgets, Bob had twinges of regret that he hadn't gone all the way with his own instincts, which told him that Letterman's was a one-of-a-kind talent. Some of Bob's friends heard his wife, Suzanne, get on him after the fact, telling him that he should have trusted his gut, because it really was just as good as anyone's on his programming staff.

Wright knew what Letterman's ascension would mean: the end of NBC's monopoly hold over late night and a sizable chunk of the profits it had generated. Putting as bright a face on it as he could, Wright concluded that the "Tonight" show could still make good money for the network—less money, but still good money. "That's not an intolerable situation," Wright said. "So our ego is hurt right now and maybe our pocketbook is lighter by some, but it's not destroyed."

Of course, everything that was coming out of NBC's pocketbook was flowing directly into CBS's, a development that galled Wright and the other NBC executives. As Littlefield saw it, CBS, which had never successfully developed anything in late night, had finally managed to establish a winner—purely out of the impossible circumstances NBC found itself in. Only by raiding NBC's late-night talent, Littlefield said, had somebody else finally broken through the NBC late-night dominance.

CBS wasn't quibbling about where David Letterman came from. All the network's executives cared about was having him, and all he brought to the network. Letterman provided instant dividends. Even with his massive contract and the expenditures on the Ed Sullivan Theater, a total figure that exceeded $50 million, CBS figured to make some profits, perhaps $10 million, in Letterman's first year.

The 4.1 rating that CBS guaranteed was so quickly eclipsed that within two months the network began releasing the commercials it had held in reserve for March and April to see if it would be forced to offer make-goods for any ratings shortfall. Advertisers got the message right away: Letterman was a late-night phenomenon. He was bringing in younger viewers in numbers the time period hadn't seen since Carson's greatest days. More than that, he was attracting the hardest viewers for advertisers to reach: Light television viewers, those who watched little or nothing regularly, were changing their habits to catch Dave.

Few shows anywhere on television had such an attractive audience makeup; high-income viewers, highly educated viewers, young men, young women, decision makers, homemakers. Young women, who were expected to be the hardest group for Letterman to reach, were actually his largest single constituency, beating even young men, who had always been his core audience. Advertisers began to line up at Letterman's door like groupies, trying to buy their way into the sold-out show. Some movie companies, quickly recognizing that the profile of Letterman's audience was almost a mirror of the main moviegoing audience, offered to double CBS's established price of $30,000 for a thirty-second commercial, if the network would move some existing sponsors out and free up the time. CBS resisted that temptation, but did free up the make-good time to try to satisfy the movie companies. Other products, such as athletic shoes and jeans, beer and automobiles, bought time in CBS's late night for the first time. Anheuser-Busch used buys in the Letterman show to help launch a new product line, Iced Bud.

Some of the sponsors buying into Letterman were new clients for CBS; they bought nothing in CBS's prime-time lineup because its audience profile was so much older. Letterman was the ultimate rainmaker for CBS; new business was flying in the door. CBS's only regret: It had badly undersold Letterman's first season. The network could have charged 20 percent, even 30 percent, more and still sold out all the time in the show.

But that was the upside that loomed in the future. CBS realized shortly into the first season that its real opportunity to cash in on Letterman's success would come the following summer, when it could walk into a hothouse seller's market, offering jacked-up prices that would still find plenty of willing buyers. And if CBS could find the right 12:30 host to follow Letterman, someone who could effectively challenge the still-green Conan, the potential was there for CBS to be the network thinking about a time period worth $50 million to $70 million a year in profits—not NBC. The transfer of funds was about to follow the transfer of power in late night.

The events of 1993 in late-night television inevitably conjured up the royal metaphor that had always been attached to Johnny Carson's reign over the "Tonight" show: When Johnny, the King of Late Night, stepped down, he took off his crown and left it on the stage to be claimed by the next great late-night talent. Jay Leno had a year and a half to pick up that crown and put it on his head. He had to survive chaotic upheaval and even a threat from within his own camp. That he did both was a testament to his resiliency and his indefatigable willingness to keep on going forward. But a year and half later, the crown still eluded Jay's grasp.

And then David Letterman came along, finally freed

to seek the crown himself. Within a month, he had picked it up, carried it off, and fixed it firmly on his head.

For Jay Leno, it was back to the familiar struggle to prove himself. He had seen David Letterman pass him twice—first when Dave zoomed past him in the comedy clubs to rapid television stardom, a move that Jay trumped by leapfrogging Dave to get the "Tonight" show; and then when Dave, with no tradition of late night at his network and a far weaker lineup of stations, cruised on by to take the leadership in late night away from Jay.

A gentle, decent guy, though a far more complicated person than ever came across on television, Leno responded the only way he knew how: He worked harder. Jay worked his phones again to the press, the advertisers, and the NBC affiliates. He reminded them all that no matter what Dave was doing, Jay was still doing well.

And he was. His ratings were off, but not drastically. The makeup of his audience had gotten older, but there were still enough advertisers buying time to ensure NBC would have a business. The quick demise of Chevy Chase had made more people aware of just how hard it was to find a host who could do a comedy/talk show five nights a week, forty-plus weeks a year. The critics in the press didn't give him the credit he deserved, but Jay could clearly do it. He was one of the few performers alive who could put a solid, late-night show on every night. He just couldn't do it as well as one other guy.

Jay wasn't the late-night leader anymore. The ratings, the almighty numbers that Jay had lived by, churned out the standings night after night, week after week—and every week that Dave won set a new record for the weeks that NBC's "Tonight" show wasn't in first place.

Inside the show, talk started early in the fall that it might be time to accept status as the second-best show in late night—or maybe even third-best, because ABC's "Nightline" was having a big year and beating the "Tonight" show consistently and even Letterman occasionally. Through the end of the year, Jay himself didn't accept that conclusion, and continued to express confidence that as time went on things would even out. "I always said it would take months and months before we really knew anything," Jay said.

NBC's view, as expressed by Warren Littlefield, was that the show still needed work. Warren and his head of late-night programs, Rick Ludwin, advanced several ideas, including one that Jay needed to add "comedy correspondents" to the show, other comics who could go to the scene of some goofy event and report back and interact with Jay. "I believe Jay has to go to the next level," Warren said. "There are a number of things he does well and a number of things that can and will progress. We have an action plan on all of them. Helen has been gone over a year. All the wounds have mended. We want more out of the show."

In November, Jay relented and accepted the need to add a head writer on the show. Reluctant as always to hurt anyone's feelings, he tried to assure his holdover staff that they were not being slighted. Jay elevated one writer, Joe Medeiros, to be co–head writer with the new guy, Joe Toplyn. Toplyn, a talented and well-regarded writer out of the Harvard club, had solid credits—he began his career writing for David Letterman.

The addition of Toplyn, the introduction of "comedy correspondents," Warren's "action plan"—all reflected NBC's unflagging commitment to Jay. But they also reflected the network's conclusion that eighteen months into his tenure on the "Tonight" show, Jay Leno's role as host was a work in progress.

More than just his doubters inside NBC were surprised at how adeptly David Letterman had changed his act to fit the earlier time period. As the weeks went on and Letterman turned in classy show after classy show, even members of his own staff marveled at his skill in modifying his comedy just enough to broaden out his audience base. He was managing to welcome viewers who might not have warmed to the quirkier style of his early years on "Late Night." Yet he was not alienating those who had come to view him as a subversive, nonmainstream comic. He had become the wisest wise guy on television.

"Dave never discussed with any of us how he was going to change the show," Robert Morton said. "That was all Dave. His instincts are incredible."

One major difference in the new Dave was simply his peace of mind. Twice within the first three months of the show, Letterman called staff meetings, an almost unheard-of development. The purpose was mainly to give everyone encouragement, and to thank them for their efforts. At the second meeting Dave told the staff that this was the happiest time of his life.

"On the 12:30 show I never managed to control Dave," Peter Lassally said. "Because Dave is Dave. And Dave was angry a lot of the time. During the three months that we were off, something happened to Dave, without, I think, our doing anything to him. Morty and I both felt there was a change in Dave. Some of the anger and frustration began to disappear."

The nightly monologue, which Lassally felt Dave used to throw away on the old show because he never committed himself to doing it well, suddenly became important enough to Dave that he went out and sold it, night after night. "I mean, he committed to it," Lassally said. "He had never committed to it before. And now he would just do a joke, stand there, and receive the laugh with a big, warm grin on his face. Well, that's something I have not seen him do before. Boy, did that excite me. I mean, like a real performer, a confident performer putting it out there. That thrilled me."

Morton said the transfer to CBS had worked a form of liberation on Letterman. "I think he felt underappreciated at NBC for all those years. And I think there was resentment that he was going out and doing his very best effort and doing good, strong shows, and the network didn't even give a damn about him. And I think now he realizes he's at a network where they really give a damn about him. And it's very enjoyable. It makes doing the daily shows that much easier when you're appreciated."

Letterman even allowed himself to admit it was a kick finally to be on at 11:30. "It really is, it's fun," he said. "I was always worried about it. I thought, well, you know, especially when I was trying to rationalize not getting the 'Tonight' show, I thought, well maybe this is my lot. Maybe 12:30 is about all I can do. But now I just think: Why were we on at 12:30 all those years?"

Many times in his last several years at NBC, Letterman would finish a show and ask Morton what could possibly be wrong with that show, why it couldn't play at 11:30 just as well as the things these other guys, like Jay and Arsenio, were doing. "I remember one time," Letterman said, "when we were talking about something we had done, and Morty said, 'Look at the guys who are on at 11:30.' And he mentioned all the guys and I said, 'Yeah, why can't I be on at 11:30 if these guys are on at 11:30?' "

Letterman had been a ballplayer hitting close to .400 year after year who was being kept unjustly down on the farm, never allowed to go to the show so he could prove what he could do. All Letterman wanted was the chance to get to the majors, to 11:30. When the time came for NBC to decide who got that chance, it picked Jay Leno.

And so the successor to Johnny Carson packed up his office, his talent, and his vision and walked out of NBC forever, taking with him the last great franchise in the network television business: late night.

POSTSCRIPT: SHOWDOWN IN MIDTOWN

I f he had been a man who traded in metaphors, Jay Leno might have thought deeply about what had been happening to him and the "Tonight" show in that fall of 1994 as he rode in the elevator surging up more than sixty floors above Rockefeller Plaza.

He was on the rise; he could feel it. For the first sustained period of time since David Letterman had taken late night by storm at CBS, Leno had momentum. His numbers were up. So was his confidence.

For months, Jay had been telling his staff that Dave was vulnerable in the very area Letterman was always credited as being superior: comedy. Jay checked out Dave's nightly monologue and found it increasingly spare of jokes. He also detected that Letterman's comedy bits after the monologue were more and more often comedy stunts: Call the phone on the corner and talk some passerby into coming into the theater. Do some goofy bit with Mujibur and Sirajul, the two Bangladeshi souvenir peddlers up the street from Dave's theater. Send out some guy in a bear suit to see if he could get a free hot dog from a street vendor.

"Where are the jokes?" Jay asked his friends. "I just don't see the great comedy writing."

In contrast, Jay had kept up his astonishing nightly joke quotient—16, 18, 20 jokes per monologue, always on the issues of the day: politics, Hollywood scandals, the hot story from the tabloids. "We're always the most quoted show," he pointed out proudly to the press. And he was convinced he was adding the bite and edge to the jokes that he had been criticized for leaving out when he first took over the show two years earlier.

From the beginning Jay had been willing to wade into the tricky waters of the O. J. Simpson murder case. He reasoned that the details of the case itself might be too sensitive for humor, but the insane media circus that surrounded it was surely fair game. He marveled at Letterman's refusal to acknowledge the case even existed. Here was a story that the public was obsessed with and Dave was still telling jokes about Ted Kennedy dropping his pants. Letterman was obviously steering clear of the entire issue, presumably on the advice of his executive producer, Peter Lassally. When radio shock jock Howard Stern appeared as a guest with Letterman that summer, he pressured Dave into explaining why he wasn't doing jokes on the O.J. trial. Letterman said he found it a hard subject to joke about.

For Jay, this was an opportunity to contrast himself favorably with Dave for all those in the press who had written him off as stodgy Jay. Here was Dave playing it safe, while Jay banged away at the O.J. case.

Jay's staff cranked out the O.J. jokes and every night that Dave didn't was a night Jay figured he had automatically "won the monologue," as he liked to put it. It certainly made sense to Jay when the Letterman show brought in a new group of comedy writers, including one team that had worked for Carson, expressly to kick up Letterman's monologue.

And in one of the first developments from this renewed emphasis on the monologue, Letterman started doing occasional O.J. jokes. Leno didn't broadcast his pleasure, but he surely sensed a degree of vindication in that move.

As he rode the elevator inside 30 Rock, NBC's corporate headquarters, accompanied by Mavis, Jay Leno carried himself with the bearing of a boxer given a shot at a rematch. He all but bounced on his feet.

Just minutes earlier he had completed the taping of that night's show, on the stage usually occupied by "Saturday Night Live," dark that week because of the Thanksgiving holiday. The taping had gone exceptionally well, Jay believed. It was a signal that this was going to be a great week of shows in New York City, in midtown, right in the heart of Letterman country.

Leno traced the spark that had lit his comeback to his previous trip to New York, six months earlier. That was the first time he had taken the "Tonight" show out of the Burbank studio, and the week in New York had supplied him and his staff with a bracing hit of adrenaline. Forced to build a temporary set, the producers had given Jay just a little platform above the audience, much in the manner of the stages he appeared on in comedy clubs. The result was a closeness to the audience that Jay had never experienced before as host of the "Tonight" show. Combined with the intensity and energy of the New York crowds, the closer connection with the people laughing at his jokes pumped Jay up like nothing else on the show ever had.

From the day he had taken over as host, colleagues and critics alike had remarked that Jay was just not as good on the air as he was in the comedy clubs, and wondered why. Now Jay himself discovered the same thing—he needed to be closer to the audience to do his best work. He came away from that first New York trip feeling as though he had found the answer: He had to reinvent the show in his own image. It was time to stop doing Johnny's old show with a new cast; it was time to make the "Tonight" show his own.

So he asked the set designers in L.A. to redo his Burbank set in the style of what they had done for him in New York. Get rid of that bleacher look that was a holdover from the Carson days. When the new set was finished, Jay felt like a man reborn. Finally he would be doing a show tooled expressly for his own talents.

And the tooling was certainly being done with that in mind. Beyond the set, the content of the show was being carefully calibrated to match Jay's strengths and avoid his weaknesses. Because of his supreme ability to craft and tell a joke, and his far lesser ability in dealing with "concept humor," the writing staff experimented with formats that lent themselves to joke telling, rather than any form of improvisation. As the year went on, the writers and producers came up with what they considered several reliable bits.

The combination of the new set and the more focused approach of giving Jay comedy he could score with certainly seemed to be working. The ratings were up about 15 percent from the previous fall . . . and Dave was coming into range.

Jay and Dave had been on the air against each other for more than sixty weeks. Jay's total number of weeks in first place: zero. Even when Letterman had a week of repeats and Leno a week of original shows, he had never managed to beat Dave. But the tide certainly seemed to be turning in Jay's favor. One week in October, with both shows in repeats, the two men had tied in the ratings. And Jay took special pride in the knowledge that Dave had actually planned on taking two straight weeks off that August only to scale it back to one week because, Jay concluded, Dave was afraid the streak would be broken.

Much more thrilling to Jay were the results that arrived in the week prior to his return to New York. In a week where both men had offered new programs, Jay had trailed Dave by just one-tenth of a ratings point.

The timing could hardly have been more propitious. Here was Jay coming to New York, ready to do battle with Dave on his home turf, and he was riding a crest. The gap had all but closed. The long humbling nightmare Leno had been compelled to live with, the descent of the mighty "Tonight" show to permanent status as the second-best late-night show, had a chance to be interrupted, if not ended completely.

Leno himself was extremely careful about leaving Letterman out of his public statements about how much better he felt about his show. But privately he could not help but be excited at the prospect of being able to say to the world for the first time: Yeah, I beat Dave last week.

NBC saw no reason for caution at all. The network's research department had taken to sending out weekly memos to the press boasting of Jay's turnaround in the ratings and comparing his performance specifically to Letterman's. In the week before Leno's trip to New York, the NBC promotion department, in a sudden spasm of cockiness, sent out a nine-page color pamphlet, which looked like a $3.00 Hallmark greeting card. It featured Jay, behind the wheel of one of his vintage roadsters, zooming along a cartoon road. Along the way road signs were posted with Jay's recent ratings gains in various cities: Chicago, Atlanta, Boston, all the places where Jay was suddenly beating Dave regularly. At the end was a final sign: PASSING LANE AHEAD.

The campaign reflected NBC's growing conviction that despite all the attention that had surrounded Letterman's first year on the air, despite the accolades in the press, despite the Emmy award, David Letterman could still be taken.

Jay believed it too. He had never stopped believing it. And now as he stepped off the elevator on the 64th floor, dressed in a striking blue suit, his hair cut longer than it had been in years (a striking contrast with Dave's noticeably thinning patch), his beaming wife on his arm, Jay Leno walked into a swirling NBC holiday party looking and feeling like . . . a winner.

Less than a ten-minute walk away, at the corner of 53rd and Broadway, in the offices of "Late Show with David Letterman," the mood was very different.

The tension that surrounded working with David Letterman never really let up, not even as Dave recorded triumph after triumph, week after week. As Letterman himself put it, "You kind of wish this could get a little easier, but it never gets any easier." In reality, doing the show was harder than it had ever been for Letterman because he was doing more shows than ever before. He was a five-night-a-week star on CBS, where he had always only done four nights a week on NBC. That meant his daily schedule was much longer, because he came to reserve several hours at night to do his remote-taped comedy pieces, which he felt were too much a signature of the show to give up.

So Letterman found himself leaving his home in Connecticut each morning at about 8:30 to drive to Manhattan. The workday would often last until 10:00 P.M. That put him home at 11:00, with very little time for anything until it was time to go to bed and start the whole routine all over again.

And though he had contracted with CBS to take ten weeks of vacation, Letterman had decided that was too much, given the continuing competition. Members of his staff began to be concerned about the pace Letterman was setting. "He is always exhausted," one of his closest colleagues said. At one point Johnny Carson called Peter Lassally and told him he didn't believe Dave could keep up the five-day-a-week schedule indefinitely. "It's going to wear him out," Carson said.

But Letterman could not back off the accelerator, not with NBC and Jay Leno spreading the word that the race was far from over. Though everyone on the show paid some lip service to the conclusion that Jay would have to win a week eventually, they all knew the week that it happened would be a grim one around Dave's big office overlooking Broadway. Letterman was in this competition to win, always to win. He watched the ratings every bit as closely as Jay did, and he questioned any falloff, trying to sense if a shift was coming. Letterman did indeed cancel one week of a planned two-week vacation that August out of concern that the show could lose some of its momentum if Jay continued to do fresh shows.

At some points Dave even longed for the good old days of 12:30 A.M. when the attention was small, the pressure slight, and the living easy. "We were lucky when we were at 12:30," Letterman said. "We didn't have everybody coming at us then."

The main somebody coming at him remained Leno, of course, and Letterman and his staff watched with some irritation as Jay and NBC mounted their campaign to sell the idea of a comeback. "I'm not surprised Jay didn't go away," Letterman said. "That would have been unlikely. How could the 'Tonight' show go away? To be on for forty years and occupy a position like that in American culture? That show will survive. Not to take anything away from Jay, but that show and the 'Today' show have been an integral part of the broadcast schedule for forty years."

That conclusion was Dave's rational mind speaking. The fact was, Letterman and his staff did not understand how Leno could have risen up again, zombie-like, from the competitive dead to pose a threat again—or at least to be perceived in the press as posing a threat again.

As Leno arrived in New York that week, Letterman saw the publicity surge that accompanied Jay—and it drove him nuts. It made him even more nuts to hear that when Jay appeared as a guest on "Live with Regis and Kathie Lee," Regis Philbin, one of Dave's most frequent guests, introduced Jay with a comment on how he was "running neck and neck with Dave." Letterman didn't watch the show but his executive producer, Robert Morton, told him about it, helping to drive Dave even more crazy.

Morton, as usual, was among the feistiest of the late-night combatants. He believed the so-called Leno comeback was a sham and did his best to get that message out into the press. Leno's improvement, as Morton saw it, had nothing to do with a new set, new comedy bits, or any other reinvention of his show. Morton argued that any tightening in the ratings between Dave and Jay was entirely due to circumstances outside each of the shows: namely, the changing fortunes of the networks the two men were working for.

In the eighteen months since Letterman had come to CBS, the network, so successfully rebuilt in the early 1990s, had undergone a transformation. Instead of leading, CBS was reeling. With shortsightedness that seemed astonishing in retrospect, the network had plugged holes in its schedule with stopgap programs and specials, most of which appealed to older audiences, instead of finding new youthful hits to capitalize on the network's success.

Much worse, CBS played hardball too long in its renegotiations for rights to the NFC package of NFL football games. After losing more than $100 million, CBS figured it was time to get a better price from its longtime partner. The other networks wanted the same thing. But none of them counted on the willingness of a new player, Rupert Murdoch, and his Fox network, to pay almost anything to get into the NFL arena.

In the end Murdoch took advantage of CBS's slow reaction and NBC, recognizing the danger, moved quickly to firm up a new NFL deal at a price the league liked. Murdoch offered more than $1.6 billion for a four-year NFL deal, an astronomical increase over what CBS had paid. When the CBS chairman, Larry Tisch, balked at matching the price, which CBS calculated would mean losses of $200 million a year or more, "The NFL on CBS," a fixture of more than thirty years' standing, was gone.

For Letterman the blow was devastating. "It was so discouraging to lose football," he said. "That really hurt us. To have your image associated with the NFL is so dynamic, so important."

If anything, the news got worse for CBS five months later when Murdoch pulled off another coup. Opening his apparently bottomless wallet again, he shelled out another $500 million to buy an interest in New World Communications, one of the largest owners of television stations. Many of the stations New World owned were affiliated with CBS, but as soon as they had a deal with Murdoch, they announced their intention of dumping CBS in favor of Fox. Huge markets were involved—Atlanta, Cleveland, Detroit, among others.

After the dust cleared, and after all the networks had made new deals to try to shore up their affiliation relationships, CBS was hurt badly. In each of those three markets, along with Milwaukee, CBS was relegated to a distant UHF station, whose signal was inherently weaker than what CBS had previously had with New World's VHF stations. In those cases mighty CBS had become the coat-hanger network. The worst case was Detroit, where CBS was forced to buy off a religious broadcaster for rights to Channel 62, formerly known as WGPR—for "Where God's Power Reigns."

"It's so discouraging," Letterman said. "In Detroit they don't even have a real building for the station. I just know we're going to be on Channel A Hundred and Seven. And I remember the days when CBS was the network everyone wanted to be with."

Winding up on a network in disarray was the last thing David Letterman expected when he decided to jump to CBS in January, 1993. He believed Howard Stringer when he said CBS was the network on the move up. Letterman thought he was boarding a moving train. He had no inkling that it was almost out of fuel and he himself would be counted on to do most of the stoking.

Every day when Morton got the overnight ratings from CBS research, he looked at how Dave was faring in the bigger cities and all but choked. Leno had started beating Dave regularly in Chicago and Los Angeles, among other places. Jay was even occasionally nosing ahead of Dave in New York. But Morton saw the context. CBS's prime-time ratings were almost in a freefall, at least on the weeknights, when Letterman was on the air. Except for Monday, CBS was at a competitive disadvantage every night.

Worse, NBC was making a serious prime-time charge. The network had boldly rebuilt its Tuesday night. Most impressive of all was what NBC had done on Thursday. Its new drama "ER" was the runaway hit of the season. Because it played at 10 P.M., that meant it led directly into the local news—and from there directly into Jay Leno.

All of a sudden Thursday night was becoming a daunting night for Letterman to try to compete with

Leno. Thanks to that powerhouse "ER" lead-in, Jay was beating Dave like a drum every Thursday. "Thursday is a tsunami," Letterman acknowledged ruefully.

As they always had in the past at NBC, Letterman's off-the-air frustrations occasionally spilled onto the air. He started taking shots at CBS for its prime-time disasters. One night, in a bit about unusual product warning labels, Letterman held up a copy of *TV Guide* with the attached label: "Warning: May contain CBS prime-time schedule!"

In mid-October, he subjected his CBS bosses to the full treatment: a top ten list: "The Top Ten Ways CBS Can Improve Its Prime-Time Ratings." Among the selections:

New Contest: Watch a week of CBS shows, get a shot at helping Connie Chung have a baby.

Send Dr. Quinn, Medicine Woman, on the road to perform complimentary throat cultures.

Let Beavis and Butthead sit in for Dan and Connie.

Judge Ito hosts Funny, Funny Courtroom Bloopers.

More shots of Dan Rather spitting.

Later Letterman had a little remorse. "I don't want to burn the network too badly," he said. "I kind of feel maybe the jokes are reinforcing the image of a network in trouble. But it's certainly discouraging. They don't seem to have a great inventory of shows."

Letterman's concerns about CBS's prime-time travails came to a head the week Leno came to New York.

It was November, a network sweeps month. CBS had begged Letterman for a prime-time special, an anniversary show like the ones he used to do on NBC. Of course, his anniversary was really in August. But that wasn't the main problem. Letterman simply didn't want to do a prime-time show. It meant more work, and more pressure. Letterman always hated going into prime time; he wasn't comfortable there. He was more exposed there.

"I just feel like it's all me. The show is all me," Letterman said. "I feel like I'm the reason people are going to watch or not watch. If I don't carry the comedy, the show suffers. I mean if Don Mattingly hits, you can pretty much count on the fact that the Yankees are going to win. It just always ends up in my lap."

It was all he needed: the additional scrutiny of a prime-time show. But CBS persisted. And finally Letterman relented. He agreed to do a show based on the best of his remote comedy pieces. Then he spent what he called "endless hours" looking at videotape, culling the best bits, such as his junk food excursion through L.A. with Zsa Zsa Gabor.

The special was scheduled for Monday night, Jay Leno's first night in New York. It was one more chip to raise the stakes on the table.

Almost every NBC figure of any significance, from Bob Wright to Tom Brokaw to Katie Couric, even to the nonagenarian Bob Hope (in town to ride a float in the Macy's Thanksgiving Day parade), was crowded into the banquet room on the 64th floor of 30 Rock. The occasion was the start of the holiday season in New

York, but it was more than that for NBC. The network was celebrating its escape from the brink of the grave.

Daytime was still a black hole, but otherwise the network was recovering on all fronts: News was improving; Sports was in exceptional shape, having preserved football to go along with the NBA and the upcoming Olympics in Atlanta; prime time was looking better than it had in years.

That only left late night, once considered the birthright of NBC. The shocking ascension of David Letterman to supremacy in late night had left a deep scar inside NBC, especially on the psyches of those executives who had a hand in passing over him in favor of Leno. All of them were still at the network. That surprised many outsiders who could not believe that the executives who had made that call, one of the most significant in the history of television, were still in place.

After all, one senior NBC executive, assessing the fallout from the late-night decision as honestly as he could, said of the decision to choose Leno and allow Letterman to go to CBS, "That was a half-a-billion dollar mistake."

But Bob Wright still ran NBC, and Wright chose not to judge his executives on the basis of one less-than-stellar decision. Indeed, the executive at the center of the decision, Warren Littlefield, had done a remarkable job of rehabilitating his image as a programmer in the eighteen months since Letterman had made him look so wrong about late-night. First Littlefield resurrected NBC's mighty Thursday night of programming, then he stuck his neck far out under the blade by moving a new hit comedy, "Frasier," to Tuesday where it faced off against television's most popular show, ABC's "Home Improvement." But that move proved to be brilliant, creating a second powerful night for NBC. The addition of "ER" on Thursday cemented Littlefield's comeback.

As Warren Littlefield entered the NBC party that November night, the sweeps month was looking like NBC's best in years. So he could hardly contain his buoyant joy. NBC was back; so was he.

"If we get a couple more shows working, we're going to have to add staff to count the money," Littlefield joked.

Though he was still among the most gentlemanly of competitors in the television business, there was a bit of an edge in Littlefield's voice when he talked about CBS. Warren said, with just a trace of bitterness, "All CBS has going for it is Letterman."

Letterman. If the name didn't actually haunt Warren Littlefield, it certainly popped into his mind an awful lot. Clearly Littlefield did not relish the prospect of his career being judged principally on the one call he made about late night. More than anything, he wanted to expunge from the historical record the conclusion that he had made one of the wrongest calls ever in the annals of the television industry.

And so he argued the point: "The jury is still out on late night," he said. It was a long race, he told everyone. Jay was coming on. Dave was starting to fade.

Warren also took some credit for the changes Jay had made in his show. He said he was very hands-on with Jay, suggesting ideas, staying in touch on an almost daily basis. The "Tonight" staff appreciated the executive support, even when they didn't exactly want to hand out creativity awards to Warren Littlefield for improving the show. "Oh, now Warren's the show's savior?" one "Tonight" staff member said. "You should hear Warren's ideas."

Jay himself maintained a good relationship with Littlefield, though his previous trials at the hands of NBC's executives had left him a bit more cynical in general about network support.

Bucked up by Jay's near tie the week before he came to New York, Littlefield gave an interview to Eric Mink in the *New York Daily News* in which he let his optimism run a bit wild. He said he hoped that Jay would pull even with Dave by the end of 1994 and that sometime in 1995, Jay would be the leader again in late night.

As bold as those words sounded, few at the NBC party that night saw reason to question them. The trend looked convincing.

And so when Jay Leno appeared at the doorway to the banquet room, a buzz went through the NBC crowd. Jay Leno had arrived and Jay Leno was hot.

Jay worked the room—and the prime-rib on sourdough—with even more than his characteristic enthusiasm. He was getting congratulations everywhere. "Oh thanks a lot," Jay said, trying to sound casual between bites. He introduced Mavis around; she seemed to be enjoying the attention he was getting as well.

Then a dark-suited figure interrupted Jay's swing around the room and asked for a private moment. It was John Rohrbeck, the president of NBC's stations division and one of the key executives who had openly and vocally supported Leno's ouster in favor of Letterman almost two years earlier. Rohrbeck had argued that Jay would be a disaster for NBC's stations.

Jay excused himself and stepped to one side with Rohrbeck, who shook his hand enthusiastically and spoke with him earnestly. Jay nodded and smiled, then Rohrbeck clapped him on the back, shook hands again, and left.

When Jay returned to Mavis he had not changed his usual controlled expression. But his report was certainly noteworthy.

"Rohrbeck just told me he was sorry. He said he had misjudged me, and apologized for that. He said it turned out I was doing good for the O and O's. I think he thought I'd be mad. I just told him, don't worry about it. This is just business. I said I was trying to bring the ship around. It was fine."

Leno did not even allow himself the slightest smile of satisfaction.

In the center of the room a small group was too busy with their own concerns to pay homage to Jay Leno. They were the staff from "Late Night with Conan O'Brien," including Conan himself, his sidekick Andy Richter, his producers Jeff Ross and Rob Smigel, and the man responsible for selecting Conan in the first place, Lorne Michaels.

Their eighteen months on the air had not gone quite so smoothly as Letterman's. Early curiosity had given way to some harsh criticism, then a period of slow growth, mostly in obscurity. One moment from the show's first year still stood out: the night that David Letterman himself had come in as a guest.

"Dave was crucial for us," Ross said. "He was not only brilliantly funny, but he gave us credibility by saying we were doing some of the best comedy on television."

Letterman had indeed said that, and it did lead to some reconsiderations of Conan. Those who watched regularly did see some of the most original comedy being done on television—on some nights. On others, they saw some of the unfunniest.

The show's unpredictability centered on Conan himself. Though he now had nights when he brought off some brilliant piece of written comedy, he still had nights when he looked like he didn't belong on television at all. What no one at NBC could seem to conclude was whether Conan had reached a plateau in his performing ability, one well short of true comic stardom, or whether he would continue to progress, although at an agonizingly glacial pace.

As a clear hedge, NBC had hired Greg Kinnear, a far slicker host type, to take over Bob Costas's "Later" show. Kinnear was so polished where Conan remained raw that many inside NBC believed it was only a matter of time before the network slid Conan out rudely and Greg in gently at 12:30.

Certainly that was the main worry of the Conan staff. They never got a message otherwise from NBC, which continued to express its doubts about Conan's long-term viability by giving him extremely short-term renewals. Every thirteen weeks. Never for a year, never even for six months. The lack of support drove the Conan staff crazy. They were left so insecure that every rumor sent a shiver through them. At one point Littlefield was openly dallying with Howard Stern. The Conan staff could only guess what Warren would have in mind for him.

In the middle of it all stood the lanky figure of Conan himself: a pleasant, clever, but still uncharismatic guy trying to figure out what it takes to be a star.

Whatever was being said about him as host, however, Conan's show was indeed demonstrating growth. If improved ratings performance was the criterion for NBC, Conan started to provide it. The talk about Kinnear began to fade, especially after one of NBC's top executives questioned whether Kinnear "had developed a comic voice."

Nor were the Conan people worried too much about the next challenge on the horizon, the backup late-night entry on CBS, a new talk show hosted by Tom Snyder. It wasn't that Conan was cocky. It was just that it didn't seem likely Snyder would appeal to any of the viewers who now liked Conan.

Snyder was Letterman's personal choice for the job. Some sneered and said the old host of the "Tomorrow" show, now in his fifties, was so passé he would only attract viewers too old to stay up past midnight. But Letterman argued that Snyder had a special broadcasting quality and backed him, even over opposition from some CBS executives who at first preferred a show hosted by another comic.

Littlefield dismissed Snyder as an act whose time had passed. "That show ought to come with a laugh track," Littlefield said.

· · ·

Only one thing seemed to be worrying Jay Leno at the NBC party that night: his bookings for the week. Coming into New York during Thanksgiving week had been NBC's idea, he said. The studio would be available because "Saturday Night Live" was dark. But nobody considered the fact that Thanksgiving week might not be the best week to line up guests.

The truth was somebody had indeed considered that—Robert Morton at the Letterman show. For weeks, since he had heard NBC's plans, Morty had worked at putting up a guest list for the week that would give Dave all the ammunition he needed to thwart Leno. The show had pulled out all its guns, starting the week with Arnold Schwarzenegger and closing it with Stupid Human Tricks, one of Letterman's most potent draws.

"If Jay's coming into our home, we have to fight any way we can," Morty said.

The other secret weapon for Letterman was his first-ever prime-time special for CBS. Despite Dave's reluctance, Morty and the other staff members concluded they needed another burst of publicity to counter the campaign for Jay that NBC had launched. The special gave them an opportunity to get press, and to get a barrage of promotions and newspaper advertisements out of CBS.

The special was well reviewed. It finished second in its time period to ABC's football game. That led viewers happily into the Monday show with Schwarzenegger. Dave opened a big lead on Jay starting with that night.

Morton, taking a cue from the CBS research department, which counseled booking a college band because so many college kids would be home for the Thanksgiving weekend, scheduled the band Candlebox for Wednesday night. The show drew a huge 7.3 rating. Stupid Human Tricks closed out the week with a 6.7 rating.

For the week, Dave had a 6.2 rating; Jay had a 4.7. The sudden one-tenth point margin had just as suddenly become one-and-a-half points, or well over a million viewers.

Jay was never in the hunt in New York.

On his way out of the city, Jay tried to be philosophical. "I think the shows looked good. Some of the critics liked us. It's just too hard to get guests in New York in Thanksgiving week—especially when the other guys are out there working against you." What bothered him more than anything was NBC's overselling the week as though it might be the one where he finally overtook Dave.

"Our goal ought to be to increase where we were last year, not to get close to Dave," Jay said.

Littlefield agreed that "it was a tough week to come to New York." But he still argued, "The show is on a roll." As for his prediction that Jay was about to run Dave down, Warren said, "All I meant to say was that if the trend continues, we feel strongly that that's where we can be. I know I stuck my neck out. I just didn't mean to stick it out quite that far."

The following week, Dave had a 26 percent edge over Jay. A week later it was 28 percent. The next week it was

33 percent. Through the end of the year and into 1995, Dave beat Jay by at least 20 percent every week after their showdown in New York. The gap between the two shows, once narrowed, had returned. It wasn't that Jay was falling back as much as it was that Dave had gained even more strength.

By the end of January, the talk of Jay's overtaking Dave had subsided to a whisper. Somewhat belatedly, NBC recast its storyline about Jay's solid showing in the ratings. Eric Cardinal, the head of NBC research on the West Coast, said, "If you had said that Jay is going to replace the King of Late Night and put up these kind of numbers, we would have been thrilled out of our minds."

And Littlefield pointed out, "Jay has put up those great numbers with Dave on against him. Johnny never had that kind of competition night after night."

He certainly never had to contend with the pressure to book guests that Jay faced on a weekly basis. Jay began to question just how much pressure the Letterman show was bringing to bear after an incident involving Brett Butler, the star of the ABC series "Grace Under Fire." Butler showed Jay's staff a letter from a Letterman producer saying that Dave was going to be personally insulted if Butler went on the "Tonight" show instead of appearing on "Late Show." Jay never discussed the issue publicly because he didn't want to raise the specter of a booking war again. But some on his staff did ask the question out loud: Are the Letterman guys starting to use Helen's old tactics?

The Letterman staff's own replay of the incident was that the only reason a letter was sent to Brett Butler at all was because she had twice before canceled appearances with Dave.

The real heat in the booking issue came not between the Letterman and Leno camps, but between some of Jay's staff and NBC. Jay was not happy that NBC did nothing to protect his booking territory the way he perceived CBS did. Jay knew of CBS stars who were asked by CBS program executives not to go on the "Tonight" show. And yet in the week after Christmas, there was Jerry Seinfeld, NBC's biggest star, on the air telling his holiday anecdotes to Dave, not to Jay.

"Jay is a little pissed at NBC," one Leno staff member said. "He's getting no backing on guests."

What made the situation harder for Jay, this staff member said, was the fact that for the first time some publicists and managers were candidly telling the "Tonight" bookers, "We're awfully sorry, but my guy just wants to do Letterman."

It was the kind of blow that Jay had been absorbing from the day Letterman had gone on the air for CBS. Tom Brokaw had gone on Dave's show that first night. Vice President Al Gore was on in the first week. When Dave did a week of shows from L.A., Carson had signaled his official stamp of approval by doing a walk-on with Dave carrying the top-10 list. Then there was the Seinfeld appearance.

But the biggest blow, the biggest and most official indication of where the two stars stood in the eyes of the show business community, was yet to come.

Ted Harbert, president of ABC Entertainment, knew early on that Billy Crystal "wasn't going to happen" one more time as host of the annual Academy Awards telecast on ABC in March 1995. In truth, despite Crystal's three highly regarded performances as host, that news did not disappoint Harbert much. Long before Crystal was officially out of the Oscar picture, Harbert had decided that there was another name that would be perfect for the role of host, a name that got Harbert truly excited about the show, a name he considered "really the home run."

"I really, really wanted David Letterman," Harbert said.

It was not the first time. Harbert had contacted Letterman and his agent, Michael Ovitz, a year earlier about taking over the host role. "But he was so new to CBS that nothing really came of the discussion," Harbert said.

In reality, Letterman had thought seriously about the offer the year before. But he had only been on the air for CBS less than six months when the offer came, and Ovitz, sensing that the timing simply wasn't right, recommended that Dave turn it down.

But when an offer came around again for the 1995 telecast, Ovitz believed Dave was ready to accept the statement that the Oscar role implied: He had become the true successor to Johnny Carson as America's host.

Harbert said that the statement was indeed accurate. More than any other star, more than anyone on any ABC show, even its own comic superstar, Tim Allen, David Letterman was the ideal host of the Academy Awards telecast.

"David Letterman has some magic about him," Harbert said. "The Oscar assignment says it all. He is *the* guy, *the* man, in American entertainment right now."

Johnny Carson did the Oscar show five times between 1979 and 1984. Before him the job was most closely associated with Bob Hope. Crystal had put his own signature on it. Now it was David Letterman's turn.

Inside "Late Show" there was the expected anxiety about what the pressure of doing this show—seen not only by an audience second only to the Super Bowl in the U.S. but also by an audience around the world estimated at one billion people—would do to Dave's always fragile psyche. The pressure of the daily Dave was enough to deal with for many staff members, who found him to be ever more irascible and difficult.

"He's angry a lot and yelling at people more than ever," one of his close associates said late in 1994. Dave's impatience with his studio audience also manifested itself on more and more occasions. If he didn't get laughs with his first couple of monologue jokes, he would be likely to turn on the audience, sometimes picking on some members of the crowd or sometimes even bagging the rest of his monologue entirely. The postmortems on the show continued to be harsh.

"I don't even want to imagine the postmortem after that Academy Awards show," one staff member said.

But there was really little doubt that Dave would accept the honor. After all, Johnny had done it. And besides, it did occur to Dave that if he had said no, there was always a chance they might offer the job to Jay.

As Morton saw it, the opportunity to host the Oscars would provide an incalculable boost to Dave's regular show. If he even needed it. "Dave will get tremendous exposure," Morty said. "And it will only cement our relationship with the movie industry as the place to go to launch your movies."

Jay Leno came out of his latest run at David Letterman perhaps more realistically aware of exactly how daunting it was going to be to turn public opinion around to the point where he could be thought of as being on an even footing with Hollywood Dave.

Jay still felt he was even or better than Dave in the first segments of their shows. "I think we win the monologues most nights, and we stay at least even with them until about the second commercial," Jay said. But even he recognized that Dave held his audience better through the interview segments.

For Jay, as always, the answer remained in hard work. He had trimmed down physically with the help of steady pounding on a treadmill. He continued to work the kinds of hours possible only to college students in exam week and other human beings for whom sleep is of no consequence. And it was music to Jay's ears to hear that Dave occasionally felt burned out by the long hours and the pressure. Because for Jay, working endless hours for days and weeks without letup was *no problem at all.*

"When I have an hour or two off, I don't know what to do with myself," Jay said. "I honestly feel that we can increase the workload another 30 to 40 percent."

Inside the Letterman shop, where they seemed already to be working at more than full capacity, nobody believed in that form of insanity. To add more work on top of what the Oscar show already represented, was to create the possibility of overwinding Letterman's already high-tension spring.

On "Late Show," as the program approached its second anniversary, the goal was more elusive: not more work, but more work of distinction, more work that touched on originality, more work worthy of the magic that now seemed attached to the man who continued to rule late-night television—America's host: David Letterman.

INDEX